Science Fiction Stars and Horror Heroes

Science Fiction Stars and Horror Heroes

*Interviews with Actors, Directors,
Producers and Writers
of the 1940s through 1960s*

by Tom Weaver

RESEARCH ASSOCIATES:
MICHAEL AND JOHN BRUNAS

McFarland & Company, Inc., Publishers
Jefferson, North Carolina, and London

British Library Cataloguing-in-Publication data are available

Library of Congress Cataloguing-in-Publication Data

Weaver, Tom 1958–
    Science fiction stars and horror heroes : interviews with actors,
directors, producers and writers of the 1940s through 1960s / by
Tom Weaver.
        p.   cm.
    Includes index.
    ISBN 0-89950-594-5 (lib. bdg. : 50# alk. paper) ∞
    1. Science fiction films—History and criticism.   2. Horror films—
History and criticism.   3. Motion picture actors and actresses—
Interviews.   4. Motion picture producers and directors—Interviews.
5. Screenwriters—Interviews.   I. Title.
PN1995.9.S26W46   1991
791.43′656—dc20   90-53528
                                                                          CIP

Manufactured in the United States of America

McFarland & Company, Inc., Publishers
    Box 611, Jefferson, North Carolina 28640

This book is
dedicated
to the fifty.

Table of Contents

Introduction

I'd like to think that someday I'll interview somebody who can solve a few of these vexing riddles: Why do the older science fiction and horror movies still have the audience that they do today? Why have many bigger (and often better) "prestige" pictures fallen by the wayside while hordes of fans still gobble up B films like *The Return of Dracula, The Creeping Unknown, Tarantula* and *Horror Hotel*? Why, in this modern age of ultra-slick moviemaking and state-of-the-art special effects, when the complete budget of *Carnival of Souls* (1962) wouldn't pay for six seconds of *Batman* (1989), do people still lionize the low-budget likes of Roger Corman, Jack Arnold and Edgar G. Ulmer? Why did the natives in *King Kong* build a wall to keep Kong out with a giant door to let him in?

These are not easy questions.

The fact is that these vintage SF/horrors do retain a following while many "better" films do not. This probably isn't fair, but it sure works to that following's advantage: The pictures still play on television, come out on video cassette and turn up in revival houses, and magazines partially or entirely devoted to them abound. (Except for horror and sci-fi, what other genres have a whole slew of current magazines exclusively dedicated to them? Or even *one* magazine?) Or whole books of interviews with luminaries of the genre?

Most of the interview subjects in this book were denizens of the Hollywood B movie mills of '50s vintage, but the '40s and '60s are also represented. British sci-fi/horror also comes under scrutiny. Performers, producers, writers, directors, a composer, a one-shot filmmaker . . . all are included. There are even a couple of participants you wouldn't call B people.

Sad to say, as we head into the 1990s, efforts to locate and interview the older filmmakers are becoming more of a race against time than ever. It's not a pleasant thought, but there are horror films from the '30s and '40s that have no notable survivors today. There are even some '50s flicks (*The Four Skulls of Jonathan Drake; The Alligator People*) well on their way down that same dismal road. The history of these pictures has to be written soon because these people are not going to be around forever, as three of the subjects from my previous book, *Interviews with B Science Fiction and Horror Movie Makers*, have already gone *way* out beyond the call of duty to demonstrate:

On March 25, 1989, Reginald LeBorg, 86, suffered a heart attack one block from the Norris Cinema Theatre, where the Academy of Family Films and Family Television was waiting to present him with its Life Career Award. LeBorg accepted his status as a horror movie director with a grain of salt, but he was unfailingly charming and enthusiastic, and he'd often call me long-distance just to chew the fat (I could never get him to call me anything except Mr. Weaver). People just don't come any nicer than Reggie LeBorg.

Jerry Warren, king of the rock-bottom filmmakers, died of lung cancer on August 21, 1988, in his Escondido, California, home. He lied about his age like an overripe starlet, but he was somewhere in his sixties when he died. Warren never really had a handle on what people wanted or expected from a film, and this was only too well reflected in his awful movies. But he was forthright enough to come out and admit that he really didn't *care*, that he was in it strictly for the bucks. You just have to take your hat off to that kind of honesty.

And on December 10, 1986, Susan Cabot, 59, was bashed to death with a weight-lifting bar by her own son Timothy in the bedroom of her Encino home. In typical modern-courtroom style, the victim became the accused: The defense said that Tim was an emotional wreck because Cabot was an over-protective, disturbed mother, and because their home was filled with such "massive filth and decay" that the conditions constituted child abuse. ("Child" Timothy was 22 when he caved in his mom's head.) None of the above was even faintly evident to this frequent visitor to the Cabot home, but there was also some legalese double-talk about steroids and an experimental hormone the kid was taking (he was born dwarfed), defense arguments that conjured up images of Cabot as *Sunset Boulevard*'s Norma Desmond, and even published accounts which made Tim the love child of Cabot and either actor Christopher Jones or Jordan's King Hussein. By the time all the hot air cleared from the courtroom, Timothy Scott Roman received a three-year suspended sentence and was placed on probation.

On a far brighter note, all of our other favorites from the earlier book are still with us and some of them are continuing to make news (not all of it good). John Agar had a co-starring role in the end-of-the-world suspenser *Miracle Mile* (1989), and to the surprise of cynical fans, he actually got a number of good reviews. He also had a small part in director Clive Barker's *Nightbreed* (1990), playing a hermit who'd like to be a monster and who is killed off by lead heavy David Cronenberg. John Ashley produced two genre-related television series in a row, the Fox Network's *Werewolf* and NBC's *Something Is Out There*, both of which were flops; he's vowed never to produce this type of show again. Robert Clarke joined the long list of veteran players that have done time in films by Fred Olen Ray, the indefatigable king of modern exploitation; Clarke is in Ray's *Alienator* (1989), a sci-fi send-up of *The Astounding She-Monster*, and *Haunting Fear* (1990), based on Poe's "The Premature Burial." Anthony Eisley turned up in a small part in *Evil Spirits* (1990), which featured a great who's-who/who's-through cast (Karen Black, Arte Johnson, Virginia Mayo,

The late Susan Cabot with son Timothy in a 1985 pose.

Martine Beswick, Yvette Vickers [q.v.], Robert Quarry). Jack H. Harris's remake of *The Blob* was a good, crowd-pleasing action/horror thriller, even though it didn't set the 1988 summer box office on fire. And Howard W. Koch, another of the all-time great guys, accepted the Jean Hersholt Humanitarian Award at the 1990 Oscarcast, receiving a standing ovation as 70,000,000 Americans watched on television. Koch also exec-produced *Ghost*, the sleeper-hit of the 1990 summer movie sweepstakes.

Scads of people aided and abetted on this book, most notably repeat offenders like Mark Martucci, always Johnny-on-the-spot with video cassettes of hard-to-find movies (and never resenting the fact that I always needed them a.s.a.p.); Dave McDonnell (*Starlog*) and Tony Timpone (*Fangoria*), two of the best editors and nicest fellas you'd ever want to run across; John Cocchi, film historian/raconteur/bon vivant; Paul and Donna Parla, the Sherlock Holmes and Dr. Watson of celebrity-hunters; and Bob Skotak, Mr. Rare Behind-the-Scenes Stills (and a good guy).

Also, for their cooperation, tapes, stills, leads, advice, lip service, and whatever, yet more thanks go to Bill and Roberta Amazzini, Merry Anders, Richard Anderson, Mon Ayash, everyone's friend and co-worker Bandit, Edward Bernds, Bill Brent (J & J Video), Hugh and Abigail Crain, Robert Day, Carl and Debbie Del Vecchio, Richard Denning, Squeamy Ellis, Tim Ferrante, Michael Fitzgerald, Flippy the Educated Porpoise, John Foster, Katie Gohdé, Bruce Goldstein, Alex and Richard Gordon, Rose Hobart, Allan Hoos, Donna Hope, Joe Jaworsky (noted scientist), the late Steve Jochsberger, Tom Johnson, James LaBarre, Richard Lamparski, Greg Luce (Sinister Cinema), Alex Lugones, Mark McGee, Gilbert McKenna, Greg Mank, Kevin Marrazzo, Dick

Miller, Cameron Mitchell, Ed Nelson, Michael Pate, Vincent Price, Fred Olen
Ray, Max Rosenberg, Mary (Bunky) Runser, Elizabeth Selwyn, John Skillin,
Jonas Slydes and his wife, Steamroller Smith, Michael Stein (*Filmfax*), Venetia
Stevenson, Herb Strock, Vladimir Strowski, Gary Svehla and the whole gang
down at FANEX, Ed Watz, Jon Weaver, John Wooley, Xerxes the Cat, and
all the other good people at *Fangoria* and *Starlog*.

Neither last nor least, my research associates (and best friends) Mike and
John Brunas, two more terrific guys. This can be one hell of a hobby when you
have friends like them sharing your enthusiasm.

And finally, the biggest thank-yous are saved for my 28 interviewees.
They are, for all intents and purposes, the true authors of this book. I just take
the credit and get paid. It's a great arrangement.

Tom Weaver

Acknowledgments

Abridged versions of the interviews featured in *Science Fiction Stars and Horror Heroes* originally appeared in the following magazines:

Acquanetta: "Where the Wild Woman Runs Free," *Fangoria* #94, July, 1990
Phyllis Coates: "Phyllis Coates, Superman's Girl Friend," *Starlog* #138, January, 1989, and "Phyllis Coates—Byline: Lois Lane," *Starlog* #139, February, 1989
Hazel Court: "Queen of '60s Horror," *Fangoria* #91, April, 1990
Richard Devon: "I Survived Roger Corman," *Fangoria* #76, August, 1988
Gene Fowler, Jr.: "'I Was a Middle-Aged Blackballed Director from Tinseltown' or 'How to Make a Terribly-Tilted Exploitation Monster Movie with Class,'" *Filmfax* #22, September, 1990
Arthur Gardner/Arnold Laven/Paul Landres/Pat Fielder: "Monster Interlude," *Fangoria* #47, August, 1985
Bernard Glasser: "The Care and Breeding of Triffids," *Starlog Yearbook* #7, 1990
Herk Harvey: "Death Comes to Kansas," *Fangoria* #86, September, 1989
Gordon Hessler: "An AIP Director Screams Again," *Fangoria* #53, May, 1986
Louis M. Heyward: "Going AIP," *Fangoria* #96, September, 1990, and "Heyward's Heyday," *Fangoria* #97, October, 1990
John Howard: "Beyond the Lost Horizon," *Starlog Yearbook* #5, 1989
Kim Hunter: "Chimp Life," *Starlog* #160, November, 1990
Robert Hutton: "Slimebuster!" *Fangoria* #87, October, 1989
Nancy Kovack: "Lady and the Argonauts," *Starlog* #151, February, 1990
Anna Lee: "Member of the Stock Company," *Starlog Yearbook* #6, 1990
Janet Leigh: "Mistress of Menace," *Starlog* #132, July, 1988
Richard Matheson: "Richard Matheson and the House of Poe," *Fangoria* #89, December, 1989, "Quoth Matheson, 'Nevermore!'" *Fangoria* #90, February, 1990, "Master of Shrinking Men," *Starlog* #150, January, 1990, and "Master of the Last Men on Earth," *Starlog* #151, February, 1990
Gregg Palmer: "The Creature Walked Beside Him," *Fangoria* #93, June, 1990
Mala Powers: "Maiden of Yesterday," *Starlog* #153, April, 1990
Robert Shayne: "Inspector Henderson Reports," *Starlog* #129, April, 1988
Yvette Vickers: "Vamp! Vixen! Vickers!" *Fangoria* #83, June, 1989
Katherine Victor: "Talking Turkeys," *The Bloody Best of Fangoria* #10, 1991
Virgil W. Vogel: "Terror on the Low-Budget Express," *Fangoria* #73, May, 1988
Robb White: "An Outspoken Conversation with Robb White," *Filmfax* #18, January, 1990

I don't criticize anything that I ever did [in films],
except that I would have liked to have done it my way....
I'm a good actress, I know that I'm a good actress,
but I feel that I have never really achieved my acting potential,
or had the right opportunities.

Acquanetta

LANDING A BLOW for feminism long before the days of women's rights, Paula the Ape Woman stood proud in the male-dominated monster world of the 1940s. Her stamping grounds were the sound stages at Universal Studios, her films included *Captive Wild Woman* and *Jungle Woman,* and the actress who portrayed her, exotic in name and appearance, was the beautiful Acquanetta. Trapped in a horror/jungle film rut, Acquanetta also appeared in such movies as *Dead Man's Eyes, Tarzan and the Leopard Woman* and *Lost Continent* before retiring from the business, although the Arizona-based actress is currently eyeing the possibility of a screen return.

The story of your early life is a little different every time you tell it.

I think many people who interview personalities add their own concepts to it, and they all write it their own way. I'm not certain *what* people have written about me; every time I picked up a paper I found things that I never said. My mother was Arapaho, and I was born on the Arapaho Reservation in Wyoming, near the Wind River. Of course I have no recollection of that, because I was given away to my father when I was approximately three years old. My father took me to Pennsylvania and gave me to his then-wife, and I grew up in Norristown, Pennsylvania, where I went to school.

And after high school you started out on your modeling career.

Right. After high school, I went to New York and became a model, and lived at the Barbizon Women's Hotel. I became a model first for Harry Conover, and then I met Arthur William Brown, who did illustrations for various magazines, while I was with Conover. We were at the Stork Club in the Cub Room one night, and John Powers was there. The following morning Powers called Brown, who then called *me* and said, "The big man wants to see you." I went to see John Powers, and he pulled open a drawer of his desk, threw a contract at me and said, "Sign!" *[Laughs.]* He said, "Harry Conover used to work for me. He's a good model, but he's never been very bright and he doesn't put anybody under contract. You are now a John Powers model." This was all really neat. I was thrown into an entirely new atmosphere, from a small town to the Big Town. And I went from a small amount of money a week, in a small town, to $100 an hour on some jobs, which in those days was incredible. This was during the war years, the early '40s, and things were moving very fast.

By the way, when I was in New York, Louis Sobol and Walter Winchell and all the scribes were writing about me in their columns. At first, when they found out that I was an Indian in New York, they said, "Oh, nobody cares about Indians." But Roosevelt was president and the big South American Hands Across the Border policy was on, and it was decided that I was now going

Previous page: **Priceless publicity pose from Acquanetta's *Captive Wild Woman*. The man in the monkey suit is Ray "Crash" Corrigan.**

to be a South American. It was almost like Pygmalion—they fabricated for me this story that I came from Venezuela. I looked the part—I was dark and exotic, and I wore these big scarfs and a big gardenia, flowered skirts, collars and capes and those kinds of things *[laughs]!* I became "The Venezuelan Volcano"— William Randolph Hearst dubbed me that. I had met Mr. Hearst and his wife Marion, they were my friends, and W.R. pushed me, he wanted me to succeed so tremendously. He was so impressed with my background *[laughs],* and he called me the Little Princess.

Somehow a bit of my background came out, that my father was a descendant of the Royal House of England—be it legitimate or not! My dad was English and French, and from what I'm told, his grandmother, who was French-Jewish, was a lady-in-waiting or something in the Royal House and she became pregnant, and out of that union eventually came my father! That's why the background was shaded in mystery—in days gone by, illegitimacy was very taboo. They actually called illegitimate children bastards, which is a horrible thing, but today it's a badge of honor—now women announce that they're going to have a baby by this married man or that married man. Everything is so changed today! But as I was saying, this business about being descended from the Royal House was true, and so of course that always impressed people like Hearst. And J. Edgar Hoover knew it—he was a personal friend of mine. As a matter of fact, because I had no birth certificate, I couldn't get a visa or a passport to get out of the country, and so Hoover arranged for that. He was a curious man. Although he had interesting stories around him, because he was never married, he still was attracted to certain types of women, he liked to photograph them. And he would come to New York and photograph us.

Your publicity also says that you were a paid escort back then.
In those days, men liked to have attractive women to escort them places. So it was almost like a job. Now, with me, I was a very innocent young girl from a small town, and I never got involved in what they called "the fast set." People were attracted to me because of that—they called me Miss Innocent. When I left Hollywood, they still called me Miss Innocent!

So how did you finally wind up in Hollywood?
I met some people from Rio de Janeiro, and they wanted me to come to South America and perform at the Copacabana in Rio. I was a natural performer and a dancer, and that's what they wanted me to do at the Copa. So I packed my things, I left the Barbizon and got on the train. We stopped in Hollywood and we went out to the Mocambo. The head of casting at Metro-Goldwyn-Mayer was there, the head of Warner Bros., Dan Kelly from Universal Studios and so on. And Walter Wanger—he was the one that really went wild over me. He tried to get me for the lead in *Arabian Nights* [1942], but unfortunately they had already signed Maria Montez. That started the big

Her original name was Burnuacquanetta (translation: Burning Fire, Deep Water), and she was an exotic presence in several Universal B films of the 1940s.

so-called "feud" between the two of us. She said, no, she would not *geev* up *thees* role — it was to be her first starring role, in Technicolor and all that. She later drowned in her bathtub, but before her demise we became friendly — never really *friends,* because there was a tremendous jealousy on her part. That is something I have never known in my entire life; I do not know what envy is, I do not know what jealousy is.

You made a test at MGM, didn't you?

    I was tested by both Metro-Goldwyn-Mayer and Universal. And before Universal even saw the rushes of my test, when they heard that I had tested the day before at Metro, they immediately signed me because they thought Metro would use me as a threat to Montez, who Universal was building then as their number one star. Dan Kelly was the one who said that my full name, Burnuacquanetta, was too long for any marquee, so I could either be Burnu or I could be Acquanetta. I chose Acquanetta.

And you ended up with a bit in Montez's Arabian Nights.

That's right—I had a small speaking part, as one of the harem girls. Universal found there was so much reaction to my appearance, my presence, whatever, that they threw me into the so-called B & B pictures.

The bread-and-butter pictures.

Yes. Those were the films that they spent less money on, but made the most money off of. And the prestige pictures were called the A's, because those were what they used to promote their studio. My films, each and every one of them, within the first few weeks of release made over a million dollars. People stood in line to see them, and somehow I caught on. However, because of the kinds of films that I was doing, I was not very happy. Of course, being the sort of person I was, I never got really close to any of those directors or producers; they were always trying to get young girls into an amorous situation. That never happened with me—that's why I never did any of these big Technicolor extravaganzas!

How exactly did you get involved on Captive Wild Woman?

I know that they were testing various actresses at the studio; I think Yvonne de Carlo was one under consideration. Yvonne de Carlo was at Universal, and in her autobiography she says I took several films from her. I think that's not the case, I think it was the opposite *[laughs]*! They were always threatening *me* with *her,* and again, like with Maria Montez, she got the big Technicolors. I think she was tested for *Captive Wild Woman,* but I'm not absolutely certain. But in any event I tested, and they said I was perfect for the role.

How did you feel, going into a picture where you would be playing a mute ape woman?

Whatever I was given, I did my best. I became a character actress. I am a natural actress—they tell me that when I was a little girl I used to gather the children of the neighborhood and put on shows! I did write a play when I was in junior high school, and I was in a play when I was in grammar school—I played an angel! So apparently acting was to be part of my life. I believe that our lives are somewhat—not pre-programmed, because we do have free choice—but I believe those choices are known. People here in Arizona call me a medium, because I do sometimes see the future—don't ask me how, it's like a waking dream. I was at a party the other night where people were standing

Mad scientist John Carradine transforms an ape into a beautiful woman (Acquanetta) in Universal's way-out *Captive Wild Woman*.

in line to ask me, "Acquanetta, what's in store for me?" I can touch their hands, and sometimes I can see what's going to happen. For some people I do not say what I see; others, I tell them. It's like channeling.

Was it exciting to be handed a leading role so early in your Hollywood career?
     You know something very curious? Nothing I ever did in Hollywood was exciting to the degree where I felt, "This is going to be my life." It was wonderful and surprising, but I just seem to have taken everything in stride. It was just another part of my destiny, and I somehow knew that, always. I did my very best, but it wasn't something that was so meaningful to me that I would give up something else for it. That's why I ended up walking away from Universal.

How did you prepare for your role as the Ape Woman?
     [*Laughs.*] There was no preparation on my part, but I sat sometimes for two and a half hours being made up by a makeup artist. They used rubber and clay, and you sat in that chair while all this stuff was put on. You could hardly breathe—it was kind of scary! I think I had more emotional feeling, being

Acquanetta in full Jack P. Pierce makeup for *Captive Wild Woman*.

made up for that, than anything that I ever did, because it was exhausting sitting being made up for those kinds of things.

What memories do you have of Edward Dmytryk, who directed Captive Wild Woman?

We had great rapport—in fact, we dated briefly. What a career he should have had—what a talent! He was my favorite director. Actually, I had *two* favorites, Eddie and Reginald LeBorg; they were the two that I really liked the best. But Eddie and I used to talk—oh, God, we could sit and talk for hours! I thought he was tremendous. Many directors seem to want to step into your skin and to tell you everything to do; they never allowed me the freedom to interpret a role the way I wanted to do it. And I resent it to this day. Eddie gave me more freedom than other directors. Nevertheless, I've always felt that I was never "me" in movies—do you know there was never a film where I was allowed to smile? And that's curious, because my personality is very exuberant. I was a happy nymph of a person in those years, and that's why people were attracted to me. I was like a butterfly *[laughs]*—I wanted to spread my wings! And I had to stifle all of that. I thought that that was an injustice at the time. But I have to say "que sera sera"—had things been different, had I soared and become the star which I could have been, my life would have been totally different. And God knows what it might have been. My people say that, for the good as well as for what we think of at the time as *not* being good, we must be thankful, because that is why we are in the place that we are in now.

Did you enjoy working with John Carradine on Captive Wild Woman?

Oh, very much so. I think of him a lot. He was great—he was always acting, you know *[laughs]!* Even when we were off the set, there was John being John! I always think of him as Dracula, always picture him in my mind's eye wearing that cloak! I wonder what he was in his past life. . . .

That was about the time that he cared more about his Shakespearean stage company than the pictures he was doing just for the bucks.

He was always doing something away from filmdom. He had it in his soul—he was an "*ac-tor.*" And he lived it in his private life! He was a character in his day, and I loved people like that. Milburn Stone was a gentleman, a real nice person, and Evelyn Ankers, too. Evelyn and I were never really close, like close girlfriends, but that could have been partly because of me. I was somewhat withdrawn in a sense; even to this day I do not have a lot of very *close* close friends. People think that they are close friends of mine, but I don't think that. I walk among, but I am not of.

Who were your close friends during your acting days?

I think Eddie Dmytryk was a friend. I don't think of Walter Wanger as a friend, because he was more like someone who thought that he could exert power over you. And when he couldn't, then he was vindictive! So, because I was not what he wanted me to be, he denied me the roles that I could have had. It was not because they were not available, it was a simple matter of exchanging a role for what I was willing to give. I wasn't willing to do that, and I never will be willing to do that! I maintained my self-respect. I had it then, I have it now—that's a very important thing. It's not what other people feel about you, but what you know about yourself.

Were you pleased with your performance in Captive Wild Woman?

Yes. You know, I don't criticize anything that I ever did, except that I would have liked to have done it *my* way. But the director's in charge. And as I look back on those films, they were effective. I'm a good actress, I *know* that I'm a good actress, but I feel that I have never really achieved my acting potential, or had the right opportunities.

You also were scheduled to star in The Mummy's Ghost, *and in fact worked on the picture for one day.*
 On *The Mummy's Ghost* I remember that we had scabs [non-union workers] on the set. We were shooting a scene where I had to walk along a path and then fall, and these scabs had put real rocks down on the path. They were supposed to put down papier-mâché rocks but they didn't—these scabs painted real rocks white! I fell and struck my head, and that's all I remember—I woke up in Cedars of Lebanon Hospital! I have the effects of that to this day: I also struck my arm when I fell, and when I had my second son, my elbow swelled up like a ball. They said that was still from that accident, because it crushed a little bone in my elbow.

What other mishaps have you had in films?
 I remember that on one of the Ape Woman pictures my costume was too tight, around the neck. The blouse part went up around my neck and was tied with a string, it started choking me, and they couldn't get it off. I'm not sure how it happened, but I fainted. Then there was another film, *Flesh and Fantasy,* which they wanted me for, but I became ill. That was a tremendous disappointment. I was supposed to be in the Barbara Stanwyck-Charles Boyer episode—Charles and I were friends always. He later came to Arizona, and died here.

How did you get involved on Dead Man's Eyes?
 I was assigned to all my films. I refused quite a number, I simply wouldn't do them. I was never handed a script and asked, "Would you like to do this?" I never reached that pinnacle of stardom.

How well did you get along with Lon Chaney on Dead Man's Eyes?
 Beautifully. He was a good friend.

LeBorg told me he was a drunk and a pain in the neck.
 Yes, but I did not see that. During *Dead Man's Eyes,* I never saw that.

You finally had some dramatic scenes in Dead Man's Eyes.
 Yes, but they still would not allow me to "come out." Everything was kind of capped; they wanted me to hold it to a low key. Emotions inside that were building, I had to hold down.

Why did you enjoy working with Reginald LeBorg?
 Because he was a gentleman—with an accent on the *gentle*. I don't like

people who are harsh, and some directors are, you know—I've seen them screaming at people on sets! But Eddie Dmytryk was my very favorite, because it was just as if I had known him forever. What a nice man. You know, when I saw him at the [1987] Universal reunion, his wife [actress Jean Porter] would not allow me to talk to him? We had very little time to visit, because she pulled him away!

Were you happy with the job you did in Dead Man's Eyes?

Pleased, let's say. As I say, the directors were always in control. When you become a big star, *then* you have freedom; then you take charge, you're in control to a great degree, and you can do your own interpretation of roles. But when you're new and you haven't had the experience, as they call it, the directors are in charge. And they like that, because they project themselves through you.

You ended up in a horror film rut at Universal. What kinds of roles would you have preferred?

Drama. Playing a woman, a *real* woman—a loving, sharing, caring person. Really, almost anything except what I did *[laughs]!* Not that I hated what I did, but I came to dislike the roles.

So you saw the rut getting deeper when they asked you to repeat your Ape Woman role in Jungle Woman?

I just did it because I was assigned to it. But once I accepted it, I did it to the best of my abilities.

Jungle Woman *really is a disappointing sequel—cheap and badly written.*

Yes, but they made money on it because Acquanetta was in it. I came to realize that I was the property, not the film. That's why I left Universal. I wanted to be a part of a film—add to it. I didn't want to be used. And I felt that I was being used.

Were you glad to get dialogue in Jungle Woman?

I thought it was really interesting to work without speaking in *Captive Wild Woman;* it was more difficult, a challenge. But, you know, I read an article once that said that I was not an actress at all, and that in fact I couldn't even talk. They didn't understand that this was deliberate, and that I had to project more—because I had to do it with my body language, my eyes, my face. Every movement had to mean something!

Did you enjoy working with J. Carrol Naish on Jungle Woman?

He helped me more than any actor or actress that I ever worked with, because he was a fabulous actor, I think one of the greatest. Why he didn't achieve stardom, other than being a character actor, I don't know. They

The popularity of the first Ape Woman film prompted a perfunctory sequel with three of the original stars.

missed the boat. But he was always offering suggestions and being very helpful and kind and gentle. What a nice man!

Naish was nominated for two Supporting Actor Oscars around that time [Sahara, 1943, and A Medal for Benny, *1945]; it's curious to find him in a stinker like* Jungle Woman.

You know, I think that he accepted *Jungle Woman* in order to work with me. He always had visions of the two of us working together in something fabulous, because he really liked me as a person and as a friend. I had met him at Universal prior to *Jungle Woman,* and we became friends—he was kind of like a mentor.

Putting the pictures themselves aside in your mind, did you enjoy working at Universal?

Oh, yes. The people that I worked with there, they were just beautiful. I never had a problem—in fact, we were just one big, wonderful, happy family. Universal was like that, but I understand that a lot of the other studios really were not. At Metro they had people working together that didn't speak to each other off the set *[laughs]!* At Universal we never had that, we had a family.

Not long after Jungle Woman *you wound up quitting the studio.*

What happened was that I went to Mexico at the instigation of the president, Mr. Roosevelt, as one of the emissaries from Hollywood. Somehow during that trip to Mexico I made lots of contacts with really important people there, plus some of the producers, and they wanted me to come to Mexico and do films. I did not speak Spanish at the time, but they said, "If you live here, we'll get you tutors." And while I was there, I met Jorge Pascal, who immediately showered me with jewels and proposed to me. Of course we had press people with us, and so it hit the newspapers in Hollywood that I was going to marry the wealthiest man in Mexico, who had proposed to me on my first night there. But I really didn't care for the man. Pascal later lured into Mexico some of our big baseball players that were jumping their contracts, and he started his own big team in Mexico. He was killed in a big air crash, on his way to Acapulco. So had I been married to him, I wouldn't be here right now!

By the time I got back to Hollywood, I was so fascinated with Mexico that I asked for a release from my contract—I wanted to go to Mexico and make films. Well, Universal wouldn't allow it. So I went to my friend Joe Schenck, who was the head of 20th Century–Fox. I told him my problem, and he said, "We'd better get this contract." He called Dan Kelly at Universal and Dan arranged for my contract release. Universal never forgave me for that. They had this *Jungle* series on the boards and they tried desperately to find someone else, and in fact they did get a girl who did one film [Vicky Lane in *The Jungle Captive*]. It bombed, and that was the end of that series.

People asked me, "You walked out on a contract, when they were ready to extend it?" and I said, "Not only that, but they offered me more money to stay." I couldn't—I had to go. It was like something drawing me, pulling me away. And I now know that my spirit guides had charge of my life, without my awareness of it. I ran into Dan Kelly at the Farmer's Market, years after I left Universal, and we sat and chatted, and he said, "Oh, if we could relive it." And I said, "This is the profound statement down through centuries. But it is for those who have wisdom to be able to perceive what is to come. Those are the ones who grasp the opportunities now." We talked like that—sat there philosophizing and just having a great time. Dan was getting old and tired, and he said, "If I could relive it, we would never have let you go."

You soon ended up under contract to Monogram.

That's right. At Monogram I had approval of my scripts because I had been so unhappy about my pictures at Universal. And I disapproved of every one! The scripts they submitted to me were mostly cowboy things. Had I done them, I probably would have gone on to be a Western star *[laughs]*! Of course they did not renew my contract, because they thought I was difficult. Again, I must say that I guess it wasn't meant to be.

Did you like working with Johnny Weissmuller on Tarzan and the Leopard Woman?

Oh, yes, very much so—he was a nice man. He'd sit and tell jokes a lot,

Acquanetta strikes a beguiling pose on the set of RKO's *Tarzan and the Leopard Woman.*

One of Acquanetta's last film roles was a minor part as a native girl in Lippert's *Lost Continent*, a *Lost World*-style sci-fi adventure.

and also episodes from his life and memories of his past. A few years after we did *Tarzan and the Leopard Woman,* Johnny was about to start the *Jungle Jim* series and he wanted me to play opposite him in the series, but I declined to do that, because it was to be shot on the backlot somewhere. And, you know, it was a very curious thing: just ten days before Johnny Weissmuller's demise, he came to my mind, and I tried to reach him in Hollywood and Acapulco, but I couldn't locate him. I felt that I needed to talk to him, and I also wanted to meet him and to be photographed together again—I had that desire. And then I read, a week later, of his passing. It was so incredible.

A few years later you popped up in the sci-fi Lost Continent, *again as a jungle character.*
  [Laughs.] Once you're cast, or *mis*cast, you become *that*—that was the sad part in those days.

You dropped out of pictures in the early '50s.
  The last film I did back then must have been *Take the High Ground* [1953]. You know, I never saw it? What happened was, after we finished a scene one day, the director [Richard Brooks] said, "You're through," and what he meant was with that particular scene. I thought he meant I was *through*! I went home and packed and went off somewhere, and I never did the whole part that they wrote for me *[laughs]*! They used the little bit I did, from what everybody tells me, but I never saw it. And they were very unhappy with me because they said I walked out, but it wasn't quite like that.

After leaving films you became a local television celebrity in Arizona.
  That was through my husband Jack Ross. My first husband, by the way, was Luciano Baschuk, a Russian, very, very wealthy, and we had one son, Sergei. We were divorced because I found out after our marriage that he was somewhat sadistic. Our son died of cancer—five years old. In the meantime, I married one of my mentors, Henry Clive. He had painted seven covers of me for *The American Weekly,* which was the most that any star had ever done. Marion Davies was on the cover three times, Sonja Henie and Simone Simon twice. No other star was ever on more than once. Then, after I separated from Henry, I met Jack Ross, who was working at a Lincoln-Mercury store in Culver City.
  Jack and I were married; I bore a son, Lance, in California; we moved to Arizona and we bought the Lincoln-Mercury dealership in Mesa, Arizona. I immediately went on television here—that's like some 30 years ago. I was on live for almost ten years, five days a week for an hour and a half, and what I did was introduce movies. It was the first program of this sort in the nation— every 15 minutes I had five minutes to come on and talk *[laughs]*! So instead of doing commercials, I started to talk about community events and to

interview people. My commercials became totally different than anything anyone had ever done. I would also say, "By the way, we *also* sell automobiles!" Time marches on—I had all of my next three children "on television." I would be on the week before they were born and the week after. I was the first person to appear on television pregnant! I would give ongoing bulletins on what was happening, and when I was in the hospital they showed pictures of me and the babies, those kinds of things. It was just incredible. My four sons now have all graduated from the university, gotten their M.B.A.s and so forth, and are doing fabulous. I couldn't ask for more—God has been very good to me.

I intend never to marry again, I have taken that vow. I am very happy where I am; feel super-great; I'm 5'7", weigh 127 pounds, and everybody in Arizona tells me I look fabulous. Whenever I hear that, it's really flattering and it makes me feel good.

I am very well known here and I'm very involved in the community, and I have been involved in the eleemosynary, fund-raising charities for all of the thirty years–plus that I have been here.

I live in a home that I was drawn to. This is a strange place where I live; this home is inhabited by the unseen. And people *know* that. People who have never had an experience have strange experiences here. I cannot tell you all of the things that have happened, because the press here would just go nuts— they have asked me not to divulge many of the things, they've said, "Acquanetta, please don't tell people about your miracles." But here is one thing which they could not cap: we had fourteen hundred people at our home for a party some years ago, and the biggest storm in the history of Arizona struck. The water was several feet deep within a couple of blocks of my home, but not one drop of water fell on our home or our garden. That was in the newspaper, of course, but they didn't spread the story beyond Arizona because they didn't want the "religious nuts" to converge here. But, oh, I have had many such experiences.

I have had a fountain spring up in my garden, for six hours, out of the earth; it watered a rose bush, which then burst into the blooms of 20 different roses. It was photographed and documented, and viewed by different people, including the clergy. All kinds of things like that.

No real regrets, then, about the way Hollywood treated you.

Had I been a big star in those days I wouldn't have my four sons, and I'll tell you, there's nothing in this world, no amount of jewels, money or love, that I would have exchanged for my life in Arizona. My four sons are worth more than anything precious that you could think of in the material sense. No way would I exchange them. Barbara Stanwyck said to me, some years ago, "I would give up my career and everything I have for your life, and what you have." Because she could see how happy I am. I am on Cloud Nine.

The actress that '40s audiences went ape for (and vice versa) recently acted in the direct-to-home video release *Grizzly Adams—The Legend Never Dies* (1989).

ACQUANETTA FILMOGRAPHY

Arabian Nights (Universal, 1942)
Rhythm of the Islands (Universal, 1943)
Captive Wild Woman (Universal, 1943)
Jungle Woman (Universal, 1944)
Dead Man's Eyes (Universal, 1944)
The Jungle Captive (Universal, 1945) (filmclip from *Jungle Woman*)
Tarzan and the Leopard Woman (RKO, 1946)
Lost Continent (Lippert, 1951)
Callaway Went Thataway (MGM, 1951)
The Sword of Monte Cristo (20th Century-Fox, 1951)
Take the High Ground (MGM, 1953)

I do take pride in Superman *because it was one of the most
loving relationships that I ever experienced. . . .
We worked like gangbusters, we did it and did it well,
and there were never any beefs or arguments within our group.
I'd have the crew come in my dressing room and have a drink
and prop their feet up — nobody drew lines in those days,
and that was a good feeling. I don't think that'll ever be again,
that kind of closeness between crew and cast.*

Phyllis Coates

SHE'S KNOWN to her friends by her real name and to countless thousands of fans by her professional name, but for untold millions of television viewers she'll always be Lois Lane, ace reporter for the Metropolis *Daily Planet*. "That's only one facet of me," Phyllis Coates stresses, but whatever other acting challenges this veteran performer has met (either in her formidable '50s career or in her current comeback), they can only be icing on the cake; her niche in entertainment history is already established. The popularity and permanence of TV's *Adventures of Superman* seem in no danger of fading, and the series' first and feistiest Lois still remains the fans' favorite after nearly four decades.

Born in Wichita Falls, Texas, the future movie and television actress (real name: Gypsie Ann Evarts Stell) moved to Hollywood as a teenager with intentions of enrolling at U.C.L.A. A chance encounter with Ken Murray in a Hollywood and Vine restaurant landed her in the comedian's vaudeville show. She started out as a chorus girl and worked her way up to doing skits before moving on to work for veteran showman Earl Carroll and later touring with the U.S.O. Coates got some of her first motion picture experience in comedy short subjects at Warner Bros. and then graduated to roles in early '50s films like *Blues Busters*, *Outlaws of Texas* and *Superman and the Mole-Men* (the feature that led to the long-running *Superman* teleseries). After a one-season stint with the Man of Steel, Coates began to divide her time between TV, B-movie assignments and serials at Republic.

How did you become involved on Superman and the Mole-Men?

I had an agent at that time who sent me out to the old Selznick Studios, where they were interviewing gals for the part of Lois Lane. I met Bob Maxwell, who was then one of the producers. I read for him and he said, "I think you're perfect for the part." It was that simple: I didn't even get a call-back on it, they just decided that I was it. And there were a *lot* of good gals up for it.

So working on Mole-Men *was when you met George Reeves for the first time?*

I met George in pre-production, and, yes, that was the first time we worked together. I thought George was a great guy, and I never did change my feelings about him. We were very good friends, and we socialized off the set. I also knew the lady he was involved with, Toni Mannix. Toni was the wife of Eddie Mannix, who used to be the production manager at MGM when the studio was in full swing. He was Toni's husband, and Toni was George's girlfriend.

And Eddie Mannix didn't mind this?

Apparently not—Eddie was very sick at that time. In their house in Bel-Air there was an elevator for him, in the home—I mean, he was really, really ill. But Eddie was the one I think was later responsible for getting George into the Screen Directors Guild.

Both George and Toni were very good to my oldest daughter. At that time she had a hip problem, and Toni Mannix used to pick her up and we'd all get

Previous page: Too-long missing from the acting scene, Phyllis Coates—TV's first and best Lois Lane—is now on the comeback trail.

Phyllis Coates (during her cheesecake days) helps to usher in a new year.

together for dinner after work. We also saw each other sometimes on the weekends. We were all very good friends, and I had a marvelous working relationship with George.

How quickly did you make Superman and the Mole-Men?

Very fast. Oh, man, we went lickety-split on that movie, and that whole series. You never knew which episode you were shooting! Sometimes we'd be shooting four or five episodes at one time — that's why I had one hat and one suit, and that was it! I didn't even dare change earrings!

Lee Sholem, who directed Mole-Men, *told me the picture took four weeks.*

I don't think we shot four weeks — my God, that would have been extravagant! Lee might've *liked* it to go four weeks, but I think we wrapped it up a lot more quickly than that. We shot in Culver City, around in that area. The studio was out there, and we couldn't venture too far away from it because of time.

Did you think that the midget actors playing the mole-men were effective?

I guess at the time they were. It was all hysterical to me—George and I laughed through the whole thing! Somebody recently sent me a still of George and the mole-men, and one of the midgets is holding an Electrolux vacuum cleaner, which was their weapon *[laughs]*! It really was funny.

Were you pleased with the final results on Mole-Men?

Well, how *could* you be? You know *[laughs]*, I took my money and went home! It was nice working together and everybody liked everybody, but in the final analysis it was a crock of crap! But I guess when you're involved in something like that, you take yourself a little more seriously. Probably if I saw it now I'd enjoy it, and maybe laugh my head off. One thing I do remember especially was that Jeff Corey, who played the leader of the mob that chases the mole-men, was very good in it. He got caught up in those damn McCarthy investigations, but Jeff has always been a good actor, and the proof of the pudding is that he went on to become one of the best acting coaches in Hollywood. Another thing I remember is that, not long after we finished it up, I was over in Scotland, visiting Edinburgh, and it was playing over there. There was this big billboard advertising the picture, and I just roared with laughter. We went directly from that *Mole-Men* feature right into the *Superman* series.

Had you been aware of the Superman *comics as a kid growing up?*

Yeah, but strangely enough I was never a comic book reader when I was a kid. I got sort of soured by *Little Orphan Annie*, who never did change, and *[laughs]* I put 'em all down!

Do you remember what Reeves's initial feelings were about the Superman *role?*

Yeah, he was not happy about it. The first time we ever got together, we toasted each other and he said, "Well, babe, this is it: the bottom of the barrel," and I felt the same way myself! George had had quite a good career going at one point, then he went into the service and it was a whole different ballgame when he came back. And he never, ever was happy. For one thing, in the beginning both of us were getting low dough—I mean, we were working for *very* little money, and George was really teed off about that. Later on, though, he really was able to get it up.

Jack Larson [Jimmy Olsen] made $350 an episode and Noel Neill [the later Lois Lane], $225.

Did they really say they worked for *that*? Jeez, then I got more than *they* did! I got $350, $375 an episode. And when I was preparing to leave the show, Whit Ellsworth [producer of *Superman* after the first season], who was trying to get me to stay, made me all kinds of offers!

What kind of money was George Reeves making?

George "Superman" Reeves is about to knock that smug look off of baddie James Craven's face, as Phyllis "Lois Lane" Coates watches approvingly. From the *Adventures of Superman,* episode "Riddle of the Chinese Jade."

As best as I can remember, George may have been getting around $1,000, maybe a little less. But we complained about it all the time.

Rumor has it that Reeves owned a piece of the show.
No, George did not. That syndicate, National Periodical Publications [now DC Comics], was very tight.

In working on the show, did you feel that your only audience would be kids?
Yes, definitely. And that was discouraging, particularly for George.

For an early TV show Superman *had very good special effects.*
The special effects were some of the best things in the old series—in fact, I don't know why Jack Larson and I stood for as much as we did. We were nearly blown up, beaten up, exploded, *exploited*—I guess it was because we were young and dumb, but we put up with a lot of stuff. Not too long ago I saw an episode *[Night of Terror]* where I got knocked out! The heavies on that show were so mean and so tough, but in real life they were the sweetest guys in the world—I worked with 'em on *Superman,* on Westerns, in gangster stuff, just all the time. The one that knocked me out, an actor named Frank Richards,

certainly was not responsible, I was. In an action show like *Superman* you had to hit your marks exactly. I missed my mark by about three or four inches, I moved too close to him, and he decked me! I was knocked out cold, and they sent me home — that left me a little black-and-blue, but I was back at work the next day. The funny thing to me is that Lee Sholem, who was directing, left that shot in! So if you watch that episode you can see that I really took a punch.

People have said that when Bob Maxwell produced *Superman* it was a more violent series, but I think it was just more action. Maxwell was, for my money, more imaginative that Whitney Ellsworth, and I thought it reflected Bob's tastes more than Whit's. As the series went on, after Bob was gone and Whit had taken over, it got a little sugary and sweet. It got cutesy-cutesy whereas before the episodes had a little bit of bite.

Do you remember anybody else getting hurt on the show?

George. He was about to do one of his famous takeoffs when the wires broke. And I thought he was going to kill me, because I couldn't help but laugh — it was just too funny! He could've been hurt and he knew it, and he grabbed me by the throat — kiddingly — and he said, "God damn it, don't you laugh, I could have been killed!" But it was just too funny for me to contain myself!

Did you have any inkling, early on, that the show was going to be a hit?

George and I had no idea, none whatsoever, that this kind of thing would develop. In fact, I wonder what it is — what is the magic about *Superman*? Is it that the good guys and the bad guys are so clearly defined?

For fans of that first season it's the dark, violent tone of the show, plus the excitement and suspense.

Well, that was Bob Maxwell — that reflects his taste. I can't tell you how many people have written me and said exactly the same thing that you just did. Maxwell was a more daring and more interesting guy than Whit Ellsworth; Maxwell just had that zip. He left *Superman* about the time that I did, and he died [in 1971] after he worked on *Lassie*. Bob had some fire and imagination — maybe that's the conflict he had with National Comics.

I guess I can see why the first season appealed to a more adult audience: I've had people write me to say that as kids they watched those early shows where the heroes were clear, the bad guys got it, Superman was really Superman and so on. I've got doctors and lawyers writing to me — really, it's amazing, the people who grew up on the series. And they all say the same thing: that that first season was the best one for them, the most meaningful in their lives.

National Comics apparently got fed up with the violence on the show, and wanted something entirely different from what Maxwell was delivering.

Well, they got it, didn't they? The new gang came in and turned it all to pudding!

I've heard people tell anecdotes that don't speak too well for Maxwell; in fact, one of the Superman *directors calls him a shit!*

Bob could be a shit, but I think anybody who has definite likes and dislikes, who's not afraid to let you know what he thinks and who shoots from the hip, is going to be a shit in somebody's eyes. I've been called that myself! I think Maxwell was tough, but I liked him — George and I socialized with Maxwell, and we *both* liked him. I just think that anybody who's definite is a bit of a shit.

Didn't Maxwell's wife also work the show?

Oh, God, did she! Jessica didn't really work the show but she was always there, hanging around on the set all the time. I can play comedy and I was always trying to slip some extra little touches in here and there, but she'd report me *[laughs]*! The directors, Lee Sholem and Tommy Carr and George Blair, were shooting and working so fast that I could have gotten away with a little — a look here, a look there — but Jessica always had her eagle eye out. I always got the feeling she was "the spy"! And she's the one who picked out that bloody suit and hat that I wore.

Did you ever tag along with Reeves on any of his frequent promotional tours?

No. He had asked me to do some, even when everybody was trying to get me to come back on the series. George wanted me back on *Superman,* and he spent some time talking to me about doing some of these personal appearances. I got talking to him about the p.a.'s he did, and let me tell you *[laughs]*, he hated 'em! It always appeared that George liked kids, but he told me some of the worst stories. Kids were always poking him, jabbing his rubber muscles — oh, God! But he did what was expected of him — George was one of those dear, sweet guys, and first and foremost he was an actor. So he would always rise to the occasion, but he said some terrible things happened on his personal appearances.

I know from several people that he had a short fuse. Did he ever lose his patience with you?

Never. But I did see him lose it a couple of times with other people, and of course he was always bitching about money. Barney Sarecky, who was head of production, used to come down and raise hell with us because George would whip out the bottle every day on the set about four o'clock. In those days we worked six days a week, from very early in the morning until six, seven o'clock at night, and we were working for short money. And so at four we drank — George and I became good drinking buddies *[laughs]*! This drove the production office crazy, and George would say to them, "Go shit in your hat!" That was really one of the reasons why I wanted out of the series: After George and I had set up this pattern, it was getting hard to break it.

George had a photographic mind, and he was such a fast study—it was great to work with him. I'm a fast study, too, but not as fast as he was. We averaged 24 pages of dialogue a day, and that's a *lot* of dialogue. And that involved only two people, not 12, 13, 15. We shot fast, we were seldom into two takes. And George was the kind of guy who, if you had a close-up, didn't let the script girl read his off-camera dialogue, he would be there—at least, he was that way for me. We just had a great working relationship as well as a good friendship.

Was he one to clown around?

Yeah, George was always telling stories. And he used a cigarette holder, and that gave him a very foppish look—George in his Superman suit, with a cigarette holder! He and John Hamilton [Perry White], they were always telling stories, and George was always pulling jokes and gags. He was a dear, sweet guy.

Have you ever seen any other actors who have played Superman?

I never did see Kirk Alyn play Superman. Christopher Reeve, the new Superman, is a wonderful actor and a good-looking guy, and really is the Superman for the 1980s. In 1988 Margot Kidder [Lois Lane in the new Superman movies] was here in Carmel, California, stumping for Jesse Jackson, and I was invited through some publicity people to attend that luncheon. And I thought it was kind of cute to be able to meet there with her. She really is my favorite Lois Lane—I think the two of them make a great team, and their relationship in these new movies is the way it should have been. But times have changed; when we did it, it was the '50s—sex was taboo. In those days, if Lois even *smiled* at Clark, they'd say [wagging her finger], "No, no, no—none of that!" I felt like a horse with a bit in its mouth! But, again, I do like Christopher Reeve, I think he's a very good actor, and I like Margot Kidder better than anybody who's ever played the role. And that includes myself.

Have you ever met Noel Neill?

In 1957 I was working at the old Eagle-Lion studio in Hollywood on a picture called *I Was a Teenage Frankenstein,* and the *Superman* people had moved their operation over there and were working there at that time. I ran into George one morning, about eight o'clock, and he said, "C'mon, let's have a drink." I said to myself, "Jesus!" George's face was like a baby's butt—he never did show it when he would drink, but I couldn't do it anymore. But anyway, I went over to his dressing room with him and he started pouring me a brandy, he was talking about the series then and he said, oh, God, he was so sick of it all. Then he took me over to meet Noel Neill. He knocked on her door and she said, "Come in." He opened the door and said, "I want you two to meet—

Phyllis, this is Noel." I said *[exuberantly]*, "Hi!" and she said, "I *hate* you!" And George reached in and closed the door!

I thought she was kidding *[laughs]*—I still to this day can't fathom this! This is the only time I ever met the lady—she can't stand me, I hear! We have never been able to appear together, have any fun together, laugh about it or anything. I did an interview on KGO-TV—Jim Eason's talk show, in San Francisco—and he told me that Noel never could call me by name, she always says "the other lady." Noel and I could have had fun and laughs, and had some cute things happen, but we've never been able to share anything. It's as though her whole life revolves around being identified with Lois Lane. I mean, if you had the suit and hat, you were Lois Lane—this is a comic strip, it's not a way of life, it was not all that serious!

People tend to say that I'm the original Lois Lane, and I *was* the first to play her in the *Mole-Men* movie and the TV series, but they forget that she did do the *Superman* serials with Kirk Alyn in the late '40s before I came on the scene. Maybe that's part of it. Noel travels and lectures at colleges and so on, and she's really milked this for whatever she could. I can understand that, but Lois Lane is not what I'm all about—that's only one facet. I really would like a career other than *Superman*.

What were your impressions of Jack Larson?

Jack is a swell guy, and we got along great together. The last time I saw him we were in Brentwood, which is where he lives; he keeps busy writing these days. The guy he lives with, Jim Bridges, is a very fine writer-director; Jim at the time was doing *Bright Lights, Big City* [1988], and Jack got cut in on that somehow as associate producer. Jack is a very sweet guy, and we always had a lot of fun with him.

Was he "the third musketeer" during that first season—you and George Reeves and Larson?

No, Jack didn't socialize too much with us then. I think later on maybe he got closer to George; early on, no.

Any memories of John Hamilton?

John was great. John liked everybody, he was a big b.s.er—he just told stories and laughed and roared and carried on. Very sweet—everybody liked John. He was a bit older than most of the other players, and we certainly all honored that. Everybody was very considerate of John.

How about "Inspector Henderson," Robert Shayne [q.v.]?

I got along great with Bob; in fact, I'm still a very, very close friend of his daughter Stephanie, who's a good actress, by the way. Whenever I have an interview that takes me to L.A. I go down and stay with Steph and her husband. And Bob is still alive and kicking—he's in his nineties, you know.

Like Jeff Corey, Bob Shayne, too, got caught up in those McCarthy investigations.

I remember the day they busted Bob—the day the Feds took him off the set. It was early in the morning, seven-thirty or eight o'clock, George and I were walking along and George looked down and said, "Those two guys with Bob are *heat.*" I said, "How can you tell?" and he said, "I just know." So we went right down to the set, where everybody was in a state of shock, and we found out what it was all about: An ex-wife of Shayne's turned him in. Well, this was one time when I really saw George with his dander up. We immediately went to Maxwell, and George raised hell. And Maxwell, who was a bleeding heart liberal, New York Jew, got right on it—I mean, everybody moved as fast as they could. We wrote letters, we did everything. Bob Shayne *had* been, I think, a card-carrying Communist, but a lot of people in Hollywood were then. I was involved with the Actors' Lab, and they were thick down there! But this wrecked Bob's career—he had to go into insurance, so on and so forth, and there were some rough years there for Bob.

That was the only time I had ever seen production stopped on *Superman,* the only time that anybody ever slowed down for anything. We didn't get going until late in the morning, and ordinarily we'd have been in front of those cameras by eight o'clock, sometimes a little bit before. But this stopped production dead.

Was there ever any danger of Shayne being bumped from Superman?

No, everybody hung on: George, myself, Bob Maxwell, we all took a strong stand.

Shayne feels very hurt that Jack Larson downplays his contribution to the show, and that he tells people Shayne wasn't part of the Superman *"family."*

Yes, he was! Number one, George liked Bob, very much, and they were always telling stories. Bob was from New York, where he had done a lot of work on the stage; he had even worked with Ethel Barrymore. Bob had a lot of strong credits behind him, and George always liked Bob. And on occasion we saw Bob and his wife Bette socially. George was a rapper *[laughs]*—you know what I mean?—and he got along with anybody who could sit around and rap. So Bob was definitely a part of the "family," and George took a very strong stand when Bob was busted. If George hadn't really cared about Bob, he wouldn't have said, "Come on, we're going to get some action." You wouldn't have stuck your neck out like that for somebody you didn't care about, particularly during that period—remember, that was a hot time. And George didn't hesitate for one second—I never saw anybody move so fast. Jack Larson wasn't even on the set that morning, he doesn't even know what happened. And in those days, George was not enamored of Jack—maybe later on they became closer friends, but I don't know because I was no longer there. George always considered Jack a kid.

When you talk about the *Superman* "family," it was not just the cast, it was the crew and everybody. My daughter was in a cast then because she was born without a right hip socket, and the grips would take her around on their bicycles and they would sit with her in my dressing room — they were just great with her. It was this kind of atmosphere. I would see George move things for grips — pick up something and carry it from one stage or one set to the next. Today you don't dare touch anything, but in those days we just were one big family and we moved like a house afire. George was very good, very fast, I was fast, it was frantic and hectic, but we all liked the pace. And that's why, at four o'clock, we all had a cocktail!

Was Superman *that much more hectic than most other TV shows?*
   The reason that we did so much and did so well was that we all liked each other. I think this was part of the problem with Noel Neill: I had some of the crew people tell me that the reason that Noel grew to dislike me was because the directors would say, "Oh, do it like Phyllis did it." So hearing that constantly would get to be a drag, for anybody.

Don't you think that your Lois was maybe a little too *hard on Clark Kent?*
   That was the way they wanted it. But I always felt that, too — that she came down a little heavy on him. In fact, I talked to George and Bob Maxwell about this, and I said, "It's almost as if she's really jealous, too much so, of him," and Maxwell said, "Yes, yes, but that's what it's supposed to be — to give him something to play off of." In other words, to really set Clark up as a softie, he had to have something hard to play against. I said, "Gee, what a ballsy broad!" and Maxwell said, "You got it!"

Did you enjoy playing tough, sassy broads?
   Well, they're a hell of a lot more interesting than those sweet, saccharine types — at least they're roles you can get your teeth into *[laughs]*!

Do actors appreciate lightning-fast directors like Lee Sholem, Tommy Carr and George Blair, or do they feel like nothing good can come of something slung together so quickly?
   We were all in the same boat — with one oar *[laughs]* — so it was row together or sink! These guys are known as action directors, and you had to bring to the roles what you could. That's why I say, if it hadn't been for Jessica Maxwell on the set, I could have gotten some *stuff* in there for Lois! They were not about to re-shoot scenes, so Jessica stood around with that sharp eye of hers and watched us, because I could have gotten away with a little bit with Lee and Blair and Tommy Carr. They were very easy to work with, sweet guys all of them, and I don't think an actor can blame them for shorting him.

Did you or Reeves ever try to pitch in creatively — suggest changes in dialogue or share ideas with directors?

Yes, George would, he was always contributing, and if there was any time he would get in there and pitch. Time was a great factor.

Your Lois is a feisty and aggressive girl. Is that you?

I'd like to be more aggressive—I'm not as aggressive as I might appear! Sometimes I am feisty, and I have got definite likes and dislikes, and that kind of thing.

Why did you leave Superman?

There were a number of reasons; one of them was that I didn't want to become typecast in that kind of thing. The minute we stopped shooting I'd bleach my hair and do other things, but for George this was it—he became typecast, and he was very unhappy about that. When I left the series and didn't renew my option, they offered me the moon. Whitney Ellsworth offered me about four or five times what I was getting if I'd come back. But I really wanted to get out of *Superman.*

A few months before he died, George came to my house. One Sunday after church he and Toni came by for brunch, and he told me that he had joined the Screen Directors Guild. He had a project he was going to do, and he wanted to know if I would play the lead. I said, "Why, if you've got the project and the money, of course." So he was preparing a picture which he really wanted to direct. It was a sci-fi—I can't remember the name of it, it was so long ago. Then the next thing I know Toni Mannix is calling me and telling me that George had been shot—you know, bullet holes around the bedroom and all this other stuff. She wanted me to go over to George's house with her and I couldn't at the time, and so she got Jack Larson to go with her.

What's your opinion about George Reeves's death?

I don't think we'll ever know. I do know that my friend Bill Cassara, who is with the sheriff's department here in Carmel, told me that he had seen a photograph of George Reeves, showing the bullet hole. They had examined that photograph and took into account the angle at which the bullet had entered the head, and they definitely determined that it was self-inflicted, that he was not murdered.

You once told an interviewer that the only TV appearance you're proud of is an episode of The Untouchables. *Does that mean you take no pride whatsoever in* Superman?

Yes, I *do* take pride in it because it was one of the most loving relationships that I ever experienced. The closeness with George, the crew—God, it was just such a great crew, I'll never forget those guys. I do take pride in it, and in the fact that we worked like gangbusters, we did it and did it well, and that there were never any beefs or arguments within our group. I'd have the crew come in my dressing room and have a drink and prop their feet up—

During the declining days of the serials, Coates made a great no-nonsense heroine in Republic's *Panther Girl of the Kongo*.

nobody drew lines in those days, and that was a good feeling. I don't think that'll ever be again, that kind of closeness between crew and cast.

I just did a picture here, after being away from the cameras for so many, many years. Larry Buchanan, who has Chaparral Productions, did a film on Marilyn Monroe called *Good Night, Sweet Marilyn* [1987] and I played her

mother, who was insane. I walked back in front of the camera and did my stuff in one take, after being away for so long—the crew couldn't believe I hadn't been in front of a camera in that long. So I'm starting back up again, and it feels good.

Early on, before you got mired in all those low-budget Westerns and then Superman, *what sort of niche were you hoping to fill as an actress?*

I really felt I could play comedy, after I'd worked vaudeville. I'd done some shows overseas with the U.S.O. and I played "straight man" to stand-up comics, and I found that I could play comedy. I did a comedy series called *This is Alice* [1958] for Desilu, I worked with Bob Cummings and Abbott and Costello and so on. In fact, another reason why I left *Superman* was because I thought Jack Carson and Allen Jenkins were headed for a comedy series, and I committed myself to a role in that. I also did a pilot film with Bert Lahr [*Thompson's Ghost,* 1966] which never got off the ground even though it was a cute idea. So I wanted to play comedy, and I hope still, even at this late date, to get into something with some comedic value.

Superman *took an unfortunate turn toward silly comedy soon after you left.*

And none of 'em can *play* comedy! That's why it turned into what it did.

I get the impression that you're not one to sit around watching your old pictures.

No, as a matter of fact, I really have never seen anything! I don't even know whether or not, if I *had* done some great things, I would sit down again to see them. Once something is done, it's done, and I never look back because you can always say, "God, I could have done that so much better." There's always that element.

Your serials for Republic, Jungle Drums of Africa *and* Panther Girl of the Kongo—*were they a hectic grind, too?*

Whew! Let me tell you, they were tough to make. In *Panther Girl* I wore a short costume in order to match stock footage from some older jungle serial [*Jungle Girl,* 1941], and I had to ride an elephant all day. And my legs were raw from the hair on the elephant—I never knew 'til then that an elephant even *had* hair! Then one of the natives fired a gun near my ear, and I was deaf for a couple of days! We'd go in this terrible lake at Republic, this water pond where the alligators would be snapping at your ass, and the minute we'd climb out of this awful, stagnant water we'd have to get a shot of penicillin so we would survive and not die of some sort of disease! I guess it was my sense of humor that kept me going through the thing. A fellow said to me one time,

Opposite: Coates ground out Republic serials such as *Panther Girl* after leaving the *Superman* teleseries.

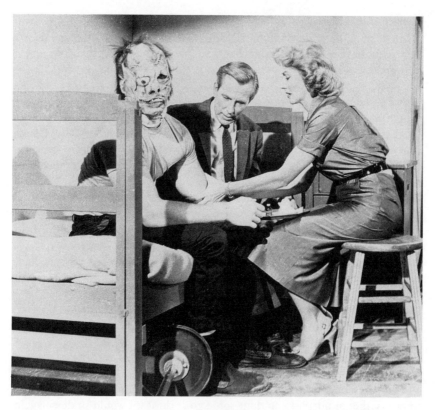

Gary Conway, Whit Bissell and Coates in *I Was a Teenage Frankenstein.*

"You were sort of the last-ditch effort at a serial queen, weren't you?" and, to be honest, I guess I was! I don't mind telling you I never read the scripts on those things—in fact, I never read the scripts on *Superman,* if you want to get right down to it. I knew the character, it became one-dimensional for me and I would just go in and wing it with George. And when I did Westerns, you either played the whore with heart, or you played the sweet mother, or you played the ingenue. In Westerns they lit the horse and the cowboy, and to hell with the leading lady! And it was the same way on *Superman.*

How did you become mixed up on I Was a Teenage Frankenstein?

I just went on an interview, I guess, and got the job. I don't really remember too much about that picture except that the star, Whit Bissell, was very nice to work with. I also remember that they had live alligators there, and they were throwing some bones to 'em—they were supposed to be *my* bones, as a matter of fact *[laughs]*!

Your worst film has to be The Incredible Petrified World.

A friend of mine from my teenage days, a fellow by the name of Jerry Warren, called me and said, "Gypsie, you have to do me a favor, I've got to get started in the business. I've got this script, Robert Clarke is gonna do it, John Carradine's gonna be in it," so on and so forth. After I read the script I said, "Jerry, I'll never work again if I do this picture!" and he said, "I promise you this picture will never show on the West Coast. I just gotta get started!" I knew Bob Clarke, who was a doll of a guy, and so I let Jerry twist my arm. And I did not take a salary, I did it as a favor.

You shot that in Colossal Cave, New Mexico.

What an awful experience! That place was full of bat guano—it was hideous! Jerry's father-in-law played the monster, and his wife was the production head.

We did have a lot of laughs over there, though; Bob Clarke's wife, Alyce, was trying to get pregnant, and I was telling them all about Vitamin E. So they started taking Vitamin E like crazy—eating it, drinking it, rubbing it on 'em and everything else *[laughs]*—and finally they did have a baby, a gorgeous son named Cameron. And it was fun working with Carradine, who was a wonderful nut—John would get drunk, and carry on with Shakespeare *[laughs]*! He was dating Della Jacques, the girl who stood in for me on *Superman,* and one time they were over at my house for dinner. I finally went to bed, I got up again about three in the morning and there he was, stark naked, "to-be-or-not-to-be"-ing in my living room! John was absolutely, marvelously insane—a brilliant, funny actor.

And then, of course, the film did *play in California.*

Oh, I could have *killed* Jerry *[laughs]*! He lost me more jobs with that film, because it did show out here. That was the biggest mistake of my life, and I never spoke to him after that.

If you could turn back the clock, what would you do differently in your career?

I would not do *The Incredible Petrified World* with Jerry Warren, that's for sure *[laughs]*! But, seriously, I don't know what I could do differently: I was in a bind, I had a child who had a physical handicap and I had to work. My mother was in and out of mental institutions, and I had a lot of heavy stuff in my life. People in Hollywood remember that I had an alcoholic grandmother who lived with me for awhile—in fact, I can remember that I was on the set of *Teenage Frankenstein* when I got a call from the police, that my grandmother was sprawled out on somebody's lawn! I had all this crap in my life, trying to handle an alcoholic grandmother who would be selling my clothes to neighbors to get money for booze, and a mother who almost drove me insane with *her* problems...! So there were great limitations on me in those days, and I had to work. And to try to work and handle this and keep it all under wraps was tough. Evidently I had some dues to pay and, man, I paid 'em!

Thanks to Superman *you're a cult actress with a large, loyal and loving fan following. Is that adequate compensation for never having broken into the big time?*

It sure is—it means a lot. The hundreds of letters I get and the requests for autographs, it's all very heartwarming. I was happy to be in *Superman;* I was also happy to be in *This Is Alice,* although the director Sidney Salkow was not very imaginative, he was one of those crank-'em-out guys. I adored working with Ida Lupino [on *The Untouchables*], she was a charge; and I loved working with Larry Buchanan in '87 on *Good Night, Sweet Marilyn.* This guy is an action guy—he's from Hollywood, he's made a lot of low-budget films and he's a very talented man. He is going to form a stock company, and I'll be a part of it. I liked the cameo role I did in *Good Night, Sweet Marilyn,* and maybe I'll do things in the future that I'm going to like even better.

PHYLLIS COATES FILMOGRAPHY

So You Want to Be in Politics (Warners short, 1948)
Smart Girls Don't Talk (Warners, 1948)
So You Want to Be a Muscleman (Warners short, 1949)
So You're Having In-Law Trouble (Warners short, 1949)
The House Across the Street (Warners, 1949)
A Kiss in the Dark (Warners, 1949)
My Foolish Heart (RKO, 1949)
So You Want to Hold Your Husband (Warners short, 1950)
Blues Busters (Monogram, 1950)
My Blue Heaven (20th Century–Fox, 1950)
Outlaws of Texas (Monogram, 1950)
Man from Sonora (Monogram, 1951)
Canyon Raiders (Monogram, 1951)
So You Want to Be a Cowboy (Warners short, 1951)
Nevada Badmen (Monogram, 1951)
Oklahoma Justice (Monogram, 1951)
The Longhorn (Monogram, 1951)
So You Want to Be a Bachelor (Warners short, 1951)
So You Want to Be a Plumber (Warners short, 1951)
Superman and the Mole-Men (Lippert, 1951)
Stage to Blue River (Monogram, 1951)
Flat Top (Monogram, 1952)
So You Want to Get It Wholesale (Warners short, 1952)
So You're Going to a Convention (Warners short, 1952)
Invasion U.S.A. (Columbia, 1952)
Fargo (Monogram, 1952)
Guns Along the Border (Monogram, 1952)
Hired Gun (Monogram, 1952)
The Gunman (Monogram, 1952)
Canyon Ambush (Monogram, 1952)
The Maverick (Allied Artists, 1952)
So You Want to Wear the Pants (Warners short, 1952)

Wyoming Roundup (Monogram, 1952)
Marshal of Cedar Rock (Republic, 1953)
So You Want a Television Set (Warners short, 1953)
So You Love Your Dog (Warners short, 1953)
So You Think You Can't Sleep (Warners short, 1953)
So You Want to Be an Heir (Warners short, 1953)
She's Back on Broadway (Warners, 1953)
Topeka (Monogram, 1953)
Perils of the Jungle (Lippert, 1953)
El Paso Stampede (Republic, 1953)
Here Come the Girls (Paramount, 1953)
Jungle Drums of Africa (Republic serial, 1953)
So You're Having Neighbor Trouble (Warners short, 1954)
Panther Girl of the Kongo (Republic serial, 1955)
Girls in Prison (AIP, 1956)
So Your Wife Wants to Work (Warners short, 1956)
I Was a Teenage Frankenstein (AIP, 1957)
Chicago Confidential (United Artists, 1957)
Cattle Empire (20th Century–Fox, 1958)
Blood Arrow (20th Century–Fox, 1958)
The Incredible Petrified World (Governor Films, 1960)
The Baby Maker (National General, 1970)
Good Night, Sweet Marilyn (Chaparral Productions, 1987)

It was on The Masque of the Red Death
that I got the review from Time *magazine that read,*
"The sexy, lusty redhead is played by the English actress
Miss Hazel Court, in whose cleavage you could sink
the entire works of Edgar Allan Poe
and a bottle of his favorite booze
at the same time." I [laughs] —
I rather liked that one!

Hazel Court

IN THE ROYAL TRADITION of Fay Wray (the 1930s), Evelyn Ankers (the '40s) and Beverly Garland (the '50s), voluptuous Hazel Court was the undisputed queen of '60s horror. Her reign spanned two continents; her regal consorts included horror kings Karloff, Price, Lorre, Cushing and Lee; and her loyal subjects were the legions of Hammer and AIP fans. In 1964 the flame-haired scream queen relinquished her throne to attend to the more pressing responsibilities of being a wife and mother, but she continues to look back with affection on a remarkable career in horror and science fiction.

Born in Birmingham, England, Court carried on a love affair with the world of movies and make-believe that made her a leading student at her hometown's School of Drama and later helped her land a contract with the J. Arthur Rank Organisation. Graduating from bits to supporting roles to leads, she made her fantasy film debut in 1953's *The Ghost Ship* and later reinforced her genre rep in British-based productions like *Devil Girl from Mars, Doctor Blood's Coffin* and Hammer's landmark *The Curse of Frankenstein*. Relocating to Hollywood, she also became a regular in Roger Corman's Poe series, acting opposite the grand old men of horror in such chiller classics as *The Masque of the Red Death* and the comedic *The Raven*.

Your first horror film was a minor picture called The Ghost Ship. *Do you remember that film at all?*

Yes, I do. That was with Dermot Walsh, who was my husband at the time — he and I made several films together. I remember the wonderful old teak sailing ship we worked on in *The Ghost Ship*. It belonged to the director of the film, Vernon Sewell, who was marvelous; he had a certain "throwaway" technique that worked *[laughs]*, and he did lots of wonderful early English films. *The Ghost Ship* was a very quick film, a low-budget picture, and to be honest with you I really don't recall much about it except that beautiful yacht. We shot everything, including the interiors, on her.

Over the years your Devil Girl from Mars *has acquired a campy, Worst Films kind of reputation.*

Devil Girl from Mars! That one really has become a "classic," hasn't it *[laughs]*? But, you know, I ran my tape of that film just the other day and I really thought it was amazing — for the time, and for what it cost. And the photography wasn't bad, for a three-week picture. And I recognized a lot of old friends that I'd forgotten: Adrienne Corri was in it, and Hugh McDermott, and others. I was just fascinated.

How about Patricia Laffan, who played the Devil Girl?

I don't remember her much. Hugh McDermott was the one with the great sense of humor — with that lovely Scottish accent, he'd seem to be sending everything up.

Previous page: **The undisputed queen of '60s horror, Hazel Court is all pigtails and sunny smiles in this candid shot from *The Masque of the Red Death*.**

Court *(left)* and space invader Patricia Laffan in the schlocky British SF film *Devil Girl from Mars*.

What about the Devil Girl's robot?

[Laughs.] It kept breaking down! It was mechanical, and it kept breaking down!

So you enjoyed working on Devil Girl from Mars?

I remember great fun on the set. It was like a repertory company acting that film: We were all friends and got on well, we rehearsed and acted and it was great fun. We kind of giggled and laughed about it all, but we were aware we were doing something different.

What do you recall about some of the behind-the-scenes people?

I remember the director, David MacDonald, he was sweet. And the producers [Edward and Harry Lee Danziger] made a lot of money out of the films they made in England. They really were very tight on budget, tight on everything—they'd even write the next script on the back of the old one! And they'd give you *a* Kleenex if you asked for a box *[laughs]*! They became very rich and I'm told they own half of Paris today.

How rushed and low-budget were these minor SF films?

Very. I wouldn't know the exact budgets on any of those things, but they were staggeringly small. We shot for like three weeks, working into the night. And you never got a chance for a retake unless the film was damaged. But they were organized, though, I must say that.

As a kid growing up, did you enjoy going to the movies?
Oh, yes. I used to go with my mother and father and we'd stand in line at the local cinema. And then on the way home I would act out the film—I walked about ten paces behind them, and do absolutely the whole film *[laughs]*! It's fun now, looking back on that time and on coming to Hollywood, seeing Sunset Boulevard for the first time and so on. I never lost my awe for it.

Is it true that, early on, your parents disapproved of your interest in acting?
They weren't that keen on it, really, but they didn't stop me. My father was a sportsman, a well-known English cricketer, and there was no theatrical background at all. At fourteen I was at the Birmingham Repertory Theater and the Alexander Theater in Birmingham. I had had my London Academy of Dramatic Art prior to that. I must have been about sixteen when Sir Anthony Asquith, who directed many wonderful British films, saw some pictures of me that my sister Audrey had, and he said, "She should be in pictures!" And Audrey said, "Well, she *is* an actress." So I was sent to London to meet him, and then he sent me to Sir Michael Balcon at Ealing Studios, where I made my first film, *Champagne Charlie* [1944]. I only had one line: It was an Edwardian film, I was up in a balcony and I'm watching the gaiety people, and I say, "I never had champagne before," as I'm giggling and laughing. That was my introduction to it.

If you had had your druthers, what types of roles would you have wanted to play?
I did love the theater and I enjoyed doing comedy—it was comedy that actually brought me to America, through doing the TV series *Dick and the Duchess* [1957–1958] with Patrick O'Neal. And then of course I ended up going back into the horror films *[laughs]*—*The Premature Burial*, *The Raven* and *The Masque of the Red Death*.

Did you see horror films as a kid?
No—never! Fred Astaire, Ginger Rogers, yes. Horror films? I wanted nothing to do with them *[laughs]*!

In making films for Hammer, did you get to meet the people who ran the company?
Oh, yes, I knew Jimmy Carreras and his son Michael very well indeed. They took over the Manor House at Bray, and the grounds became the studios.

It was all on a shoestring, but the amazing thing is that I remember incredibly beautiful sets. And I never had cheap costumes there, I had the best of everything. We didn't get much money for working in Hammer pictures, and they didn't cost a great deal, but they made a fortune.

Did the Carrerases enjoy making horror films, or did they make them only because they saw the future in them?
I think they had a feel for horror films *and* they saw the future. They were both wonderful men.

Had you seen any of the old Frankenstein films before making The Curse of Frankenstein *for Hammer?*
No. But we ran the original film with Boris Karloff—and little did I think that I would act with Boris Karloff years later, in *The Raven.* We didn't really know what we were doing, but Terence Fisher had a wonderful eye for all that and he would get it all on film without any fuss. He was marvelous in that way. We were always at great ease and we were never pressured; with Terence Fisher you had all the time you wanted.

A screenwriter named Chris Wicking, who wrote some films for Hammer, says that Fisher looked upon his horror films as "a bit of a joke."
Terence Fisher may have thought of them as a lark, but he had such a good technique that he did a good job. He was excellent—a good, solid, well-informed and knowledgeable director.

Were these Hammer films one-take pictures?
No, we'd go two and three takes on those.

How did you like working with Peter Cushing on The Curse of Frankenstein?
He was a wonderful man, a trained actor from the Old Vic. Peter Cushing was born a century too late—he really comes from the nineteenth century. A lovely man. I don't remember too much about Christopher Lee, to be honest with you, even though I worked with him twice, in *The Curse of Frankenstein* and *The Man Who Could Cheat Death.* He was a very funny man, a great raconteur with lots of stories.

Your daughter is also in Curse of Frankenstein.
That's right—she's a little girl of three or four. They wanted someone who looked like me to play me as a little girl, in one of the flashback scenes, so I suggested Sally. She hated it—*hated* being in it! I think it was all very foreign to her, and she didn't understand it. She still remembers it today, and still doesn't like it!

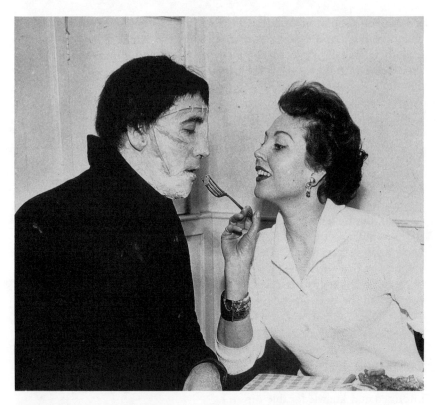

Beauty and the Beast: Christopher Lee (in Phil Leakey monster makeup) accepts a morsel from Hazel Court, behind the scenes on Hammer's landmark *The Curse of Frankenstein*.

The gory and sexy scenes in The Curse of Frankenstein *were groundbreakers in 1957. What did you think of them at the time?*

    You know, we took it lightly, and kind of almost tongue-in-cheek, even though we always played it seriously. But it was fun. The [slasher] films they make today are horrible—I think they're awful! So many fans write to me and say that it's not the "true" horror anymore. They're just nasty films, whereas the Frankenstein films and all the other ones we made there were tongue-in-cheek—played for real, but kind of tongue-in-cheek, and fun. Today's films have different connotations. I honestly believe that the films which I appeared in are among the last of the really well-done horror films.

    The Curse of Frankenstein had its opening night at the Metro-Goldwyn-Mayer Theater in Leicester Square. If you remember the picture, after Peter Cushing has participated in some particularly bloody scene, the film cuts to me having breakfast with Peter the next morning, and he says, "Pass the marmalade, please." The whole house roared with laughter—and now it's become a line that's quoted!

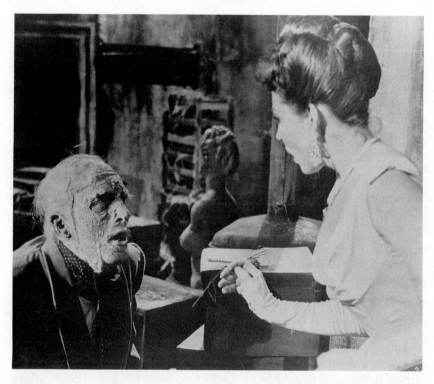

Hazel Court went nose-to-nose with a record number of movie monsters, including a withered Anton Diffring in *The Man Who Could Cheat Death*.

Your other film for Hammer was The Man Who Could Cheat Death *with Anton Diffring.*

That was a lovely movie. It seemed to me that they took greater pains with *The Man Who Could Cheat Death* than with *The Curse of Frankenstein,* and that it was a more elaborate movie. I remember there was a nude scene in there, too—that was one of the first! In the domestic version you see only my head and shoulders, in the scene where Anton Diffring is sculpting me, but we also shot a European version and there I am—front and back *[laughs]*! Somewhere in Europe there must be a print of that floating around.

Were you comfortable doing that?

[Hesitantly.] Y-e-s. It was new in those days, but it was a beautiful setting and supposedly I was being sculpted, so . . . it didn't worry me. Actually, to make that bust, a plaster cast was taken of my body, including my face; I remember having the straws out of my nose and my mouth, for breathing. It's a terrifying thing, and they ask you to keep it on for as long as possible. (I didn't keep it on very long!) I'm sure that bust is still somewhere in the property department at Pinewood Studios!

Anton Diffring always gives such icy performances. Was he any "looser" off-camera?

He was just the same off-camera as on film. He was from the old Berlin school of acting, and he was a very good actor, very renowned as a stage actor in Germany. Anton Diffring was charming, a very educated man. He died just a while back [May 1989].

In preparing for this film did you get to watch the older version, The Man in Half Moon Street?

No, but I remembered it, from seeing it as a young girl growing up. I loved it, thought it was wonderful, and it had been very prominent in my mind always.

When you started getting roles in horror films, one after another, did this suit you or did you feel they did you no good?

No, I was looking for something more, much more serious roles. But that didn't happen. It almost started to happen with *Carnival* [1946] which I won a British Critics Award for playing a crippled girl. But it never really came about.

What memories do you have of Doctor Blood's Coffin?

That it was shot in Cornwall, England—I love Cornwall, it's a wonderful part of the world. *Doctor Blood's Coffin* was one of the first films of Sidney Furie, who went on to direct lots more films. He was always interesting; he was always trying to find ways to shoot something differently. I saw his future potential, absolutely—it was right there for all of us to see.

What can you remember about the rest of the cast?

Kieron Moore, who played Dr. Blood, seems to have dropped out of movies. He was a beautiful Irish actor and I don't know what happened to him—I would like to know! He was lovely to work with and a very attractive man. And Ian Hunter was a lovely man, too, he was very good.

Were the cave scenes shot on a set?

No, in a cave—the real thing, at Cornwall. And very wet!

Throughout this late '50s–early '60s period you were back and forth to Hollywood a number of times.

I did the TV series *Dick and the Duchess,* which we did in England, and then CBS brought me to America, where I did several episodes of the Alfred Hitchcock TV series. I did four of those—in fact, my present husband, Don Taylor, was the director of the first episode I did, which was called "The Crocodile Case." So I was doing a lot of going back and forth.

Hazel Court is less than pleased to find her husband (Paul Stockman) has been revived from the dead in the climax of *Doctor Blood's Coffin.*

Did you get to know Hitchcock at all?

Yes, I knew him well, and I am also great friends with Pat Hitchcock, who is his daughter. Of course Hitch never cared much about actors, it was always the camera, you know. So you were always fighting that. But he was fun — he was a great storyteller and a very funny man.

One of your Hitchcock *episodes,* Arthur, *was directed by Hitchcock himself.*

Oh, yes, with Larry Harvey. Two thousand chickens and me and Laurence Harvey! I remember Harvey saying to me, "Are you as nervous as I am?" and I said, "Yes, I am!" I remember us both saying, "This is *not* going to be our best day" — we were very nervous.

Did Hitchcock put you at ease?

[Laughs.] Halfway!

Then in the early '60s you moved here permanently.

That's when I also did *The Premature Burial* and *The Raven* . . . my God, I did do a lot of horror films *[laughs]*! No wonder they call me a scream queen! But I had fun, I must say that — lots of fun. It was sheer delight to be working with Peter Lorre and Karloff and Vincent Price, who I became a lifelong friend of. He was instrumental in getting me started in my art—he thought I had great talent—and which I've gone on to do ever since. He's a wonderfully interesting man, and still my mentor today. He's written quotations for me, on my brochure about my painting, and now he's going to do one about my sculpting. He, like Peter Cushing, was born in the wrong century.

Your first horror film over here was Roger Corman's The Premature Burial.
That's one of my favorites. There was a mood to it, a strangeness and a mood. And working with Ray Milland was lovely—when I was asked to do the film, I thought it would be wonderful to work with him, and in a Poe story at that. Roger Corman was fun, he and I got on well—we all got on well. I enjoyed working with Roger very much; he was efficient, never went over budget, never went over time. He was quite marvelous.

Corman's stepped on a lot of actors' toes, and some have come away bitter.
On the pictures I did with him, if you wanted more time, you'd just say, "I've got to do it again." He did rush, there was no question about that, but you had to rush with him *[laughs]*—you had to stay right alongside Roger! I never had rows or anything with him, it was always fun.

Did he really direct you, or was he a camera director?
He directed a little—mostly he was camera in those days.

Did you enjoy making so many period pictures?
Even as a kid I always did—I was always dressing up with crinolines and shawls and things. So it was kind of a natural follow-up for me—I dwelled in the past a lot! So I enjoyed all the costumes and so on.

What about your Premature Burial *co-stars?*
Well, I discovered that Ray Milland was a marvelous poet, which I didn't know—he used to write beautiful things. He was Welsh, and the Welsh do write poetry. He was charming. *The Premature Burial* was Richard Ney's last film. He was involved in the stock market, and he was more interested in that than in the acting at that point; then I think he really went into it in a big way, became a broker or something. He made a lot of money at it. And Alan Napier was sweet, it was nice to work with him. There's a song that's called "The Grand Old English Gentleman," and that's what Alan Napier truly was.

You must have a story about the scene where you're buried alive.
Yeah, I was really in there—I did it. They actually did bury me! On rehearsals I had a straw in my mouth, and in covering me up they didn't cover the top of the straw. But on the actual take I had to hold my breath for a minute—a full 60 seconds—covered up with cork. It was horrible!

You appeared with a trio of top horror stars in The Raven.

That was a fun one. Boris Karloff was a great gentleman, but the raconteur, of course, was Peter Lorre, who had great sex appeal, and great charm for the ladies. You always felt that you were the only one in the world he was talking to. He used to make me laugh—a highly intelligent man. Peter Lorre was not well at all on that picture, I think his heart was bad—he perspired all the time, and his eyes were always teary. But nothing would hold him back, he was a wonderful pro. And I remember, too, that Karloff's leg was hurting him, very badly.

They say Peter Lorre ad-libbed a lot on The Raven.

Yes, he never quite got the lines right *[laughs]*—he'd just do his version, and the rest of us would just muddle along! But then there were three of them at it—Vincent and all of them! It was wonderful to be with them, because one would tell a story, then that would spark another one, and then that would spark Vincent, and on and on. This round robin of stories would keep going, and you'd just sit there fascinated and your eyes would go from side to side...!

Would Corman crack the whip on these oldtimers like he did most of his other actors?

Oh, no—there was no problem at all, he never did that. We used to make him laugh a lot—I was always giggling. He never told me off!

Did you see any spark of stardom in Jack Nicholson?

You would look at him and you never would think that this little Jackie Nicholson would turn out to be this big star! He was so young, and so much fun—like a little stuffed elf popping around!

Did you ever encounter James Nicholson or Sam Arkoff?

Oh, yes, I knew them quite well and they were nice people, and great to work for. I'll always remember Sam Arkoff—he didn't like "dark" pictures, he said, and it was funny because on these pictures it was *always* dark!

In your Corman films you played scheming vixens to perfection. Did you enjoy these roles?

I loved doing them—I liked sacrificing myself to the Devil and branding myself in *The Masque of the Red Death* and all that. But that's not me at all! It was on *The Masque of the Red Death* that I got the review from *Time* magazine that read, "The sexy, lusty redhead is played by the English actress Miss Hazel Court, in whose cleavage you could sink the entire works of Edgar Allan Poe and a bottle of his favorite booze at the same time." I *[laughs]*—I rather liked that one!

Much more money was spent on *The Masque of the Red Death*—it was a more opulent production. It was a big production, lots of costumes and a wonderful cameraman, Nicolas Roeg, who photographed me beautifully in that. I think I was like two or three months' pregnant when I was doing the film!

What else do you remember about the picture?
    Working with Jane Asher. She was in love with Paul McCartney, they were seeing each other at the time and she wanted to marry him—I kept telling her she was too young *[laughs]*! And of course she didn't marry him. And she was knitting balaclava helmets—the kind of knitted helmet they wore in the war, in cold climates, with the face showing. These balaclava helmets were for the Beatles, so they could go out at night and they wouldn't be recognized. I liked Jane Asher, she was talented, and she still is a good actress today.

Many fans think Red Death *is the best of the Poe films.*
    I think *The Raven* is.

Why did you turn your back on acting after The Masque of the Red Death?
    I had my son Jonathan, and I firmly believe that you cannot have a marriage, a career *and* bring up a child in Hollywood. It was a decision I had to make. By the way, right now Jonathan is managing a marvelous rock-and-roll band called The Rotters, and I think they're going to break out—I think their sound is going to be known very soon.

In 1981 you surprised everyone by turning up in the third Omen *film,* The Final Conflict.
    I was on vacation in Cornwall with Harvey Bernhard and his wife. Harvey was the producer of all three of the *Omen* films: *The Omen, Damien—Omen II,* which my husband directed, and *The Final Conflict,* which was then shooting. And Harvey said, "Would you mind just popping in and doing this?" I giggled and laughed and accepted, never thinking that anybody would see me. Well, I tell you *[laughs]*, *everybody* saw me! They all asked me, "What were you doing there?" and I'd say, "Well, that's supposed not to be seen." It's a foxhunt scene, and I'm handing around a stirrup cup.

And today sculpting is your new passion.
    Oh, sure. I study in Italy part of the year every year, I'm in many big collections and I've had shows in Los Angeles, in La Jolla and in Pisa, Italy. I'm in the Dupont collection in New York, I'm in Vincent's collection—many prominent people. That's my life now, and I'm becoming very prominent.

What favorites, among your horror films?
    The Premature Burial I loved doing; I don't know why, but I did. If it isn't that, then it's *The Raven*, because it was so much fun working with "the boys."

What would it take to lure you back to acting?

Hmmmm ... a small role, one that had some substance to it. But I have no great desire to do that, I'm well and truly wedded to my art. It's a whole new dimension, a whole new direction, and it's very exciting. New people, a new career—it's wonderful.

HAZEL COURT FILMOGRAPHY

Champagne Charlie (Ealing, 1944)
Dreaming (Ealing, 1944)
Carnival (General Films Distributors, 1946)
Dear Murderer (Gainsborough/General Films Distributors, 1947)
Holiday Camp (Universal, 1947)
Meet Me at Dawn (The Gay Duelist) (Fox, 1947)
The Root of All Evil (Gainsborough/General Films Distributors, 1947)
It's Not Cricket (Gainsborough/General Films Distributors, 1948)
My Sister and I (General Films Distributors, 1948)
Showtime (Gaiety George) (Warners British, 1948)
Forbidden (British Lion, 1949)
Bond Street (Stratford, 1950)
The Ghost Ship (Lippert, 1953)
Undercover Agent (Counterspy) (Lippert, 1953)
The Scarlet Web (Eros Films, 1954)
A Tale of Three Women (Paramount, 1954)
Devil Girl from Mars (Spartan, 1955)
Behind the Headlines (Kenilworth/R.F.D. Productions, 1956)
The Narrowing Circle (Eros Films, 1956)
The Curse of Frankenstein (Warners, 1957)
Hour of Decision (Eros Films, 1957)
A Woman of Mystery (United Artists, 1957)
The Man Who Could Cheat Death (Paramount, 1959)
The Man Who Was Nobody (Anglo Amalgamated, 1960)
Model for Murder (Cinema Associates, 1960)
The Shakedown (Universal, 1960)
Breakout (Continental Distributing, 1961)
Doctor Blood's Coffin (United Artists, 1961)
Mary Had a Little ... (Lopert Pictures, 1961)
The Premature Burial (AIP, 1962)
The Raven (AIP, 1963)
The Masque of the Red Death (AIP, 1964)
Madhouse (AIP, 1974) (filmclips from *The Masque of the Red Death*)
The Final Conflict (20th Century–Fox, 1981)

*Anything that costs a penny over his minuscule budgets
turns Roger Corman into a monster. He is a dual personality:
You meet him in his office and he's absolutely charming.
That boyish face of his, he digs his toe in the carpet,
all of that jazz. You get him on the set,
and he's Attila the Hun.*

Richard Devon

YET ANOTHER talented member of Roger Corman's early stock company, actor Richard Devon provided consummate villainy in such B productions as *The Undead, Machine-Gun Kelly* (1958), *War of the Satellites* and the cumbersomely titled *The Saga of the Viking Women and Their Voyage to the Waters of the Great Sea Serpent.*

Devon wanted to be an actor from the time he played a small part in a first grade grammar school production. After finishing high school he answered a small ad in a Los Angeles newspaper which offered training to the novice. This drama school, "Stage Eight," allowed him to work his way through as he hadn't money for tuition. He painted walls, built sets, waxed floors and strung lights. It was during this time that he made his first live television appearance for the experimental TV station W6XAO, atop Mt. Lee in the Hollywood Hills.

Amidst much additional work in television, radio and little theater, Devon also played a recurring character on the kiddie-oriented teleseries *Space Patrol* (when Devon asked for a pay hike, his character was put into permanent suspended animation!). He made his major motion picture debut in Metro's Biblical spectacle *The Prodigal* (1955) with Lana Turner, appeared in his first film for Corman two years later, and picks up his own story from here. . . .

How did you first become acquainted with Roger Corman?

I became acquainted with this boy wonder on a film called *The Undead.* There was an interview, I got the role and I appeared in the film as the Devil. As far as my part was concerned, *The Undead* was shot entirely in an abandoned market on Santa Monica Boulevard. Roger got ahold of some phony boulders and he filled the place with dead shrubbery and all of that. They had a bee-smoker to create the dreadful-smelling fog, and a camera, and the whole thing was shot there. As you know, Roger was not great on budgets and he was extremely tight on schedules.

What else do you remember about working with Corman?

His temper was really quite awesome. On *The Undead,* someone had left one of my speeches out of the script, and naturally I couldn't learn what wasn't there. And he was not just upset, he was *maniacal.* Anything that costs a penny over his minuscule budgets turns Roger Corman into a monster. He is a dual personality: You meet him in his office and he's absolutely charming. That boyish face of his, he digs his toe in the carpet, all of that jazz. You get him on the set, and he's Attila the Hun. With Roger, if anything costs more than what he has figured, it's a disaster for everybody that's around him.

So what exactly happened when you skipped that Undead *speech?*

He was just screaming his head off. Everybody was telling him that it could be rectified, and I said, "Roger, it's all right, don't worry about it. We'll

Previous page: **Richard Devon is still active in Hollywood doing occasional acting and voiceover jobs.**

get somebody to write it out on a card or something and I'll read it." So one of the prop guys wrote it out on a little cardboard box of some sort and I read it—we did it in one take—and that was it. Roger never did another take unless it was absolutely impossible to get around it. If something went wrong or if a take was blown or something like that, what he would do was give it to the editor, and use some footage to cut around.

Did Corman give you enough creative freedom as an actor?
Roger's direction didn't consist of too much beyond, "Let's get fifteen pages in the can"—I mean *[laughs]*, Roger was a quick-buck boy. Roger was great for saying, "Let's try the rehearsal on film"—that kind of thing. I didn't know very much of his background; I understood that he took a course at one of the colleges in cinematography, he finished the course and that was it—he was on his way. He did a picture called *Monster from the Ocean Floor,* which he made for about twenty cents, and he sold it for something like 250 grand! He bootlegged most of the footage—this is Roger. You're talkin' about Roger, you're talkin' about bootleg.

And he never got away from working that way, even when it seemed like he could have.
He did have chances at really getting up there and being a good producer and a good director of big films. As a matter of fact, at one point he was given a film at Columbia [*A Time for Killing,* 1967] to direct. He was given a fine budget and stars and everything else. But what happened was, he started shooting the film and he just couldn't get out of his old ways. He was pushing the actors, they were upset, the crew was upset, so on and so forth. The Columbia brass looked at the rushes and called him in and said, "You know, Roger, we want something to be on the *film*—we don't need this fast kind of attitude that you've had in the past. There's a talent there, there's an ability—stretch it out." But he couldn't hack it. And he was replaced on the film.

Do you think you were chosen for the Devil role in The Undead *because you "looked" the part?*
I think so. My agent was good, and I'm sure he sold me well to Roger. And the fact that I was able to cope with the hectic pace impressed Roger very much. Anybody that could save Roger a buck impresses him tremendously.

How did you get along with the other Undead *cast members?*
I got along with the people fine—everybody knew what they were supposed to do, so we just delivered.
One thing that Roger did look for was people that were going to deliver; that was extremely important, because his budgets were like twenty cents. Every time you worked for Roger it was up-and-go, quickly.

Richard Devon in full costume and makeup for his role as the Devil in Corman's *The Undead*.

Anybody that blew a line, it was like the kiss of death—really and truly. But Roger had a penchant for getting together people who could get along. The problem was getting along with Roger *[laughs]*!

Did you find it difficult trying to keep the dialogue in The Undead *from sounding too awkward?*

    I didn't, but a number of the other people did. It was stilted, and there was just no way to get a flow into it. Mel Welles just played everything off the top of his head and he came out all right, but it was difficult to keep from looking foolish. Pamela Duncan pressed very hard and Dick Garland worked hard, too, but everything was against them as far as the dialogue was concerned. It was just coming down around their ears. But as I recall everybody that was on the show was quite professional and they really tried — they really put forth an effort.

The Undead always struck me as a film that was just a little too bizarre, and that probably left a lot of young audiences very cold.
Very definitely. I took friends to see it, when they had the preview in Redondo Beach, and *[laughs]* I don't think they've ever forgiven me! It's a film where you keep trying to figure out what exactly is going on. This was a problem which I tried to distance myself from; I knew what my character was and what I was doing. But some of the other things in there just didn't work — they just didn't go together.

Weren't you next scheduled to appear in Corman's Attack of the Crab Monsters?
Yes, I was. However, I was slated to do another film at the same time, and there was just no way at all to work out the scheduling. Richard Cutting did the part that I was supposed to do in *Crab Monsters.* Later I turned down a part in Roger's *Teenage Caveman.* I looked at the script, and I just didn't believe it. I simply walked away from that picture, and *[laughs]* I was delighted to be able to do so! Bob Vaughn said it was the worst picture ever made.

I guess he never saw Saga of the Viking Women.
[Laughs.] You're probably right! Frank de Kova got stuck with that *Teenage Caveman* part. I ran into him some time after that and asked about it, and he said, it was . . . *okay.* Whatever that means.

Did you enjoy playing the Grimault chief in Viking Women?
That was a disastrous film to work on. It was as if Roger were really trying to short his skimpy shooting schedules, even *more* than what he had done. He was trying to beat his own record. He didn't waste a frame, nor did he spare anyone's feelings on the set. He was an absolute demon. As I said before, in his office he would purr like some wide-eyed kitten — but he could be dangerous. I remember some jokes on the set where the people freely discussed him as the sea serpent's brother. On the sets of my six Corman films there were several "Roger-isms," whispered softly among cast and crew alike. I don't know if he ever heard any of them, but it would be difficult to believe that he had not heard at least a few. "The Sultan of Trash," "The Doge of the Dreadful," "The Lord of Film Litter," and this one, which seemed quite popular: "The Robin Hood of Rubbish."
In one sequence in *Viking Women* I had to ride this horse through a small cave. It was like seventeen and a half hands tall, and that's a tall horse. I was leading the other Grimaults through the cave on this huge horse, and the

sucker hung me up on a wall and damn near tore my kneecap off. As I recall, there was never any nurse or any first aid people on the set; Roger said "uh huh" to my problem, and, "Let's get on with it." You can see the bruises on my right knee in the film; I doctored it up with makeup the best I could, but it's still there. And there was a lot of pain connected with it.

What do you remember about working with the other members of that cast?
   Abby Dalton was a delight—Abby you could kid around with and she'd kid back. Lynn Bernay was a lot of fun, and Betsy Jones-Moreland also, in a quiet sort of way. Susan Cabot was a *bit* standoffish; I think she and Roger were close friends at the time. She never really got involved with any of the cast members or anything like that, but she was pleasant and she knew her work, and that was swell.

Where was Viking Women *shot?*
   We shot up at Iverson's Ranch, which was out in the San Fernando Valley—that's where all the exteriors were done, and some of the cave stuff. We also shot in the caves in Bronson Canyon, which is off Bronson Boulevard. And the interiors were done at the old Ziv Studios on Santa Monica Boulevard. They're long gone now.

What about the scenes on the beach?
   That was a condemned beach at Cabrillo. Nobody bothered to tell us it was condemned. They used to post signs when they condemned a beach; somebody had picked up the sign and threw it in the bushes, but I found it. And then we saw the water, and there was a tremendous undertow—it was sort of scary. We were all down there on the day when Roger shot the scene where the Viking women launch their ship. If you recall the film, the rudder falls off the boat. Needless to say, that was not supposed to occur, but Roger is undaunted—nothing stops Roger. They just kept going. The girl who swam after the boat was swimming to save her life, because of the undertow. She got to the boat, and they pulled her in. Then when we got on the stage, to shoot dialogue scenes in front of a process screen, they did a bit of a rewrite. The girls are in the boat, and one of them is hanging onto an oar which she's presumably using as a ruddder. She has a line to Abby, something to the effect that they can't make this long journey using an oar for a rudder. And Abby has to reply—straight-faced—"We *must!*" So *[laughs]*, they go on this tremendous voyage with no rudder on that boat! But to Roger it didn't make any difference; with Roger you just drove ahead. Period. If something went wrong—give it to

Opposite: Rare behind-the-scenes still from Corman's *Saga of the Viking Women.* Brad Jackson is tied to the stake; prop man Karl Brainard (face partially hidden by stake) watches the action. Moving right from Brainard are Jay Sayer, key grip Chuck Hanawalt, Richard Devon and Lynn Bernay. Abby Dalton is at far right.

the cutter. If you could pick it up in another shot—that's fine, too. But there was no backtracking.

There's a scene in there where we're chasing the Vikings—me as Stark and my men, the Grimaults. We dismount from our horses and jump into these canoes—

You used the same beach for the Viking and Grimault coastlines?

Oh, sure—the beach worked for everything! We climbed into the boat, and I asked the guy behind me what Roger had told him to do. He said Roger told the guys to keep rowing out to sea until they heard him yell *cut*—and not to stop until they heard it. Now, what Roger had told me was that these guys would row out a very short distance, and he would cut the scene. Quickly I became aware of the fact that Roger had no intention of yelling *cut*—and we were going into some dangerous water. I was furious. I turned around, I screamed an obscenity at Roger and I bailed out of the boat. The water was about waist-high, but the waves were coming in. So I spewed out a couple more expletives at Roger—and if I could have gotten to him...!

The wardrobe I was wearing consisted of Indian moccasins; heavy sheep-skin leggings; East Indian rompers; some sort of velvet shirt you wouldn't want to be buried in; a ridiculous belt; upper torso armor over which was flung this huge, heavy sheepskin; and a fur-trimmed hat with earflaps and some kind of point on the top. I looked like Genghis Jerk *[laughs]*—I mean, it was unbelievable! Just then a huge wave hit me from behind, the sheepskin and the armor filled with water, and I went down and under. I couldn't get up; I was struggling, I was furious, and I thought I was going to drown, right there, on this ridiculous seashore. Somehow, through anger I guess, I got to my feet, I tried to move toward the shore—shouting everything at Roger that I could think of—and I remember screaming, "If I ever get my hands on you I'll strangle you!" But I was constantly being knocked down by waves—every time I'd get up, the damn things would hit me again. I struggled and struggled and I finally got to shore. Roger, very tactfully, moved offshore—when I got to the shoreline he wasn't around. People on the shore said they could see me shaking my fists and arms but they couldn't hear me, because of the surf. Anyway, Roger had disappeared for a while, so I cooled off.

Did you enjoy being typecast as a villain in Corman pictures and in other pro-ductions as well?

Not really. I had a penchant for comedy, and I've rarely been given an opportunity to play it. I did a series called *Yancy Derringer* [1958–1959] where I was a recurring character called Jody Barker, and that was a delight. The first time I did the show, I was a heavy on the street—I was a pickpocket, but I held up somebody with a gun. After that first show we talked and decided that it would be a good idea if, the next time he appeared, there was a change in the character—to make him cowardly, and to get away from the gun entirely.

Devon as the barbaric Stark in *Saga of the Viking Women:* **"I looked like Genghis Jerk!"**
(Photo courtesy Robert Skotak.)

So then Jody became the Jody that you see in the shows: He's fussy, he's funny, he's upset and nervous all the time, and *hates* violence. It was a lot of fun to play.

You toiled briefly on the right *side of the law in* Blood of Dracula.

I really don't have a lot of memories on that one. Herb Strock directed it, and Herb was from the Corman school: Get the footage in the can; push it; shoot the rehearsals; and don't fiddle around with everything. Never mind *creativity;* if you've got something in mind, don't discuss it with me. If you had something that you wanted to do character-wise or something that you thought should be done, just keep your mouth shut about it and do it, because nine chances out of ten it was going to be printed. So if you had a good solid idea where you wanted to go with the character, just hang loose and go with it.

By the time of Corman's War of the Satellites *you had worked your way up to star.*

What had been happening was that I had become progressively more impressive to Roger, as a performer, through the things that I had done. It was apparently a logical chain of events, and he felt that I would be the right person for this film. I always knew my lines and I could handle any situation that came up unexpectedly, which was paradise for Roger. Anything that would not get in the way of his budget or cost him extra bucks was wonderful — *Eden.*

You really did have a good part in Satellites *playing that dual role, one sympathetic and one villainous. Did you enjoy the opportunity?*

Very much so, yeah — that's one of the few I really did like.

What do you remember about those satellite sets?

They were practically non-existent; I think if Roger could have gotten orange crates and made them work, he'd have done it *[laughs]*! They built two corridors, and they made them work for about twelve dozen in the picture. Our sets were basically just flats, more along the lines of what you'd have in a stage show. And that was it! They were endlessly re-dressing them, to make them look like different parts of the satellite. Most of Roger's sets consisted of two walls, and you played the third like it was really there.

Now, the punchline to this story is that a few years ago I got a very strange phone call from someone who wanted to know whatever happened to the sets from *War of the Satellites!* I mean *[laughs]*, how should I know, and why should I care? He took me completely off-guard, I didn't know what to say to this fellow. As far as I know, they perished — you could fold them up and put 'em in a cigarette pack!

Satellites *is really a study in corner-cutting: the same sets used over and over, some actors playing multiple parts, and even Corman himself turning up in two parts. Did you resent all of this economy and wish you were working in bigger-budgeted films?*

A thing that I learned a long, long time ago is, "Pay close attention to your own garden." I'm the one that's ending up on the film, and what I want to occur is up to me. And if I start letting these things bother me, I can start nitpicking and destroy whatever I might have in mind or what I might be trying to do. I was fully cognizant of the fact that this was not a big-budget picture, and that anything that I could bring to it would be a plus factor for me. But I couldn't get into the area of being worried about cheap-here and cheap-there.

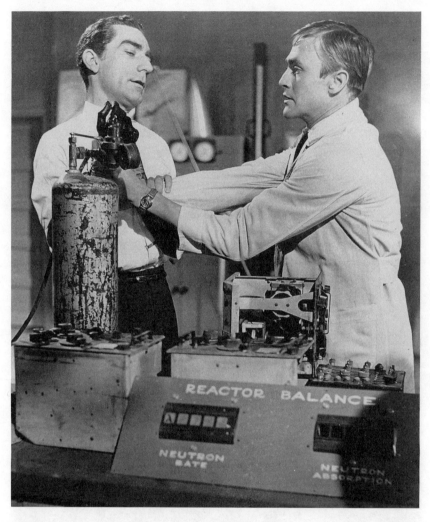

Devon grapples with Jerry Barclay in a tense scene from Roger Corman's *War of the Satellites*.

The silliest scene in Satellites, *the one that really torpedoes the picture, is at the end, when you create a heart for yourself and start making love speeches to Susan Cabot.*

[Laughs.] The direction on that was, "Do something, Richard." What do you do when somebody says to you, "We need you to create a heart"? I grabbed at whatever I could, trying to figure out who this person was, which was difficult because his background was totally splintered. So whatever I built into it I built in step-by-step. I figured if I played it the way that I did play it, that it would work, at least for me, under the circumstances.

The climax of *War of the Satellites* finds Devon duking it out with Corman perennial Dick Miller.

You also had a good supporting role in one of Corman's best pictures, Machine-Gun Kelly.

We were beginning to grate on each other, Roger and I, by the time of *Machine-Gun Kelly*. We weren't getting along too well and so on, but work is work and you try to smooth things over and keep going. The wardrobe on that film was a nightmare; on all of Roger's pictures you sort of did it yourself, and you can see on the film how it turned out. Somebody handling the wardrobe said, "It's near something like the 1930s" — so you did whatever you could with that kind of a situation. Charlie Bronson and I got along just fine; we've also worked together on *Kid Galahad* [1962] and in his *Man with a Camera* TV series. But for Roger nothing had changed. In his office he was Peter Pan and on the set he was an ogre. Without any discussions we kept our distance from each other, and that was it.

Corman's "war movie" Battle of Blood Island *[1961] gave you your most sizable film role.*

It was a two-character film, and several parts of the film worked very well for me. Unfortunately you can do a great job in a rotten film, and—you're in a rotten film. It doesn't make any difference; none of the nuances are watched or anything. I've got a drunk scene in that picture that I *loved*—it played well and it worked well, but we were in some stupid cave in Puerto Rico doing this damn thing.

That was your last film for Corman, wasn't it?

Yes, it was; I had pretty much had it at that point. When this film came up I asked my agent, "Where did this film come from?" and he said, "Well, Roger is in the background on it, but he's not involved in it at all." I asked him if he was sure about that and he said that, yes, he was. *Battle of Blood Island* was directed by a fellow named Joel Rapp; Stan Bickman was the producer; and it was based on a short story called "The Forgotten Ones," which was also our shooting title, by the way.

After being reassured by the agent that Roger really didn't have anything to do with this film, I flew down with the cameraman, Jack Marquette, to the airport in Puerto Rico. And who's there to greet us but *Roger*. And the first words out of his mouth are, "Why don't we all have a strawberry daiquiri?" So I looked at Jack, Jack looked at me—we both knew Roger—and we were wondering what was going to be happening next. He took us to the baggage area and we had the daiquiris and we were chatting, and I finally said, "Roger, where are we staying?" Roger was very exuberant when he said, "We're all staying at a villa." Now, *that* gets you a little shaky. So they put us in a little dinky car and they took us to this *house*. I mean, it's a house—and a small one! And everybody who's concerned with this film, or with the other films that they were doing back-to-back with it, is chucked into this place. Robert Towne, who ended up writing *Chinatown* [1974], was there—he was involved with Roger, and he was writing a script, in longhand. It was the script for the next film they did down there *[Last Woman on Earth],* and Roger wanted to know if I would play the lead. I turned it down because I had three shows waiting for me in Hollywood; Tony Carbone flew in and played the part.

Anyway, Towne was writing in longhand and people were cooking their own meals in the kitchen—it was a disaster, the whole thing. Jack and I got together and we said there was no way we were going to go along with this. We wanted some decent accommodations. So we talked to the rest of the people there and we said, "C'mon, let's move out of here, let's do it all at one time." They said it was a good idea, but when the chips were down and it came time for all of us to talk, it was only me and Jack. But Jack and I were very smart in one way: We had round-trip air tickets in our pockets. I was doing the lead in the film and Jack was the cameraman; if they lost us, they lost everything. There was a lot of dialogue, back and forth—we didn't want anything out of bounds or fabulous or anything like that, just clean—and they finally put us up in the Caribe Hilton, which was delightful. And then everybody was mad at us, because we didn't have to live in the villa! But that got smoothed over after a while.

Blood Island *was entirely shot in Puerto Rico, right?*
    Yes, and all exteriors. There were a lot of problems on the show in that we were working in rain forests and jungle, and several of the crew guys were eaten so badly by the bugs that they just had to be shipped back. We were all a mass of welts. Of course, no doctor, no nurse.
    One of the sequences in the film was done with a guy who was the house detective at the Caribe Hilton. They hired him to play a Japanese that I was supposed to fight in a scene on the beach. The guy was not an actor, he was a detective. I gave him a crash course in "picture-fighting" and we started shooting. While we're going through this, the tide's coming in, more and more—nobody bothered to check the tides in this area. The detective got so involved in the scene and in the fact that he was doing a movie that he ran straight at me during a take where I'm holding a bayonet—he scared me to death, because I damn near ran him through. I dropped the bayonet, off to the side, I spun him around and threw the punch. He took the punch and threw himself back into the water—and hits a coral reef! He hit it on his chest, and it just shredded him. And by that time the water had come in completely, and the sand crabs were jumping in and out of our jackets! But this was typical of a Corman film: he was in the background this time, but you had the feel, you knew that he was there . . . !

Was that what finally tore it for you and Corman?
    No, it was one day when we were out on location, and Roger came out bringing lunch. There's a large group of us out there, and he brought dry sandwiches with some indeterminate kind of meat on them, and two quarts of milk. For the *whole crew.* I had gone through this whole picture, I'm eaten alive by bugs, and we're all tired, just wiped out. So I just blew my stack—I said, "Get him off the set. If he doesn't go, I go." People were trying to settle me down, but I said, "Get him off. *Now.*" Boom. And that was the kiss of death—that was the end for Roger and I. Roger had just cut every corner in the world where

I was concerned and where everybody else in the film was concerned. I mean, the fulcrum of Roger's life is a dollar bill, and not in a singular sense. And anything in the world that gets in the way of that monetary move—forget it. You're in deadly, deadly trouble.

Have you seen Corman at all in recent years?

I haven't seen him in many, many years. I don't know whether he's changed—I don't really believe that people basically change. Maybe he has, I don't know—I read things about him in the trades and that kind of thing. But that's pretty much my adventure with Roger.

In 1988 you returned to the horror genre with the supernatural suspenser The Seventh Sign.

When I first met the casting director on *The Seventh Sign,* the only hitch was that she thought I was too young to play the cardinal. I told her that I work all different ways, that I could do the part with gray hair and all, and it should work out just fine. As usual with films, the role was much larger when I first read it; it was trimmed down and trimmed down and so forth. But we worked out the deal and I did it. The entire sequence in the film that is supposed to take place in the Vatican was shot at the Wilshire Ebell Theater on Wilshire Boulevard.

How active are you in the business today?

I'm living up here in San Francisco now, but I do go back to Los Angeles for various things. I also do TV voiceovers and radio spots up here in San Francisco.

I don't know whether this belongs in the interview or not, but it is very important to my wife, Patricia, and me: This winter [1989] we are going back to Paris (the one in France, thank goodness, not the one in Texas) to celebrate our 30th wedding anniversary—it seems like barely 30 minutes! It'll be cold and blustery, but when you're in love, who cares?

Do you enjoy or resent being permanently associated in the minds of many fans with the Corman stock company?

I don't resent it, not at all. When you're starting out and you're trying to be an actor, you just go after whatever you can get. You hope you can get some decent breaks, but you still go after whatever you can and do your damnedest to make it the best that you possibly can.

And I have no regrets whatsoever for any of the things that I did with Roger; I did the best job that I knew how and I worked hard, and that was it. When films are finished and you get to see them, of course you re-evaluate and find things in there that you would like to re-do. But you say, "Hey—move on." And that's what I did.

RICHARD DEVON FILMOGRAPHY

The Prodigal (MGM, 1955)
The Racers (20th Century–Fox, 1955)
Escape from San Quentin (Columbia, 1957)
The Undead (AIP, 1957)
The Saga of the Viking Women and Their Voyage to the Waters of the Great Sea Serpent (AIP, 1957)
Blood of Dracula (AIP, 1957)
3:10 to Yuma (Columbia, 1957)
The Buckskin Lady (United Artists, 1957)
Teenage Doll (Allied Artists, 1957)
The Badlanders (MGM, 1958)
Machine-Gun Kelly (AIP, 1958)
Badman's Country (Warners, 1958)
Money, Women and Guns (Universal, 1958)
War of the Satellites (Allied Artists, 1958)
Gunfighters of Abilene (United Artists, 1960)
Battle of Blood Island (Filmgroup, 1960)
The Comancheros (20th Century–Fox, 1961)
Kid Galahad (United Artists, 1962)
Cattle King (MGM, 1963)
The Three Stooges Go Around the World in a Daze (Columbia, 1963)
The Silencers (Columbia, 1966)
Three Guns for Texas (Universal, 1968)
Magnum Force (Warners, 1973)
The Seventh Sign (Tri-Star, 1988)

There were a bunch of these exploitation pictures
being made ... [in the '50s], but at that time there didn't
seem to be a very big market for them. I guess the other producers
must have been spending just about the same amount of money that we were,
but their pictures were such shit. I did not try to make
just an exploitation picture. I was trying to do
something with a little substance to it.

Gene Fowler, Jr.

BEFORE 1957, who would have suspected that horror movies and true confessions would have combined forces to produce one of the most successful exploitation film phenomena of the '50s? Certainly not Gene Fowler, Jr., and he directed the movie that kicked off the trend, *I Was a Teenage Werewolf*, as well as *I Married a Monster from Outer Space* one year later. In a decade filled with spectacular film titles, these names stood in the forefront of no-holds-barred '50s sensationalism and earned a notoriety that has lasted to this day. Much of the credit for their box office (as well as dramatic) success is due to the professionalism and dedication of the doubting director Fowler, who was so surprised by the popularity of a werewolf in a high school jacket.

After years in the cutting room, you made your directorial feature debut with I Was a Teenage Werewolf *in 1957.*

I was working in a cutting room next door to a fellow named Herman Cohen. Herman kept dropping into my cutting room and we talked pictures, naturally, and one day he came in and said, "How would you like to direct a feature?" I said I would. He said, "It's got the worst title in the world, but it's a very good script." He gave it to me to read, and it was a thing called *I Was a Teenage Werewolf.* I remember I read the thing as I was lying in the bathtub one night, and after I read it I said to my wife, "I can't do this god-damned thing!" She said, "How was the script?" and I said, "Fair." She said, "Look, why don't you do it anyway? You'd like to do a feature, and nobody will ever see it." There were a bunch of these exploitation pictures being made (I know Roger Corman was making the damn things), but at that time there didn't seem to be a very big market for them — they were very specialized showings. I guess the other producers must have been spending just about the same amount of money that we were, but their pictures were such shit. I did not try to make just an exploitation picture. I was trying to do something with a little substance to it.

What kind of a producer was Herman Cohen?

I enjoyed working with him. We had our normal fights and so on, and there was a lot of rewriting of the script to be done. It was the usual kind of mad scientist picture, which I disagreed with. In the script, after the first interview with Michael Landon, a maniacal gleam comes into the scientist's eyes and he rubs his hands together. I always figured that a villain, in his own eyes, was a very good, very nice fellow. So I tried to make the villain that — he was actually trying to do good for the world. I tried to get some sympathy for him, or at least some understanding. I remember talking to Whit Bissell, who played the doctor, and telling him, "Keep in mind you're *not* a bad man."

Previous page: **Son of the famous author/scenarist Gene Fowler, Sr., Gene, Jr., turned his hand to directing after years as a film editor.**

I'm surprised that Cohen let you rewrite. Herbert Strock told me Cohen was touchy about things like that.

He didn't know it, while I was doing it! Otherwise he'd have fought me every step of the way. Actually, Herman wasn't too bad. He generally came on the set in the morning and was there for about an hour and left. He was busy promoting other stuff, and he left me alone pretty much.

There's a scene in *Teenage Werewolf* where Michael Landon argues with his father, Michael gets mad and the old man leaves. And Michael is left standing there, boiling. I said, "The scene needs a capper, to show that the kid is a little unstable." So I figured that, since Michael had in his hand a big bottle of milk, I'd have him throw it at the wall. I told Herman and he was against it, but finally I figured I was going to do it anyway—I was all set up, and I might as well do it. And Herman liked it after he saw it. In the dialogue I wrote, I tried to give the characters dimension, to show where they came from, instead of just moving them around and having them say the obligatory lines. I tried to give them a reason for these things. For instance, the milk bottle was not a big production thing; the only thing I was trying to do was give a demonstration of how screwed up this kid was.

Is that a mask on Landon, or applied makeup?

It was applied—it took about two hours to put on the damn thing. We had to do an awful lot of shooting around him while that was going on. I think he did an incredible job.

Teenage Werewolf *was shot by Joseph LaShelle, who was a superb photographer.*

Joe LaShelle was an old friend of mine. When I was over at Fox, he was the operating cameraman for Artie Miller, who was one of the premier cameramen in Hollywood. He and Gregg Toland, in my opinion, were the two best. I became a very good friend of Artie, who was an amateur still cameraman as well; I used to go up to his house all the time and we'd make stills together. To me he was a genius. He asked me one time if I would like to become a cameraman; maybe I was a fool to say no, but I did. Anyway, Joe LaShelle was his operator and I got to know Joe very well. He was one of the sweetest men in the world. So when I got this assignment to do *I Was a Teenage Werewolf,* I called Joe and said, "How 'bout it?" He said, "What's the title?" I told him and he said, "You're kidding! I don't want to do something like that!" I said, "Well, I didn't, either *[laughs]*, but this is my first feature and I could sure use some help." So he said all right, and he did it with me, strictly as a friend.

Did he pitch in creatively on Teenage Werewolf?

We worked together. I worked with the art director, the cameraman and the head of pre-production, and tried to lay out everything in the most

Years before he co-starred in TV's *Bonanza,* **Michael Landon frothed and foamed as the "I" in the Fowler-directed** *I Was a Teenage Werewolf.*

economical way we could. (The theory being, if you know what you're doing, you can do it faster!) Joe did contribute, there's no question about that. And so did the art director, Les Thomas—there was another sweet guy. I've always claimed that all art directors must have to take a course in being a nice guy before they can get the job, because I have yet to find an art director who is a shit! They're marvelous people. On *Teenage Werewolf* Les and I really cheated on sets—we were building them out of spit and polish.

So it was all this planning that helped you bring the picture in so quickly.
    Well, I had no choice, it had to be done quickly, and that's how we did

it, by planning. We made the picture in six days—no, five and a half days, because we got rained out one day. Our budget was $82,000—not very much *[laughs]*!

Who cast the movie?
Oh, we all did that. Herman Cohen brought a bunch of kids in and we worked together picking them. I think *I Was a Teenage Werewolf* may have been Michael Landon's first picture. I loved Michael—he was a very young kid at that time, maybe twenty years old, but he was good, a hard-working guy, always knew his lines. You could ask him to do anything and he'd do it. It became kind of "family," the way everybody was working together on it. All of these guys were tremendously cooperative; we treated the picture as though it were *Gone with the Wind* and we didn't make fun of it. I told the crew, before we started, "Look, anybody who can give me a suggestion, I'll consider it." That is, anybody except the producer—I won't even listen to him! *[Laughs.]* That's a general rule of mine!

The screenplay of Teenage Werewolf *is credited to someone named Ralph Thornton. Was there really such a person, or did Cohen write it himself?*
No, no. *Teenage Werewolf* was written by a novelist named Abe Kandel. He wrote a lot of novels and he wrote a lot of pictures, including some very famous ones. He was a very nice fellow.

Why the pseudonym?
'Cause he probably didn't want his name on a thing called *I Was a Teenage Werewolf [laughs]*!

Any other Teenage Werewolf *anecdotes that you can recall?*
Because of the half day that was rained out, we had to go back and pick up a couple of shots. We had already used a police dog in a scene, but we couldn't afford the dog anymore so we were going to do without that scene. But I owned a police dog and it matched the first one pretty well, so I said, what the hell, why not use my own damn dog? We were up there at Bronson Canyon, and my dog Anna was having a hell of a time running in the forest while Michael was getting his werewolf makeup on. Finally he came on the set, Anna turned and took one look at him and ran like hell *[laughs]*! What eventually happened, I guess, was she figured that since Michael *smelled* like a human being he must *be* a human being, and we got some very close and very quick shots of her loving him to death! That seemed to work all right.

What do you think of I Was a Teenage Werewolf *today?*
I guess it's all right. Looking back at it, I can think of many things that I wish I had done, but to be realistic there wasn't time to do them anyway!

Did you have an opportunity to meet with AIP heads Nicholson and Arkoff?

Only on the wrap party. The last shot I shot was the destruction of the lab, and everybody came down to look at it. I think I went about a half-hour over schedule, and everybody was trying to hurry me up so they could open the bar! So, no, I didn't know Nicholson or Arkoff that well, all I know is that *I Was a Teenage Werewolf* was the picture that put 'em in the black.

Were you surprised by the film's success?
Indeed I was. I think the thing, when it was first released, grossed something like $6,000,000, maybe even $8,000,000. Which, for a picture that cost $82,000, is a hell of a profit! And apparently that put them on the map.

Did you work for a salary, or a percentage?
A salary. I was *offered* a percentage, and I turned it down because I didn't believe it would make any money *[laughs]*!

Cohen himself turns up in one short scene in Teenage Werewolf.
He very well might have. I remember we used to do those "in" things all the time. Even I would do it occasionally—I remember having my shoes shined by the producer on some picture, I don't recall which one.

Are you in either Teenage Werewolf *or* I Married a Monster?
No—only my hands. I always did my own inserts, in all my pictures. That I got from Fritz Lang—Fritz and I were very, very close friends, and Fritz always put his hands in the picture.

What were some of the things you learned from Lang that came in handy on movies like Teenage Werewolf *and* I Married a Monster?
Firstly, prepare. I remember one time when I was going up to San Francisco to do the *China Smith* shows for TV [1952], he asked me, "Have you prepared?" and I said, "Heck, I haven't even seen the sets yet." He said, "Look, a window's a window, a door's a door. Prepare your show and just adapt yourself to what the set is, and you'll have no problem." Which I did. So he taught me preparation, and he taught me use of the crane; this man really knew how to move the camera and so on. I used to work very closely with Fritz. As a matter of fact, I would lay out the following day's work, then Fritz would come over and say, "Well, why do you want to do it this way?" and I'd tell him. And he'd say, "I think it'd be better *this* way, don't you?"—and we'd work together. That's a unique situation. He didn't teach me much about acting, because *[laughs]* he and I always differed on what actors should do. He was probably righter than I was, but we both were very stubborn people. And, my God, he was a master of suspense!

How were you able to break into the movie business?
I got into the business by being introduced to Allen McNeil, who was

a fellow that my father had interviewed while writing a book called *Father Goose*. *Father Goose* was the story of Mack Sennett, and Allen McNeil was the chief editor for Sennett at the time. McNeil asked me, "Would you like to get into the cutting department?" and I — not even knowing what the cutting department was — said yes. So I started working there at night, and going to U.S.C. in the daytime. The first picture I ever worked on was a Fox picture called *Thanks a Million* [1935], which was directed by Roy Del Ruth and written by my future father-in-law, Nunnally Johnson. I remember the first time I walked into the place — I never saw so much film in my life! It was all off-reels and trimmed ends and so on, and I was just stunned, and couldn't figure out how the hell anybody kept track of anything. But he taught me the business, and I was cutting there until 1941.

At what point did you decide that you wanted to become a director?

Around 1950, or maybe a bit earlier than that. I thought at the time that my experience in the editing room was a helluva good background, and it turned out to be true. I worked at first in TV, on *China Smith,* a very popular show in those years. It was a half-hour show — it starred Dan Duryea, we made it in San Francisco, and shot it on 16mm. We started out by making two of those a week. Dan was on salary, $250 a week, guaranteeing that he wouldn't make more than two shows a week. But, as time went on, we suddenly started making three shows a week — that translates to two days per show *[laughs]*! We made a lot of those things, and then when I finished with that I did a lot of other television stuff.

Why didn't you stay on with Herman Cohen and AIP?

I don't remember exactly but, to be honest, I don't think I wanted to. Anytime you wanted something a little special for your picture, you'd have to fight like a dog for it. I remember directing pictures for Bob Lippert, a man whose eye was on the budget at all times. One thing I always wanted to do, particularly in these low-budget pictures, was have one day with a crane. Well, the crane cost maybe $250 a day and $250 for the operator. I remember shooting *The Oregon Trail* [1959] for Lippert, and I traded 25 Indians for the crane *[laughs]*! It sounds stupid, but that's the way you had to work. Lippert was releasing pictures through 20th Century–Fox; he had a deal whereby he'd make pictures for $125,000, and if the picture came in for less than that, he'd steal from the top. That was Lippert, not me — I didn't get *any* of that *[laughs]*!

That Lippert experience was wonderful in a way because we had the run of the Fox lot; whatever sets happened to be still standing, we'd use those sets. My partner, Lou Vittes, and I would walk through these sets that'd already been used for much more expensive pictures than we could make, and we would pretty much write out scripts around the sets! I did a number of pictures for Lippert: *Showdown at Boot Hill, Gang War* [1958], *Here Come the Jets*

[1959] and *The Oregon Trail*. *The Oregon Trail*, that was a son of a bitch—
Lippert really screwed that one up. He made a bet with Spyros Skouras [presi-
dent of 20th Century–Fox] that he could make a big outdoor Western without
ever leaving the Fox lot, and like an idiot I agreed to direct it!

As a former editor, did you supervise the editing of your films?

I have a theory about that. I think you should allow the editor to put the
picture together without any kind of supervision whatsoever. Because he
sometimes can find things that you don't even know you shot. So I stayed out
of his way, and I only came in after the whole thing was assembled. Directors
shouldn't be allowed to edit their own movies, unless they have a helluva lot
of training. Directors have an awful habit of remembering how difficult the
scene was that they shot. And the thing is just crying to be cut in half or thrown
out *[laughs]*! Just the other night I saw Sam Peckinpah's *The Wild Bunch*
[1969] on TV, and it was advertised as his cut, as opposed to the one that was
released. I looked at the thing and I said, "I am sure that the studio was more
correct than he was"—it was a very self-indulgent thing. I hope I was never
guilty of that.

George Gittens edited I Was a Teenage Werewolf *and George Tomasini did*
I Married a Monster from Outer Space.

Tomasini was Hitchcock's cutter; I was in the army with him. And George
Gittens was a funny guy—he was deaf as a post. When we'd run *Teenage
Werewolf* with Herman Cohen, Herman would say something to George and
I had to write it down. George couldn't hear and I didn't want Herman to know
he was deaf *[laughs]*! So afterward I would have to transcribe all my notes, go
up to his cutting room and show him what had to be done. George was Louis
Loeffler's assistant at one time; Louie was the man who cut most of Otto Prem-
inger's pictures. Louie's eyesight was going and George's hearing was going,
and they'd both collaborate on cuts. One could see and the other could hear
[laughs]!

How did I Married a Monster from Outer Space *come about?*

Lou Vittes and I had worked together over at Lippert's, and Lippert would
always work from a title. He'd say, "Oh, I've got a great title, here it is, now
write a story about it," and that's what we'd do! So both of us were trying to
break away from that, and try and find a subject we could write about. So I
said, "Let's do what they did on *Teenage Werewolf*. Let's find some absurd title
and write a good script for it." And actually the script, for what it is, is all right.
But I looked at *I Married a Monster from Outer Space* just the other night and,
boy, all I can say is that there are an awful lot of things I would have done
differently.

Such as?

In the first place, I hated the main title—it really looked like the cover of a comic magazine. And then within the picture I would have done a lot of things differently. Just little things.

What extra responsibilities did you have as producer?

Oh, pretty much all of it except where sometimes the studio heads would come in and insist on something. I remember they were the ones that wanted the glowing effect on the monsters. I didn't want that; I think that without the glow it would have been a little more subtle. But I guess it worked out all right. I designed those monsters, and I designed them with only one thing in mind: so I could get rid of the god-damned things [*laughs*]! I gave them a vulnerable spot, those tubes on the outside of their bodies, which gave the dogs something to grab hold of. That was the only reason for that! We had two costumes, which we used over and over to make it seem like there were a bunch of them.

Is that your dog in I Married a Monster *as well?*

Oh, yes. Having dogs kill off the aliens was probably the cheapest thing we could think of [*laughs*]!

Tom Tryon gives a wooden performance that doesn't do much for the picture.

You're right, he *was* wooden. He did not want to do this picture—there was no *way* he wanted to do this picture. But this was at the time when the studios had all the power, and they'd say to an actor, "You do this picture or you're put on the blacklist." So he did it, much to his chagrin. But then about halfway through we became good friends, he eased up a bit and started doing things. And Gloria Talbott I love. She's another person who'll do just about anything you ask her to do.

How much of a spaceship did you actually build?

Almost nothing. I think it was just a door, and the rest was foliage. Then the interior was just some plain curved flats, that's all. We suspended the actors inside with harnesses and piano wire.

Did you shoot the whole picture at Paramount?

No. We did some shooting up in Bronson Canyon, and then also out on the streets. That was the dumbest damn thing in the world. We had to shoot a scene on a public street and I was told, "Make it very convenient, find a location near the studio." So I picked a spot about two blocks away. Well, when I went to that location to shoot that scene, I saw more god-damned trucks than I ever saw in my life! They had honey wagons, they had grip trucks—we must have had fifteen or twenty trucks to shoot that simple silent scene! When I was on location on *China Smith* in San Francisco years before, we had two trucks and a station wagon. One little truck carried the camera equipment and the sound, and then we had a regular two-and-a-half-ton truck to carry whatever

Posse members, led by Steve London (holding dog), examine the body of a slain alien in *I Married a Monster from Outer Space.*

other crap we needed. The station wagon was for us, and we had cardboard inserts that we would put up against the windows so that Dan Duryea could change his clothes while we were driving to the next location! And we would shoot all over San Francisco. I'd see a good location, we'd come screeching to a stop and within five minutes we were shooting.

Did you learn your lesson and work for a percentage this time?
     I did work for a percentage, yes—I owned 25 percent of *I Married a Monster.* But they "bookkeeped" me out of everything they could—they told me the picture never made any money. And yet I'd go out and see kids lined up around the block to see the picture on a Saturday, and I'd say, "You mean to say this picture isn't making any money *yet?*" Our budget was $125,000.

I Married a Monster *is so well-done that nearly every reviewer at some point apologizes for the title.*
     Well, that was the purpose of that title, the exact purpose. I mean *[laughs]*, we were certainly capable of coming up with a decent title! This was strictly an exploitation picture. But there again I tried to put characterization into the monsters. The so-called monsters, the aliens, were very sad people. One of the things I've always found is that you've got to accept the premise,

regardless of how ridiculous it is. If you accept the thing as very realistic and very honest, then you can come up with very honest performances and make a fairly honest picture out of it. And this premise was kind of sad; these aliens, all of their women had died off, and they were searching the galaxy for women to propagate their race. They were desperate. What they were doing, as far as they were concerned, was very honest and very necessary. The fact that they were kicking the shit out of Earthmen made no difference!

Why did you turn your back on directing after only seven pictures?

I didn't turn my back on it, it was the result of something I didn't even know was happening. My father-in-law had written a script called *Flaming Lance** and a producer, whose name I won't divulge, heard about it and he wanted me to get my father-in-law to give it to me, for him to produce and me to direct. I said I wouldn't do it, that he should be paid for his script. And the producer got very upset about the thing. Suddenly I stopped working, and I didn't know why. For a year. Then a friend of mine stopped by my house at seven o'clock one morning, and he said that he had been in a poker game with the producer who was upset with me. He told me that there was someone at the poker game who was about to make a picture and this producer asked him who he was going to hire to direct. The fellow said, "I was thinking of getting Fowler," and the producer said, "You can't hire him — he's a *Communist.*" Well, that was his way of getting back at me for not giving him a free script. I went back into editing some time after that.

Aside from Fritz Lang, some of the other name directors you edited for were Stanley Kramer and Sam Fuller.

Stanley's very nice. He used to say after he finished a picture that we should run it and then take all the gags out. Stanley did not have a very good sense of humor *[laughs]*! And Sam Fuller? Christ, he's a maniac! I remember he was doing a picture called *Run of the Arrow* [1957] up in St. George, Utah, and I kept getting film back from him — I got twenty reels of film, all silent, and I had to run this god-damned stuff. What they were, were shots of a wagon train; you'd see the wagon train in the distance, it would move slowly across the frame, kept *going* and *going,* and then it would disappear over the other horizon. A thousand feet *[laughs]*! And every so often the picture would jump or jerk around. So I went up to St. George and I told Sam about this jerking action and said, "Sam, there's something wrong with the camera or the film." Finally I found out what was happening: Sam always used to cue actors with guns, and he'd shoot this .45 right next to the camera operator's ear! And the operator would jump every time *[laughs]*!

Sam did a picture called *Park Row* [1952], about the newspaper business, and he wore a green eyeshade; when he did *Run of the Arrow* he wore a cowboy

*Later made into *Flaming Star* (20th Century–Fox, 1960), an Elvis Presley Western.

hat; and on *The Big Red One* [1980] he wore a helmet! Whatever picture he was doing, he wore the hat that went with it!

You've worked with a lot of filmland's top talents in your long career. Are you pleased with what you've done in Hollywood?

I guess more or less; Lord knows, I don't think *any*body's ever achieved *all* the things they set out to do. But I must say I've had a lot of fun doing it. I think back to the days of working with Fritz Lang; my wife worked with me on those, she was my assistant. We were young, and to work with Fritz you had to be young, because he'd work you into the ground. But I learned a helluva lot from him, and Margie did, too. And directing I loved—I'm just sorry that I didn't do more. There was a certain sense of achievement in it—you seemingly expressed yourself a little more fully than you do in any other field, with the possible exception of writing. What I did do was a lot of fun.

*We thought we could take our sense of good picturemaking,
apply it to science fiction, and in so doing enable our company
[Gramercy Pictures] to keep the momentum going, pay the rent....
It was in that spirit that we started to develop some ideas
and brought them to UA. They went along with our thinking,
and we were in the science fiction business....* —Arnold Laven

Arthur Gardner
Arnold Laven
Paul Landres
and *Pat Fielder*

UNDER THE DIRECTION of Jules V. Levy, Arthur Gardner and Arnold Laven, Levy-Gardner-Laven Productions has been a consistent supplier of well-crafted entertainment, from such films as *Vice Squad* (1953), *Geronimo* (1962) and *The McKenzie Break* (1970), to TV series like *The Rifleman, The Detectives Starring Robert Taylor* and *The Big Valley*. During the 1950s, the company (then calling itself Gramercy Pictures) applied their professionalism to the science fiction and horror genres in four films, three of which rank with the best of that decade's independently produced thrillers: *The Monster That Challenged the World, The Vampire* and *The Return of Dracula*.

Levy, Gardner and Laven met while serving in the Air Force's motion picture unit during World War II (the same unit that included Capt. Ronald Reagan, Capt. Clark Gable and Lt. William Holden). The ambition to create a Levy-Gardner-Laven production company was born during the war but was not realized until 1951, after each of them had accumulated some film industry experience at already existing studios. With Levy and Gardner producing, and Laven directing, the newly formed company made several successful, modestly budgeted pictures released by United Artists. In 1956, they entered the currently popular field of sci-fi/horror. Their first venture, *The Monster That Challenged the World,* was written by Pat Fielder, a woman promoted from Gramercy's production assistant, and was directed by Laven; the directing chores for the next three Fielder-scripted horror films were then handled by Paul Landres. We are fortunate to have here a four-way interview with Gardner, Laven, Fielder and Landres.

What prompted Gramercy Pictures to enter the horror/sci-fi field in 1956?

Laven: We really were not successful at certain periods of time in getting some of our story ideas and scripts into the kind of shape where our parent organization, United Artists, was willing to finance them. It occurred to us that the field of science fiction was one which we could enter and, if we used the knowhow which we believed we had, make better films for lesser money. We thought we could take our sense of good picturemaking, apply it to science fiction, and in so doing enable our company to keep the momentum going — pay the rent, keep up production activity and maintain an ongoing relationship with UA. It was in that spirit that we started to develop some ideas and brought them to UA. They went along with our thinking, and we were in the science fiction business for a couple of years making those four films.

Did your production unit have complete creative freedom making these films for UA?

Gardner: We had a reputation for bringing our pictures in on budget and on schedule, so we really had complete creative freedom. We only showed the pictures to UA after they were completely finished.

Laven: They were the ideal company to work with. The earlier films we had made all showed profits — really very good profits, based on the cost of the

Previous page: Using a little business savvy and a lot of production knowhow, Jules V. Levy, Arthur Gardner and Arnold Laven parlayed their minor production company into a major purveyor of motion pictures and television series.

pictures. They showed a profit of 50 to 75 percent of each investment. UA trusted us: They knew that we were scrupulously careful and tremendously devoted to putting every dollar on the screen. With that assurance, they really let us do pretty much anything we wanted.

Fielder: That was the good thing about UA in those days — they put up the money but they really didn't inhibit their filmmakers from doing what they thought was best.

What sort of budgets and shooting schedules were these films allotted?

Gardner: *The Vampire,* I believe, was $115,000, *The Return of Dracula* around $125,000, and *The Monster That Challenged the World* was the most expensive of the four — that was $254,000. *The Flame Barrier* was the cheapest; I think that cost $100,000. I would say that the average science fiction film being made at that time probably had a cost of anywhere between $25,000 and possibly $200,000.

While most of the sci-fi films of that era were geared toward teenage tastes, your added production values and use of respectable actors seem to indicate that you aimed for a broader audience.

Laven: Part of our sales pitch to United Artists was that we could make these films look as though they were more expensive, to look richer, to have a greater market presentation than the competitive science fiction films, because of our knowhow and our design in writing scripts that would allow us to *use* our knowhow.

Fielder: We had a limited area that we could travel to in order to make a picture; we really had to deal with the elements that we had close at hand, and find a story that would fit into those parameters. We also had certain titles that we could work with, and often we would start with a title and construct a story around it. We would discuss the type of film that we were going to make, and then I would prepare some kind of an outline for the story and talk it through with Arthur and Jules.

How did The Monster That Challenged the World *come about?*

Fielder: There was an article in *Life* magazine, a true story about ancient shrimp eggs being discovered and reconstituted after millions of years buried in a salty pond. We transposed it all to the Salton Sea. There was an earlier draft on the screenplay [by David Duncan] which was not used at all — UA had decided that they wanted a rewrite on that script. So because of my strong desire to write and the fact that I was right on the scene, I convinced Levy-Gardner-Laven to give me an opportunity to rewrite it, to see whether I could do the necessary work. I plunged into it, and found that it was great fun and I loved doing it. We even made a survey research trip down to the Salton Sea prior to the shooting — Arnold Laven and I took a trip down to the unit where

they did the parachute jumping, which was in El Centro, and around the area
of the Salton Sea.

Did you pattern parts of your screenplay after Them? *The two films seem quite
alike.*

    Fielder: I had seen *Them!* and so had Arthur and Jules. It was a fine pic-
ture, and I'm sure that it was the inspiration in some ways for *Monster.* I think
it inspired a whole bunch of pictures of that era, but our independent research
had allowed us to develop an awful lot of other material, too. Once we had
gone down into the Imperial Valley, there was so much that was exciting and
interesting about the area, and it only took a skip of the mind into fantasy to
see how such an incident could have really happened. But we did try to keep
within the realm of reality, because the best science fiction is something that
you can strongly believe could have happened.

    Gardner: *The Jagged Edge* was our original title for *Monster,* and we
thought at the time that it was a very good one. In retrospect, we all feel that
The Monster That Challenged the World was not a very good title. We may
have been better off releasing the picture as *The Jagged Edge.*

*Western hero Tim Holt and eccentric character actor Hans Conried seem odd
choices for the top male slots in* Monster.

    Laven: I suppose in a way they were, except that we knew both those
gentlemen to be marvelous actors. I had been a fan of Tim Holt's from the time
that he did *The Magnificent Ambersons* [1942] and *The Treasure of the Sierra
Madre* [1948]. When I was a script supervisor, some years before I became a
director, I had worked on a low-budget Western that Holt did, and I
remember having a very nice relationship with him and finding him to be a
fine quality kind of person. There's no star temperament or that kind of thing
in Tim Holt's makeup. And the same goes for Hans Conried; I can't remember
exactly how we cast him, except that I know that either I or all three of us were
aware of the fact that there was a very rich acting background in Conried's past.
He was noted more for comedy and for slightly cliched or stereotypical parts
like in *The Five Thousand Fingers of Dr. T,* and some of the other things that
he did. But we knew better—we knew that, beneath some of the lighter things
he did, he did have a background in classic theater, and it would be an interesting, maybe slightly offbeat performer for *The Monster.* We always looked
to find those actors who could bring something special to a part, and who
might be just a little different so there's a freshness to the films.

Where exactly was The Monster That Challenged the World *shot?*

    Laven: In and around the L.A. area. We went down to the Salton Sea and
to Barstow, where the water irrigation system had little locks—a very visual atmosphere that fitted in with the whole development of *The Monster.* The
underwater sequences were shot outside Catalina, with "Scotty" Welborn,

who is a very well-known underwater cameraman, and Paul Stader, who was the underwater director. He has since gone on to be quite a well-known and highly praised second unit director. The nice thing is, whenever I see Paul, he comes up and shakes my hand, because *The Monster* was the picture that got him a director's card. Prior to that, he had just been a highly acceptable stunt-man, especially around water sequences.

Gardner: The underwater scenes were shot after the bulk of the film was finished. We then went back to the sound stage for underwater inserts, shooting through water-filled tanks that had artificial seaweed in them, for closeups of the actors peering at the camera from behind the tanks.

Were you involved at all in the underwater scenes, Mr. Laven?

Laven: I tried to go down a couple times—I found that I was not a very good scuba diver. But I did view the sets and review what was to be photographed underwater, with Paul, before it was shot.

Talk about your giant mollusk prop.

Gardner: The mollusk monster was conceived by us and executed by a very good special effects man named Augie Lohman. Augie went on from that picture to do many, many famous special effects films. The monster stood around ten feet high, and the exterior was made of fiberglas. All the movements were controlled by Augie and two assistants—it took three men to operate it. It worked with a series of air pressure valves. I believe it cost around $15,000 to build, and weighed about 1,500 pounds.

What became of it after you finished the picture?

Gardner: We sold it to the Ocean Park Pier, where it was a children's attraction for several years afterwards.

Were you pleased with the way Monster *turned out?*

Laven: Through the years, people who have a rapport with science fiction films have made me aware that *The Monster That Challenged the World* has made a mark of some kind in the catalogue of SF films, and that's very pleasing to me. I remember when I finished it, I felt that I had done a good job, and thought it came out pretty well. It wasn't meant to be an elaborate, over-whelming film at that time, but just good, strong, effective entertainment.

Then why is Monster That Challenged the World *your only sci-fi credit?*

Laven: Partly because of the damn snobbishness that existed, especially around that time. Thank God, since then George Lucas, Steven Spielberg and others have broken that barrier down. But at that time sci-fi was, overall, regarded as a lesser credit for directors. I can give you a very specific example: I had directed, before *Monster That Challenged the World*, a film called *The Rack* [1956] that launched Paul Newman's career. It was made at MGM and

Barbara Darrow struggles with the giant mollusk in this publicity shot for Levy-Gardner-Laven's *The Monster That Challenged the World.*

critically it was a highly regarded film — a character study of a man who became a collaborator in Korea. It was from a Rod Serling teleplay, adapted by Stewart Stern, who wrote *Rebel Without a Cause* [1955]. Wendell Corey, Walter Pidgeon, Eddie O'Brien and Lee Marvin were some of the other people in the cast. It was a really fine screenplay, a pretty damn good movie, and I did get some interesting attention after *The Rack.* Subsequent to *The Rack,* Art, Jules and I were trying to find a script of some significance — something that maybe we could look to get an Academy Award for, or something like that. But, as I explained earlier, we went into the business of making sci-fi films. I almost didn't direct *Monster,* but I felt I owed it to the company — to Art and Jules, for their confidence in me, and to UA—to do the first one. But I knew at the same time that it was not going to enhance or advance my career as a director.

The specific situation came up after *The Monster That Challenged the World,* when I was in contention to do a picture called *The Dark at the Top of the Stairs* [1960], which came from a highly acclaimed play by William Inge. It was going to be a very important film on the Warner Bros. schedule. As I understood it, they were debating between hiring me and another director. I went on an interview with a man who was then in charge, under Jack Warner, of production at Warners. I thought it was a very good interview—we talked about *The Rack* and my relationship with Paul Newman, who had subsequently become a star. I felt that I was making some points. Then he looked at a memo on his desk and said, "I see here that you also did a film called *The Monster That Challenged the World.*" I realized when he started to talk about that, that I was going to be put into a slightly embarrassing position because the actors who were scheduled to be in *The Dark at the Top of the Stairs* would not necessarily be impressed with a man who just recently directed a monster snail. I realized that the interview had taken a downturn. I didn't get the picture. Maybe I wouldn't have gotten it even if I had *not* directed *The Monster That Challenged the World.* But I do know that the idea of directors doing low-budget science fiction didn't fit in with their concept of the kind of director they wanted for the pictures that I truthfully would like to have done. I love pictures that are rich in human characterizations, and where the story has maybe some social or psychological significance—the kind of film that, if you were to make a broad generalization, could be nominated for the Academy Award. I've come close, but never quite achieved the identity that would get me those assignments.

So Paul Landres stepped in and directed the remaining three SF/horror films.

Landres: I first met Art Gardner when I was doing a film at Allied Artists in 1952. At that time he was production manager for an independent company releasing through AA. He suggested to his producer that I read and give a critique on a script they had. I gave the producer a comprehensive critique with positive suggestions to correct and help the script. The producer was so impressed that he offered me the picture to direct when and if it was made. Unfortunately the picture was *not* made, but Art Gardner was also impressed with what I had done and he suggested that I meet his partner Jules Levy. Together they had an option on a property called *Invaders from Mars.* They asked me to come in with them as director of that property if it was made. We worked long and hard on that story, but they lost the option on it.

Was that the Invaders from Mars *that Edward Alperson later made?*

Gardner: That's right. A writer named John Tucker Battle brought the story to me, we optioned it, and then Jules Levy and I worked with Battle on the screenplay. Jules worked for Eddie Alperson at the time, and Alperson became involved in the picture, too. Through a series of circumstances, our option expired, and Alperson picked it up and went on to make the film.

Extensive outdoor photography is a major highlight of The Monster That Challenged the World, The Vampire *and* The Return of Dracula.

Landres: Shooting in a studio is and was very costly. Not only did a company renting studio space pay top dollar, but there was an additional overhead charge that I believe was about 25 percent. This doesn't mean that we never shot in the studio—we did when we had small sets and it was convenient to do so. But when we wanted scope and realism from a location, we went outside if it was at all possible. Also, the less shot in a studio, the longer the shooting schedule was.

Laven: We learned from the earlier pictures that we did that the richest, most visual, effective sequences, production-wise, were those that were shot outdoors, where even a low-budget film is in a sense on equal standing with the most high-budgeted pictures. When you shoot the Pacific Ocean, or meadows, or city streets, those are the same visual backgrounds that the highest budgeted picture will shoot; they can't change or alter them any more than we can. We would look for things such as the Salton Sea locations; the ability to shoot the underwater sequences, by planning, with a minimal camera unit and almost no overhead. The fact that our company operated with as small an overhead as probably any company in town was again one of the reasons we were able to put whatever dollars were spent right on the screen.

Miss Fielder, did the films of Val Lewton influence your writing?

Fielder: I was very much influenced by Lewton. I thought *Cat People* was one of the great masterpieces. But I also have always loved horror films, and horror in general. I loved Poe; the darker side of storytelling has always been appealing to me, putting it in terms of American life.

Jack Mackenzie, who photographed several of your pictures, had also worked for Lewton.

Fielder: Certainly he was responsible very much for creation of mood, but of course you can't get there without first having it indicated in the script. Suggesting the frightening aspect of any film is probably more effective than actually showing it in detail. I suppose you finally get to the point where you feel that you must satisfy the audience's curiosity as to what "it" really is, although there've been a few great films where you have never seen the monster other than by suggestion. On *The Vampire,* the theme of the father potentially destroying the thing he cared about most—the ultimate victim being his daughter—seemed to me a classic theme around which to build a story. It seemed to have a particular kind of horror, going back to the Greeks, to Oedipus and Medea, all the great classics.

While The Vampire *and* The Return of Dracula *stand with the better horror films of the '50s, surely they must have represented a comedown for actors like John Beal and Francis Lederer.*

Gardner: John Beal and Francis Lederer did not consider it a comedown to appear in these films. Even in those days actors were actors, and if the film had any sign of being anywhere near a quality production, they would agree to appear in them.

Landres: I had no feeling whatsoever that they were in any way condescending to play these parts. As a matter of fact, it was just the opposite—they were both most cooperative. And because of their cooperation and friendliness, the feeling of camaraderie on the set was wonderful and affected not only the cast but the crew as well. This is the feeling I believe you sense when you see each of these films.

What was John Beal's reaction to the grisly makeup he had to wear in The Vampire?

Gardner: John Beal is a real trouper. He loved playing the vampire, and he did everything—he played the monster in the long shots, and in most all the action scenes.

Fielder: He thought it was one of his best jobs. He also liked the chance to come back to Hollywood—he had been living somewhere on the East Coast, and had really not been in Hollywood that much.

The Return of Dracula *was certainly the eeriest of these four films.*

Fielder: For the *Dracula* picture, I was influenced by the original Bram Stoker story, of course—the angle about the friendship of the two girls. Also, I'm sure that Thornton Wilder's film for Hitchcock, *Shadow of a Doubt* [1943], had an influence on my thinking. It was fun to create a character that was so suave, so evil—so far from Transylvania, and right on our own back doorstep.

Francis Lederer gives an outstanding performance.

Fielder: Francis Lederer had not been in that many recent films at that point; he was conducting a theater school, I think, at the time. And certainly he couldn't have been a more handsome, suave, marvelous Dracula. Both Francis Lederer and John Beal were a delight to work with, and they brought a tremendous professionalism to the sets and to their parts.

How was the effect of the gushing blood achieved in the female vampire's staking scene?

Gardner: We accomplished the effect by getting a goat bladder, filling it with makeup blood and taking it down to the stage with an insert crew. I remember that I held the goat bladder full of the makeup blood while Jules Levy, off-camera, plunged the sharpened stake into the bladder. We had to do

Top: Stage and screen star John Beal played his most offbeat role in the 1957 horror thriller *The Vampire* (with Coleen Gray). *Bottom:* Francis Lederer, a Continental leading man in the 1930s, made a fine Count Dracula in 1958's *The Return of Dracula.*

Count Dracula (Francis Lederer) meets a grisly fate in the climax of *The Return of Dracula*. Notice the movie light by the Count's left foot.

it three or four times, and when we finished I had makeup blood all over my clothes.

What prompted the decision to film this scene in color?

Landres: Obviously it was done for shock value. Color was not in common use at that time, so what could be more shocking than to suddenly have the rich red color of blood practically come popping off the screen? The decision to do this part of the film in color was the producers', and a very good one it was. However, it entailed a considerable amount of effort and money to do this. The original cost of the color film and the camera was the least of it. It got involved in negative cutting, the number of color prints that were made and, most important, cutting the color footage into all of the theatrical prints. All I can say is that it was not inexpensive. Art and Jules deserve a great deal of credit for doing this.

The Flame Barrier *is indisputably the least of the four sci-fi/horror Gramercys.*

Gardner: It really was the most inferior of the four, and the only reason I can give for it coming out the way it did is that the screenplay, obviously, wasn't as good as the others. Without a good screenplay, you just can't make a good film.

Fielder: I think we were kind of following a pattern of other jungle movies of the time—but there *had* been the event of a Sputnik going up with a monkey on board. We had fun making *The Flame Barrier,* but we shot it entirely on a sound stage, and we had a very limited budget and schedule.

Gardner: I think that three of the four films turned out as well as we hoped. We were disappointed in *The Flame Barrier.* And if we were doing them again today we would, of course, try to make them better. But at the time we did the best that we could with the budgets we had, and with the screenplays and casts that we had.

If you were remaking these films today, what elements would you change?

Landres: If we were shooting these films today, I would shoot *The Vampire* and *The Return of Dracula* without change. As for *The Flame Barrier,* I would not do it!

Considering the high quality of The Monster That Challenged the World, The Vampire *and* The Return of Dracula, *why has Levy-Gardner-Laven neglected this genre in recent years?*

Gardner: To be honest with you, the four films we did make were not very profitable. That may sound strange because of the low cost, but I don't believe United Artists really knew how to release this type of film at the time. We'd have been far better off if we had made them for a distributor like American International or one of the other, smaller releasing companies.

Laven: UA didn't have too much experience releasing science fiction films, and I think for that reason the maximum probably was not gained from the films. Columbia, which made the Sam Katzman sci-fi films, and some of the smaller companies that dealt in sci-fi, probably had a better knowledge in where and how to release them. But UA did their best, and we in no way complained about the fact that maybe they didn't do as well as some other studio because they did give us their backing and they did invest their money and show confidence in us. That whole company now has changed around considerably, but they were indeed a marvelous organization to work for.

Which is your personal favorite of the four films, and for what reason?

Arthur Franz and Robert Brown battle an extraterrestrial blob in the last (and least) of the Levy-Gardner-Laven science-fictioners, *The Flame Barrier.*

Laven: It's always one's own work which one tends to most admire, so— *The Monster That Challenged the World.* It's funny, I do a certain amount of television work these days—*The A-Team, Hill Street Blues, Mike Hammer*— and, in truth, I hardly look at any of those shows except when mine are on, and then I look with great fascination! Such is the nature of this particular director and, I suspect, of most all directors.

Gardner: My personal favorite is *The Vampire.* I think that we got the most out of that screenplay, and the most for our money. Of the four, it really did the best at the box office.

Fielder: It's gotta be *The Monster That Challenged the World,* because it was really a super picture. It was a bigger production and a great experience for me because it was my first picture. It was very, very special.

Landres: Of the three shows that I did, *The Vampire* was my favorite. It was a very successful combination of all of the elements necessary to make a successful show—producing, writing, directing, acting, editing, camera, etc. And the feeling on the set, from top to bottom, was one of great camaraderie, one of every person involved trying to do his best. It was a wonderful feeling and doesn't happen very often.

[I was told] many times that my music was better than the picture.
Years back, in the '40s and even into the '50s, the reviewers in town
would never even mention the composer. Once in a while they would mention
a top guy like Steiner or Korngold. But us little guys in the Bs, never.
All of a sudden you would see, "Al Glasser did an outstanding job."
They would never say that about anyone else.

Albert Glasser

A CONVERSATION with Albert Glasser reminds one of Sydney Greenstreet's classic line to Humphrey Bogart in *The Maltese Falcon*: "I like talking to a man who likes to talk." Glasser has had a long and lucrative career and certainly has a lot to talk about. One of the most prolific Hollywood composers, he started off as a copyist in the music department at Warner Bros. in the late 1930s, learning the art of film scoring from scratch while working under such big guns as Max Steiner and Erich Wolfgang Korngold. He graduated to orchestrating and by the mid-'40s was composing and directing his own scores.

A hard, fast worker, Glasser found his musical skills were put to the test in the frantic, down-to-the-wire world of B-picture making. He can certainly boast of a voluminous filmography, having scored a staggering 135 movies between 1944 and 1962, not counting at least 35 features for which he received no official credit. In addition to scoring 300 television shows and 450 radio programs, he arranged and conducted for the noted American operetta composer Rudolf Friml and orchestrated for Ferde Grofe (with whom he first collaborated on the science fiction classic *Rocketship X-M*).

Glasser probably holds the record for composing more sci-fi music than anyone else in the 1950s; he scored practically all of Bert I. Gordon's special effects epics and even worked for Roger Corman and William Castle. Glasser's style was unmistakable: pounding, hard-driving rhythms and crashing crescendos which set the pace for the lurid, action-packed quickies they accompanied.

How did you become interested in music?

It started when I was in high school here in Los Angeles. I fell in love with medicine because I had two broken noses in two fistfights. The guy who fixed my nose was a great plastic surgeon, so whenever I had the spare time I would run down to his office and hang around for an hour or two watching him work. I was just fascinated and decided to become a doctor. I started to take all of this pre-med stuff in high school. About halfway through, around eleventh grade, I started to hear music in my head that you couldn't believe. I was playing the flute and my sister was a fine concert pianist. I wanted to switch courses, but they said I couldn't do that. Well, screw *them [laughs]*! There was a lot of yelling and screaming, but finally they said, go ahead. From there I graduated and went to a junior college and started taking harmony classes. Finally I got a scholarship at U.S.C. for a violin concerto in 1934.

How did you break into the movies?

When I finished up at U.S.C., a lot of my friends were saying, "Hey, Glasser, as long as you're so inventive in your god-damned music, why don't you get a job at the studios? They need musicians." This was a period when the studios were getting guys from New York and Europe, anyone who could come here and conduct, play a fiddle, blow a trumpet, any damned thing. The soundtrack had only just come in in 1929–30 and they were always looking for

Previous page: Al Glasser at home, 1987. Glasser is today happily retired. He maintains a full schedule of writing and is an ardent photography and ham radio buff.

good people to work in the music department. But the next question is, how do you get into the movies? It's *still* a good question *[laughs]*! I went to the movies two or three times a week just so I could write down who the musical directors were for all of the studios. For Warner Bros. at that time it was Leo Forbstein. I called up the Warner Bros. music department. "This is Mr. Forbstein's office," the secretary would say. "This is Mr. Glasser. I'm a composer." "Sorry! We've got plenty of composers. Goodbye!"

And the same result for each of the other studios?
Exactly the same. So I figured, there's got to be a way of finding these guys—I had to go to them directly. So I figured out a little pattern and it worked like a charm. I hiked to Warner Bros. and went to the head cop at the gate. "Hi, officer. Has Mr. Forbstein come out yet?" "Oh, no. Around five o'clock, usually. Did you see his new car?" I said, "What new car?" and he said, "He's got a gorgeous new red Packard." Now I walked across the street and sat on the curb and waited and waited. Finally the cars started coming out and here's this great big red Packard. I *got* him! That's *him*! He's the man sitting in the back seat with the chauffeur in the front. I got the license number, that's all I wanted.

The next morning I hitchhiked to the license bureau and got his address. By now I had been orchestrating all kinds of stuff: Bach, piano sonatas, the *Toccata and Fugue* like Stokowski made, my own personal stuff. I had a mountain of music. So I got dressed up one Sunday morning and brought this whole bundle along. I rang his doorbell. I was all ready to put my foot in the door in case the butler would tell me to get the hell out of there. The door opened and here's a short fat man in a bathrobe who hadn't shaved in a couple of days. I said, "Mr. Forbstein?" and he said, "That's me. What do you want, kid?"

I told him who I was. He said, "I'm making breakfast. Come in." We went into the kitchen and I'm jabbering away a mile a minute. He said, "Just a second, kid. Let me see what you got here," and he was looking and looking at my stuff. And I'm so happy. Here's the guy who runs the whole goddamned music department for the studio, he's looking at my music. Later on, I found out that this was bullshit. He couldn't even read music. He was a fiddle player from St. Louis. He was a good musician, and a good, sharp cookie, a good businessman. He became the musical director in the theater in St. Louis and then when Warner Bros. was looking for people, he talked them into giving him a job. But he couldn't read an orchestration, not a god-damned thing!

Did he like your music?
He said, "Hey, your writing is very good. Better then we have. Tomorrow morning call my librarian, Vito Centroni, and you come and work for us." Holy shit! The door is opening up! I ran home, I was flying! The next morning, first thing, I called up the music department. "Vito Centroni, please. Hello,

I'm Al Glasser. I talked to Mr. Forbstein." He said, "Oh, yes, he just told me about you. I'm so busy I can't talk now. Goodbye!" Boom! He hangs up.

So that was the end of Warner Bros. for you?
  Temporarily. I tried the same trick on all of the others, found out where they lived, tracked them down one way or another. Some were very nice like Forbstein, others were sons of bitches. *Get out of here, don't bother me, you little snot!* Finally I call up again this Centroni guy. He says, "All right, kid. Come in tomorrow morning. I could use you." So I go hitchhiking the next morning, a car stops and I jump in. The guy says, "Where are you going?" I say, "Warner Brothers." "Do you work there?" "Sure. In the music department." So, he dumps me off at the front gate. When I finally walk into the music department, who's sitting in the front desk? The guy who picked me up, Centroni himself *[laughs]*!

What was your first job at Warner Bros.?
  I was a copyist. From there on, I just took off. I corrected things I wasn't supposed to at times. All of the other copyists wouldn't bother correcting obvious mistakes, they couldn't have cared less. But I could tell a mistake in two seconds. I was good, so to speak. Soon, other studios like Paramount and Universal called. I went from studio to studio. (Except Universal. Very cheap!) So, in a hurry I was making money and moving up! I learned the ropes. I watched Max Steiner. I used to pull out his original sketches, take them home and stayed up to three, four and five o'clock just analyzing every god-damned thing that Max Steiner was doing. The transpositions, the resolutions, the whole bit, the mechanics of it. The best school in the world for pictures was right there. [Erich Wolfgang] Korngold came along right after that. I started to study his sketches. He was unbelievable, a great genius. I decided to get out of the copying racket because you could be locked in forever. I saw others who tried to get out, but they waited too long.

When did you finally quit?
  I quit in 1943 when I was working with Dimitri Tiomkin. I started working on orchestrations exclusively at MGM. Composing was something else, where they would ask me to write something because they knew I could, and I would knock out whatever they wanted. In 1946 Johnny Green called me to write the overture for the Academy Award show. When they got through playing it, the whole audience stood up, cheering and clapping for Johnny Green. Green said, "Ladies and gentlemen, thank you so much, but it's not for me, it's for Mr. Albert Glasser who did the show." So, I was on the way up and starting to get credit.

What was your first movie as composer?
  I did *The Monster Maker* for PRC—for $250 I composed, orchestrated,

Glasser received $250 for writing the score of *The Monster Maker,* the 1944 horror cheapie starring J. Carrol Naish and Ralph Morgan.

copied, conducted, worked with the music cutter. What the hell? If I didn't want it, they had ten guys waiting. I wanted credit. I did about three or four of them for [Glasser's agent] David Chudnow—for $300, then $325, then $350. I did a picture called *In Old New Mexico* [1945] and the producers were so impressed that they called me in for another one. They said, "What did we pay you last time?" I said I got $350. They said, "Wait a minute! We paid $3,000 for that!" I said, "You paid Chudnow $3,000! He gave me $350." They said, "Oh, that son of a bitch! From now on, forget about Chudnow, you come straight to us and we'll hire you for $3,000."

How much time did they give you to score The Monster Maker?
One week. Luckily there was very little for me to do. Mostly piano work for that. It was the story of a pianist who gets acromegaly; his hands get big and he cannot play anymore. I had to find a concert pianist to record all of the piano stuff and write a couple of cues here and there. Nine times out of ten, all I had was a week. Occasionally two weeks.

What size orchestra would you use for a typical PRC film?
About 20, 22. It was way too small.

The studios have their own orchestras?

That came later, in the '50s. In the '40s, all of the best musicians in Hollywood were drafted. I was working with Dimitri Tiomkin at the time, orchestrating the scores he was writing for the War Department. We got all the stuff recorded with the Army bands. They had the best damned orchestras in the world.

How did your collaboration with Ferde Grofe during Rocketship X-M *come about?*

That was a helluva situation. I was with Lippert Productions at that time. I was the head honcho, which worked out very well. They fell in love with my stuff, and you couldn't blame them. I gave them some very good scores—*I Shot Jesse James* [1949], *The Return of Wildfire* [1948]. . .

Lippert, the boss, called me in one day. Short, fat guy. He said, "Look, Al, we're going to do a big one, a science fiction thing called *Rocketship X-M* and we've got to work very fast. The guy who wrote the script tried to peddle it all around town for a couple of years, no one wanted it. Why? It's science fiction, who gives a shit about science fiction? But now, that big idiot, that asshole George Pal is making one about going to the moon. He's been making it for a year and a half, and there's trouble, trouble, trouble—all of those special shots, the photographic tricks and whatnot. He even took out a five-page ad in *Life* magazine, announcing that *Destination Moon* is on the way and will be out in about three or four months."

So, Lippert said, "We're going to knock *Rocketship X-M* out in three or four weeks. We'll do it real cheap, and get ahead of him. George Pal is making everyone conscious about moon pictures. *We'll* give 'em moon pictures!" So he did. We worked day and night, like sons of bitches.

How did Ferde Grofe become involved?

Lippert said, "We have to have a high-class name, we're going for class now. We know you're good, and don't get me wrong, but I had a long talk with a guy named Ferde Grofe last night. He's going to compose the music, but he wanted so much more money for the orchestration and the conducting! Holy cow! Half the budget would go to him! So I made a deal for him to compose and I want you to orchestrate and conduct it. Which means we'll save a big chunk of money." I think they paid him $5,000 for the composing only.

Were you looking forward to working with Grofe?

To work with Grofe! What an honor! What a *privilege!* So, I went out and met the old guy. We had a ball. First they had to finish the movie. It took about two or three weeks. They worked every day and half the night, two crews going, just to push it through. Grofe started writing, and I started orchestrating for him.

Glasser *(left)* conducts alfresco on *The Return of Wildfire*. The comely cowgirl is leading lady Patricia Morison.

Rocketship X-M *had an innovative score for its day.*

We wanted some different sounds, something unusual, once they got out into outer space. The theremin at that time was really hot, since Miklos Rozsa's score for *Spellbound* [1945]. So I met the guy who invented it, he was a foot doctor. He followed my orchestrations as closely as he could and it worked like a charm. Grofe was a doll to work with, a wonderful man. He was enormous, fat as a pig! An old beer-drinker from way back.

Did you visit the set of Rocketship X-M?

Oh, yes. Many times. Kurt Neumann, the director, was very nice, very gentle, very intelligent. A good, hard worker. He wrote his own scripts.

Preparing to soar through space to the sound of music orchestrated by Albert Glasser are Noah Beery, Jr., Hugh O'Brian, Lloyd Bridges, Osa Massen and John Emery—the crew of *Rocketship X-M*.

What's your opinion of the movie?

I loved it. I'm an old science fiction fan from way back. When I was in junior high school, I wrote two science fiction stories.

You worked on a few SF films with the production team of Jack Pollexfen and Aubrey Wisberg. How well did you work with them?

Aubrey Wisberg was a helluva nice guy; in fact, we got very close with him. A very fine gentleman, very direct and honest. But in the last picture I made with them, I got screwed. They wanted me to sign an agreement that

I'd take 10 percent now and the balance when the movie was released. This is an old trick that I heard about many years ago. But I took a chance.

Do you remember scoring Invasion U.S.A.?

Oh, yes. That was for Albert Zugsmith. He's a wild man! I thought I wrote a pretty good score for it; there were some good scenes in it. I tried to imitate the Russian national anthem. I turned it around, upside down, to give some flavor. That's one picture I don't have the tape on. In most cases, I saved everything I had. From the very beginning, I would get copies of what I was doing. Most of them now are in the University of Wyoming. Sixteen crates! I'm living in a fire zone here. We had a big fire in 1961 and it burned up half of the area; about four hundred homes went in two hours. If my music got burned up, I'd shoot myself!

Sci-fi fans probably remember you best for your long association with Bert I. Gordon. Did you and he get along all right?

Wonderful guy. We had more fun with him! He got me into ham radio for which I am very grateful. I met him right after I finished *Huk* [1956]. That was the biggest job I ever had, the biggest orchestra, forty men! It paid off just beautifully and almost came into the last runoff for the Academy Awards. Anyway, I was laying the tracks in with a film cutter. Suddenly the door opens and Bert Gordon comes in and says, "Who wrote that stuff? It's marvelous. I'm working next door finishing up a picture I just made and I'm looking for a composer." He wanted to hear some more of my stuff and so he came over to the house. He said, "I want *you*! I've done two pictures so far but I'm not very happy with the music, it didn't give me the lift that I wanted. Your kind of stuff has *balls!*"

Which brings me to another story. During the war, when I was working with Dimitri Tiomkin, we used to record all of his stuff at the army camp and one of the things we had to do was *Battle of Britain* or *Battle of Russia,* one or the other. We were running out of time, and Tiomkin asked me to write one section for it. So I knocked out one big number, about four or five minutes. Later on, when he went to conduct it for the recording, the whole orchestra, a hundred musicians, got up *[clapping]* — "Bravo, Dimi, bravo! That's the best thing you ever wrote!" I cringed! Tiomkin said, "Gentlemen, thank you very much but I can't accept that. Mr. Glasser, come up here. Here's the man who wrote the music: Mr. Albert Glasser, my assistant."

Later, when I drove him home (I was his chauffeur), we pulled up in front of his house, he got out and started yelling! "You son of a bitch! I hate you! You lousy bum! You piece of shit! I worked two weeks on that music, day and night, you do one lousy number and for you, they clap and for me, I get nothing!" The next morning when I came to pick him up I was trembling. I see him walking towards me, laughing and happy. Tiomkin got in the car and said to me, "Do you know what's wrong, why I got so god-damned mad

A 1952 Manhattan shattered by enemy bombers (and still cleaner and safer than modern Manhattan) was the setting of *Invasion U.S.A.*, scored by Glasser. Pictured here are Gerald Mohr and Peggie Castle.

yesterday? The difference between you and me is that the music you write, it has balls! Mine doesn't!"

What was the first film you scored for Bert Gordon?

    The Cyclops. He paid me $4,000 for the whole thing, including the orchestra. I had fun with it—it was a cute little picture, well done. From then on, I was his boy. The next one was *The Amazing Colossal Man* and then *War of the Colossal Beast*. I was fascinated. I used to watch on the set as much as I could while he was doing the effects. He used to work a lot out of his garage, where he had his equipment. The funny one, of course, was *Attack of the Puppet People*. On the set, they made chairs ten feet high so when the actors would sit on them, they would look little. It was cute, a lot of fun. In fact, we wrote a song for that for which they're still paying me—*[singing]* "You're a dolly, you're a dolly." I can't believe it.

So you got to know Gordon well.

Oh, yes, we had a lot of fun. He even gave me the ham radio test to get my license. I still hear from him but not too often. He keeps to himself a lot. His father used to manufacture a certain part for the old Studebaker, the door handles or something, and so they lived very well. When he was growing up, Bert had a fascination with movies. When he was ten or eleven years old, he made a movie by himself. He would take pictures one at a time, and when he played it back real quick, it started to move—the basic element of movie technique. He made a movie, it wasn't very long, of about two or three hundred pictures. He showed it at his birthday party and the kids loved it. His parents almost had an orgasm. *Look at what our son did! He's a genius!*

When he got out of college, he wanted to get into making movies. He borrowed some equipment and figured out a gimmick how to make commercials—television was just getting started. Eventually he started making a lot of money in this little city outside of Detroit. Then he got married and came out here. In the meantime, his family started raising money for him to make a movie. He had all of these gimmicks and tricks of moving animals, of animals getting big. He developed a system and it wasn't bad. You've got to hand it to him, he did it all by himself. He sold these pictures, made a profit, paid back his family. It was a good investment for the family, but eventually they started to lose money—the science fiction thing was disappearing. I worked on four or five of his pictures.

You worked with Roger Corman, also.

He walked into the cutting room where I was doing this science fiction stuff. He said, "Hey, I need you. I did a little picture recently and it's so bad that nobody wants it. Even the music was terrible. Can you give me a good score on this?" We went down to the projection room and put it on and ran it for about an hour *[groans]*—*Viking Women and the Sea Serpent!* That was a weird one, *very* bad! I said I'd try. He said, "Give it all you have!" When it got wild, I gave it wild music. When they were on the boat in the middle of a storm, I gave it storm music. That's easy, any asshole can write that kind of music. When we got through, he said, "You saved my picture! You saved my *life!* I just sold it and it's all set. The music did it!"

That I heard many times, that my music was better than the picture. Years back, in the '40s and even into the '50s, the reviewers in town would never even mention the composer. Once in a while they would mention a top guy like Steiner or Korngold. But us little guys in the Bs, never. All of a sudden you would see, "Al Glasser did an outstanding job." They would *never* say that about anyone else. I cut them all out for my scrapbook.

Did the B directors have any input or suggestions on these scores?

Very seldom. Only Sam Fuller, when I did *I Shot Jesse James.* He was a wild character, very dramatic, but he got good results. There was one scene when Jesse James [Reed Hadley] was talking to his wife, he's saying that one of these days he's going to buy a farm out in Oklahoma. And it's getting sadder and sadder. Reed Hadley was a marvelous actor. I started to cry while I was watching it, so did the electrician and the cameraman. The whole god-damned company was sitting there crying!

Memories of Giant from the Unknown?

You mean *The Giant from Devil's Crag?* They changed the name, the crooks! That was a little cheapie that I never paid much attention to. We had to record it in a lousy, half-assed recording studio because they were broke.

How would you rate some of your colleagues who worked in B movies? Like Ronald Stein and Gerald Fried?

I knew Ronald Stein quite well, we used to work together on the science fiction stuff. Nice guy. I didn't care for his *music* too much, but he was adequate, a good musician. Gerald Fried was one of the top oboe players in New York. He came out here in the mid-'50s because he wanted to compose. He did good work. Never great, but good.

Raoul Kraushaar?

Kraushaar was a nice person, but his work was never worthwhile. He was good for a cheap Republic Western.

Leith Stevens?

Leith Stevens was a good man, very good. When work started to slow down in the late '60s–early '70s because the B movies were out, I couldn't get a god-damned thing to do. So I went out to talk to Stevens. He said, "Bring along some of your stuff. I like your work." So I brought along the record of *Huk.* I put the record on and he started to listen to it and all of a sudden he said, "Jesus Christ!" I knew I was dead because he didn't want any competition. If I had done anything with him, I might supersede him, so I had cut my own throat. He said, "I'll be in touch," but he never was.

Did you have much contact with Bernard Herrmann?

I met him once or twice. He scored *Jane Eyre* [1944], which I happened to catch on TV. What struck me was the music. *There* was a fine composer; I was just thrilled! So I stopped what I was doing and watched the whole god-damned movie just to listen to the score and it was marvelous. When I got through, I got him on the telephone. I said, "I want to congratulate you. I just saw *Jane Eyre* and your score was so god-damned beautiful, so fantastic, I still have goose pimples!" There was a long pause. He finally said, "So what do you want?" I said, "I'm congratulating you for the marvelous job you did. All of your stuff is great but this is the best score you ever wrote. I'm *proud* of you!" He said, "Well, what do you *want?*" I said, "Oh, fuck you!" and I hung up *[laughs]*!

Was there much rivalry between the top Hollywood composers?

I'll tell you a story. When I was working with Tiomkin at the War Department, the telephone rang. It was Miklos Rozsa. He said, "I just got my draft notice from the Army. I want Dimi to call Washington to have me transferred to your place. I'll do anything—I'll orchestrate, I'll conduct, I'll clean the toilets! As long as I can stay here in town." Later, when Tiomkin walked in, I said, "Dimi, you got a phone call from Rozsa. He wants you to call Washington 'cause he has to go for a draft call, and he wants you to transfer him over here. We can use him." We were scoring Frank Capra's war shorts at the time. Tiomkin blew up: "Hell, no! The dirty bastard. Let him suffer like all of the other boys are suffering!" As it turned out, when Rozsa went for the draft, he was kicked out anyway. He had a bad foot or something and he was too old.

What was Tiomkin's problem?

Tiomkin was making big money for his scores, but the problem was that he was charging too much. His price was going up and up. He had scored a big musical show, an extravaganza over at MGM, and he wanted the violin section to sound so rich and so warm that he rented about 25 Stradivarius violins, at about $5,000 to $6,000 apiece. It was an enormous bill and MGM was paying for it. The next picture he made for Capra the orchestra bill was so steep, the studio said, "Get this guy out of here and *keep* him out of here!" By 1940, all of the studios said, "Hands off Tiomkin. He's too expensive, he's a crazy Russian!" Tiomkin couldn't get another feature for about a year. Here comes Rozsa, moving up fast, getting all of the biggest and best pictures. Tiomkin hated him! He said, "The son of a bitch is taking all of my pictures away from me!"

How about contemporary composers like Jerry Goldsmith?

Excellent! I wrote him a fan letter years ago. Whenever I hear good work, I drop off a note or phone. Including Johnny Williams. I even wrote a letter to John Barry. Marvelous writer, one of the top group.

Of the more than 100 film scores you've written, which is your favorite?

I like 'em all!

The production of motion pictures, especially overseas,
was an exciting way of earning a livelihood. It was a method
of providing the necessities of life for one's family and having
a great time in the process. Oddly enough,
I didn't consider it a career.

Bernard Glasser

ONE SCHOOL of film criticism holds that the director is the one and only true author of a motion picture, while others consider the writer's contribution the most vital. The only time these two camps seem to fully agree is in ignoring the role of the producer, without whose participation no movies would exist at all. During the '50s and '60s Bernard Glasser worked as a producer in both TV and films, sometimes turning his talents toward directing and writing as well. His list of credits range from a Three Stooges Western (*Gold Raiders*, 1951) to the Cinerama war epic *Battle of the Bulge* (1965), and also include frequent detours into science fiction via such well-remembered genre titles as *Return of the Fly*, *The Day of the Triffids* and *Crack in the World*. Glasser left the business after twenty industrious years of squeezing dollars, stretching budgets and making successful pictures, and now looks back without regret at his Adventures in Filmland.

The Chicago-born Glasser grew up in what he calls "the movie generation" and fell in love with pictures at the ripe old age of four. In the late '40s, while working as a teacher at Beverly Hills High School, he got his feet wet in the film industry by working as a production assistant. In 1950 he invested in an old motion picture studio and turned it into a rental lot. Glasser leased his Keywest Studio out to producers like Roger Corman (*The Fast and the Furious*), Burt Lancaster (*Apache*) and others as well as using the facilities to make a five-day, $50,000 film of his own (*Gold Raiders*), directed by his friend Edward Bernds. When Glasser's studio lease expired in 1955, Glasser and Bernds combined forces on a series of budget features for Robert Lippert's Regal Films, with the pair making their joint SF debut on 1958's *Space Master X-7*.

How did you hook up with Robert Lippert's organization?

While shopping for a release for *Gold Raiders*, I was introduced to Bob Lippert, and he invited me to his house to screen the film for some of his associates. Lippert was pleasant, but the deal he offered for distribution was not. A few years later I purchased a Western novel entitled *Long Rider Jones*. The property was submitted to David Brown, then the story editor at 20th Century–Fox, and Brown indicated that the studio was interested in the property. After a meeting with Brown and [Fox production chief] Buddy Adler, I was told that they would buy the story but I could not produce the picture for Fox. I thanked Brown for his interest, but told him that my goal was to produce *Long Rider Jones*. Several weeks later I received a call from Brown. He said that Bob Lippert had just signed a multiple picture contract with the studio for the production of second features, and that if I was interested in making a budget Western, he would recommend my project to Lippert. I accepted his offer. *Long Rider Jones* was retitled *The Storm Rider* [1957], and it was one of the first productions made under Lippert's Regal banner for 20th Century–Fox distribution.

What were your impressions of Lippert and his organization?

Bob Lippert knew how to choose capable employees to supervise his

Years before his producing career veered off into science fiction, Glasser *(center)* turned out the low-budget Three Stooges Western *Gold Raiders* (1951), co-starring George O'Brien (in cowboy hat).

company. Harry Spalding was one of these capable men. He had been a newspaperman in Seattle when Lippert hired him as the chief booker for Lippert theaters. When Lippert entered production, he sent his scripts to Harry for comment. Harry had a good story sense and a tactful way of making criticism. Bill Magginetti was another capable Lippert employee. Magginetti was originally a bookkeeper in Lippert's office, but as production activities expanded he became proficient in analyzing budgets and supervising the Regal operation.

My relationship with Bob Lippert was always friendly and productive. On occasion he asked me for advice regarding pictures that were experiencing difficulties.

What are your recollections of Space Master X-7?

After Ed Bernds and I had made several Westerns for Regal we decided to widen our horizons. One of us mentioned outer space as about as wide as a horizon could get. That afternoon I called my agent and asked him if he knew of an inexpensive idea for a space film, and he described a property involving trains and a submarine. The script had been turned down by several producers as being too expensive to produce. Ed and I read the script and agreed that we could make it work, but the writers, Dan Mainwaring and George Yates, wanted more money than we could afford. I told Harry Spalding that I would find the extra money somewhere in the budget, and he approved the purchase. Ed rewrote the script gratis because we were already over budget in the story department. We had seen some exciting stock footage of an airliner "wheels-up" landing and decided to utilize it for a "big," inexpensive ending for the picture.

What were your budget and shooting schedule?

$125,000. But we had to pay Mainwaring and Yates $25,000 for their script—$15,000 that had been set aside for it, and then an extra $10,000 that they insisted on. That left us an even $100,000 to lavish on our production. Bill Magginetti's approval of the budget of *Space Master* was necessary before we could start shooting, but he rejected the budget because it was too low. He was correct, but what he didn't know was how we planned to shoot the inserts, special effects and "documentary" footage. At a luncheon meeting in Lippert's office, the conversation went something like this:

Lippert: "Bill tells me your script calls for a lot of location shots as well as special effects, planes, trains and I don't know what else. Are you sure you can make it for $100,000?"

"$90,000," Magginetti corrected. "He paid $20,000 for the script."

"We're going to do the special effects at Mercer's [an old-time special effects house in Hollywood]. Ray Mercer has given us a flat deal which includes everything, even the titles. Our principal photography is about eight days. I don't know how long the second unit will take, we're handling it ourselves. John Link, the editor, has made a flat deal which includes everything—sound effects, music, even negative cutting. I've 'locked in' most of our costs," I replied.

"What about the creeping fungus?" Magginetti asked.

"We're going to do that ourselves," I answered.

Magginetti shook his head "no way."

"Well, Bill, what do you say?" Lippert asked.

"It's his ass if he goes over," Magginetti said.

That ended the budget discussion. We were subsequently given the green light.

Ed Bernds told me Norman Maurer helped out quite a bit on Space Master. *How did he get involved?*

Moe Howard of the Three Stooges had asked us if there was a place on our production team for his son-in-law, a comic book illustrator. Moe said that Norman would work without a salary in order to learn the film business. Norman

With today's high-priced, high-tech special effects, it's hard to believe that the alien threat in *Space Master X-7* cost "less than $1,000."

invited me to his house to show me his artwork. He was an enthusiastic person brimming with suggestions for the special effects in the script. We became fast friends, and he went to work the next day. Upon the completion of *Space Master,* my friend Sid Pink asked me if I wanted to help him produce a science fiction film *[The Angry Red Planet].* I suggested Norman for the producer position and described his abilities as a conceptual artist as well as a practical executive. Sid Pink hired Norman for the picture.

Who devised the fungus effects in Space Master?

Norman Maurer did. This effect was composed of a foam rubber rug about a yard square. Several different models were made at a latex factory in Hollywood. Norman and I supervised this operation while Ed rewrote the script. These latex "rugs" looked like miniature volcanoes. In the vortex of each volcano, Norman inserted a plastic tube. Compressed air forced a red powder through the tube and out of the vortex. Compressed air was also utilized to make the rug sections undulate. The entire effect cost us less than $1,000.

According to Space Master's *publicity, you rushed it into production ahead of schedule to capitalize on publicity surrounding the Explorer liftoff.*

Yes, we did, a bit. Most of the publicity surrounding *Space Master* was generated by Marty Weiser, Lippert's staff publicity man. Marty gave *Space Master* special treatment, and the trade papers assumed that Ed and I were making a big-budgeted science fiction picture. This didn't hurt our feelings. We had no money in the budget for anything except production. Marty also suggested the title change from *Missile into Space* [the film's shooting title] to *Space Master X-7*. He claimed that his title was more imaginative and less "on the nose," and we agreed with him.

What were some of the cost-cutting measures you used?

We tried to lock in most production expenditures: music, editing, transportation, set construction, electrical, set dressings and props, etc. Most of the companies we dealt with were willing to give us a flat deal because we had a continuity of production. If the companies lost money on a particular production, they knew that we would try to make it up to them on the next show. We photographed the second unit with a handheld Eymo 35mm camera. We shot police car run-bys, inserts, airport scenes, etc., at all hours of the day and night, and without compensation. Our team consisted of Norman Maurer, [stuntman] Joe Becker and myself. For our studio facilities we returned to Keywest. That place went back to the days of silent serials, according to what people told me; it's still standing, but it's deserted now. It's at the corner of Santa Monica Boulevard and Van Ness in Hollywood.

In order to make a picture "for a price," you have to be acquainted with all elements of production. As an example of "hands-on": Most of our set construction was done at night, and I would have the construction foreman call when the sets were completed. Sometimes this would occur at three or four in the morning; I would go to the studio and approve the sets, whatever the time. We couldn't risk any surprises the next morning.

Have you appeared in any of your own films?

Space Master was my only screen appearance. Ed Bernds suggested that I appear; he wanted an extra "extra" to fill the camera frame in the bunker scene. My wife [Joan Barry] was also in *Space Master;* she had been an actress prior to our marriage, and it was practical to call her, especially when an actress did not report on time. With four children in her care she didn't appear as frequently as she would have liked. Our oldest son and daughter obtained their Social Security cards at a very early age — they were the children seen in *Space Master* and *Return of the Fly*.

The finale to Space Master *is a slight letdown. Was the climax of the original script utilized?*

For the most part, we followed the script. In editing we deleted an office tag scene by the government official who opened the film. We felt that once the plane landed, the movie was over.

Was the film a moneymaker?

Space Master did very well for Lippert and Regal. Fox billed *Space Master* with *The Fly,* and this combination outgrossed many of the more expensive Fox productions. Lippert became a celebrity on the Fox lot, and the Regal low budget films were the main topic of conversation in the Fox commissary. The Fox distribution department then pulled *Space Master* from the bill and replaced it with an expensive Fox picture that was not getting good grosses. The revised bill did not do well. The chemistry of two science fiction pictures on the same bill was the key.

How exactly did Return of the Fly *come about?*

The Fly was the sleeper everyone had hoped it would be. It was Harry Spalding's idea to make a sequel. He suggested that Ed and I be given the project. *Return of the Fly* was supposed to be just another Regal project. Perhaps it was the quality of Ed's script or revised thinking on Lippert's part that upgraded the project.

Robert Lippert was originally supposed to produce the original Fly.

The Fly was an "in-house" project; Regal purchased the short story by George Langelaan that appeared in *Playboy* magazine. Lippert felt that he had something special with this project, and he requested and received additional funds to produce the picture. If Bob relinquished producer credit, it must have been for a good reason; I'm sure that he could've had producer credit if he felt it was important.

You did have a better budget and shooting schedule on Return of the Fly.

Our budget was increased to $275,000. The production department of the Fox studio asked Lippert to move *Return of the Fly* to the studio instead of our shooting it at an independent lot. Of course this meant an increase in production costs and no controls. Because of the inefficiency of the slower Fox crews and the added charges and surcharges for set operation and construction, it was impossible for me to lock in any expenditures. Most of our money was being spent unproductively. The net result was that Lippert had to obtain additional production funds. I had been reluctant to make the move to Fox and had predicted problems. Bill Magginetti backed me in this opinion, but Lippert didn't want to antagonize the Fox big brass. But shooting on the Fox lot greatly enhanced the production values of the picture.

What about your shooting schedule?

Still tight, because of the slower Fox production pace.

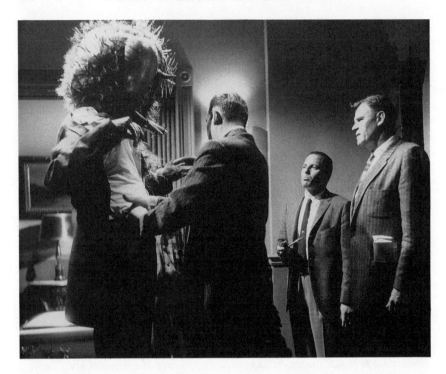

Glasser (with pipe) and director Ed Bernds watch as Ed Wolff is prepared for the cameras, on the mortuary set from *Return of the Fly*.

What can you tell me about working with Vincent Price?

We were surprised when Lippert approved Price and his salary. Perhaps Price had been a good luck omen for Lippert. It began with Price appearing in Lippert's *The Baron of Arizona* [1950]. Or perhaps Lippert was playing a hunch. At any rate he approved the additional expenditure for Price, $25,000. Price was always a gentleman, always ready and prepared, but as I recall he was not overly enthusiastic about the screenplay!

What do you recall about your Fly portrayer, Ed Wolff ("Hollywood's Tallest Actor")?

Just that he couldn't stand on his feet for long periods of time, and he had great difficulty breathing while wearing the Fly head. Our friend Joe Becker, the stuntman, did most of the closeups wearing the Fly's head. Joe did all the action sequences for Wolff.

How did Return of the Fly *do at the box office?*

One afternoon Lippert took out his tally sheet from Fox and pointed to *Return of the Fly;* our grosses were just a tad lower than some very large Fox productions. I have to assume that the film did very well.

You split with Lippert around 1960.

When I informed Lippert that I was leaving Regal to pursue other film ventures, he was disappointed. He said he was ready to commit for a budget war film if Ed and I could satisfy Harry Spalding with a storyline. (Gene Corman got this project.) I thanked Bob for giving me the opportunity to make films for him, and we exchanged a warm goodbye. I recall walking down the stairs of Regal headquarters, knowing it was the last time I would visit the office. It was time to close the chapter and move on.

You worked with Philip Yordan several times in the '60s. How did you hook up with him?

Yordan was represented by attorney Herbert Silverberg. Silverberg, who was also *my* attorney, had knowledge of my attempts to sell my television series idea. He calculated, and correctly, that with Yordan's name associated with the project he might possibly make a sale. Yordan and I were partnered in Liberty Enterprises and we produced 39 episodes of *Assignment: Underwater* for NTA.

Did you enjoy the experience of working with Yordan?

Yordan was primarily a deal maker, more concerned with the next deal than with the current production. It was a fascinating and educational experience working for, and with, Yordan. He was an original character. He made a study of each person whom he dealt with, and knew the exact buttons to push to further his objectives. He had a charm about him that was most compelling. Yordan could also be vindictive when someone did not go along with his plans. He extended to me complete autonomy and support during our association. Also, the basis of my business relationship with Yordan was cash—I didn't want any promises or percentages of pictures. I was paid a handsome salary plus a living allowance for my efforts. I have no regrets concerning my association with him.

As a result of my long production association with the Bank of America, the Yordan pictures were financed by the Bank of America. Our pictures were negative pick-up deals with the various distributors. We set the "pick-up" low enough so that the distributors were not concerned about recoupment.

How did you become involved on The Day of the Triffids?

During a visit with Yordan in Paris, he handed me a script of *Triffids* and asked me to read it. The next morning, after a discussion, he offered the project to me to produce. I also was the financial liaison between the Bank of America and the production company.

Why does the producer credit go to George Pitcher?

In order to qualify as a British production and receive a film subsidy, Yordan formed a British company and *Triffids* became a British production. In

Top: Behind the scenes on *The Day of the Triffids* are *(left–right)* co-director Freddie Francis, actress Janette Scott, producer Bernard Glasser, troubleshooter Lester Sansom and actor Kieron Moore. *Bottom:* A tree monster accosts Janette Scott in *Triffids.*

order to effect this qualification, two-thirds of the above-the-line elements had to be British. The producer was considered one of those elements. The screenplay and star artists were also elements of the one-third above the line. It was obvious that with the script and two foreign stars [Howard Keel and Nicole Maurey] we had reached our quota. By employing a British producer— in name only—the quota would be maintained. George Pitcher, who had been in retirement, was a pleasant older gentleman happy to be back at a studio with the title of "producer."

You could have taken producer credit on non–U.K. prints of Triffids, *couldn't you?*
  [Laughs.] That's one of my pet peeves. My contracts on *Triffids* stipulated that I would receive credit as producer on all U.S. prints, and I didn't see one until I came back to the States. When I finally did get a chance to see it, and saw Pitcher's name on the credits, I was just burned up. My kids asked me, "How could you have produced this picture when your name's not in the credits?"

What recollections do you have of director Steve Sekely?
  Sekely brought the project to Yordan with the understanding that he would direct. He was a gentleman of the old European tradition, a tall, thin man with a large head, closely cut gray hair and well-trimmed gray military mustache. These features accentuated a somewhat bulbous nose. Sekely spoke English with a slight accent that was part French, part Hungarian. He was a capable director who worked well with the cast and was always understanding and cooperative.

Who was responsible for the Triffid effects?
  Wally Veevers was the special effects supervisor at Shepperton Studios. He was a rolypoly kind of a man, turned-up nose, sparkling eyes and an easy smile. He reminded me of an Irish gnome from nursery rhymes. His appearance was deceiving; Wally was a brilliant special effects technician. He enjoyed problem-solving: If he was at a loss about how an effect could be done, he would think about it for several days, recommend a technique and generally it would work.

Was all of the work on the Triffids done in pre-production?
  No, *during* production—Veevers had a backlog because of the volume of production requiring special effects at Shepperton. The design of the Triffids had constituted another production delay. We experimented with various designs: When we had a Triffid that looked exciting, we could not get it to move properly. We settled for a motor-driven model designed by an artist named Hugh Skillen. Every step of the way was experimentation and exasperation. We had three motor models which were also articulated with compressed

Despite difficulties encountered in production, *The Day of the Triffids* remains the best—and best-remembered—of Glasser's SF forays.

air. For the most part our Triffids were engineered and built by a theatrical prop company in London. The Triffid sound effect was another challenge. Most of the sound effects didn't work with the appearance of the Triffids. The least objectionable sound appeared to be a clicking noise.

Did you have to contend with effects problems during shooting?

Yes, we did. Many effects had to be deleted because they were too difficult or too expensive. We had a lot of mechanical troubles; some sequences were working, others were not. It was a most frustrating experience. Several times a week I would call Yordan in Madrid and during our long conversations I would tell him what scenes were not working. The main difficulty was getting the Triffids to perform action called for in the script. [Screenwriter] Bernard Gordon was in Madrid working with Yordan on Samuel Bronston projects. Yordan kept assuring me that all the script problems would be remedied by Gordon, that there was nothing to be concerned about. But the script revisions were not forthcoming, and the delays forced schedule changes.

Some prints of Triffids *give screenplay credit to Yordan, others to Gordon.*

As the producer and as a faithful employee, I always saw to it that Yordan had screen credit on any picture that I was associated with, when most of the time we had a team of writers that did the work. Phil did very little writing. He wore very thick glasses and he suffered from cataracts, so writing for any length of time was a great strain on his eyesight. He never told anyone that he had cataracts, and he was also color-blind—these cataracts seemed to show everything in sepia.

Reportedly, Howard Keel rewrote his own dialogue, either because he was displeased with it or because there wasn't enough of it.

In one of the sequences Keel and the women were escaping in a van. The scene didn't play for one reason or another and Sekely asked me what I could do about it. I wrote some additional dialogue that seemed to fit the mood. As I recall, Keel was unhappy that I had written this material. I suggested that he rework it. He did and was pleased with his efforts. The changes were minor.

Did you ever meet John Wyndham, who wrote the Triffids *novel?*

Yes, on the second day of production he came by, and we chatted briefly.

Sekely's version of Triffids *came out disastrously short.*

Sekely wasn't to blame. After completion of principal photography, he asked me if I wanted him to stay for the second unit work. Because of the delay by the studio in completing our effects, I informed him that he could leave and perhaps return at some future time to see the rough cut. He was pleased to return to sunny California. Once we had deleted the special effects sequences that did not play, the picture was short. Steve Broidy, the head of Allied Artists, was on his way to see this short version which I knew was not satisfactory. Yordan kept advising me that he would come over with Gordon and solve the problems, and he told me to screen the picture for Broidy. Broidy was unhappy after seeing *Triffids,* and he suggested that he would send his editor and troubleshooter Lester Sansom to view the film and make suggestions. When Yordan received Broidy's reaction, that the film was too short, the alarm bells sounded for the first time and he came to London with Gordon. Gordon, Yordan, Les Sansom and I spent several days looking over the outtakes, looking for ways of stretching the picture. Some of the footage played very well but did not have a climax. We had to find a way of cutting away from the action and then returning to the scene after the chaos was resolved. I was too close to the film to see the very obvious solution.

The lighthouse scenes that were added, you mean.

Right. The lighthouse sequences were written in conjunction with the existing footage and directed by Freddie Francis at MGM Elstree. Freddie was a former lighting cameraman, and he understood the difficulties inherent in lighting the Triffid sequences. He was a marvelous person to work with, a fine cameraman and a good director, too.

Did Francis mind working without credit?
    No, not at all. People that have talent and ability really don't mind, it's just another job.

After Sekely left, you also shot some second unit scenes in Spain.
    Right, all of the carnival van scenes, using Spanish doubles for Keel, Nicole Maurey and Janina Faye. We also did a sequence in which the Triffids walk into the sea. In the original script, the van had loudspeakers and the Triffids were following the music, so when the van drove into the Mediterranean the Triffids followed. We hired 150 or 200 Spanish extras for the scene and had Triffid wardrobe made for them. I was on a platform out in the Mediterranean with two cameras, and it just wasn't working—the poor Spanish men and women felt so ridiculous dressed as these Triffids that they were embarrassed, and because they were embarrassed they started to joke, and sashay to the music...! The whole thing was just a fiasco. So we had to go back to the drawing board.

Where in Spain was this scene shot?
    At a place called Sitges. The cathedral at the end of the picture is the Cathedral of Sitges. Bill Lewthwaite, who was one of our editors, directed those scenes as well as some retakes that were shot in London.

What was your budget on Triffids?
    As I recall, the total budget, including special effects, was $750,000. Rank Film Distributors guaranteed a portion of the budget in return for U.K. distribution rights and Allied Artists guaranteed a portion for the U.S. and Canada distribution rights.

Was Triffids *a moneymaker?*
    The picture did very well for Allied Artists, so well that Steve Broidy asked Yordan to make two more pictures for AA, *The Thin Red Line* [1964] and *Bikini Paradise* [1967].

Any final comments on Triffids? *What do you wish you had done differently?*
    In retrospect, the original shooting script for *Triffids* was deficient because it assumed that the Triffids could perform action just like an actor. We were terribly limited in what the models could do and how much it would cost to get them to do it. It was surprising that the production did not exceed the funds available. As for doing anything differently, the services of a good special effects specialist, like a Eugene Lourie, would certainly have been a must.

How did Crack in the World *come about?*

While I was in London completing *The Thin Red Line,* Yordan and Gordon arrived. In a meeting Yordan suggested that we look for a science fiction subject for our next production. He suggested a visit to Foyles, a large London bookshop, and a search of the racks for an idea. In the meantime he was going to contact a few literary agents and see if they had any suggestions. One of the agents suggested that Yordan meet with the novelist Jon Manchip White, who currently was teaching at a university. Jon was a bit austere and standoffish at first, but Yordan with his usual charm put him at ease and before long we were bouncing ideas back and forth. Jon came up with the basic premise for *Crack in the World,* Yordan liked it at once and made a deal with Jon to write the story. Gordon wrote the screenplay with a dialogue polish by his friend Julian Halevy. Gordon did an excellent job on the screenplay. (Yordan on more than one occasion jokingly asked, "Why should I write when Bernie does it better? If Gordon could make deals for pictures, I would let him do it, and I would write the scripts.") Our shooting script for *Crack in the World* was technically authentic thanks to the work of my neighbor Dr. Tom Slowdowski, a geologist working for a major oil company in Spain.

What prompted the decision to make this film, and several of your other films, in Spain?

During the production of *Triffids,* Phil Yordan was developing projects for Samuel Bronston Productions in Madrid. He observed the lower production costs and the ease with which pictures were shot in Madrid. Above all, he felt that having his unit in Madrid would be more convenient. On *Crack in the World,* we utilized the Bronston Studio in Madrid and the C.E.A. Studio, near the Madrid airport, for all the interior shots, special effects and some of the exteriors. The underground complex required a large stage that had to be integrated with the hanging miniature that Eugene Lourie created. We took space at C.E.A. for this set. The United Nations meeting hall was shot in a museum in Madrid. The main unit shooting schedule was about seven weeks.

Where were the exteriors shot?

The opening sequence was filmed in a mountainous region not far from Madrid. The company traveled to the coast to do the island sequence. The exterior of the bunker was constructed at the Bronston Studio "ranch" at Las Matas.

The scene in the volcanic shaft?

The exterior of the shaft was shot at the Bronston Studio just outside the stage. The interior was a combination of interior set and special effects.

What can you tell me about working with the celebrated Eugene Lourie?

Lourie was what I would term a "team" art director. This is said not to denigrate Lourie's abilities. He was an artist and thoroughly understood the

Ad for *Crack in the World*.

special effects process. Much of his knowledge of special effects came about when he directed and supervised a monster picture called *Gorgo* for the King Brothers. On *Crack in the World*, Gene had the good fortune of working with the Bronston Studio special effects chief Alex Weldon. Weldon constructed and supervised the physical effects, explosions, etc. For the construction of miniatures, Gene contacted and brought to Madrid a team of three French special effects men that he had known. All of these people were supervised by Lourie. The special effects costs accounted for about 40 percent of the budget.

Lourie told me Crack in the World *was "a tremendously cheap picture."*

Lourie didn't have any accurate knowledge concerning our productions in Spain. He probably was not familiar with the much lower production costs in Madrid (we worked a five-day week). He did, however, realize that his department was functioning efficiently with rather stringent cost controls. The special effects (without principals) was not bound to a schedule, but rather to a limit of expenditure.

Was it Lourie who designed and built your miniatures?
Lourie designed the miniatures and they were constructed by the French special effects crew under the supervision of Henri Assola, one of the crew members.

The train wreck scene is a highpoint of the picture. How large a miniature was involved?
The individual train cars were about three feet in length. The special effects set including the backdrop was about 100 feet wide.

Dana Andrews had a good, dramatic part. Did he seem to enjoy himself?
Andrews felt an identification with the role of the older scientist, and he had an immediate rapport with Janette Scott. The music for their love scene, which we jokingly referred to as "I Want a Baby," was beautifully written and scored by the English musical talent Johnny Douglas.

Why do Janette Scott and Kieron Moore turn up in so many of your films?
Kieron and Janette were sensible actors, always prepared for the day's shooting, cooperative even when the locations were difficult. Hiring them made casting in Spain simpler for us. We were never disappointed with their work.

Were you happy with the finished film?
I considered *Crack in the World* a good picture of its type. [Director] "Bundy" Marton and Gene Lourie worked well together and were responsible for the look of the picture. Lester Sansom and a competent editorial staff supervised the many details of editing and sound effects. As with all our Spanish productions, we worked with a distributor's guarantee. All our films were financed by the Bank of America, without a bond of completion. It was my personal relationship with the vice-president of the bank, Al Howe, which made this working arrangement possible. As I recall, the pick-up for *Crack in the World* was about $875,000.

Why did you retire from the picture business?
After directing *Todd* [1967], my enthusiasm for production was greatly dampened. Ted Sewell, the vice-president of Four Star Television, proposed that I join him in developing a program of budget features. Only one film was

produced [*Madron*, 1970] — Four Star experienced severe financial difficulties and I thought it was a good time to retire. Which I did.

What keeps you busy these days?

Over the years, between assignments, I involved myself in commercial real estate development. What started out as a method of providing activity and income during the lean times has evolved into a going business.

Are you pleased with your movie career?

The production of motion pictures, especially overseas, was an exciting way of earning a livelihood. It was a method of providing the necessities of life for one's family and having a great time in the process. Oddly enough, I didn't consider it a career.

Which of your films is your personal favorite?

Ed Bernds and I did a Western called *Escape from Red Rock* [1958]. We made it for $100,000, starring Brian Donlevy and a cast of unknowns. The script had all the elements of an A picture. It was a warm personal story and also contained the action necessary for the genre.

How do the sci-fi films stack up, in your estimation?

I was surprised and not unhappy to learn that *Return of the Fly, Day of the Triffids* and *Crack in the World* are considered cult films. The films were well done, especially when you consider the economical production and that they were produced independently outside of the Hollywood system.

Any Famous Last Words?

They say that hindsight is 20/20 vision. I have tried to avoid the "should have, could have" syndrome. A production executive should consider all the alternatives and make a decision based upon the facts at hand. I made the best calls that I could. I have no regrets.

I remember one night ... I was sitting outside by myself
putting makeup on. I have no idea where they came from
or where they were going, but these two little boys came walking by
and saw me. I didn't have a chance to talk to them, I just turned around
and looked at them. And they didn't say a thing, didn't scream
or yell or anything, but, boy, did they take off —
they ran like hell!

Herk Harvey

IT ISN'T EVERY DAY that a low-budget, Kansas-made indie captures the fancy of an entire generation of horror fans—in fact, it's happened only once. The story of a church organist (Candace Hilligoss) who survives a near-death experience only to be stalked by the cadaverous embodiment of death, *Carnival of Souls* has been raising goosebumps on late-night TV viewers for nearly a quarter-century. And now the man behind 1962's spookiest shoestringer steps out of retirement to reminisce about the near-legendary cult favorite he crafted.

Colorado-born Herk Harvey majored in theater at Kansas University, directing and acting in stage productions and later returning to the school in a teaching capacity. Harvey broke into the film business as an actor in some of the films being made by Centron Corporation of Lawrence, Kansas, an educational and industrial production company for which he subsequently went to work as a director. In 1961 he took a working vacation from Centron to try his hand at feature filmmaking: producing, directing, co-starring (as *Carnival*'s footloose phantom) and writing a new page of horror film history.

How did you come up with the idea to make Carnival of Souls?

I was on location in California shooting an industrial film for Centron, and decided to travel home by car. Driving back, I was passing Salt Lake, and I saw for the first time an abandoned amusement park called Saltair. Saltair was an amusement park that was built probably at some time in the '30s, a terrific park in its day, built right on the edge of the lake. Its attraction was that people could go there and bathe, and because of the salt content in the lake they could float very easily; supposedly it was also medicinal to a certain degree. They had all of the amusement park facilities there also—a roller coaster, games and a big pavilion.

Well, with the sun setting and with the lake in the background, this was the weirdest-looking place I'd ever seen *[laughs]*! I stopped the car and walked about a half or three-quarters of a mile to the place, and it was spooky indeed. And I thought, "Gee, what a tremendous location!"—because it's completely isolated from everything and everybody, and at that time it was completely defunct. But most of the things were still standing—the only thing that wasn't was the roller coaster. I came back and talked to John Clifford, who was a writer at Centron and a co-worker, and told him that I needed a horror script that would revolve around Saltair. So basically in talking we came up with some of the general plot, and he wrote the script in a matter of a couple weeks.

How did you go about raising money to go into production?

A man here in town named Joe Traylor had told me that if I ever had an idea for a feature film, he would be interested in getting some local businessmen to help out. I told him about our idea on a Friday night, and by Monday morning he had raised $17,000. I figured we could defer $13,000 and

Previous page: Abandoning his plan to devise an elaborate makeup for his own character, Harvey emoted from beneath a simple coat of greasepaint in *Carnival of Souls.*

do the film on a budget of $30,000, and so we started production. John and I made up the name Harcourt Productions just for that show, I took three weeks' vacation and we shot the film.

Did you do any "ad-lib"–style shooting?
Oh, sure. Often it was a case of find-what-you-can-on-the-streets, as in the scenes where Candace Hilligoss goes out of touch with reality. That also happened when we got to Saltair—some of the scenes there, how the dance was staged and so on. That sort of situation, it's not something that you plan in detail.

Where did you shoot all those street scenes?
All of those we shot in Salt Lake City. The department store, all the scenes in the street and in the bus station, all of those are "grab" shots. For instance, we just walked into that department store and asked, "Can we film here?" Everything in Salt Lake City was shot in a day.

For the most part, did you shoot on sets or in actual locations?
Just about everything was location. The organ factory scene was shot at the Reuter Organ Factory here in Lawrence; we knew it to be a fine location, and so the idea of making the lead character an organist came about because of that! What we were basically trying to do was to get everything we could out of Lawrence and Salt Lake City, so that we wouldn't have more locations to go to. The church was here in town, and still is; the rooming house was a house that was vacant at the time. Joe Traylor was in the real estate business, and this was a house they had not rented for that month. I asked if we could just rent it for a week, he said sure and so that's what happened. Some of the interior car scenes we filmed at Centron, using a projected background. Only one scene, the doctor's office, was a set, built at Centron.

The psychiatrist's office, you mean.
Well *[laughs]*, he really isn't supposed to be a psychiatrist. I've always felt that that doctor character just didn't come across, mainly because of the situations we put him in. The actor who played it was fine, but everything was too pat in his character. Both the doctor and the minister have the sort of stereotypic character that doesn't add anything to the film. There are quite a few things like that in *Carnival of Souls [laughs]*, and as we look at it now we hope that people can realize that we knew better! But when you write a script in two weeks or three weeks, and you shoot it in that same amount of time, you just make it happen rather than sitting and fine-tuning it.

What can you tell me about some of the other creative people involved on Carnival of Souls?
[Director of photography] Maurice Prather was, again, in the educational

and industrial film business. At that time, Calvin Company in Kansas City and Centron here in Lawrence made this area one of the hubs of educational and industrial production in the Midwest, and Prather worked for a number of different companies of this type. [Assistant director] Reza Badiyi, who was also working in this field, worked with Bob Altman a lot in Kansas City. Then when Bob went to California, Reza went with him, and later became a successful television director — as a matter of fact, I got a call from him just the other day and he has just finished his 350th television show. Almost any adventure show you could name, he's directed; in fact, I would imagine he is now as prolific a director as exists in Hollywood.

How large — or small — a crew were you working with?

I think we had a crew of about six — me, a sound man, a cameraman, an assistant cameraman, an assistant director, and then a gaffer or two. In those days we were using the old blimped Arri camera, which weighed about 75 pounds, and the sound man was using the Magnasync tape unit for 16mm magnetic sound, which also weighed like 35, 40 pounds. In comparison to the way you go now, it was a real giant operation.

How did you happen to select Candace Hilligoss for the lead?

The fellow that played the part of John Linden, Sidney Berger, was a theater major here at Kansas University and had acted for me in some of the shows I did. He was going back to New York on vacation and I said, "We've got to have a lead for this show in a hurry. Could you find me a good actress from New York?" So he talked to an agent he knew there and came back with Candace.

When I first saw Candace at the airport, she just didn't look like what I thought a Candace Hilligoss would look like, and I thought, "I don't think it'll work out." She looked very dowdy, very "hippie" and this sort of thing, and I asked myself, "How am I going to tell her tomorrow that we can't use her?" But the next morning when she walked in, she was gussied up and looked exactly like what I wanted in the show, and that took care of that. We paid her $2,500 for three weeks' work.

How did you enjoy working with her?

Very much, as a matter of fact. Most of the time she was very eager to do the best she could. She was a method actress, though, and that made for problems a couple of times. For instance, in a scene where she was to walk across the street to the doctor's office, she said, "What is my *motivation?*" It was noontime in Salt Lake City and the street was very busy, and I told her, "Your motivation right now is to get across that street without getting killed!" Well *[laughs]*, she understood that, and she did it! But at other times I really did appreciate her attitude because, being an actor myself, I do respect actors and actresses and their desire to do a good job and to get into the part. And she

"So far out—it races ahead of time!" Pressbook cover for *Carnival of Souls*.

was really attempting to do that in a logical and professional manner. But with this kind of a budget and shooting off the cuff in many instances, a director really doesn't have time to say, "Do it because of this and this and this."

But overall you were happy with her work?

I was very, very pleased with Candace, yes. She had the look and the ability to do what I wanted. There was a scene at the end where she was in the car, dead, with the other two girls; this was shot in late September [1961] and the Kaw River here in Lawrence is very cold at that time of year. We put the car in the water and the other two girls climbed in and shook and shivered, and Candace put her foot in the water and said, "I'm not gonna do it." I tried to reason with her, to convince her that the show had to have that scene; she understood that and put her foot a little further in the water and, once again, "It's too cold, there's no way I can do it." And so finally *[laughs]* I just had to grab her and *throw* her in the car and get her underwater. There was an officer from the sheriff's department standing there, and he just turned around and left, because he knew he was either going to have to arrest me or do something if he stuck around. He must have said to himself, "Let *them* take care of it!"

Did any one scene present a particularly interesting challenge?
   The opening sequence at the bridge [where a car topples into the river] was an interesting one for me; I just wasn't that sure of myself, I hadn't done that many action scenes. We had no people here to do stunts for us, so we had to do it all ourselves. The bridge was between two counties, Douglas and Jefferson, and I had to talk to both of them about my plan to shoot on the bridge — to run a car through the railing and into the river. Douglas County said they didn't think they would be interested, but if I could get permission from Jefferson, they would go along. So I went to Jefferson and told them that I *had* Douglas's permission, and they said, "Then, fine, it's okay with us!"
   One stipulation they placed on me was that I had to get the car out and I had to pay for damages to the bridge. So I crossed my fingers and hoped things worked. I got two old cars and painted them the same color; if it didn't work the first time, at least we'd have another car. Luckily it did work the first time — we put mannequins in the car and used cables to drag it off the bridge.

So everything went smoothly shooting that scene?
   In dredging the river for the car, they managed to grapple it and get it out of there in a matter of about a half-hour, which was great, and when I left they were repairing the bridge. And when I got a bill for it, it was for twelve dollars *[laughs]*!

Why is Candace Hilligoss's Mary Henry such an uptight, standoffish character?
   What we had in mind was, here is a woman who had never really lived. She played an organ and she lived by herself, and nothing had really happened in her life. And so the fact that she was passive in her life before the accident gave more credence to the fact that she now really *wanted* to live. When faced with death, she refused it and came back as a poltergeist or what-have-you. I'm not sure, though, that we got all this across in the show; the way we developed it, you really didn't get much indication of this. We tried to point it out by showing her character as being very passive, but I think there were other things that would have been good to play up in order to get this point across.

I wonder if that didn't hurt the picture. A leading character who was a little more real might have gotten more audience sympathy.

This surrealistic collage of images captures the spooky flavor of *Carnival of Souls.*

It probably would have. As I say, Candace kept wanting to know how to get into her role, and for the most part I didn't want her to get into *anything* — I just wanted her to sort of walk through it. Basically this is how we explained it to her, but in some of the scenes she still wanted to know, "Am I warm? Am I this? Am I that?" And we had to explain *again* that she was nothing, neutral, very passive. That is very hard for someone to do — they say, "If I'm passive, how am I going to interest anybody in this character?" As an actor I can certainly understand that.

Some of the neatest moments in the film are when she goes "out of touch" with reality.

I'd probably have to give John Clifford the credit for coming up with that, because I think most of the ideas in the developing of the show were his.

What can you remember about some of the other people in your cast?

Frances Feist [Miss Thomas, the landlady], who is now dead, was an actress at K.U. and had been in the Broadway production of *Harvey*, in the female lead. Stan Levitt [Dr. Samuels] is an actor from Kansas City, and he's done several industrial films for me; Art Ellison [the minister], the same. Art Ellison has probably done more industrial and educational films than any other actor in the country — a huge number of them.

There's a long castlist at the beginning of Carnival of Souls, *but no one seems to know what roles any of these minor actors play.*

[*Looking over castlist.*] Tom McGinnis was the man in the organ factory; Forbes Caldwell was a carpenter in that same scene. That organ factory scene originally went on longer and those two discuss Candace's character, that she's a very strange girl, and bring out the fact that she's never lived; the distributor, Herts-Lion, cut that out. Dan Palmquist played a service station attendant in another scene which was cut; he was the assistant editor on the film. Bill De Jarnette, who also did some editing, played a different service station attendant, the one who puts Candace's car up on the hydraulic lift. Steve Boozer was Sidney Berger's friend in the dance club; Sharon Scoville and Mary Ann Harris were the other girls in the car in the opening scene; [production manager] Larry Sneegas was one of the guys in the other car. The other names in the opening castlist must have been the people who played the ghouls; we used a dance class from Utah University for the scene where the ghouls are dancing. Reza Badiyi, who doesn't get a screen credit, plays the little guy in the bus station who's trying to buy a ticket as Candace comes up.

What prompted your decision to play the head ghoul in the film?

Economics [*laughs*]! Also, the fact that there were no lines, and I didn't have to memorize anything. We had to go fast and furious, and in playing the ghoul I had nothing to do except to stand around.

If you had had a few extra bucks in the budget, would you have still played the ghoul?

[*After a pause.*] I probably would have. Call me an egoist! However, I did not take a screen credit for appearing in the film; it just seemed a little much, producing, directing *and* starring, I mean.

What kind of makeup sessions were involved?

Very short ones! That again was a compromise, because originally I had intended to use egg white and make it so it would flake off, and I really was going to work on the makeup to quite an extensive degree. But I realized that between getting into the water and some of the other things I had to do, that that type of makeup would not be feasible, and I finally got down to using just greasepaint because the other just wouldn't have worked. I put the makeup on myself.

I remember one night out at Saltair, the crew was inside setting up lights and so forth and I was sitting outside by myself putting makeup on. I have no idea where they came from or where they were going, but these two little boys came walking by and saw me. I didn't have a chance to talk to them, I just turned around and looked at them. And they didn't say a thing, didn't scream or yell or anything, but, boy, did they take off [*laughs*]—they ran like hell!

Did you feel any concern as you were making Carnival *that perhaps it would be too weird, too dreamlike a movie for mass consumption?*

Very much so. Not so much during the time we were making it as when we started putting it together in the editing stage. I thought it was kind of far-out for its time; most horror films, even then, really weren't that far-out as far as inter-dimension, the character of Death coming back to reap his just reward and things like that.

As with many other films of this type, the music really helps do the trick.

Gene Moore, who did the music for us, was in charge of music at Calvin Company in Kansas City. I gave him a 16mm print of the movie and he looked at it a very short time and said, "Okay, I'm ready." So we went over to an organ sales company that had a big Thomas organ, and he simply sat down and started in. Most of it he had scored, but some of the music, just for general effects, he just sat and ad-libbed. We started around eight o'clock in the morning and probably by two o'clock in the afternoon we were done.

Did you get a positive reaction from audiences when you first showed Carnival of Souls?

No, I didn't. The reaction was very neutral. When we had the opening here in Lawrence, we had a big premiere and a full house—the Granada Theater brought out searchlights and that sort of thing and we really did it up. The audience was very nice but they just didn't know how to react to the film.

What was your own initial reaction to the finished film?

I shared their skepticism. Also, some of the things I let go because of budgetary restraints have haunted me forever—footsteps being out of sync and a lot of other stuff. I should have taken time and said, "No, I am not going to let this film go out this way," and waited until I got more money and done it right. But when I told the investors that I would have it done by a certain date, that became the foremost thing in my mind, rather than the quality of the film.

If you could turn back the clock, what would you do differently?

I would sound-effect it completely different. Also, we lost a roll of film through the lab—General Labs in California did the processing, and there was one roll of film that was lost. That was the ghouls coming out of Salt Lake. We had a scene of them coming out from behind pilings, out of the lake itself, white hands coming up and grasping the railings, black silhouettes coming in, getting ready for the Danse Macabre. It should have been very effective, but I never saw it.

How did you get mixed up with the Herts-Lion company?

A friend of mine, the president of General Labs, turned me on to Herts-

Harvey returned to directing for Centron after completing *Carnival of Souls*. Here he directs actors Jim Claussen, Ross Copeland and William Kuhlke in a futuristic skit for AC Spark Plugs.

Lion because they were a newly formed distribution company. He didn't know Ken Herts, the president of Herts-Lion, but he said it was a public-held company and that they did need product. I had already had the experience of taking the film to New York and showing it to people like United Artists — they looked at it and their reaction, too, was very neutral. At that time independents were kind of a new thing, and I really don't think the majors wanted independents in the business — at least that's the excuse I made to myself, rather than blame the film!

So I took *Carnival of Souls* to Herts-Lion in Hollywood and showed it to them, and they said, yes, they would be interested. I guess they already had *The Devil's Messenger,* which was a Lon Chaney, Jr., film, and they thought that that film and *Carnival of Souls* would make a good double feature. There was no money up front but they offered a good percentage on the distribution. Then I took off on a trip to South America to shoot seven films down there, for Centron. When I got back I saw all these reports — the film had shown primarily in the Southeast, in drive-in theaters — and these were glowing reports, that the film had been doing well, and that they owed me so-much money. Well, pretty soon I started realizing that they *owed* me money but I wasn't *gettin'* any. I called Herts up and said, "I'm going to get some money or I'm coming out there," so he sent me a check and it *bounced*. Then I knew we really had trouble. By the time I got ahold of Herts again, he was in Europe and the company had folded. Con men are con men and he was a good one. I'd sure like to meet him again—I would *love* that.

Why did Herts-Lion cut your film prior to release?

Basically, I think Herts-Lion wanted it cut because it was going to be part of a double feature and they wanted a certain length. Then, too, they just thought artistically it was better that way. Herbert Strock, who was the director of *The Devil's Messenger,* did the final cut on *Carnival*—he edited it down about nine minutes.

If we had simply shown *Carnival of Souls* in theaters here in Lawrence and in Kansas City and in Salt Lake City, the film would have made the money back. I'd have just hand-carried it around and made arrangements with the theater owners and explained that it was filmed in the area. Our receipts here in Lawrence were very good, and I think that would have worked.

Are there deeper meanings in Carnival of Souls, *as some of the artsy-fartsies claim, or is it simply an exercise in weirdness?*

It's an exercise in weirdness. Some of the "deeper" meanings in there, like the call of death and that sort of thing, John Clifford and I intended, but a lot of the things that have been read into it have happened because of audiences. Shortly after the film was released, a teacher here at the Spooner Thayer Museum went on a vacation in Sweden and brought me back a review. And the Swedes were really, really reading things into it—the dimensions of death and so on—because they're much more preoccupied with death than we are. They were also comparing it to Bergman and that sort of thing—not so much the story as the *look* of the film.

Given the fact that the film lost money for all its investors, do you regret having made it?

No, because basically what we did was right, and what we intended to do was righter. John Clifford had also written another show called *Flannigan's Smoke,* a kind of experimental comedy and a much better script than *Carnival.* We did *Carnival* because we thought that the horror genre at the time was much more apt to be bought by a studio than something that was very experimental in comedy. We thought we would do *Carnival of Souls* first and then, if we could make any money on it at all, that would give us an avenue to make *Flannigan's Smoke.*

I assume you had no desire to dabble in features again after Carnival *went bust.*

It was one of those things where you're too busy with your own job to start over again. And by that time, of course, Mr. Traylor and all his investors knew

Herk Harvey still remembers how to turn on The Look.

that they had been burned by Ken Herts, and nobody was really all that interested. But I want you to know that all of the people who put money into *Carnival of Souls* were very understanding. I was never hassled by anybody — not by a soul — and I think that's fantastic. Nobody told me they were sorry they did it, I think everybody just kind of got a kick out of taking their shot at making a movie. But I never would have had the guts to go back and say to 'em, "Well, we're gonna try it again, you want to put up some more?" So that was basically what happened.

Looking back on the film today, are you proud of Carnival, *and happy that it's your claim to fame?*

A 1989 reunion of the makers of *Carnival of Souls* brought together production designer Larry Sneegas, actor Sidney Berger, writer John Clifford, actors Candace Hilligoss, Stan Levitt and Art Ellison, and director/star Harvey (left to right).

I have to say yes and no. When you work someplace for thirty-five years making educational and industrial films, and the one feature that you make is really what you're known for *[laughs]* — a film on which you spent a total of maybe five weeks — that to me doesn't seem right. Some of the things I'm much more proud of, we did in the industrial area. We shot hour-long films in two days, musicals with people like Eddie Albert and Ed Ames and so on. Some of those with skits and original music and all that, are really kind of interesting. And I think that many of the other films that we made in the educational and industrial area really had something to say. Yet, as you say, I'm known for *Carnival of Souls.*

John Clifford and I are both surprised that *Carnival* "came back" the way it did because there was a long period there where it was just plain dead. Ken Herts had left and the movie had stopped and there was nothing. Then the TV rights were sold to Walter Manley, and through his efforts the film started showing on late night TV and I started getting letters from people all over. And that was kind of interesting.

But you must be pleased by the film's ongoing popularity.

Of course. At that time in our lives *Carnival of Souls* was an expression of our desire to get into moviemaking. It was an exciting time for all of us that worked on it, a very enjoyable time. Even though we worked long hours, it was a feature film where we were expressing ourselves, doing new things, trying to make do with little money. All of that adds a great deal to the general excitement of doing and moving and making things happen. *Carnival of Souls* was certainly an enjoyable experience.

*I think Hitchcock's early films
were the great, great films that he did....
But later on he lived in some kind of an ivory castle —
he was like an emperor at Universal Studios, he became less and less
accessible to people, and he moved in and out of the studio
rather mysteriously. I felt he seemed to lose
that common bond he had with people.*

Gordon Hessler

PROVING THAT there is indeed Life After Corman, director Gordon Hessler took the reins on AIP's Poe series in the late 1960s and helmed the English-based productions of *The Oblong Box, Cry of the Banshee* (both starring Vincent Price) and the Spanish-made *Murders in the Rue Morgue*. While these films have not attained the following that Roger Corman's trendsetters enjoy, Hessler's Poe adaptations were unique and intricately plotted productions which reaped handsome profits for AIP and typed Hessler as a horror/suspense "specialist" who continues to work in the genre to this day.

Gordon Hessler was born in Germany, the son of a Danish mother and an English father. Educated in England, he moved to the United States while in his late teens and spent several years working in documentaries. At Universal Studios, "I guess because I had an English accent," Hessler was placed under contract to Alfred Hitchcock and went to work on the master director's video series *Alfred Hitchcock Presents* and *The Alfred Hitchcock Hour,* climbing the ladder from story reader to associate producer and finally to producer in the series' final year. A novelette rejected for the show became the basis for *The Woman Who Wouldn't Die* (1965), Hessler's first feature film as director.

When production of the AIP Poe series was shifted to Britain, Hessler collaborated with producer Louis M. Heyward (q.v.) and horror enthusiast/screenwriter Christopher Wicking on the aforementioned Poe films and on the science fiction shocker *Scream and Scream Again.* Carrying on in the fantasy field, he also directed the Ray Harryhausen stop-motion swashbuckler *The Golden Voyage of Sinbad* and additional small-screen suspensers like the *Psycho*-inspired *Scream, Pretty Peggy* with Bette Davis and *The Strange Possession of Mrs. Oliver* with Karen Black.

Apart from directing a handful of episodes, what input did Alfred Hitchcock have on Alfred Hitchcock Presents *and* The Alfred Hitchcock Hour?

He approved all the stories before they were shot, but really it was an entity of its own. Hitch looked at all the scripts, and if he didn't like something we had to change it. And he did all the introductions, but you know of course that they were all done in one day. Joan Harrison, who wrote some of the scripts and was Hitchcock's personal assistant, was the actual producer of the show. Norman Lloyd, who was an actor in his own right—he was in Hitch's *Saboteur* [1942]—was also a producer, and was sort of my boss. When he moved up from associate producer to producer, I became the associate, then when he moved to executive producer I became producer. He was always one step ahead of me *[laughs]*!

Early on, what did your duties as story reader entail?

To locate stories, work with writers, develop new stories and then present them to the management—that would be Joan Harrison and Hitchcock. Hitch was very, very tough on stories; there were some stories you'd be angry that he wouldn't use, but he was adamant. It was a very tough job.

Previous page: Gordon Hessler, who worked on the *Hitchcock* teleseries early in his Hollywood career, and has since become a frequent presence in the horror and suspense genres.

The great thing was that all the scripts were finished before any of the shows were shot, so you could really get the best actors in town and give the scripts to them long before they were booked. If you look at the roll call of that *Hitchcock* era of television, you'll see that many of those people turned into big, big film stars.

Were you at Universal when Hitchcock was making Psycho?

Oh, yes. It was made with the same television crew that made the show, so he made that in a very short space of time. Bob Bloch, who is a very famous short story writer, came up with this very pasty, B-picture story, but Joseph Stefano, who wrote the screenplay, did a wonderful job. It was a very modern and dangerous kind of film, far away from any of Hitch's concepts, which were kind of fairy-tale suspense stories.

Later in your career, pressbooks for the films you directed labeled you a Hitchcock protégé.

[Laughs.] I don't know how that got in there. I was under contract to him — to Shamley Productions — but that's really not a fair thing to say. Obviously, since he was my employer, I watched his films more closely than I would otherwise.

What do you remember best about working with him?

The extraordinary thing was how well he prepared everything. When he directed an episode, he would finish it up much more quickly than any of the young hotshot directors; he "cut in the camera" as he was shooting, so there was no waste of film. He would only put on film what was going to be in the finished episode. He was able to use very little film and he used little time because he knew exactly what he wanted — it was all pictured and storyboarded in his mind very, very carefully beforehand.

Is it true that Hitchcock was mistrustful of writers?

Well, he liked to work with them very closely, and he had a very good relationship with Ernie Lehman [*North by Northwest* (1959), *Family Plot* (1976)] for many, many years. But he had a problem when the new writers were introduced because they were posing *their* ideas and he was very authoritative in *his* picture-making ideas. He had very, very clear visual images of what constituted suspense and what didn't. I think Hitchcock's early films were the great, great films that he did — some of those silents were absolutely brilliant, way ahead of their time. But later on he lived in some kind of an ivory castle — he was like an emperor at Universal Studios, he became less and less accessible to people, and he moved in and out of the studio rather mysteriously. I felt he seemed to lose that common bond he had with people. You know his father was a poulterer in England and he came from a sort of middle-class background. It's a shame, but in later years he didn't make his films as magical as the early ones were. But still, Hitch was one of the great masters; if there *are* any great picture-makers, he certainly was one of the greatest.

Why was production of AIP's Poe series shunted to England in the mid-'60s?

Samuel Arkoff, who was the head of AIP, saw the great advantage of shooting in England because the dollar was very high and the pound was very low, and you could shoot there very, very cheaply. You also got the advantage of all the backlots that were full of wonderful sets that we could "steal" for our pictures, plus the very talented art directors and cameramen and the classical actors that this kind of film needed. Louis "Deke" Heyward, who executive-produced these films, was an extraordinary character, an American who I had first met at Universal Studios. He got a job with Arkoff as his right-hand man, and then he opened up AIP offices in London. He ran the whole company in a marvelous and very creative way, and we had a wonderful time there. It was then that the whole of America was making movies in England—Fox, Columbia and Warner Bros. were all shooting pictures in Europe like mad.

How did you get involved on The Oblong Box?

I was producing a film called *De Sade* for AIP. *De Sade* was a film that was going to be the biggest production that they had ever made; they had asked me to produce it and Michael Reeves was going to direct it. Michael was an American, living in England, who was having severe mental problems at the time. He was a wonderful man and he would have been one of our most brilliant directors. I flew to England to talk with Michael about *De Sade,* but he was sick at the time. Michael was not able to do *De Sade* because he was getting mental treatments—electric shock and all those horrible things. They put another director, Cy Endfield, on it.

I got fired, virtually, on that picture, and I thought my career was over. But they came to me and said, "Look, there's another film *[The Oblong Box]* which we'd like you to produce in Ireland." Michael Reeves was going to direct it but, again, he was not up to it, so I took the film from Ireland, put it into Shepperton Studios and directed it myself. AIP was so worried about their "big" production in *De Sade* that they didn't pay any attention to us. We just made the film we wanted to make, they were very happy with it and we got a contract to make another three pictures after that: *Scream and Scream Again,* which I think was our best; *Cry of the Banshee,* which none of us liked particularly, but we weren't really allowed to change it; and *Murders in the Rue Morgue,* which I think *would* have been my best picture.

Would you agree that The Oblong Box *had a story that was hard to follow?*

I would, yes. The story was sent to us from America—written by an American—and we had to try to re-adapt and save it. Chris Wicking, who is an absolute horror buff, rewrote the script. We only had three weeks to shoot it, and the budget was very small—we're talking about $175,000, maybe a little bit more. An incredibly small amount.

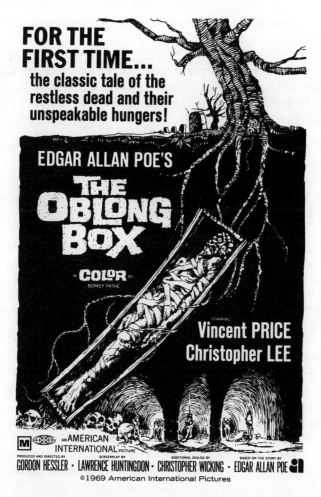

FOR THE
FIRST TIME...
the classic tale of the
restless dead and their
unspeakable hungers!

EDGAR ALLAN POE'S

THE
OBLONG
BOX

IN **COLOR** BY
BERKEY PATHE

STARRING

Vincent PRICE
Christopher LEE

AN AMERICAN
INTERNATIONAL PICTURE

PRODUCED AND DIRECTED BY · SCREENPLAY BY · ADDITIONAL DIALOG BY · BASED ON THE STORY BY
GORDON HESSLER · LAWRENCE HUNTINGDON · CHRISTOPHER WICKING · EDGAR ALLAN POE

©1969 American International Pictures

Hessler made his horror movie debut with *The Oblong Box,* an AIP thriller from the tail end of the studio's Poe cycle.

How did you enjoy working with Vincent Price and Christopher Lee on The Oblong Box?

Vincent Price is an extraordinary man. We had a prince from Nigeria come to lunch with us at the Shepperton Studios; we were showing him around the place and we asked Vincent if he wouldn't mind coming along. Many actors have to talk about themselves or their careers and so on, but not one word of that from Vincent. All he talked about was African art, by region and in such detail that this prince was absolutely amazed! Vincent Price is a wonderful personality. Christopher Lee is made of much sterner stuff: very exacting, very correct. But he was very well educated and has a great deal of charm. I enjoyed working with him as well.

As you mentioned before, Scream and Scream Again *probably is your best film from this period.*

We got a pulp magazine–type story [*The Disoriented Man* by Peter Saxon], which if you read you know was just trash, but the ingenuity that Chris Wicking brought to it made it a film of a much grander scale. He showed his potential talent on that because it really was just pulp — he really uplifted it, made it something very, very different.

Sort of like the difference between Robert Bloch's book Psycho *and the Hitchcock movie.*

Robert Bloch is a wonderful short story writer but he's not really that good at scripts. The fellow who did the screenplay for *Psycho,* Joseph Stefano, really whipped it into shape. I thought he did a marvelous job.

Did you get to know Max Rosenberg and Milton Subotsky, the heads of Amicus Films, while making Scream and Scream Again *with them?*

I had not that much contact with Max Rosenberg; Milton Subotsky was a kind of line producer on *Scream and Scream Again.* They had sold the whole project to AIP. Early on Subotsky wrote a script for *Scream and Scream Again* and it was pretty bad — that was when we put Chris on it.

Fans' complaint with Scream and Scream Again *is that, except for one short moment with Price and Lee, none of the horror stars have scenes together.*

That was an unfortunate thing but it just worked out that way. It was a last-minute Deke Heyward decision to try and get all three stars together in one picture, and we hadn't designed *Scream and Scream Again* for anything like that. But I enjoyed working with Vincent Price and Christopher Lee again, and then of course Peter Cushing, too. Peter Cushing is just a wonderful individual to work with; you couldn't have a better professional than that man.

And you remain happy with the film?

It was ahead of its time, I thought, and we tried to figure out some kind of stylistic approach. But again, these films were made in three and four weeks.

Cry of the Banshee *turned out to be a pretty unpleasant and kinky movie, and it isn't well-liked by the fans.*

I agree. Again, we were sent the script from Hollywood, we read it and we were all unhappy with it. It was a dreadful script — what we got from AIP was something unbelievable — and so I asked if I would be allowed to change it. Chris Wicking and I went to Scotland and we were planning to do a completely different, very, very interesting movie. We wanted to shoot *Cry of the Banshee* there; all the witchcraft seemed to emanate from Scotland, "The

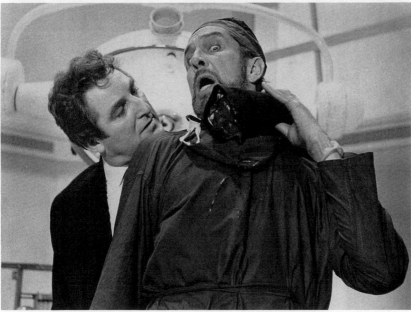

Top: Hessler *(right)* directed horror icon Peter Cushing in the AIP/Amicus thriller *Scream and Scream Again. Bottom:* Vincent Price, on the receiving end for once, is manhandled by Marshall Jones in the climax of *Scream and Scream Again.*

Land of Witches," and we thought that would be a wonderful place to film it. As a matter of fact *[laughs]*, we *met* a number of witches, Chris and I, while we were doing the research in Scotland! We were trying to get inspiration to do something very different, but as it turned out we were never really given the power to do that. We would have had to change the script so much that the AIP people in London got worried. They felt that the original script had been approved and pre-sold, and if we changed it very drastically we might be cutting our own throats. They said, "Ten percent is the maximum amount you can change," so that was about all we could do.

What sort of changes did you plan to make?

What Chris wanted to add into it was that those of the "old religion," the people that everybody thought were so terrible, were actually the *good* witches. But as I said, we rewrote it so far away from the original script that Hollywood had sent us, that Deke got a little worried and said, "Look, this is not the story that everybody's bought. You're going to have to go back to the original concept."

What is there in The Oblong Box *and* Banshee *that makes them Edgar Allan Poe films?*

There isn't anything; that was a pure and absolute lie.

Banshee *was Elisabeth Bergner's first film in 29 years. It wasn't much of a comeback picture.*

No, it wasn't. I really can't say why she agreed to do that part, except maybe because there was very little film work in London at the time. Deke Heyward had an amazing ability to persuade actors to go into pictures.

Were you happy with the demon makeup in Banshee?

Not really, we just didn't have the money to do it. *Banshee* cost maybe $450,000, $500,000 maximum, with perhaps four weeks' shooting. We had an incredible English musician named Wilfred Joseph do the music for that, and the music was on the first print. Wilfred Joseph gave the picture another level with the music — it was really marvelous. But when it went back to Hollywood AIP took that music off and put a very lame piece of music on in its place. The new score was by Les Baxter and it was totally inappropriate, it was just *so* bad, especially when you know what a fantastic score Wilfred Joseph did. It was such a pity. There is at least one print floating around somewhere with the original music on it, and I wish I could get hold of it. It would have made a tremendous amount of difference. *Cry of the Banshee* did all right for AIP but it was, I think, the least interesting of all the films I did for them.

Did you encounter Sam Arkoff and James Nicholson while making these pictures?

Yes, I knew them both pretty well. They would come over when a film was finished, look at it and then take us out for dinner, that kind of thing. I liked them both very much—in the way that you like executives *[laughs]*! They were characters, they had their own niche in the film world and they made pictures that were highly successful. They dissociated around this time, but they were necessary to each other. I haven't been in contact with Arkoff for some time now—he's not really that much involved in the film business. He's got his new company [Arkoff International Pictures] but I think that Arkoff by himself is probably a little bit lost.

Cry of the Banshee *had a wrap party honoring Vincent Price, didn't it?*

We had an incredible party, everybody dressed in costume. After-picture parties are always so boring and so uninteresting, so I said, "Anybody who wants to come to this party, executives included, has to wear a costume." We got all the costumes from the Richard Burton movie *Anne of the Thousand Days* [1969]—we had rented them from Berman's—and they were marvelous costumes. (We used them in *Cry of the Banshee*.) Everybody had to wear one of those costumes, including Arkoff and Nicholson. Vincent was very upset at the time for some reason to do with his contract, and he was having a fight with Arkoff—I don't really know what the details were. And Vincent didn't want to come to the party. I said, "Vincent, you've got to come, this is a party in your honor." He refused and refused, but finally I persuaded him to come. But by the time he arrived, he had drunk too much.

What happened next?

What we had done, we'd got a big cake and there was a naked girl supposed to pop out of it. And Vincent was supposed to cut the cake. I had told Arkoff he had to make a speech, to present the cake and all that sort of thing, but when Vincent found out that Arkoff was going to make the speech, he said, "If he does, I won't be there to cut the cake!" So, we had to rush back to Arkoff and tell him *not* to make the speech! I remember also that we couldn't find a knife to cut the cake, and Vincent, who was roaring drunk, said, "Use the knife that's in my back!" *[Laughs.]* I thought, "God, this is going to be disastrous!" but everything turned out all right—the party was great fun, a lot of liquor was flowing, we had a band and dancing and I think everybody enjoyed themselves.

Murders in the Rue Morgue *owes a lot more to* Phantom of the Opera *than it does to anything Poe ever wrote.*

The problem was that the Poe story, which is a mystery where the *monkey* did it, was not the kind of story you could do anymore. So we used *Murders in the Rue Morgue* as a play-within-a-play; the Poe story was being done on the stage, and we developed a mystery that was going on around the Poe play.

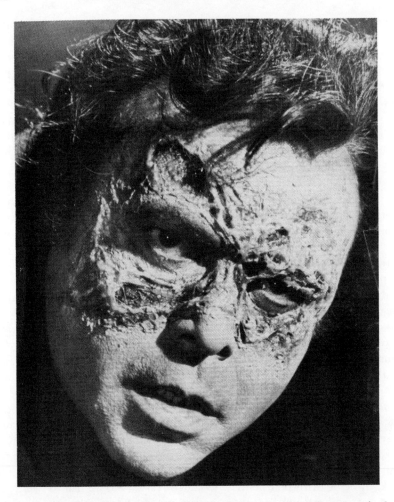

AIP recruited Herbert Lom to play an acid-scarred Phantom-of-the-Opera type in their made-in-Spain *Murders in the Rue Morgue*.

This time around you shot in Spain.

Murders in the Rue Morgue was made in Spain, on a budget of maybe $700,000. I was very disappointed when that was sort of re-edited in Hollywood. When James Nicholson came to Spain and looked at the final cut, he was very, very excited about it. But apparently when it went back to California they didn't like it. Now I must say that it was a very different film from anything they'd ever done, and to me it was one of the best films I had ever made. But they took out a whole end sequence and made the film unintelligible! I almost begged them just to put back that end sequence, but they never did it. Our original finish was a wonderful twist ending, but they took it all out and I was very unhappy.

Can you speculate on why they did that?
England was where practically all the AIP pictures were being done at that time; literally, the Americans were doing little or nothing. There was a great rivalry there, and I suspect that's probably one of the reasons why *Rue Morgue* was re-edited, so all the editors in America could re-assert themselves. Lilli Palmer had a marvelous role in the picture — she was the catalyst for the film to shift into a new gear, and her role made the whole story make sense — but it was almost all cut out! *Incredible!* They cut it down so she was almost like an extra. I don't know what she must have thought when she saw the film.

Any anecdotes about working with Jason Robards?
Jason realized after we started that he had taken the wrong role — he suddenly realized he should have been playing Herbert Lom's role. But he realized that a little bit too late *[laughs]*! He was great fun to work with, though.

Your Poe films never gained the following that Roger Corman's have. Can you guess at the reason for that?
I don't know; I never really thought about that. That's a good question *[laughs]*! Well, maybe Roger's are better!
Nobody's really liked my films that much in Hollywood, for some reason or other. Roger Corman, who's a wonderful director, is a great hero in Europe — the French just love him — but over here they just think he's a bum director because he was working on low-budget films and he took short cuts and so on. But he was a great cinema-maker, and he *taught* Hollywood how to make low-budget pictures, which they didn't know.

What was it like working on a stop-motion film like The Golden Voyage of Sinbad?
That film is all Ray Harryhausen's; as you certainly know, he's a marvelous effects man, an American living in London. It was a great education for me to make a film like that. *Golden Voyage* was filmed in Spain, in Palma de Mallorca and in Madrid.

What were your impressions of Harryhausen and producer Charles Schneer?
I got along well with both of them. Ray Harryhausen is a real sort of Victorian Anglophile, a super guy, just wonderful. I learned a lot from him, because I knew nothing about that area of special effects picture-making — knowledge which he supplied. He was marvelous. I pressed him to do more and more things special effects-wise, and he would do anything you asked him — he said, "There's nothing you can't do on film if you've got the time and the money."
Charles Schneer is a real character in every way. He can be very difficult, and very hard to get to know. (Somehow I got on well with him.) He's enormously hard-working, works harder than anybody else; he sees every single

play that comes to London. His taste hasn't come along with the same depth as the amount of work that he does, to see all these plays, but I must say he's a wonderful producer, really. He's one of those producers who goes all the way through with a picture and is involved in every phase; everything that is being done in the picture, all the way through to the very end, he's absolutely, totally involved in it. And he's very tough with a buck, but anything he says he'll give you, he gives you. While we were making *Golden Voyage of Sinbad* there was a young fellow who was running Columbia Pictures, Peter Guber, and actually that was the only picture that was being made by Columbia at that time—Columbia was in a very bad way. And the way Charles Schneer treated Guber—if Guber didn't return Schneer's phone call in a few seconds, Schneer would treat him like a nobody! I think Charles must have had an enormous number of shares of Columbia, to have such power there. Now he's retired, and enormously wealthy.

Golden Voyage of Sinbad was a very tough picture because we were only allowed eight weeks on it—formerly you'd get about fourteen weeks. By the skin of my teeth I managed to finish it on time *[laughs]*! And I know the film did well.

Was it difficult directing a film of that sort?

No, it was surprisingly easy because we had Ray, a man who had done so many of those, on the set with us all throughout shooting. What was great was that I kept asking him if we could do more and more difficult things—"Couldn't we do this, and this, and *this?*"—and he had no problem accomplishing any of them.

Did you stick with the film throughout the months of post-production effects work?

No, I didn't. I made another film, *Embassy* [1972], in between there, and when I came back we did the final editing.

What hurts Golden Voyage *is that John Phillip Law's performance lacks the necessary dash.*

He was the best we were able to get on the budget that was made available to us. He did lack the style that made stars of an Errol Flynn or a Douglas Fairbanks.

One of your newer films, Pray for Death *[1985], ran into trouble with the censors, didn't it?*

You know, there's a double standard in the Motion Picture Association. If you're working for a major, they really let you show heads being blown off and all of that sort of thing. If you're not a major—*Pray for Death* was made for Trans World Enterprises—they just come down on you. They took out a sort of rape scene—it was not a voyeur scene, it was a necessary story point to

John Phillip Law battles to rescue Caroline Munro from the Centaur's lair in the stop-motion adventure *The Golden Voyage of Sinbad*.

show the villainy of one character and make the hero's revenge so much more satisfying. It's the same sort of rape scene that you can see at the opening of *Jagged Edge* [1985], but they arbitrarily took *ours* out. You've got five old women making these decisions, and you cannot argue with them, you can't discuss it or use logic, you're finally blackmailed into accepting their wishes and cutting down, because a small company has just got to get the film released. The people here would not give it an R rating and we had to cut some very, very good sequences out of it.

Pray for Death was a horror film as well as being an action film; there are great horror overtones in it. It's a very good picture and I think it's very different from any martial-arts film that you've ever seen.

You recently made another film that's being described as Hitchcockian.

Yes, and I'm very, very happy with it. It's called *The Girl on a Swing* and it's from a novel by Richard Adams—you may know him from *Watership Down*. It's a love story that goes awry, the story of an Englishman who meets a German girl in Denmark and falls hopelessly in love with her. He gets involved with this girl, and she has something terrible in her past—*we* know it, and *he* begins to sense it. And then everything awful begins to happen. There's suspense in it; it's a kind of love/suspense story, and a very unusual picture. We shot it in England, Denmark and here in America, in Florida.

After many years of working extensively in TV, you seem to finally be back in features again.

I did a tremendous amount of TV, but now I *am* going back more to features; I've sort of almost lost touch with television. What I'm involved in now is very interesting: Trans World asked me to do two films and I am preparing them. One is a kind of remake of *The Mummy;* it's being written by Nelson Gidding, a wonderful writer who wrote *The Haunting* and got an Academy Award nomination for *I Want to Live!* [1958]. And then the other picture is an H. Rider Haggard novel called *Ayesha.* So I'm preparing those two projects, and those will probably be the next pictures I'll be directing.

[My AIP experience] ... was a period
that had never existed before and will never exist again.
My first cousin was Irving Thalberg; he existed at a time and in a place
where things were just right for him. Things were just right for
the American producer in England when I was there for AIP.
It was the right time, the right place,
and a great opportunity
to learn and grow.

Louis M. Heyward

THERE'S JUST a (very!) thin line separating horror from humor in low-budget thrillers, and no one knows this better than Louis M. Heyward. A specialist in both categories, Heyward honed his comedy craft while working in TV with such small-screen comic luminaries as Ernie Kovacs and Milton Berle, and later learned the fine points of horror filmmaking during his long stint at AIP. Merging the two divergent genres, Heyward helped to create the most popular AIP horror character, Dr. Anton Phibes, in the campy classic *The Abominable Dr. Phibes*.

Born in New York City, Louis Heyward ("Deke" to his friends) was headed for a career as a lawyer while at the same time moonlighting as a writer of scripts for various radio series. After a six-year Air Force hitch, he landed a job with the Associated Press but continued to dabble with radio scripts, and later found an eight-year home as a comedy writer on daytime TV's *The Garry Moore Show*. Other jobs in New York TV included writing comedy material and skits for *The Ernie Kovacs Show* (the program was Emmy-nominated in 1956, the same year Heyward won the Sylvania Award as its top comedy writer) and developing *The Dick Clark Show*.

Migrating to Hollywood, he held executive posts at 20th Century–Fox and MCA before joining forces with AIP, first as a writer, then as their director of motion picture and TV development and ultimately as head of the company's London-based foreign arm. During his years with AIP, Heyward worked alongside many of its top stars and directors on a wide assortment of exploitation films, from froth like *Pajama Party* and *Sergeant Deadhead* to the horror thrillers *The Crimson Cult* and *The Oblong Box* and cult favorites like *Dr. Phibes*, *Dr. Phibes Rises Again* and *Conqueror Worm*. Now the vice-president of development at Barry & Enright (producers of game shows, features and TV movies), the funny, feisty Heyward looks back with affection (and frustration) on the glory days of AIP.

How did you initially hook up with American International Pictures?

I heard about The Jolly Green Giant, which is what AIP was known as in those days, and I went up to see Jim Nicholson, who was a wonderful man. Strangely enough, he knew me as a writer, I don't know why or how, and he'd heard of my association with Ernie Kovacs—he was a Kovacs fan. Of the two, Nicholson and Sam Arkoff, I felt that Jim was the more literate. There was Arkoff, puffing his big brown cigar and pontificating on the lack of art in the business, but really not doing anything *but* business, and Jim, really being involved in film. Jim truly loved film, and he also loved horror—he was the one who came up with the idea of doing the Edgar Allan Poe films. He was doing all these pictures with no money; we were doing things with spit and pennies, and nothing more.

So it was Nicholson that initially got you aboard.

He said, "Look, I'd like to ease you into the company, but horror is a very involved thing and you don't know that much about it. But you're funny. Can you write a funny script?" I said, "Of course I can." He said, "In two weeks?"

Previous page: **Louis M. Heyward, who made the switch from TV comedy to AIP fright films, proving that the line between comedy and horror was often thin indeed.**

The first one I did for him was called *Pajama Party*. I tried to write this particular thing as a cartoon and indeed, if you look at it, it's done almost in cartoon cuts, in four-strips. That was a large part of it.

Did you know in advance, on a picture like Pajama Party, *who would be playing the various parts?*
    You could never be sure. It was dependent on the budget, and the
budgets were sometimes virtually non-existent. If an actor was out of work and
hungry enough, you were going to get him — that's substantially what we fed
on at AIP. I knew that I wanted Buster Keaton; I had used him when I was
doing *The Faye Emerson Show* way back when, and he and I became friendly.
I regarded him as a wild genius that nobody really appreciated. (They've
rediscovered him since.) I sat down with him and we worked out gags.

*Were these beach pictures as much fun to make as they seemed to be on the
screen?*
    It was the old "Hey, kids, let's put on a show!" atmosphere. It was great,
because everybody contributed. It wasn't you standing there alone and naked
with your two weeks' or three weeks' worth of script; everybody pitched in and
came by with ideas. This was wonderful, it was "the old college try."

Pajama Party *is sort of like the* Mork and Mindy *of the '60s.*
    Yes, it pretty much was. At the time, I was very pleased with the way the
picture turned out, and it did well financially, for its price and for its time.

Both of the beach pictures you wrote incorporated SF or horror elements.
    I also did *Sergeant Deadhead*, which had a lot of science fiction to it. I
grew up on horror and science fiction films; as a matter of fact, as a high school
kid I was adapting Edgar Allan Poe to radio. I sold the same *Tell-Tale Heart*
three times, to three different buyers *[laughs]*!

In writing The Ghost in the Invisible Bikini, *did you anticipate that Basil Rathbone and Boris Karloff would be in the cast?*
    That I knew, and I knew that Susan Hart would be in it. She was Jim
Nicholson's girlfriend. I had met her at a party: I sidled up to her and I said,
"Whose girl are you?" She pointed with her eyes, I turned around and there
was Nicholson, and he said, "Mine. Lay off. She's in the next picture."
    I want to jump ahead. Jim said to me one day, "We're doing *Dr. Goldfoot
and the Bikini Machine*," and I said, "What's the story?" He said, "You're the
writer, I want *you* to tell *me* the story! But I got an idea. Vincent Price is a crazy
scientist, and he's got a machine that turns out rowboats." I waited a proper
period, because I'm not about to contradict the president of the company, but
finally I said, "Rowboats?" and he said, "Yeah." And I waited again *[laughs]*!
"Jim, I don't mean to be disrespectful, I think it's a great idea, but I've never

Torn between two lovers (Aron Kincaid, *left,* and unidentified ghoul, *right*), Nancy Sinatra doesn't know whether to laugh or cry. An amazingly bad posed shot from the even-worse *The Ghost in the Invisible Bikini.*

seen a rowboat machine." He said, "Not rowboats! *Rowboats!*" I said, "Jim. Help me." He spelled it out: "R-o-b-o-t-s. Rowboats!"

Susan's acting talents at that time were limited. I later discovered that the reason that he wanted "rowboats" in the picture was ... the ... way ... she ... moved ... her ... arms ... and ... the ... way ... she ... walked ... and ... turned—she *needed* to play a rowboat!

Where were these AIP pictures shot?

We shot them at Producers Studio for the most part, where we had what we used to refer to as a leftover deal. Any sets that people had used in prior shooting, that were not hauled away or destroyed, we had the right to use. It was a grungy studio—oh, God, you couldn't walk there barefoot, because the floors were wood and splintery. A lot was lacking, but the spirit was there, and I think that was a large key to AIP's success. There were times when Jim would say, "Hey, come down with me and let's look at the sets that are left over," and two or three weeks later, we'd have a script.

What kind of input did Sam Arkoff have?

During those years, precious little; he stayed in the background and let Jim carry the ball. Remember, it was initially Jim's company, and then Sam came into it as Jim's lawyer and then as Jim's partner. During the period when I joined them, Jim had the big office and Sam had the ancillary office nearby. It wasn't until Jim left the company that Sam took over command functions.

Did you meet Basil Rathbone on Invisible Bikini?

Of course. I had a horrible experience with him, because I have a penchant for twisting names in my mind; I am aware of it and I don't want it to happen, and I said to myself, "I must *not* say Mr. Nosebone." So when we were introduced, I said, "I'm so pleased to meet you, Mr. Nosebone," and he glared along that bony nose of his and said, "Are you making jest of me, sir?" And relationships were strained for the first few weeks thereafter!

How about Boris Karloff?

The Boris Karloff I knew was a studious, delightful, funny funny *funny* fellow, and I don't think anybody has talked about him being funny! He had a wry sense of humor, and he would say sly, funny things. By "sly," I don't mean "naughty," they were just cute, they were words within words, totally encapsuled. If you understood it, great, and if you didn't, also great. When he found that I understood almost half of his little secret jokes, he would nod his head and his eyes would twinkle, which was a kind of precious thing to have with him. Now, skip a number of years. When I used him in England, on *The Crimson Cult,* he was confined to a wheelchair and I was told we could not get insurance. I've been told that with a number of people. I said, "Screw it. Here is one of the greats of our time. He goes on." And no one came in as well prepared as Boris. He was the consummate, thorough professional, with respect for his craft and respect for his fellow workers. He was just a total delight to be with.

Your first encounter with Karloff was on Invisible Bikini, *right?*

No, I had written a script where he was a babysitter for radio, and he played the part of the babysitter with his lisp. He was cute and he was funny. He wanted to do comedy.

He got chances on TV, but almost never in movies.

The comedy that he did in TV was at his own expense, it wasn't with "precious words." He poked fun at what he had become, and that to me is sad comedy.

What kind of shape were Rathbone and Karloff in on Invisible Bikini?

They both moved well. Rathbone moved almost like an aging athlete, he did have a grace and style to him. He had tremendous panache.

What do you think of Invisible Bikini *today?*

I just saw it again very recently and it was bad — *unbelievably* bad! It left me in a state of shock.

What kind of money went into these movies?

Pajama Party I'd say we did for about $200,000, *Invisible Bikini* about the same, maybe a bit less. I wasn't really happy with *Invisible Bikini*, it was a "created" picture. There was no reason for it to be made, other than Jim's trying to prove that he could make Susan Hart into a star.

How did you get involved on War-Gods of the Deep?

I was here in the United States, doing whatever nonsense I was doing for AIP. *War-Gods* was being shot in England and they ran into problems with the then-producer. I don't remember his name, but he was English and he was causing some sort of problem. I called, and he said, "Dear lad, the script's impossible." I said, "*Most* of our scripts are impossible!" (And the ones that weren't impossible were improbable!) He said, "I cannot possibly shoot." So I went to Sam Arkoff and I said, "Sam, we are having genuine trouble." Sam clutched his breast and said, "It's gonna cost money!" *[laughs]*, and I said, "Yes. They don't like the script." He said, "Well, dictate something over the phone."

I said, "Sam, that isn't the way you do scripts. I've got to see what they've shot, see how I can blend whatever it is that I'm going to write into it, find out what's lacking." So I went to England, and found there was a war between [co-producer] Dan Haller and the English producer, which is always very, very destructive. And they were getting nowhere. Dan Haller had been a scenic designer prior to this, and a protege of Jim Nicholson's. Dan was an extremely good scenic designer, and he came up with some awfully good sets on *War-Gods*.

Did you end up reworking the screenplay?

Yes, I did. The one thing that I felt was missing was humor, and that's where the chicken appeared. There was no chicken in the script, so I wrote it in along with the David Tomlinson character. Tomlinson was enjoying great vogue at that time because he had just done *Mary Poppins* [1964] for Disney. At the point when the English producer saw that I had written in a chicken, and knew that whatever I wrote was going in, he quit — he said, "I don't do chicken pictures!" And Dan Haller took over the reins.

Did things go smoothly after that?

No, there were continuous problems there, because Dan at that time did not really know how to do what Sam used to refer to as "take over the power." I called Sam and said, "Okay, I've completed the rewrite, but I think I better stay here 'til the picture is finished." Again, I had a mental picture of him clutching his breast and thinking in terms of dollars, but I did stay, because there had to be someone backing up Dan. Dan turned into a very good producer later, but he couldn't do it alone in the face of an English crew who probably resented the fact that the other producer had walked off.

Where does Jacques Tourneur fit into all of this?

Poor Jacques! Jacques was, again, at the nadir of his career, but he wanted to direct another picture or two. He was overly agreeable, and there was a sadness to that. At AIP, it was the same with directors as with actors. If you were a young director, AIP was giving you a chance; if you were an old director, your career was on its way down when we inherited you. You were usually afraid to fight because it would influence the next picture. But face Jacques with a technical problem and he would come up with answers. He knew his craft and he knew his media.

What was the point in continuing to stick Poe's name on all these movies that had absolutely nothing to do with him?

As I recall it, Jim Nicholson had a vision. He believed in television, and thought that if he could get together enough Edgar Allan Poe movies, he'd have a television series. I admired him for being a visionary, which he very much was. There'd be times when he'd come into my office with advertising for a picture, magnificent advertising. But the picture didn't exist, the script didn't exist, we hadn't cast it! He sold on the basis of advertising. He was enough to inspire you with his own enthusiasm for things.

War-Gods of the Deep *has a Jules Verne flavor.*

It felt *very* Jules Verne, and *to* whom did we attribute it? Poe. This was Jim. Give him any script—*Broadway Melody of 1938 [laughs]*—and he'd derive the title from an obscure Edgar Allan Poe sonnet! And you could always find something to validate it—if you're easily satisfied!

Did you know the original War-Gods *screenwriter, Charles Bennett?*

Oh, yes. The screenwriters out here, most of us know one another, and it's senseless to attempt to work with someone unless you get along. I had a number of meetings with Charlie, and in fact I worked with him on another picture shortly thereafter. He did as good a job as he could. I remember that Charles's credits were very heavy and he was used to working for the majors, so when I said to Charles, "You've got two and a half weeks to do this script," a little question mark lit up in the middle of each eyeball *[laughs]*! He said, "You mean for corrections?" and I said, "Not for corrections—to do the *script!*" So we worked on that one together, and he did as good a job as any man could do under the circumstances and for the money.

Did anyone actually sit down and read any of these Poe stories or poems for ideas?

The most
fantastic
journey
ever
dared !

AMERICAN INTERNATIONAL STARS

VINCENT   TAB
PRICE · HUNTER

SUSAN   ALSO   DAVID
            STARRING
HART   TOMLINSON
        AS HAROLD TIFFIN JONES

WAR-GODS
OF THE DEEP

COLORSCOPE

Directed by   Produced by   Screenplay by   Underwater Photography   Executive Producer
                                                                                    and
JACQUES TOURNEUR · DANIEL HALLER · CHARLES BENNETT & LOUIS M. HEYWARD · Direction: JOHN LAMB · GEORGE WILLOUGHBY

No. *No. No-ooo-ooo [laughs]*!

What do you think of War-Gods of the Deep?
There was a lot that was satisfying. The worst thing in it was my own contribution. The chicken didn't belong there in a diver's helmet, not really *[laughs]*. It was insanity. But that's the way we were doing things. There never was any time, there always was a crisis.

Did you enjoy working with Vincent Price throughout this period?
We had a thing. I collect art, have collected since I was 14. I bought my first Paul Klee, my first Henry Moore when I was a kid, and paid for 'em five dollars a week. Vincent of course is famed as an art collector, and so we started talking art. I also enjoy cooking, and Vincent is well known for that. So Vincent and I had a community of interests to keep us busy talking between takes. Occasionally he would read a line, then look at me and say, "Deke—dear, sweet Deke—you are screwing my career into the ground!" And indeed I may have *[laughs]*! But I appreciated his frankness about it. He was a delight to work with.

That was about the time you started getting involved in AIP's overseas production.
It was just the beginning of co-productions and films acquiring their own nationalities and having a life of their own. If you were an Italian picture, great, they could show you in Italy and derive benefits therefrom. If you were a German picture, they could show you in Germany, and so on and so forth through the countries of Europe. But then someone said, "Hey, what if a picture is both German *and* Italian?" And then somehow laws were passed there that allowed you to say, "With American participation." So if an American production company came in with, say, one-quarter of the money and sold off bits and pieces to various countries, it could walk back and get the entire western hemisphere. Put down 25 percent of a picture and bring along a star with whom you have a contract, and you were in business!

And the picture would play in all those other countries, too.
That's right. The advantages in shooting there were, one, prices were lower; two, very little union problem; and, three, the fact that you could give the picture a series of nationalities that would lower the cost of a picture below what we could do here.

What was the story on Planet of the Vampires?
Planet of the Vampires was Mario Bava, shot at Cinecitta in Rome. Again,

Opposite: AIP's *War-Gods of the Deep* was Jules Verne-ish in flavor, but AIP prexy Jim Nicholson insisted on marketing it as a Poe film.

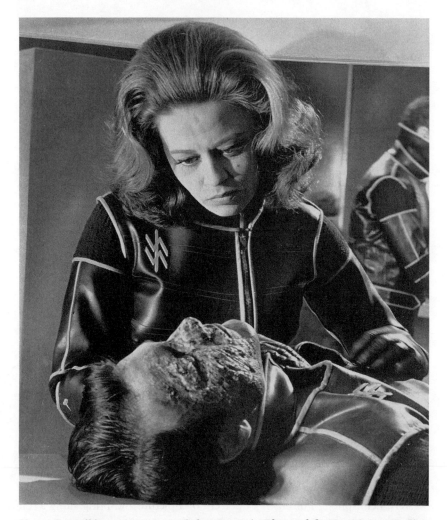

Norma Bengell hovers over a mangled astronaut in *Planet of the Vampires*. According to Heyward, Mario Bava's "hots" for Bengell may have caused trouble on the *Vampires* set.

I think there were a lot of strange things going on. At that time Mario, genius that he was, was undergoing a number of problems, one a typical Italian mental dichotomy between girlfriend and wife. It bothered him during this period; he was a mass of guilts and he wasn't even Jewish. I think that may have interfered with the tempo of his shooting. On *Planet of the Vampires* we had Norma Bengell, a Brazilian lady with enormous boobs—which I think were a testimonial to her talent [*laughs*]. She could only speak Portuguese. And I think Mario fancied *her,* too! It turned into a real mishmash, a disaster. I was rewriting the Italian script day by day, virtually line by line. As an executive of a company you do a helluva lot of rewriting and you do producing; you fill in in all ways. I would go to the Italian producer, Fulvio Lucisano, and say, "Look, the lady is standing behind the man naked. What is the sense, what is the motivation?" And Fulvio would look at me sagely, rub the side of his nose and say, "She's a-wanna have something to do with him!" Well, *that* I could have figured out, I think, given time *[laughs]*! But it was not good writing. So we had to get rid of these extraneous things which appealed then to the Italian market and the Japanese market, where they wanted to see as many naked ladies as they could at one time. I was busy taking naked ladies out and he was putting naked ladies in!

You also had Ib Melchior over there helping out.

Ib was wonderful. Ib is a very competent, very good writer, and he was an enormous help. When we originally got that script in, it was a typical Italian script on long sheets of paper, larger than legal, divided into audio on one side and video on the other, and an Italian student's translation into English. Nothing ever made any sense, and Ib was forced to try and make sense out of the first draft. And he did as good a job as he was capable of. We had not worked together before, but he was a delight and we became close personal friends.

That was an AIP co-production, of course.

AIP, American participation; Fulvio Lucisano, for Italian International; there was a German company involved; and somehow I think there was a South American company involved. It was a Tower of Babel, because we were shooting virtually silent at the time, everything to be dubbed into English. There'd be one voice talking in Portuguese, another in Italian, another in German, and there was no communication, just a lot of facial writhings. Barry Sullivan was the star of the American version; each company star-billed the player that was important to their country. In fact, we had to try for line balancing: "Your star has got more lines than my star!" "Okay, I'll trade you two of my star's lines for one of yours." Which ain't the way pictures should be made. And they ain't never gonna be made that way again *[laughs]*!

Was Mario Bava better to work with on Dr. Goldfoot and the Girl Bombs?

Emotionally, yes; craft-wise, sometimes superb, like on his glass shots. He was great, he would paint them himself. But then there were periods of extreme forgetfulness—he'd forget what he had shot the night before, and so how do we match it the next day? There would be fights, and you had to wait until the dailies came back and you could match it.

You worked without credit on Dr. Goldfoot and the Bikini Machine.

I did. Robert Kaufman's name was on that as writer; I brought in [director] Norman Taurog, who was a personal friend, and we screwed *his* career into the ground! In Italy I did the rewrite on Kaufman's script, but I didn't take a credit on that one.

You don't know the number of pictures I've done. I've been on over 80 films. But you don't always get credit. You do a tremendous rewrite, and I would say under the Writers Guild here you would be entitled to credit. But Sam Arkoff would say, "What do you want credit for? I *pay* you, don't I?"

Was that first Goldfoot *film really successful enough to warrant a sequel?*
It didn't take that much. Remember, we were grinding these things out. That may have cost $300,000, and if we grossed $2,000,000, there was a lot of profit in it. Also remember that we were grinding out a lot of them a year.

You also did some borderline horror and SF films like The Glass Sphinx *and* House of a Thousand Dolls.
I remember a lot about *The Glass Sphinx.* I loved the adventure of going to Egypt, and I loved working with Robert Taylor and Anita Ekberg. While I was in Egypt I had (with the government's permission) entered two or three tombs that had been sealed. I was also given handfuls of scarabs, with hieroglyphics on them! *Glass Sphinx* was with Fulvio Lucisano and, again, there were day-to-day rewrites. But my compensation was in looking at what to me was a living legend, namely Robert Taylor.

House of a Thousand Dolls we shot in Madrid, in a palace that had belonged to a Spanish prince who was a member of the House of Hapsburg. The palace had later turned into a whorehouse, which was kind of setting the pattern for what the picture was about. And I remember the casting of the B-girls, at various of the gin mills in Madrid *[laughs]*! Vincent Price approached me when we had about five girls there and he whispered, "Deke, please, give 'em some garlic. They *stink*!" Which is beautifully anomalous to me! *Thousand Dolls* was done in partnership with Harry Alan Towers. We had some horny scenes in there, and I wondered how we got away with it—there was a lot of nudity in *Thousand Dolls* that was excised for the American version.

One day I come onto the set, which is a jail set, and I see a guy with a stovepipe hat . . . a beard . . . a wart on the left side of his face . . . and a frock coat. And I'm struggling to think of the scene to be shot, because standing before me is Abraham Lincoln! I go over to Harry and I say, "Harry, what are we shooting?" and he says, "Just be calm." What had happened was, he had a copy of the script of *Abe Lincoln in Illinois* that he had submitted to the Spanish censors to get permission to shoot. And whenever the censor came by, there was this fucking Abe Lincoln walking back and forth *[laughs]*!

Your most famous AIP film is probably Conqueror Worm.
I had just gone over to England on a permanent deal as a result of a conversation I had with Sam Arkoff. I told him, "Look, I'm running around like

Behind the scenes on *Conqueror Worm. Top:* Vincent Price consults with the "real" witch hired by Heyward as a technical advisor for the film. *Bottom, left–right:* Heyward, Price and Sam Arkoff huddle between takes.

a doctor, fixing things that shouldn't have to be fixed, they should be right in the first place. I'm putting Band-Aids where 35mm film should be. And this is wrong. Why don't we open an English office?" Sam was very wise, and he saw the possibilities of this. And he had a strong ally in Fulvio Lucisano in Italy. To show how close they were as friends, Sam went on Fulvio's honeymoon with him *[laughs]*, which I never really understood! So we opened an office in London, right opposite the American Embassy—a gorgeous townhouse.

Now this is how *Conqueror Worm* came about. There was an English producer named Tony Tenser. Tony had [director] Michael Reeves, about whom I really had not heard anything except just a few whisperings; he had a script called *Witchfinder General,* which was in some sort of condition but not completely correct; and he had some good locations scouted. What he *didn't* have was the full amount of money for total production, and he didn't have a star. We had a contract with Vincent Price, so what we did was make a trade: We gave 'em Vincent Price and a few dollars, and in exchange we got western hemisphere distribution rights.

Did you have confidence that a director as young as Reeves could pull it off?

Not initially, but a very strange thing happened in our relationship. I was very dubious of him, and I exerted a lot of controls. But little by little we developed a relationship that to me was a very touching thing. He virtually became my son. After the picture was completed, he'd come to my office in the penthouse there, and just sit on the floor. He'd say, "I just like being here. I like being with you. I like to be around. Is it all right? Am I bothering you?" It was sad.

Ian Ogilvy was in all three of Reeves's pictures. Do you remember knowing him?

I thought Ian was tremendous, and that he deserved a much bigger career than he's enjoyed. I thought he would become the ultimate Bond, that he had the capacity of being the next Olivier. And yet somehow his agents did not guide his career correctly, in my opinion.

What other memories do you have of Conqueror Worm?

We had a girl named Hilary Dwyer on *Conqueror Worm,* the typical English rose, and Tony Tenser was fighting for a nude scene. I have spent a large part of my career concealing nipples, and with this particular English rose I did *not* want to shoot her nipples. Michael also did not want to do the nude scene, there was no necessity for it. At a point where Vincent was supposed to be plucking at some child's breasts, I could see Michael getting very tense and very tight, and I became conscious that there was a problem of some kind. That required my going over to him and giving him a nip in the back of the neck and saying, "Hey, everything's all right, you're doing a beautiful job. If it

bothers you to shoot this, we'll change it. Let me know, let me be the bad guy."
I think that was what solidified our friendship.

Did anyone worry during production that the film might not get past the censors?

The English did; we didn't. The English censorship was very heavy at that time, violence more than nudity. Poor Tony Tenser would run with edited clips to the English censor, daily—"Hey, can I do this? Can I do that?" Yes, there was a lot of worry.

Was Conqueror Worm *a success right away?*

In the United States, yes; in England, after all of the horrified letters came in to *The London Times,* yes. In Germany it was so successful that, two weeks after we delivered the prints to the distributor, a bootleg company came out with *Conqueror Worm II [laughs]*!

It's become fashionable to say that Reeves would have gone on to become a major talent.

I couldn't agree more. He was wonderful. He saw pictures in his head, which is what good directors do; he knew what the pictures would be before he shot them. *Conqueror Worm* was made for $175,000 and it didn't look it; at the time, it looked rich and full and complete to me. That was thanks to the genius of Michael Reeves. I think *Conqueror Worm* is a good film for that genre and that time, and it may be one of the better things that Vincent Price has done.

Michael and I started talking, post–*Conqueror Worm,* about doing *De Sade.* I had a vision on *De Sade* and I wanted to do the picture desperately, to accommodate the vision. I described scenes that I would like to have written and scenes I'd liked to have shot, and I could get very enthusiastic about them. *De Sade* started with a dream of mine—it may have been an erotic, self-pleasuring dream. I had an idea of a marble floor with a number of naked female bodies on it, and a pair of boots walking amongst the naked bodies. That's as far as I went. It tied into the Marquis De Sade because I was interested not in what he had done, but why he had done it. Also, I was interested in experimenting on a number of time levels. I broached it to Nicholson, and when you say Marquis De Sade to an exploitation king, he has *got* to respond. And I felt there was only one person who could write it, and that was Richard Matheson [q.v.]. Matheson did not want to write horror, which suited my purposes entirely. I've got to tell you that of every script I've held in my hands, his script for *De Sade* has got to be one of the best; if there are any fuck-ups in it, it's my fault, and in no way do they reflect on the writer, who in my opinion did a beautiful job in handling time. I recently reread the script and it's a good script, fine writing.

Once Michael Reeves died, Cy Endfield got the picture.

Reeves really was never in the picture 'cause there was no script when Reeves was alive. Just my concept of naked bodies and boots behind the opening titles — that's all that existed. Endfield had directed *Zulu* [1964], which was a brilliant piece of picturemaking. I should have wondered why he agreed so readily to do *De Sade* — apparently he had been having difficulty getting work, and I do not know the reason. Also, a mistake on my part: I should have examined more carefully the content of his other films, to see if he could handle the sexual aspects and if he could handle things of moderate delicacy in terms of time. I did not.

Move ahead. We are shooting in Germany (West Berlin for the most part, but other locations as well), and running fairly much on schedule, which is the one thing I always prided myself on. Then, as we approached the sexual scenes, there was a slowing-down. I came on the set one cold morning and there were about twenty naked girls sitting around doing nothing. And Endfield was there playing a recorder. I said to myself, "Oh, dear God, we're in trouble." We lost almost a day's shooting. I got on the phone and told Arkoff, "Sam, I think we're facing a problem." Next day I come on the set and we're falling *further* behind. And I suddenly realize that Endfield, for whatever reason, either did not want to do the orgies, or was incapable of handling them, or distressed at being faced with them. Or perhaps he felt then as I feel now: that they were out of place. But he wasn't working, and every day you don't work, you're losing money. Then Endfield caught the flu, and he was sent to the hospital. All we had left to do were the orgy scenes. I told Sam I would do the setups on them, and that he should send over Roger Corman to finish directing. That's eventually what happened. We sent Endfield the rushes, at the hospital, every day.

How much contact did you have with Corman throughout those AIP years?

We were old buddies from AIP from the West Coast and it was my request that he come out to Germany. I respect Roger totally. He is a fast craftsman. You go to McDonald's and you get the masterpiece of hamburgers, the best one of which they're capable. Roger does that with pictures. We had talks before this on *The Wild Angels* [1966], which was an initial concept of Jim Nicholson's. I went out to do the research on it and came back with tons and tons of it. I also did research on *The Trip* [1967], which was an original concept of mine that Corman changed totally because he was working with Jack Nicholson at the time. Which is fine — I get no credit on it, and I don't deserve any. Roger Corman was charming and wonderful, and good to be with.

De Sade was another of your international co-productions.

We had a partner named Arthur Brauner who put up half the money, and he was co-executive producer or co-producer, I don't remember. (I don't remember what *I* was!) Arthur Brauner was a wonderful partner and a good fellow. A Jew who had escaped from a concentration camp, he was owner of the CCC Studios in Berlin, which is where they made the gas which killed the Jews. It was kind of an ironic thing: Arthur, escaping from the concentration camp, came out with hundreds of pairs of shoes that he had taken off dead bodies, went to Berlin, sold them and parlayed that into the studios and a real estate fortune.

You could always josh or jolly Arthur into going along with you, with a little bit of caviar and German champagne, which is about the foulest thing known to man or God. He would cry into the caviar, which Heaven knows was salty enough, then agree to another $25,000, $50,000, a few more days of shooting or whatever. Remember the pin that De Sade wore, shaped like a figure-eight—the snake swallowing its own tail? I had drawn a sketch of it which Arthur took to a local jeweler, and he was going to have it cast in *[laughs]* some kind of cheap tin compound, and then dip it to make it look like gold. I said, "Arthur, it has to be gold." He said, "For a movie it doesn't have to be gold!" I said, "It *does*. Think of the actor's psyche." A little question mark lit up in the middle of each eyeball—"What's a psyche? I'm not gonna argue with this guy." He said, "All right, it can be gold." Then I said, "And I want real rubies, too." He cried out, "You're meshugana!" but I got my way. 'Cause in the back of my little head was the idea, I was either gonna steal it or buy it back for my then-wife, whoever she may have been *[laughs]*!

Speaking of your star's psyche, how did you like Keir Dullea?

Keir Dullea had a problem on this picture in that he had just gotten engaged, and had brought along his fiancée. I could not bar her from the set, but for her to sit there through the nude scenes was very hard. She would always go over to Keir at the end of a take and say, "Keir, you don't have to be so *close!*" or "Keir, you're *touching* her!" It got to be a bit of a problem. Keir was good to work with, he came in prepared, but I always had the feeling he felt he was above the picture.

And how about John Huston?

John Huston was wonderful. He and I would sit in a gin mill at night, pouring down the wee drops. He was an Egyptologist. Remember those Egyptian scarabs I told you about before, when we were talking about *The Glass Sphinx?* I would take them down to the gin mill at the Berlin Hilton, and with his Irish charm Huston would read me the hieroglyphics, which always knocked me for a loop. Here is a drinking Irishman, reading hieroglyphics *[laughs]*! As an actor, he handled himself well. I went to him when I was having the problem with Endfield and I said, "John, how do I handle this?" He looked at me with some love, because he had a sense of humor and we knew the same Irish drinking songs and we had a very strong rapport. He said, "Dear Deke, you hired me as an *ac-tor*." That last word was in italics and underlined; the meaning was, "Hey, don't ask me about directors—we have our own fellow-ship." I had to respect that.

Richard Matheson told me that Huston later said to Jim Nicholson, "Why didn't you ask me to direct De Sade?"
  I wonder if he would have. If he had, he would have done a superb job, I think.

Was De Sade a moneymaker?
  It was a moneymaker, but not as much as it could have been. Most of the things we did were moneymakers, because we brought 'em in for such low budgets. Is it the picture I wanted it to be? No. Is it the picture it *could* have been? No. A lot of mistakes were made, but with my name on it as producer, I've got to accept the brunt of it. Those orgies didn't belong in there and that irks me to this day. They lessened the quality of the picture.

Although they weren't released here until 1970, you also did The Crimson Cult *and* Horror House *around this same time.*
  That was Tony Tenser again—Tigon Productions. My involvement on *The Crimson Cult* was the rewrite of the script; the bringing-in of the American elements; sitting on it to the degree that we controlled the budget, and AIP could not be penalized if it *did* go over-budget. But creatively, not that much. Tony Tenser didn't do that much, either. Vernon Sewell was an extremely capable director whom you trusted to run with the ball.

What do you recall about Christopher Lee and Barbara Steele?
  Christopher Lee was a personal friend, and still is. He's a dear, sweet man of many talents, easy to work with, has a charming wife and I love him. Barbara Steele I really don't remember, I just know that there were mutterings about someone who was modestly notorious. But what she was notorious *for* I never could quite figure out *[laughs]*!

The Crimson Cult *is the picture where Karloff had to shoot scenes outdoors in cold weather, and caught the cold that killed him.*
  If it was so, I was not aware of it. I am strongly disinclined to believe it. However, Karloff was a good enough person and a strong enough actor that if he were told to sit outside, he would sit outside. Like a good soldier, he would not abandon his post, so it is within the realm of possibility. I never heard that before, but if it is so, it's sad.

And Horror House?
  I have no recollection of it; a merciful Heaven has struck me amnesiac with regard to it.

COME FACE
TO FACE
WITH
NAKED
FEAR
ON THE
ALTAR
of EVIL!

HIS FINAL
EVIL ROLE

**BORIS KARLOFF
CHRISTOPHER LEE**

**The
CRIMSON
CULT**

GP ALL AGES ADMITTED
Parental Guidance Suggested

STARRING
MARK EDEN·BARBARA STEELE·MICHAEL GOUGH
INTRODUCING   GUEST STAR
VIRGINIA WETHERELL· RUPERT DAVIES · COLOR
                                                                    MOVIELAB
DIRECTED BY   SCREENPLAY BY   ADDITIONAL MATERIAL BY   EXECUTIVE PRODUCER   PRODUCED BY
VERNON SEWELL· MERVYN HAISMAN AND HENRY LINCOLN· GERRY LEVY·TONY TENSER· LOUIS M. HEYWARD
A TIGON BRITISH-AMERICAN INTERNATIONAL PRODUCTION   AN AMERICAN INTERNATIONAL RELEASE

©1970 American International Pictures, Inc.

Boris Karloff's death resulted from the cold he caught on the set of *The Crimson Cult,*
prompting AIP publicists to (falsely) play up the film as the actor's final role.

The Oblong Box was originally supposed to be shot in Ireland, with
Michael Reeves directing, so it was Reeves's death—that got Gordon Hessler
[q.v.] the picture. And he stepped in with maybe two days' notice, and we did
it in England, on location. Gordon always turns in a workmanlike job. In
Scream and Scream Again he did shots that are impossible—you would swear
Hitchcock had done them. The pull-backs and the follow-throughs in the
police station—shots like that are destructive to a director's stomach, and he
did 'em! I had known Gordon from my days at Universal, when he was

Hitchcock's protégé. I realized how good Gordon was, and I had a script called *The Oblong Box*—again, nothing to do with Edgar Allan Poe *[laughs]*! In trying to get this picture in on budget and on schedule, knowing Gordon as a quick director, I propositioned him to do it for an infinitely small sum. He accepted it. But Gordon is a little more than a director, he also happens to be a tremendous producer and a tremendous respecter of budgets. Once you tell him a budget, he will keep it inviolate. Gordon saved my ass on that picture, because we didn't have the money to do it. Gordon pulled that picture through.

Price was pretty disgruntled about the quality of some of the later AIP scripts, and in fact he feuded with Arkoff about it.
    This is very possible. Arkoff at times was difficult to get along with, and so was Vincent, in his own way. There is an alternative, however. If Vincent did not like the scripts, he either had to tell me, "I would like a rewrite on it," and I would have obliged him; or, he could have told Arkoff, "I don't want to do it." You can't bitch about a script after it's made.

Arkoff told me that he was bummed by how frugal Price could be.
    What we would do is pay Vincent X-number of dollars, whatever the fee was—not great, but considerable. Vincent would breeze into London, not spend a penny on lunches or dinners, expecting you to take him out. That's fine. I remember one day when I was picking him up at this little hotel near the railroad terminal in London. I was up in the room waiting for him. I said, "Vincent, where's the lavatory?" and he said, "It's down the hall, dear chap." I said *[reprovingly]*, "Vincent . . . !" and he said, "Have you considered how little time you spend in the toilet? There's no sense in paying for it." That was his attitude. But what he would do—and he would very proudly recount it to anyone who would listen—was save as much money as he could, and then go on an art-buying spree at the end of the picture.

What do you remember about Cry of the Banshee?
    That was Gordon again, Gordon with his wild, wild enthusiasm. We had Essy Persson in *Cry of the Banshee,* and she had just come off *I Am Curious—Yellow* [1968]. We had a rape scene in *Banshee,* it was in the script and she knew it beforehand, and I told her we had to have a nude scene there. But after having done *I Am Curious—Yellow* in Scandinavia, she wouldn't take her clothes off for Gordon so the guy could rape her! And I'll tell you, it made Gordon into a total nervous wreck. So in that scene there are some very goofy camera angles concealing the fact that she is not exposed at all.

Was she difficult in general?
    In that we had a language barrier. She spoke some English but it was difficult to understand. We also had Elisabeth Bergner in there, making her

first picture in like 30 years. Why she would do a picture like *Cry of the Banshee,* I don't know. Actually, as I remember it, I don't think the picture was that bad — it could have been worse. Which is about the best you can say for most of the AIP pictures *[laughs]*!

Where in the world did all these half-assed scripts come from?

[Laughs.] Most of 'em came from Hollywood. They would send us scripts that couldn't be shot, *shouldn't* be shot, and yet we had to fill a schedule for the distribution arm.

Is it tough to care about the quality of your pictures, when your own bosses have this sort of hit-and-run attitude?

Not for me it wasn't. I prided myself on doing the best I could with whatever I did. When I did *Ernie Kovacs,* it was the best show of its kind; when I did *Garry Moore,* it was the best show of *its* kind; the same thing when I produced *The Dick Clark Show.* I busted my ass to do the best job of which I was capable, whether or not the people involved were concerned with quality. AIP was an atypical case in that they had to feed that enormous distribution machine, and I think that was their prime concern.

Hessler and Chris Wicking did an extensive rewrite on Banshee, *but said that you couldn't allow him to shoot that version.*

I can tell you that whatever Gordon tried to put together was probably infinitely better than what we went with. But there was a problem with Nicholson at that time — he wanted, "No more changes! No more changes!"

AIP tried to promote two of Price's movies as his 100th, Abominable Dr. Phibes *and* Cry of the Banshee.

This is most probably one of Jim's promotions, and I'm surprised he didn't do it several more times. And let me also add that I'm sure *neither* picture was Vincent's 100th *[laughs]*!

How much contact did you have with Milton Subotsky and Max Rosenberg (Amicus Pictures) in making Scream and Scream Again?

A lot. They brought in the project, which was a paperback, and they were two guys full of enthusiasm. If I recall correctly, I had Subotsky thrown off the set, and Rosenberg allowed to come on. I felt there was too much interference going on. They were earnest, they were well-meaning, but they got in the way of production. I didn't have that much traffic with them, but it was very difficult. I don't bar people from sets too frequently, but when you're trying to protect time and a budget, you have no recourse. You can't fight about the little things.

Gordon Hessler says Subotsky's initial script was so bad it was unusable.

Chris Wicking was brought in and together with Gordon they fixed it. Because it was a script that had not come from Hollywood, we could get away with tinkering with it. I was protecting the future I hoped to have when I left AIP *[laughs]*!

It was your idea to put all three of the horror kings—Price, Lee and Cushing—into Scream and Scream Again. *Did it work well?*

Not as well as it could have. It was interesting to have them all in the same film, but they should have had contretemps between them, utilizing all three in one scene in a face-to-face showdown. But there was no way of doing it. We just brought them in to take advantage of the names, for marquee value.

Cushing was the one that got the short end of the stick.

He really did. I played that film just the other night and I asked myself, "Why did he accept it?" I think the reason is, the British are so damn nice as actors—again, they're good soldiers and they'll do what they're told. They're dear sweet people and they're professionals.

Any other Scream and Scream Again *anecdotes?*

I felt Michael Gothard was going to be the biggest thing that ever happened. He had that insane look and that drive, and he was wonderful. Here is a kid who really threw himself into the picture wholeheartedly. Do you remember the scene where he appears to be walking up the cliff? That's a stunt that, as an actor, I would not have agreed to; I'd say, "Hey, get a double or get a dummy. I ain't either one." But the kid agreed to do it, without a double—he was that driven. He had a lot of class and a lot of style. Gordon came up with the idea of using an overhead cable to give that illusion of his walking up the cliff.

What did you contribute to The Vampire Lovers?

Vampire Lovers was done with Hammer—Jimmy Carreras. I was allowed first look at the girls who were to be nude, as a courtesy, and I think that was the limit of my involvement with it *[laughs]*! Hammer was like a ship without a rudder; they were reduced to, "The script doesn't mean anything, the picture doesn't mean anything, it's the deal." It was a question of, "Can we crank out *one* more picture? *Two* more pictures?" I don't think anybody really cared. And that's a pity, because it was a good house at one time. We kind of stumbled through that picture; I had precious little to do with it other than playing floor monitor, protecting the money again.

Why was Murders in the Rue Morgue *shot in Spain?*

Budget. That was a Spanish-Italian-German co-production, and we shot in Spain because Spain was the signatory country. Lilli Palmer and Jason

Heyward felt that the Hammer Film company was on its last legs by the time he got around to collaborating on *The Vampire Lovers*. (Peter Cushing and Ingrid Pitt are pictured.)

Robards would sit down in a gin mill and they would talk fine points of acting to a degree that was well beyond my knowledge or ken. They both knew more about acting than I, a poor, lowly, self-appointed producer, did, and there were impassioned discussions. I think Herbert Lom was having wife problems at the time; he was married to an English lady agent, and he was more concerned with his domestic life than with his craft. Gordon Hessler filled the opera house (I believe it was in Seville) with a group of gypsy-extras, and he got them all to work for free by giving away a refrigerator. He called me and said, "I'm giving away a refrigerator," and I said, "But there's no electricity in the gypsy caves!" He said, "It makes no difference. This one has no motor!" *[Laughs.]*

This was another of those slapdash Hollywood scripts.

Right. It arrived in the mail in one form and Chris Wicking did a job on it. He was a good rewrite man.

AIP Hessler says re-edited that picture, making it incomprehensible.
That's correct. They didn't understand what Gordon was trying for. Gordon had a lot of dream sequence effects in there that were integral to the story, and once they cut out the background they destroyed the story.

Sounds like De Sade *all over again.*
You betcha.

Most of these later AIPs have quite a nasty edge, and probably could have used a bit of humor.
You're totally correct. As I said, they would find a script in America and send it to us in England, and they would not look kindly upon rewrites. I think it was Jim, protecting what he considered his sense of integrity. And he did have it—I'm not demeaning Jim in any way. Jim was a guy who came out of nowhere and started making pictures instead of talking about making pictures, and you gotta give credit to the guys who really make them. I think he felt each script was like a personal possession—"This is my script. Even though I didn't write it, I found it and I'm sending it to you to make." Now, they could not interfere in a thing like *Conqueror Worm,* on which I'd say I did a 50 percent rewrite, because that was a script that was in existence over here. They had no idea what the script was, they only had an idea of what the deal was. This was during the period when the deal was as important as the script, which is a fairly interesting concept. "We need a film, 90 minutes of screen time—whatcha got?" That's the way things were working.

However, I am now in England a couple years, there's a feeling of power that is growing within me, and I had to say to myself, "I do not like particularly the script I am about to shoot, and I am going to try and change it." And then you start pulling rewrites. Like on *The Abominable Dr. Phibes.* A fellow by the name of Ron Dunas found the script by James Whiton and William Goldstein and brought it to Jim. Ron was a real estate developer who always wanted to be a producer. Whiton and Goldstein were good writers, very competent, but the script had that edge of nastiness to which you refer. Here is a man [Dr. Phibes] on a vendetta, killing people. It could have been a gross piece of nastiness. It was changed by doing slight rewrites here and there.

But not changing the plot.
Right. The plot was even intellectual in spots, when it went off into the Talmudic background of the killings. But here's what I thought up. You know that I was head writer for Ernie Kovacs for four years. Ernie did a little schtick where he minced and pranced and did imitations of Vincent Price. It occurred to me, if Vincent were to do an imitation of Kovacs-doing-Vincent Price, we

might have something strange here! And indeed it could be a *black* black comedy. That was the hope I had for it. So there were a lot of funny little things that were inserted into the script, to take advantage of this concept. To the point that, when Sam came to London to see the film, he clutched his breast, rolled his eyes upward and said, "I am undone!" *[Laughs.]* He said, "You got a cockamamie comedy here! Take my name off it!" So I took his name off it. Then we won some film festival award, and he said, "Put my name on!"

Do you remember specifically any of the things you added?
No. They were nuances, they were moues, they were stage directions.

Did Price enjoy playing what was essentially a non-acting part?
I think it *is* an acting part. Remember the scene [in *Dr. Phibes Rises Again*] when he's in the tent, eating fish with Vulnavia [Valli Kemp]? He seems to swallow a fish bone, and he takes it out of the little vent in the side of his neck. He does it with such delicacy that it's great acting, and funny funny *funny*. That's the way Kovacs would have done it. I would say that Vincent enjoyed himself as Dr. Phibes.

The "look" of the film attracted a lot of favorable comment.
We had a guy named Brian Eatwell do the scenery, which I think was superb for a budget show. He did it for pennies — pennies and brains. He did a number of pictures for me, and he eventually ended up here in Hollywood. And I'd welcome an opportunity to work with him at any time, because here is a scenic designer who puts in a helluva lot more than he gets.

Robert Fuest, who directed, has gotten most of the credit for the way the film turned out. Is this fair?
For the most part, I would say yes. Bob Fuest had a great sense of style and flair. He struck up a very good rapport with all of the actors; being an ex-scenic designer himself, he knew how to guide Eatwell, and I think that was a very strong key to the picture. He conceptualized a lot, and he also had a very sly English sense of humor. I would say, "Hey, wouldn't it be funny if...," and he'd ponder; he was a very serious young man. I was always expecting him to say no, and he'd say, "Yes, but I think it would be *funnier* if...," and he extrapolated upon any thought I had. And he was a working director; when we did the River Styx scene [in *Dr. Phibes Rises Again*] he went in the water up to his waist — he didn't have to. (Maybe he had to pee!) Also, he was very conscious of budget, which I'm sure doesn't mean diddly-squat to your readers, but it means a lot to a producer.

Ron Dunas gets a co-producer credit. What did he contribute?
Ron was a very wealthy guy who fancied himself a patron of the arts. He

Vincent Price had one of his best roles...

may or may not have put some money into *Dr. Phibes;* they shipped him over to England and told me to treat him nicely. I found him a source of difficulty on the set.

Did you like Joseph Cotten and Hugh Griffith on Dr. Phibes?

Cotten was just like Boris Karloff, the original gentleman. He also was not in good health at that time, but he went home and he studied, and came in the next day knowing his lines letter-perfect, attempting to contribute, using every one of the tricks that he had acquired over years in the business to enhance the picture. He was a big plus.

...as the vengeful two-faced killer in Heyward's *The Abominable Dr. Phibes.*

It was around this time that Cotten seemed to be trying to establish himself as a horror star.

I don't think that's quite right. Bette Davis, poor thing, discovered that when your career is on the way down, you will do a horror picture, just as you will when your career is starting. You don't do them in the middle of your career, you do them on the way up and the way down. Cotten was on the way down, and the job was available. People really don't want to do horror pictures, they are driven into them.

And Hugh Griffith?

When I got to England, Hugh could not be employed, he had a reputation as an alcoholic. But I desperately wanted to use him, and I knew he could use the work. I told him, "I will accept the fact that you are uninsurable. You've got to accord me the same respect I give you." He said, "I give you all the respect in the world, guv'nor." I said, "That ain't it. The respect I want is a promise. From the moment you come on the set, you don't touch a drop. When we yell *cut* and it's a wrap for the day, do whatever you want, I don't care. But you give me your hand-to-God promise that you're not going to touch a drop while we're shooting." He held out his hand and said, "Lad, you've got it." Well, I did five, six pictures with him, and he adhered to that promise.

You came up with a sequel to Dr. Phibes *in fairly short order.*

I don't know if you saw the reviews, but the reviews on the first *Phibes* were great and, strangely enough, the English reviews on the second one, *Dr. Phibes Rises Again,* were even better. I brought out from L.A. a writer named Bob Blees, a dear friend; he did what was for me one of the best emotion-laden pictures ever made, *Magnificent Obsession* [1954]. And he also had a sly sense of humor which I felt would fit in with *Phibes.* Now, Bob Fuest wanted to write this second film, and the two of 'em did not see eye-to-eye on *anything.* They were two men with great senses of integrity, but one protecting director's viewpoint and the other protecting writer's viewpoint. The visions that Fuest enjoyed were in his head; the visions that Blees had were on paper, and easier to handle. So suddenly you were referee, placed in a position you did not want to be in because they were both right. It was a question of allowing them to go as far as they could, and then saying to yourself, "Don't worry, there'll be a rewrite at the end and we'll straighten out whatever doesn't seem to work." That's of course what followed.

Was Rises Again *as good as the first movie?*

In some ways better, in some ways worse. It did not hit some of the beautiful, beautiful highs that I felt we had in the first, but there was a steadiness to it that I liked. Because after all the fighting was done, it turned into a very good script, one that I think could be used in writing classes. Indeed, if I ever get around to teaching again, I will use that as one and *De Sade* as the other.

Where were your desert scenes shot?

Ibiza, off the coast of Spain. It's a little bit of a desert and rosemary grows wild all over and the air is scented with it. And the sheep shit that beautiful smell of rosemary *[laughs]*! The rest was shot in England.

Do you remember your impressions of Robert Quarry?

I enjoyed working with him. I felt he was misunderstood, he was being given short shrift by AIP. He had a decent role in *Rises Again* but I felt that his career was being mangled. He deserved more, I felt. He was a delight to work with.

AIP was supposedly grooming him as a replacement for Price.
They were. Those were my instructions. But I was not privy to any fights or discussions or animus between them.

There was talk about a third Phibes, *which never happened.*
This was such a personal venture, I felt Phibes was mine. AIP made attempts to get scripts — they even went back to Whiton and Goldstein — and apparently they couldn't lick the script problem. Because again there's a philosophical approach to making a picture of this kind. You're treading a funny middle ground between humor and murder. Precious few pictures have stayed on that tightrope.

What's the story on Who Slew Auntie Roo?
Curtis Harrington brought in a script by Jimmy Sangster; Bob Blees was brought in to rewrite it. Harrington directed, and all we had at the time was Shelley Winters and a very nervous Jim Nicholson, who said, "Don't say no to her on anything." 'Cause Shelley Winters was a big name for AIP. Then I also got Ralph Richardson, which as I said before is the wonderful thing about the English: They will say yes to a small part if it's a good part. We got Richardson, Hugh Griffith, Lionel Jeffries — a lovely, very good cast. The picture was a delight to make, and it did good business — not great, but good.

Curtis Harrington has a good reputation as a creative director.
I thought he was wonderful. Over and above being a creative director, he was a pleasure to be with. He was never demanding, he was always smiling and suggesting rather than insisting.

And, on the flip side perhaps, how about Shelley Winters?
No comment — except to say that *is* the flip side *[laughs]*!

Gordon Hessler told me there was great enmity between "American AIP" and "English AIP." Sam Arkoff told me that was bullshit.
There wasn't great enmity; Sam Arkoff was best man at whatever wedding it was I had at that time, so there was a fondness between Sam and me. But beyond Sam, they had gotten in a new head of production who did not want there to *be* a European AIP, who wanted all the pictures to originate in America. Now, I can't blame the man for wanting to do that. We were doing nothing but making money with our pictures and we were helping to keep AIP going, but for me to fight a battle 3,000 miles away, I gotta lose.

And you did lose.

    What happened is that somehow Sam and I got into a tangle, and I don't remember what it could have been—we were very, very close friends. And we mutually decided to part. I remember a party in Cannes (we always had the best parties in Cannes) and Sam Arkoff making an announcement that we were going to do a sequel to *Wuthering Heights* [1970] and we were going to do *Camille*. The BBC covered it, and it was a very tearful thing, Sam and I both knowing we were going our separate ways but putting on a show for the BBC, to allow them to believe there was going to be continuity. Now, after I left, they had three other people in rapid succession take my place in England, and I don't think any of them made a picture, over a period of two or three years. It was a sad break-up.

Can you sum up your AIP experience?

    What it was, was a period that had never existed before and will never exist again. My first cousin was Irving Thalberg; he existed at a time and in a place where things were just right for him. Things were just right for the American producer in England when I was there for AIP. It was the right time, the right place, and a great opportunity to learn and grow.

I've always been disappointed
that movies have not done the job
they could do with science fiction....
I've done a lot of science fiction movies,
but I never was satisfied with them—
they always looked dumb to me.
Unimaginative. Not poetic.
Not done the way they
ought to be done.

John Howard

ALTHOUGH BEST KNOWN to film buffs as the dapper star of Paramount's *Bulldog Drummond* series and as the rich and stuffy fiance of Katharine Hepburn in *The Philadelphia Story* (1940), actor John Howard is no stranger to fantasy and science fiction films. In the 1937 *Lost Horizon,* Howard starred with Ronald Colman and Jane Wyatt in the timeless James Hilton tale of survivors of a Tibetan plane wreck spirited away to the gleaming monasteries of Shangri-La. He later added to his list of credits such horror and sci-fi titles as *The Mad Doctor, The Invisible Woman, The Undying Monster, The Unknown Terror* and *Destination Inner Space.*

A native Ohioan, John Howard (born John R. Cox, Jr.) had no interest in working in theater until schoolmates at Cleveland's Western Reserve University turned him on to acting. After some work on his college stage, he made his movie debut in a bit part in Paramount's *One Hour Late* (1934) before moving up the Hollywood ladder to featured parts and ultimately landing his own series (the *Bulldog Drummond* mysteries). An avid lifelong reader of science fiction books and stories, John Howard can boast a career in fantasy, horror and sci-fi films that has spanned a full five decades.

Your first fantasy film was Lost Horizon *with Ronald Colman. Do you remember how you became involved on this film?*

Frank Capra was making tests of lots of people for this particular part. I was under contract at Paramount and Frank was working for Columbia, so I thought it was kind of peculiar when Paramount phoned me and said, "Frank Capra wants to test you for a part in *Lost Horizon.*" At that moment I didn't know what *Lost Horizon* was, but I said yes—naturally! After all, Capra was a big name at that time, after *It Happened One Night* [1934]. So I went out, grabbed a copy of *Lost Horizon* and read it. But as yet no one had said which part I was going to play. When they told me I was going to play Mallory, I said, "Wait a minute! That's a terrible part—the guy is an absolute jerk!" But Paramount said this was going to be a big picture and that I should do it. So I made the test, and afterwards Frank told me that I was going to play the part. Then he asked me if I would mind acting opposite some girls who were testing to play the part of Maria. Naturally I couldn't say no. Strangely enough, I didn't make a test with Margo, who got the part eventually, although I had worked with her many times previously—she was a real close friend of mine. You might be interested to know that one of the girls I did make a test with was named Rita Cansino. She just didn't work out as far as Frank was concerned, but later on she turned out to be Rita Hayworth!

This whole experience, of course, was a pivotal moment in my career. Without *Lost Horizon,* I doubt very much whether I would have survived in Hollywood.

What made Capra think of you?

Previous page: John Howard puckers up for a peck from *The Invisible Woman* (who, unaccountably, isn't making a hole in the water). Of this experience Howard says, "My feeling was, 'Jeez, I'm going to look like an absolute idiot here!'"

I asked him that. I said, "Frank, this character ought to be British, right? He's the brother of a man who's going to be the prime minister of Britain if he ever gets back to England. How in the world did you think of me?" And he had a rather equivocal answer; he said, "It's just something that I saw in you in a picture which was about the Naval Academy." That was a picture I'd made for Paramount, *Annapolis Farewell* [1935]. How in the hell he figured out from *that* that I had the kind of quality he wanted for *his* picture, I don't know. Bless his heart, I'm glad he did, but I'm not quite sure still to this day that I was right for that part. And a lot of British actors, including David Niven, Richard Greene and a number of others, had also made tests for it. Of course I couldn't object to the fact that Frank picked me, but I also couldn't understand why!

We talked about this as the picture went on, and of course we had some different opinions about how this character ought to be played. And even though I was a dumb kid, I was brash enough to occasionally say to Frank, "I don't think this guy would do such-and-such a thing." And then Frank would explain to me why he thought I should do whatever it was. It was a nice relationship.

There were some changes between the character in the book and the character you ended up playing.

Mallory is a very important character in the book because he's the guy that louses up everything. They changed it in the picture into a different kind of character, but he still does the same job of messing things up. I guess [screenwriters] Capra and Robert Riskin also felt that it would be a good idea to make this character the brother of the leading character, Conway [played by Ronald Colman], and I think they were right about that. In fact, the author of *Lost Horizon,* James Hilton, actually *said* that—he said, "My gosh, if I would have thought of this, I would have made him Conway's brother to begin with!"

So you got to meet Hilton?

Yes, he was on the set quite a lot. He was a very interesting fellow—really, the first major author that I had ever met in my life. Such a shy little man—he just didn't want to talk at all, he sat in corners of the stage and it was very difficult to get him to talk. But when he did, he spoke like a Cambridge don: with great understanding, and a delicious sense of what was wrong with people and with the world. He had a great love for humanity, and a strong feeling that humanity was doomed to some kind of horrible fate unless they picked themselves up. I think all of his novels kind of reflected that.

On the other end of the spectrum, possibly: Was Harry Cohn on the set very much?

No, not at all. I had a good relationship with Harry, personally. I was just

Margo and John Howard in a publicity photo for Frank Capra's *Lost Horizon*.

a little jerk, so I don't want to make this thing into a big deal, but I did several pictures for Harry and he was always very nice to me. I never found him to be the awful ogre that other people made him out to be. On the other hand, I didn't give him any trouble *[laughs]*! But, no, he seldom came on the set of *Lost Horizon;* I think when Frank made the deal with Harry, he must have said, "Look, you stay off the set!"

Because Lost Horizon *was being made by Columbia, which was then a Poverty Row studio, Ronald Colman initially had misgivings about the project. What were your feelings about having to work at Columbia?*

In those days everybody was a slave; "sold down the river" was a real term then. We couldn't control our lives. If you were under contract at MGM or Paramount or Warners, you belonged to them, and they just sold you. It wasn't an awful thing, usually, although I did a couple of pictures under these conditions that I didn't like at all. But in this particular case I realized that this was a real chance, because *Lost Horizon* was going to be one of the big pictures of the year—or, for that matter, of the century! My feeling about Capra, of course, was a matter of worship; I thought this guy was the greatest director to come along in a long time. To have a chance to work with him was great.

Howard *(left),* Margo and Ronald Colman in *Lost Horizon.* Howard's role in this hall-of-famer ensured his niche in Hollywood history, but 50 years later he remains unhappy with his performance.

How did you like working with Colman?

I enjoyed it tremendously. He was a difficult man to know—a man who had a kind of "shutter" on his personal relationships. He would close the shutter and you just couldn't get any further with him. On the other hand, a couple of times I was privileged to have him open up about his past life, and that was fascinating. I thought, and still think, that Ronald Colman was the acme of film actors. He had this amazing ability to do *nothing,* and let you look into his eyes and imagine everything that *you* thought he was thinking. I wasn't ever convinced that *he* was thinking the things that the audience thought, but at least he gave them the chance to put their thoughts into those big brown eyes.

Where was Lost Horizon *shot?*

The exterior Shangri-La sets were built on the Columbia ranch. They raised doves and pigeons there, from eggs, so that they would never leave—they were always floating around in the air there. They also planted all the trees and plants, so that they grew there. The first time we walked onto this set, we couldn't believe our eyes. It was paradise! Everything was blooming, the birds were flying around making cooing noises—it was very exciting. Personally, I thought at the time the design of the temple was wrong, because it looked too art-deco; I thought it ought to mirror the actual temples in Tibet. But I must say that I think maybe they were right and I was wrong; it made people in the movie audience sit up and take notice, because they'd never seen anything like it. Maybe that's what made it exciting.

The scenes at the airport were shot out in the San Fernando Valley. The scene where we land our plane in the desert was done out in what's now called Antelope Valley—in those days it was complete desert. Some of the aerial stuff, flying over the Himalayas, was done over the state of Washington; some of it was clips of the actual Himalayas. The rescue scenes after the plane crash were done in an ice house in downtown L.A. They had several machines that chopped up ice and they blew it around, and it looked like snow. The temperature in there was *just* below 32°, just enough to keep everything frozen, and we worked there for two or three weeks.

At that particular time—1936, '37—somebody discovered that you could take a film can cover and flip it through the air, and make it glide. Does that sound familiar? During our lunch break, all of us went out into the street outside the ice house and we had great games flipping this film can cover around. But none of us had brains enough to realize that we could develop this into something that would be commercial—

The Frisbee!

Right! Every day we'd get out there and play this game. It was in July, I think, and the temperature was around 100°. We got all boiled up, sweated like mad, and then we went back into the ice house, where it was like 28°. We all thought we'd die of pneumonia. Well, nobody got even a cold—nobody had any problems at all, which I always thought ought to have been investigated by scientists.

It was in this same area of downtown L.A. that Frank found the old woman who stood in for Margo as the ancient crone. They found her on the street! They had tested all kinds of people—they even put old-age makeup on Margo—before they finally noticed this old Mexican woman whom Frank found while he was wandering around during the lunch hour. They signed her for like $50 a week and put her on Ronnie Colman's back for that final scene, and she played the part. She didn't have to do anything, of course, except look incredibly old—and she did! It was not makeup, she was just an ancient, *ancient* crone.

Looking at the reconstructed Lost Horizon *recently, it struck me that a few of the cuts made over the years may have been for the better.*

I've got to disagree with that. As far as I'm concerned, the reconstruction is marvelous, but then *[laughs]*, I have a reason! They put back two scenes that I was in that had been lost for years. When I used to see the cut version on television, I always felt that my character didn't make any sense, because they had taken out those two very valuable scenes which explain why this idiot kid did all these dumb things. So I appreciate the reconstruction from that standpoint: I still think that I did a bad job of *playing* the character, but the motivation for what he did now makes more sense.

You don't think you did a good job in Lost Horizon?
No. I began to feel this way the first time I saw the film, at a preview! Damn it, I thought I was too brash, too uncontrolled, too unbelievable. And I've wished always that I could go back and do it again.

Did you ever see the Ross Hunter remake [1973]?
[Groans.] Oh, God! I didn't—I didn't want to. People told me, "Don't watch it—please! Don't go and see it!" And I have not seen it yet.

How did you become interested in becoming an actor?
I actually wasn't. My father studied drama at Carnegie Tech, and as a little tiny kid I remember going to see productions that he was in. But I never thought anything about doing it myself until I was in high school. They suddenly put me into the senior play, much against my will *[laughs]*, and as I think back on it I must have been absolutely awful—*ghastly!* Then when I got into college [Western Reserve University, Cleveland, Ohio], through my fraternity I met a couple of guys who were really fascinated with the theater and knew a lot about it, and they educated me. I began to see that this was something worth doing. I'd always been interested in doing something artistically—playing some instrument, perhaps. And at that point I thought, "Well, this is something I can do, and I don't have to compete with trombonists and pianists. I can just do this on my own." So I got fascinated with the idea of theater, and the more I got involved, the more excited I got about it.

And then how did you break into pictures?
A talent scout from Paramount came to Cleveland to see a local stock company, but they had a dark house that night—the leading lady was sick or something, and they closed down. The talent scout called William McDermott, who was the drama editor of *The Cleveland Plain Dealer,* and said, "I've got a free evening, where can I go?" And McDermott said, "Go out to the university and see the show." Our show, incidentally, happened to be the first production ever made of Stephen Vincent Benét's *John Brown's Body.* The talent scout picked out me and a girl in the show and said, "How would you two like to come to New York and make a test for films?" I wasn't quite sure—I thought he was nuts *[laughs]*! I didn't really believe that he was a talent scout. I thought he was one of these guys that wanted to pick up little people and milk them for their money. But of course he was legitimate. I called McDermott and he said, "No, no, this guy is a big wheel!"

So I went to New York and made the test, and they said, "Would $75 a week get you through your New York experience?" Seventy-five dollars in 1934 was a fortune—it was like a *thousand* dollars today! I swallowed a bit and said, "I *guess* I can get by on that." Actually, I'd been living on three dollars a week! So that's how I got into the business—completely by accident.

How did you get involved on The Mad Doctor?

I was in a funny kind of state at Paramount at that time: I was right at the end of my contract, and they didn't know quite what to do with me. I had done the *Bulldog Drummond* pictures and several other things like *Disputed Passage* [1939], which was one of my favorite pictures but didn't make any money. So Paramount came and said that *The Mad Doctor* was going to be a good picture for me because Basil Rathbone was going to play the title role and I'd be playing the hero who defeats him in the long run. Also, I was secretly in love with [co-star] Ellen Drew; we'd sort of grown up together at Paramount, and I thought she was great. So I felt that *The Mad Doctor* was going to be a marvelous opportunity.

How did you like working with Rathbone?

I think he was a superlative actor. That's the first time I'd ever really met him personally, and I didn't realize he was such a robust conservative. He was trying to sell everybody on the idea that America could not survive unless we had some kind of a really strong, conservative government—and, of course, at that time I couldn't have disagreed more with that kind of philosophy! So we had a lovely running argument for the six or seven weeks it took to make the picture. Also, we were both stamp collectors, and we got into a situation where he was trying to sell me his stamps and I was trying to sell him mine. And nothing happened, because I thought he was a crook *[laughs]*! And I still think so!

The Mad Doctor *was a B picture with A picture length and A picture pretensions. Strange as it sounds, I think with a little* less *effort it might have been better!*

I'd go along with that, they tried to make too much out of it. But *The Mad Doctor* was a real experience for me because I actually learned a lot from Basil Rathbone. Not in the sense of copying what he did, but in seeing the kind of timing that he had in his readings. I really did appreciate working with him. I also loved the director, Tim Whelan. He was a great, marvelous guy, and I just couldn't understand why he didn't go on to become really famous.

Did you enjoy yourself when you made Universal's The Invisible Woman?

Yes, I did. That movie was absolute hilarious fun. I'd worked with John

Howard remembers his illustrious *Mad Doctor* co-star Basil Rathbone as a superlative actor, but he wouldn't buy a used stamp from this man.

Barrymore before, several times, and I just loved the guy—I adored him! After all, how many people have achieved the stature of John Barrymore in the theater? I thought it was fantastic just to be able to sit in the same room with him. We had a good relationship. Barrymore was an ordinary fellow; he wasn't stuffy, no pretense whatsoever. He kept saying, "I never wanted to be in the theater. I wanted to be a cartoonist." He wanted to be an artist, actually, but couldn't do it that well, so he decided he wanted to be a cartoonist—at which he was very good.

Even in pictures that you felt weren't up to snuff, I don't think he showed any disdain. We knew perfectly well that *The Invisible Woman* wasn't going to be an award-winner, but it was fun to do and interesting to those of us who never did one of those invisible things before. Which included the whole cast, I guess.

Curt Siodmak, the writer of The Invisible Woman, *told me that Barrymore was at the point where he couldn't memorize dialogue anymore.*

That was true even before *The Invisible Woman*. When we did the *Bulldog Drummond* pictures at Paramount, the first few starred Barrymore and I was second-billed as Drummond. And he had great problems. It wasn't that he couldn't memorize lines, he did fine with that; the problem was that he got so petrified that he couldn't remember the first line. For instance, if he and I happened to be walking together into a scene already established, he would grab my arm with a vicious grip — he was very strong for a small fellow — and he would say *[frantically]*, "What's my line? What's my line?" I'd tell him, we'd go in and he would be brilliant from that point on. But later on, in the second picture, he began to develop a kind of aphasia: he would get going well, but then he would lose lines during the scene, which wasn't true in the first picture. So he developed, with my help, a system of cutting up the script and putting it down on the set: behind vases, behind phones, in drawers, on the backs of other actors, whatever! They were like cue cards, although this was long before television. This way he could just look around and find the lines. And of course he was such a superlative actor that it looked as though this was an inspirational way to *say* the lines! It worked very well, but it must have driven him nuts — he must have realized what was happening to him, and I felt terribly sorry about that.

Did you get along well with the rest of the cast?

I loved everybody in that picture. It was a ball from start to finish. Working at Universal was fun. Not as much fun as Paramount, but still a relaxed kind of atmosphere. I never really had any contact with the front office at Universal; we worked for a producer and that was it. In fact, most of the time I didn't even know who was running the place! But it was fun to work there in the sense Universal was kind of at the second level — it wasn't really a major studio, but it had a history of making good pictures.

Were any of the "invisible" effects achieved before your eyes on the stage?

Yes, some of them were achieved right there. You know of course how they made a person "invisible" on film — dressing them in black garments and then shooting them against a black background. But there were other things, like footprints on the carpet, which could not be done that way. They were achieved in a very strange way that involved putting springs and wires under the carpet, to get the imprint to go down. The same thing when an invisible person sits in a chair: How can you indicate that they're sitting there except to show the padding in the chair become concave? That, too, was done mechanically.

The thing that was difficult for me was that I had to work opposite *nobody*—to talk to a non-existent person. The first time I mentioned this to a reporter he said, "Well, that's no different from doing a scene with anybody who's not there, and *that* happens all the time in pictures." But it's not the same, it really isn't. There is a difference between trying to deal with somebody "invisible" compared to somebody who had played a scene with you before, and now just doesn't happen to be there physically. There's a kind of funny transition that you have to make, and I think it's a different technique in a sense. I'm not sure we did it well, but we tried.

I always wondered whether actors working in Invisible Man films felt silly going through all these bizarre motions.

That's exactly what I'm talking about. My feeling was, "Jeez, I'm going to look like an absolute idiot here!" For instance, how can I kiss an "invisible" hand? Am I going to look as though I am *pretending* to kiss an invisible hand? That would throw the whole picture out of kilter. As an actor, I have a responsibility—I have to make this thing look believable. But how can I do it? I have no experience in my life that deals with this kind of thing *[laughs]*! This is pretty frustrating! Of course the director's no help, 'cause he doesn't know, either!

How do you feel about science fiction, fantasy and horror films in general?

I guess I was one of the original science fiction buffs of all time. In the '20s I used to smuggle science fiction books and magazines into classrooms, and put them inside of history books. Science fiction I love, and always have. Horror movies I always loved to go and see, just for the fun of it, but I don't think they really fall in the same category. I still read a lot of science fiction, more science fiction than fantasy; I make a great distinction between the two. I think *real* science fiction is the only remaining area where imagination can really work—the imagination of authors or poets or dreamers. So I'm still very devoted to it; I still read *Omni* and *Discover* and everything else I can find.

I've always been disappointed that movies have not done the job they *could* do with science fiction. Movies are the real medium for this kind of thing, but it's never really come about as far as I'm concerned. I've done a lot of science fiction movies, but I never was satisfied with them—they always looked dumb to me. Unimaginative. Not poetic. Not done the way they ought to be done.

The Undying Monster *was one of your last films before going into the service during World War II.*

It was *the* last film. Here's the story on that: Instead of waiting to be drafted into the army, I decided that I wanted to be in the navy. So the navy picked me up and put me "on hold," so to speak. My agent said, "The navy says you won't be called up for six or eight months. Wouldn't it be a good idea if we got a contract with some studio? That way, when the war is over, you'll

Ultra-rare closeup shot of Howard in full werewolf makeup, from the climax of *The Undying Monster.* **(Photo courtesy Steve Jochsberger.)**

have something to come back to." I thought that made sense, and so, months later, he got me a contract with 20th Century–Fox. Fox didn't do a damn thing about it for a couple of months, and then suddenly they came up with this picture, *The Undying Monster.* I couldn't refuse it, and yet I didn't really feel I belonged in the thing. It had a British setting, and I thought I was out of place.

What about James Ellison? He was a cowboy star, and he played a Scotland Yard sleuth in it!

   [*Laughs.*] To have Jimmy in that picture was absolutely stupid. It wasn't his fault, he did a good job, but again, why in the world put this guy in that particular part? It didn't make any sense at all. To be honest, until I finally saw the film, very recently, on television, I had forgotten that Jimmy was even in it! When I saw him in there, I was just shocked.

The leading lady, Heather Angel, was the only star who seemed to belong, but her character is so high-handed and standoffish that you just don't care about her.

I don't think they thought much about what they were doing. I didn't really care, though, because about three weeks after the darn thing was over I was already on my way to Casablanca. So I was not really concerned with it; I was only concerned with the idea that I'd have some place to come back to.

The director, John Brahm, now has something of a reputation as a horror specialist.

[*Laughs.*] John and I had an adversary relationship going way back to a picture that we made together at Columbia, *Penitentiary* [1938], with Jean Parker. I got sold again by Paramount for that particular picture; Brahm was the director, and we had some difficulties. He's a German, after all, and he expected people to listen to the director and to *obey* the director. I didn't really feel that way; I thought I could listen, but that I didn't have to obey. He wanted me to do a lot of things that I thought were just hammy and stupid. We had quite a long to-do during that picture, and neither one of us wound up liking the other much. So when I found him also directing *The Undying Monster* I was not too happy about that [*laughs*]! But everything went okay — he wasn't worried about my performing like a German actor. Maybe he had changed — maybe *I* had changed! — but we got along fine. I respected him for being a technically good director, but I just didn't like his Germanic attitude.

That whole movie was done indoors, even the scenes on the moors, right?

Yep. Really, the only thing I remember about *The Undying Monster* — with great pain! — is the scene in which I changed from a werewolf to a human being. I was clamped down in some kind of vise while they put this makeup on, and this was not fun at all. It took about four hours, and in the picture it only lasts about thirty seconds. As I said, I had never seen the picture until recently, and I was astounded. I remembered this thing as being a long, long transformation, but from what I see in the film now, it's *nothing.* And I thought, God, I spent all those hours in agony there, with no real result!

The camerawork and art direction were the best things about Undying Monster. *Despite its classic rep, it's pretty poky and drawn-out.*

I couldn't agree more about that. I thought it was dull. The intention was good and the whole ambience was good, but I don't think that it held up, or that it had any great appeal. It certainly didn't keep *my* interest [*laughs*]!

After World War II your feature film career never really seemed to get back into gear.

I got out of the service early because I got a medal, and according to the rules if you get certain medals you get out early. I thought that was a good opportunity to get a jump on all the other actors who were coming out later on. So I wired my agent and said I was being released, and that I could be in Hollywood in a week. "Call Fox and see what they've got going," I told him. He did, and he wired me back to tell me that they didn't have anything for me. Most of the people who were under contract to Fox were not out of the service yet; how could this be possible? I got the feeling that they just didn't give a damn.

A man named Leland Hayward, who had been an agent in Hollywood and became a producer in New York during the war, called my agent and said, "I want to talk to John about doing a play in New York." I read the script, thought it was very exciting, called my agent and said, "I love this thing, but how can I get out of my contract with Fox?" Eventually what happened was that I flew back to the Coast, we went to Fox and talked them into letting me out of the contract. This accomplished, I went back to New York and we tried to make this play work—and it just didn't work. We opened it in New Haven, we went to Boston, we went to Pittsburgh and we closed in Pittsburgh because everybody realized it wasn't going to work. The New York critics would have killed it; it just had something missing. I went back to Hollywood, but really I had nothing to go back to. I was an actor who had not worked in five years, coming back from a flopped show. How could they sell me? I had to scrounge around and do lousy little pictures until television raised its ugly head, when finally I got a chance to start again. But it was a long, long period of absolute dearth.

How did you land your part in The Unknown Terror?

The director, Charles Marquis Warren, was a guy who had a great reputation: He created *Gunsmoke, Rawhide* and several other TV series, and he was a good director. I don't know where he glommed onto the idea that I should play in this picture, but I was approached. I had just finished doing my TV series *Dr. Hudson's Secret Journal* [1955–1957], and I was delighted to get a chance to work with him.

It was a good script, basically; as far as science fiction was concerned, it was all right. I had seen Mala Powers [q.v.] in *Cyrano de Bergerac* [1950] and thought that she was absolutely delightful, so I also looked forward to working with her. She turned out to be a fascinating person. And since the film was shot at the Producers Studio, which is where I'd made *Dr. Hudson's Secret Journal* and several pictures, it was like old home week.

So you enjoyed the experience?

It was a delightful picture to work on. I thought everybody involved was

They dared enter the **Cave of Death** to explore the secrets of HELL and find the...

UNKNOWN TERROR

A **REGALSCOPE** PICTURE

starring JOHN **HOWARD** · MALA **POWERS** · PAUL **RICHARDS** · MAY **WYNN** and Sir Lancelot King of the Calypsos

Produced by ROBERT STABLER · Directed by CHARLES MARQUIS WARREN · Written by KENNETH HIGGINS

An Emirau Production · Presented by Regal Films, Inc. · Released by 20th CENTURY-FOX

Howard played his last film lead in the science fiction quickie *The Unknown Terror*.

very good at his craft; in my opinion, [co-star] Paul Richards was one of the best actors I've ever run across. He was just superb. Mala was good and so were all the other people. It was fun to do.

Where were all the cave scenes shot?
　　All of them were done right on the set. I had never heard of the word "spelunking" before; to have to climb down those damn rope ladders and swing across crevasses was a challenge, and made it kind of exciting. There were no stuntmen involved, and these were not easy things to do. I will tell you, in case you have to run down a rope ladder someday, that you had better learn how to do it first. The thing sways around like mad, and you've only got a little

four-inch place to plant your foot—it's hard to find where those rungs are. And swinging on a rope across a 12-foot gap was no fun, either. That chasm was about twenty feet deep! They had tried desperately to find a way to film us swinging across from above; they wanted to have a rolling stream down there, and to show us swinging across the chasm from that high angle. That didn't work out, but it was still a 20-foot drop! We couldn't miss—to drop off in the middle would have been a disaster.

I never could figure out where your character in that film was coming from.

I couldn't figure that out, either, and that was one of the things I talked to Charles about! I was just a set-up *[laughs]*—obviously Paul was the hero and Mala was in love with him, so why was I there at all? I didn't understand, and he couldn't figure it out, either!

Were you around when they shot the cave scenes with the fungus?

I was out of there by the time they got around to those scenes; I wasn't involved with that at all. In viewing the movie, I thought that it looked like soap bubbles coming down the cave walls. I didn't see how this could frighten anybody, but it sure frightened the hell out of my kids—they were scared to death! So if all the movie set out to do was to scare young people, I guess it worked!

How about the fungus people—did you find them effective?

Nah, that was just nonsense. I didn't think *The Unknown Terror* was a very good film at all. But I thought what they did with the Indian ritual angle was good—I thought those scenes gave you a pretty eerie feeling that strange things do go on, that modern people don't really know about. I liked that part, and thought they should have made more of that and less of the monster stuff.

The Unknown Terror *was your last sizable film role. Why? Because you went into teaching?*

Not quite. The actual fact is that no one gave me any decent offers for a couple of years. I did many, many appearances on television shows, so I was making a living, but nobody came to me with a picture. I did go into teaching, but it was several years after that. I went into teaching with the provision that I could do a picture or a television show whenever I got a chance, and I did. But gradually I began to be aware of the fact that every time I took off from school and had fun on a set and made a lot of money out of it, I was having to ask some fellow teacher to take over my class. I began to feel pretty bad about that *[laughs]*—I felt like saying, "I made $400 today and *you* ought to get $385 of it for doing my job!" Also, the longer I was with the school, the more involved I got in the operation of it, and I finally became a kind of principal there. At that point I just didn't feel that I had time enough to go and do little movie jobs, one-day bits and things anymore. So my acting career petered out

Flanked by the Fabulous Brunas Boys (Michael and John), Howard smiles for the birdie in the backyard of his Los Angeles home. (Photo: Jon Weaver.)

because I was working twelve hours a day at school and feeling that it was worth it. And since I retired from the school, I haven't even attempted to get back in the business because I just don't like what I *see* about the business. I think it looks like a crock of shit! I probably shouldn't say that, but it's true—I just don't like what I see.

Your last genre assignments were smallish roles in Destination Inner Space, The Destructors *and* So Evil, My Sister.

There was a fish-man in *Destination Inner Space*, I was some kind of an engineer, and I just don't remember anything else about that picture! I've also completely forgotten everything about *The Destructors* except that it involved laser. *So Evil, My Sister* was a real under-the-rug production, a very strange picture, made on a shoestring. We didn't have any sets at all; we worked inside of little houses in Pasadena and on sidewalks in Burbank and so on. Very weird—it's the only picture I ever made like that. It was a good attempt with good people in it, but it was made for no money at all, just buttons.

Lost Horizon *is unquestionably the film you'll best be remembered for. Why does it hold up so well after so many years?*

Jane Wyatt and I did a lot of tours with this new reconstructed version, since we're the only players left, and that question always came up. It's so easy to say that it's a dream that people have of a world where there is no danger;

it's a dream that we could establish a place on Earth where there is absolute peace and love and happiness—which, of course, we all would like to see. I think it's more than that; I don't think people like the film only because of that. I think they like it because the people involved are led into this world at peace sort of against their will. All the characters, even Conway, are originally repelled by this idea. This is kind of a reflection of the way most people think about the world: They love the *idea* of a world at peace, and yet they tend to question what this would be like. We are a contentious bunch of people, aren't we? We are basically still animalistically fighting to survive and trying to make ourselves interesting and better. Maybe that's part of it.

JOHN HOWARD FILMOGRAPHY

As John Cox, Jr.:

One Hour Late (Paramount, 1934)
Car 99 (Paramount, 1935)
Four Hours to Kill! (Paramount, 1935)

As John Howard:

Annapolis Farewell (Paramount, 1935)
Millions in the Air (Paramount, 1935)
Soak the Rich (Paramount, 1936)
Thirteen Hours by Air (Paramount, 1936)
Border Flight (Paramount, 1936)
Valiant Is the Word for Carrie (Paramount, 1936)
Easy to Take (Paramount, 1936)
Lost Horizon (Columbia, 1937)
Let Them Live (Universal, 1937)
Mountain Music (Paramount, 1937)
Bulldog Drummond Comes Back (Paramount, 1937)
Hold 'Em Navy! (Paramount, 1937)
Bulldog Drummond's Revenge (Paramount, 1937)
Hitting a New High (RKO, 1937)
Penitentiary (Columbia, 1938)
Bulldog Drummond in Africa (Paramount, 1938)
Bulldog Drummond's Peril (Paramount, 1938)
Touchdown, Army (Paramount, 1938)
Prison Farm (Paramount, 1938)
Arrest Bulldog Drummond (Paramount, 1939)
Bulldog Drummond's Secret Police (Paramount, 1939)
Grand Jury Secrets (Paramount, 1939)
Bulldog Drummond's Bride (Paramount, 1939)
What a Life (Paramount, 1939)
Disputed Passage (Paramount, 1939)
Green Hell (Universal, 1940)
The Man from Dakota (MGM, 1940)

The Philadelphia Story (MGM, 1940)
Texas Rangers Ride Again (Paramount, 1940)
The Invisible Woman (Universal, 1940)
The Mad Doctor (Paramount, 1941)
Tight Shoes (Universal, 1941)
Father Takes a Wife (RKO, 1941)
Three Girls About Town (Columbia, 1941)
A Tragedy at Midnight (Republic, 1942)
The Man Who Returned to Life (Columbia, 1942)
Submarine Raider (Columbia, 1942)
Isle of Missing Men (Monogram, 1942)
The Undying Monster (20th Century–Fox, 1942)
Love from a Stranger (Eagle-Lion, 1947)
I, Jane Doe (Republic, 1948)
Motion Picture Mothers, Inc. (Columbia short, 1949)
The Fighting Kentuckian (Republic, 1949)
Radar Secret Service (Lippert, 1950)
Experiment Alcatraz (RKO, 1950)
Models, Inc. (Mutual, 1952)
Make Haste to Live (Republic, 1954)
The High and the Mighty (Warners, 1954)
The Unknown Terror (20th Century–Fox, 1957)
Destination Inner Space (Magna, 1966)
The Destructors (Feature Film Corporation of America, 1968)
So Evil, My Sister (Psycho Sisters) (Zenith International, 1972)
Capone (20th Century–Fox, 1975)

Becoming a star wouldn't have bothered me,
but what is a star? A star isn't anything.
An actor acts. That's the important thing.

Kim Hunter

BY HOLLYWOOD'S skewed standards of normal behavior, Kim Hunter probably qualifies as "the eccentric type": She lives in a Manhattan apartment and not in L.A.'s smoggy climes, her Oscar statuette is tarnished and inconspicuously displayed, and she doesn't give two hoots in a barn about owning any of her films on videotape. But in Hunter's case, "eccentric" also translates into warm, intelligent and charming. On a bleak spring afternoon, an electrician is rummaging through her Greenwich Village digs as rain spatters the windows and lights flicker off and on, but Hunter is unruffled and unfailingly pleasant, giving her full attention to an interviewer whom any "normal" Hollywood actress would have gladly kicked down the stairs on such a trying day.

Née Janet Cole, the future stage, screen and television actress began her acting career fresh out of high school, first as a member of a Florida stock company and later with the Pasadena Playhouse. A talent scout for Hollywood mogul David O. Selznick spotted her in one of the Playhouse productions, and Selznick quickly placed the young actress under contract. Hunter film-debuted in the Val Lewton chiller *The Seventh Victim* and has since gone on to appear in more than twenty films and close to a hundred stage roles. One of her finest and most challenging roles was as Stella Kowalski in Broadway's *A Streetcar Named Desire* (she later reprised the role in the 1951 film version, copping a Best Supporting Actress Oscar), but by her own admission she is best remembered today for playing the chimpanzee psychologist Dr. Zira in the '60s classic *Planet of the Apes* and two sequels. Truly a class act, Kim Hunter has more than made her mark in the annals of fantastic filmdom.

How did you get involved on Val Lewton's The Seventh Victim?

Val Lewton knew me because he had been in charge of the screen test that got me my contract with David O. Selznick, and Jacques Tourneur had directed it. In fact, Tourneur and Val were around when Selznick said my name had to be changed. Val had worked for David during the time of *Gone with the Wind* [1939], and Val was assigned to get audience comments during the intermission. He didn't want to do it, and what he finally ended up doing was making up a list of comments and inventing names to go with them. David later found out what Val had done, and when he sent me over to see Val at RKO, he said, "I'm sending you to a man who's very good at making up names!" *[Laughs.]* Anyway, the three of us sat in Val's office — Val Lewton, Tourneur and me — thinking up first names, and Val's secretary was writing down a whole list of last names. *Hunter* was among them. And in our list of first names I suggested Kim, only because I remembered it from *Showboat* — I sort of liked it, thought it was kind of fun. And Selznick put the two together — I had nothing to do with that. He called me and asked, "*Kim Hunter* — do you like it?" *[Laughs.]*

What were your impressions of Val Lewton?

Previous page: Petite (5' 3½"), brown-haired, hazel-eyed Kim Hunter, Oscar-winning actress of *A Streetcar Named Desire* fame and a frequent visitor to the SF and horror genres.

"Terrified to move a muscle," Hunter had a classic case of first-picture nerves on the set of RKO's *The Seventh Victim*. The bookworm is Erford Gage.

A darling, gentle man—so wrong to be known as the king of the horror films *[laughs]*! Just a sweet human being.

Was he on the set of Seventh Victim *much?*
I don't remember his being on the set all that much, I really don't. He saw all the dailies, I know that, and he insisted that I not! He had brought me in to look at my tests, and I damn near burst into tears, and so he said, "Oh, no, no, keep her out! She's one of those that has no objectivity about her own work." Actors do that, they just sit there and criticize everything.

Did you have first-picture jitters?
It was just all so new. I remember them telling me to be very, very careful because the camera exaggerates everything, and what an actor might do on stage is not necessarily a good idea on film because it looks five times as large. Which meant that I found myself terrified to move a muscle *[laughs]*! Every now and then Val would say, "Would you relax, please? You look like you're embalmed!" So I had to find a way, somehow, and I concentrated on trying to understand the medium. Camera marks, those were hard to get used to, and the silence drove me absolutely crazy. There is nothing quite as silent as the

silence during the shooting of a film in a studio. It was [director] Mark Robson's first picture, too, so we were hangin' onto each other for dear life *[laughs]*!

What do you think of the film today?

Oh, I don't know—it's very hard for me ever to see myself. I keep seeing things I wished I'd done, or not done, or what-have-you. I just know from what I'm told and what I read that it was considered one of the best of the whole lot of horror films that Val Lewton did. But Lewton's way of dealing with horror films, I thought, was so marvelous, letting the audience use its imagination rather than showing all the blood and guts and all of that.

Another one of your early pictures was When Strangers Marry *[1944], once called the best-ever B movie, directed by William Castle.*

I liked working with Castle very much, but *When Strangers Marry* was a very peculiar experience. In a way, it was a horror film of its own type *[laughs]*! The King Brothers produced it, and they had quite a reputation in Hollywood for having notches on their guns—little things like that! Mama kind of ran the gang, but it *was* a gang, those guys! They slapped a ten-day schedule on the film, and Bill Castle said *[whispering]*, "Would you all mind if we sneaked a rehearsal period for about a week in my apartment?" And we said *[still whispering]*, "Yes, we'd love to do that!" So we had an illegitimate week's rehearsal, Dean Jagger, Bob Mitchum and I. That saved our lives, in order to do that film in ten days.

The King Brothers were absolutely fascinated with Mitchum, and Bob was very glad when the ten days were over. Because frequently, while Bob was waiting to do a scene, two of the King Brothers' "henchmen" would come over to him, one guy would stand on one side of him and the second guy on the other, and he swears they had guns in their pockets. They would say to him, "You really oughta leave MGM and move over to the King Brothers. They really want you under contract." Bob said, "No, I don't think I can get out of my MGM contract," and they said, "We'll manage it, we'll get you out of it!" They were at him the whole time, and he was glad when he was able to get out!

How did you land your role in A Matter of Life and Death?

While I was under contract to Selznick, I got a call asking if I would mind coming into the studio and substituting for Ingrid Bergman in tests that Hitchcock wanted to make for *Spellbound* [1945]. I said hell, yes, because I wanted to go and watch the guy work. He would shoot the back of my head, testing various male minor roles, and it was very exciting—I worked with him for about three days doing that, and we had lunch together each day. And that was the end of that. A year later, Michael Powell and Emeric Pressburger came to this country looking for somebody to play the WAC in *A Matter of Life and Death*. They saw people in New York, then they came to California and had dinner with Hitch. And Hitch said, "Well, there *is* a girl you might see..."

That's how I got brought to them, and we just sort of talked. I had just finished making a film with Lizabeth Scott, *You Came Along* [1945], and they asked to see snippets of that. I didn't know anything more until some time later, when my agent got a call saying that I should go to London, etc., etc. — I was *in*. Later, talking to Mickey [Powell], I found out that he had hired me on a hunch and it was not *You Came Along* — in fact, seeing that film almost turned him against me, because he didn't like the hairdo!

You liked Powell?

God, what a gorgeous man! I was so sorry when he died, but he had been quite ill so it was probably a relief. He was on morphine almost 24 hours a day toward the end. I saw him just before he went back to England, where he died — he was dear, but he wasn't "in" the conversation, because he couldn't hear, couldn't relate. So sad. I had much more contact with Mickey than I did with Emeric during the making of *Life and Death* because Emeric didn't come around the set all that much. His work was basically done when they had decided on the finished script. The two of them worked pretty closely together in writing it — the first draft would always be Emeric's, then Mickey would get his hands in it, and then Emeric would tidy it up! So as I said, Emeric didn't really come to the set that much, but I got to know him because of various little gatherings. Another dear, sweet man.

Where was Life and Death *shot?*

In Denham Studios in London — I believe the whole film was shot there except for one scene at Saunton Sands, where they did the opening shots on the beach. But most of it was in the studio. I liked England very much; the work was very good, very exciting, particularly after Hollywood. The attitude was so much more concentrated on the work — that was the important thing. How you lived, what kind of car you drove and what-have-you didn't mean a damn thing; it was each to his own taste over there. I'll never forget when I bought my first car in California, a Ford business coupe, and I drove it up to my agent's office and I said very proudly, "Look!" And he said, "You're crazy — take it back!" He said, "When you're well-known, you can be eccentric and drive a Ford business coupe, but until you get to be a star you need a Cadillac!" To impress. And that's insane. It was such a relief to find that that attitude just didn't exist in England.

Life and Death *was a fairly prestigious picture for England, wasn't it?*

Yes, it was. And it was the first Royal Command Film Performance — it took place at the Empire Theatre in Leicester Square. It was quite a show that night, because there were so many of us involved. There was a stage show as well as the film, and actors from all over the world were there. From Sweden, from Greece, from France and the States, and of course all the top English people. After the show we went upstairs to the Royal Lounge and they had us all

Congregated on the *Stairway to Heaven,* Marius Goring, Kathleen Byron, Robert Coote, Roger Livesey, unidentified players, Joan Maude, Abraham Sofaer and Raymond Massey look on as Kim Hunter reaches out to David Niven.

lined up in a semi-circle and the Royal Family came around us. Mickey said later that when King George got to him, he was very complimentary, and then he said, "*I* know what you did! *I* know how you got the film to go from black-and-white to color and back!" What Mickey had done was shoot the black-and-white scenes on color film and then print only one of three color matrices — you had to print all three to make it color. The King said, "That's how you slid back and forth, isn't it?" He was right, and he was terribly pleased with himself that he had figured it out!

Then when the film was released, all the critics laced into it, calling it an anti–British film! In the trial scene, Raymond Massey had all these marvelous things to say about America and terrible things to say about England, and Roger Livesey just sort of sat there quietly and once in a while said, "But you're wrong..." Roger won the battle, but because he didn't say enough, the critics all thought ultimately that Massey's character had won! It was crazy.

Why did they change the title to Stairway to Heaven *for U.S. release?*
    Jock Lawrence [head of the Rank Organisation in the U.S.] said, "You've

Hunter's finest hour on the screen was Elia Kazan's 1951 production of *A Streetcar Named Desire*. From bottom in this photo are Vivien Leigh, Marlon Brando, Hunter and Karl Malden.

got to change the title because nobody in the United States will come to a film with *Death* in its title." So it became *Stairway to Heaven*—this is the only country in the world where it's called that. Also we're the only country in the world that had various little cuts, like the little goatherd boy on the beach. He was perfectly decent *[laughs]*—the way he was sitting, you couldn't see his parts!—but no, no, you couldn't have any nudity in the United States.

The color in Life and Death *is very striking.*

Powell was relentless, he kept sending prints back to the lab until he got it exactly the way he wanted it. He was marvelous.

You also appeared in scenes for Powell & Pressburger's A Canterbury Tale.

They had already made that film, and they wanted to shoot a few new scenes and bring it up to date for release in the States. So they brought back [actor] John Sweet and they used me in those scenes as well. Mickey knew he was going to do it before he got me to London, because he had me shopping in New York for a hat and clothes and what-have-you for *Canterbury Tale*. I was just in the prologue and epilogue for American audiences.

In 1951 you starred with Claude Rains in an acclaimed play called Darkness at Noon.

That was fascinating, because Claude was a dear to work with, absolutely marvelous. He was so generous to the entire company of *Darkness at Noon,* because [writer/director] Sidney Kingsley—bless his heart—was a beast *[laughs]*! Sidney was terribly insecure about that particular play of his; I talked to him before we started rehearsals, and he was a perfectly reasonable, intelligent, gentle, nice man. Then we got into rehearsals! Because of the McCarthy idiocy during that period, he was terrified that people might think the play was slightly pro–Communist, so this beautiful play that he'd written he damn near ruined by insisting that everything be either black or white—no grays. And he'd written a lot of lovely grays, but didn't allow any of them to be on stage for fear that people would get the wrong impression. So he was very difficult during rehearsals. I think Claude and he had a lot of controversies and disagreements, but Claude kept them absolutely private so that the rest of the company was not involved in their fights. Whatever Sidney said during rehearsal, Claude just went ahead and did, and then had his fight with him afterwards, away from the company. Which was very generous of him, believe me, because everybody was so on edge.

Sidney was almost going to fire Claude—he was trying to find someone to replace him while we were in Philadelphia, but fortunately all the agents in town were on Claude's side and nobody that Sidney suggested was available at all! Claude finally opened, and Sidney was there every performance. Finally after one matinee Sidney came backstage to Claude's room and said, "You were marvelous this afternoon, Claude! Very, very good! What happened?" And Claude said, "Well, I just said to myself, 'Fuck Sidney Kingsley!'" Sidney's jaw dropped, and he didn't come back after that *[laughs]*!

You also had Jack Palance in Darkness at Noon.

Claude and Jack worked quite differently, and one time Claude asked Jack if he couldn't sort of do something like the same thing each performance, so that Claude at least would have some notion as to what to expect from him! Well, Jack was one of those people who on one side of his nature was the sweetest, gentlest person in the world and on the other side was really terrifying! He got into one of those moods, and after the curtain call he went after Claude. Claude was in his dressing room with the door locked, and Jack was pounding on it and screaming. Claude wouldn't leave until Jack finally gave up and left, because he thought Jack was going to kill him! Jack and I were in *Requiem for a Heavyweight* [on live TV] and the people there were really scared to death, because one scene called for him to hit Ed Wynn. Well, Jack was absolutely marvelous on that one—he faked it beautifully. But going into it *[shaking with terror]*, everybody was like *this!*

You once said that you got into the business to be an actress and not to be a star.

That's fully accurate, I think for a great number of us. Becoming a star wouldn't have bothered me, but what *is* a star? A star isn't anything. An actor *acts. That's* the important thing.

Why don't you collect your own films on video?

Generally I've seen my pictures once, and *[laughs]* I'm not a big one for repeating the experience! So why save them? They just take up space!

Do you even own A Streetcar Named Desire?

No. I've seen it enough *[laughs]*!

Do you remember what your initial reaction was when you were asked to play a chimpanzee in Planet of the Apes?

I was sent the script by my agent in California, and he wanted to know whether I'd be interested in his following through on it. I read it, I thought it was a damn good script and I said sure. But from reading the script I knew that we were all supposed to look like real apes, and I asked my agent how they were going to deal with this. He said, "Don't worry about that, 20th Century–Fox is a reputable firm. They'll find some way—put little bits of fur here and there." I didn't hear anything more for a while, and then I got a phone call from Fox, from somebody in casting, and he asked, "Miss Hunter, how tall are you?"—which I thought was a very peculiar question. I said, "Five-three and a half, why?" He said, "No, that's fine, thank you very much," and he hung up *[laughs]*! Then later I heard from my agent that the role was mine. Well, of course, I hadn't realized that all the apes had to be short and all the astronauts over six feet, and they wanted to make sure I wasn't going to be too tall!

Then came the shocker. The first call was to go out for a fitting, and all I could think of was costumes, right? *Wrong!* First they stuck me into a death mask or a life mask or whatever the hell it is, which was quite different from most of them. Usually you had straws in your nostrils, but we had a block of wood between our teeth. We had to breathe through our mouths because

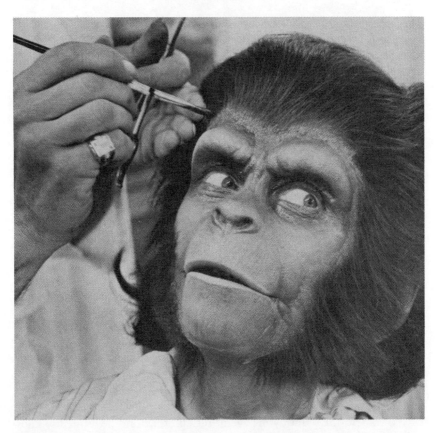

The price of movie stardom: a four-hour morning makeup session (and an hour and a half to remove it at night) to transform Hunter into Dr. Zira for *Planet of the Apes*.

everything else was covered—you'll notice in the film and in photographs that the lips of the apes never come together, because that was the only way we could breathe. The noses above were purely aesthetic, they had nothing to do with reality. Then [makeup man] John Chambers showed me some photographs of some of the testing they'd been doing, and what it would look like eventually. I thought to myself, "Oh, boy, what am I getting into?" But I came back again, and the next session was to do full testing with the appliances. The first time it took four and a half hours just to get the face on.

Did it take that long to put on the makeup every day you worked?
    During the filming they brought it down to three, three and a half, but that initial time took four and a half. Roddy McDowall and I were there and they found out our voices weren't coming through properly, so we were sent off to a sound studio and we worked on that until we finally figured out just where to place the voice so it wouldn't be nasal and fuzzy. Anyway, a short time later I

came back here to New York and I went to my doctor right away, and I said, "I need some help for this one, because this is going to be terrible. I need some kind of a tranquilizer for the makeup period, and then I have to be sharp as a tack once we start working." He gave me Valium, and that really was the only way I could get through it.

Did other ape actors have that problem?

It was just insane, for all of us. Psychological problems for everybody— everybody, without exception. We went through hell. I remember on the third one, *Escape from the Planet of the Apes,* Roddy and I were hugging dear Sal Mineo like crazy. Fortunately his character got killed right off so he wasn't in it all that long, but we'd hug him 'cause *[shaking violently]* he was like *this!* Just crazy, the whole time! Roddy and I both kept saying to the other apes, "Everything's fine, don't worry about it, you'll get used to it"—*nobody* got used to it, but we kept trying to reassure 'em. One of the gorillas came to me once and said, "My wife tells me that I've started talking in my sleep, and I've never done that before in my life!" One of the gorillas *[laughs]*!

Who was your day-to-day makeup artist?

We each had our own, and mine was Leo Lotito. After about three weeks I thought to myself, "Oh, come on, I don't need the Valium anymore," so this day I didn't take it before I sat in the makeup chair. And when we got to the set, Leo said, "You bloody well better take that pill from now on, or you get somebody else to do your makeup!" He practically had to hold me in the chair that morning, and he was a wreck!

How uncomfortable were you in that makeup, in that heat?

That was odd. In the heat we damn near died, and in the cold we nearly froze to death. It was no insulation one way or the other, which was very strange.

Did you really faint a number of times because of the makeup?

No, that was publicity. They had fans for us all over the place and they did their damnedest to help us all survive, but it was very hard, very difficult. We had to use straws for drinking, there was no other way, and for eating they brought in makeup tables and mirrors for everybody. [Producer] Art Jacobs provided us with lunch every day because we had to look into a mirror to eat, in order not to mess up the appliance. If you ruined it in any way, that was hours out of the shooting schedule to replace it! My mouth was a good inch or more behind the mouth of the makeup appliance.

And how long to take the makeup off at night?

Four hours to get it on in the morning and an hour and a half to take it off at night. Nobody said lightly, "You're through for the day"; they made

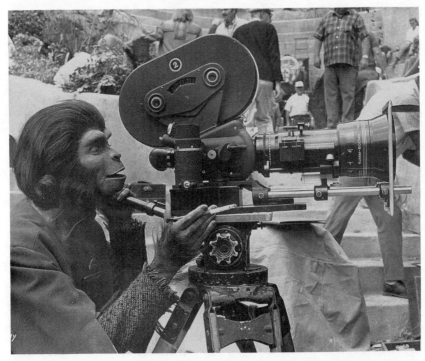

Taking a break between set-ups, Hunter monkeys with the camera on the set of *Beneath the Planet of the Apes.* Note the cigarette holder, required for smoking while in makeup.

damn sure you were through *[laughs]*! Our days were very long — mine started at four A.M. and I'd be lucky to get home by 9:30 at night. Leo and I had a little routine: He had his Scotch and I had my gin, through a straw, while he took off the makeup! One time Roddy pulled at the makeup to take it off — and it took his whole eyebrow off. But just to get it *off*...!

But you came back sequel after sequel.
    The second one *[Beneath the Planet of the Apes]* they had to talk me into — I mean, they *really* had to talk me into. They said, "Look, it's only ten days' work and it's continuity. Please!" Roddy didn't do the second one because the timing was bad for him, he was making a film in England and couldn't, so somebody else [David Watson] took over for him. But I said all right, and I came back. And *Escape*, the story was good enough for me to want to come back, even though I still had my reservations about the makeup! And I was very glad I got killed on the third one! Roddy went on and did the last two, playing his own son, but for me three was enough, thanks a lot.

Did you get a chance to rest at all during the day?

Yes, but that was dangerous, too. You had to lie on your back, absolutely flat, and one time I did fall asleep and I had the nightmare of my life. "It's happened," I said to myself. "I have *become* one!" I couldn't see down below, but I was sure that my legs and everything had become like an ape's! I told myself, "No more sleeping! None of that foolishness!" *[Laughs.]* I gave up eating, too, I didn't like looking at it anymore.

Were there discussions about how you would move and act playing an ape?
No, but Roddy and I both did our own research, he in the L.A. Zoo and me at the Bronx Zoo. I found a chimpanzee up at the Bronx Zoo who was the only chimp up there—they had orangutans and gorillas, but only the one chimp. Which was unfortunate, because he saw me watching him and it got him very angry! I kept trying to hide, I'd get behind groups of people that came into the ape building, but he'd spot me and turn his back *[laughs]*! I really felt badly, and, believe me, I understood exactly how he felt while we were shooting. We felt like *we* were in a zoo! We finally got Fox to stop bringing around visitors, because they'd come up and poke our faces with their fingers—they literally did that to us. I couldn't believe it!

What happened was that Roddy and I got together before we started shooting and exchanged our observances, and we kind of mushed around and figured out the best way to move and all of that. We were basing it on what we had seen real chimps do, but we also knew that we were playing *evolved* chimpanzees, which made it kind of crazy! We brought all of our thoughts to the director, Frank Schaffner, and he said, "Great, it's up to you, you guys figure it out." So we taught everybody else what to do. The one thing that Frank did tell us, something he found out after a few days of dailies, was that we had to keep those appliances moving. He said, "The minute you hold absolutely still, it looks like a mask." So that's why Roddy and I ended up twitching our noses a lot *[laughs]*, to keep them moving!

If audiences had found Planet of the Apes *funny, it would have been the Hollywood embarrassment of all time.*
John Chambers said, "We're either gonna be real or it's gonna be Mickey Mouse. And we won't know until it gets on the screen."

What do you remember about Apes *producer Arthur P. Jacobs?*
I had known Art for a long time because he was a publicity agent for years before he went into producing films—he was my publicity agent when I won my Oscar! So we'd known each other for a long time. Art was a good producer, very sweet and very generous to us—he brought all the straws on the set so we could drink, cigarette holders so we could smoke, food and so on. I think one of the reasons why we weren't allowed to go to the commissary was that they were afraid that no one else would go *[laughs]*—that no one could look at us and eat, too. It would have killed their appetite!

Did Rod Serling ever show up on the set?

Rod came by once, yes, and I even remember the scene — it was the court-room scene. Of course it wasn't his script anymore; he had done the original script, and then they reworked it into what we ended up with. I knew Rod from *Requiem for a Heavyweight* and from other television things I had done with him. I liked him.

What role was Edward G. Robinson supposed to play in Planet?

Dr. Zaius, the role Maurice Evans ended up playing. Robinson tested and then told his doctor what he had to do, and the doctor told him not to do it, that it would be very bad for his heart. But he would have been right for the role. There were others who were asked to be in *Planet of the Apes,* and then they got a load of the makeup and said no — I think Mickey Rooney was one. I think all the short people in Hollywood were approached *[laughs]*!

What kind of an army of makeup people did you have on that film?

At one point when we were out on the Fox Ranch, I think we had just about every makeup artist in Hollywood — there were something like 65 of them working for a few days. If the camera was far enough away, actors could wear overhead masks, but if it got at all close you could see the difference *[snap of the fingers]* like *that.* There was one section where the camera had to see a lot of different people — chimps and orangs and gorillas and such — and an incredible number of makeup artists had to come in. But even with just the few of us, our regular group, we not only had makeup trailers but the lab had an awful lot of people working because each day we had to have a new set of appliances. I suppose if they had used acetone to take the appliances off, they might have been able to save them from day to day, but acetone would have killed us so they had to use alcohol. So every day the appliances were new.

Where did you shoot Planet of the Apes?

At the Fox studio itself; the Fox Ranch; and Lake Powell, which is on the Arizona/Utah border. We were also at Point Dume, up above Malibu.

Any special memories of Charlton Heston?

Chuck was very dear — Roddy called him Charlie Hero. I remember we were up at Point Dume, which is where we shot the ending — the Statue of Liberty, the caves, all that stuff. We were out there quite a while, a good week or more; the first day we met at Fox, we were made up and then driven all the way out to Dume (over an hour driving). Then that night we had to be driven all the way back to Fox and the makeup taken off. That first day was just insane. Chuck was the one who said, "Look, you've got to do something for Roddy and Maurice and Kim," and so they got us a helicopter and took us back and forth that way from then on. That cut the time down considerably.

The picture of wedded bliss, time-travelers Hunter and Roddy McDowall are (temporarily) attuned to 20th century life in *Escape from the Planet of the Apes.*

Linda Harrison? Maurice Evans?

Linda Harrison later married Richard Zanuck, she was his first wife. She was a contract player at Fox at the time, I believe, and Zanuck was very interested in her, so we saw a lot of him — he wasn't part of the picture, but he'd hang around because of Linda. She was very pretty and very bright. And Maurice Evans *[laughs]*, I remember they had to keep taking his wig off all the time because he perspired so! They'd take it off and *[fanning the top of her head]* try to cool his head down! Fortunately, as an orangutan, he had a little less makeup than the rest of us, but he survived absolutely marvelously. We were a little worried, because of his age and everything else, but except for the heat he had no problems.

A lot of actors would probably insist on a stand-in whenever they could get away with it on a picture like that.

The only time I insisted on it was when we were all on horses, waiting for the blowing-up of the cave. I'm not that good a rider—I'm not an expert at all!—and I was terribly afraid I wouldn't be able to control the horse if it were bugged by the sound of the explosion. I said, "It's dumb to take a chance on that, since I don't know what I'm doing on a horse!" I just didn't think it made any sense for me to tackle that one, since we still had a few more scenes to do and they couldn't write me off. They got a guy to put on my makeup.

But that's you in the other riding scenes?

Yes, and it was tough. Our "ape feet" were much longer than our real feet, and they had "thumbs" jutting out to one side. So to put your foot in a stirrup was really silly. You could put the whole foot through, including the thumb, and then you could never get your foot out; or you could put only the toes in, and then it was floppy. There was no control at all.

How long were you on Planet of the Apes?

About three months. *Beneath* I was on longer than I expected because the weather was cockeyed and most of my stuff was outdoors. *Escape* was then cut short, of course—budgets change when you're making sequels, don't they *[laughs]*? That one only took a month or six weeks.

It posed a few heavy questions, but Escape *was the most light-hearted and charming of the* Apes *pictures.*

I liked that one. I mean, it wasn't any easier in terms of the makeup—in fact, it was very peculiar, because Roddy and I were the only chimps. Although the atmosphere on the set was very friendly and fun and all of that, Roddy and I both felt sort of out of it. John Randolph, an old, old friend of mine, was in it, and I grabbed him and asked, "Am I being paranoid or something?" He said, "The problem, Kim, is that I know in my head that underneath all that makeup it's you, but I can't keep that in my mind all the time!" For some reason the [human] actors tended to keep us at arm's length on that one *[laughs]*, because they couldn't quite ignore the barrier of the difference!

Did you think Beneath *and* Escape *were worthy sequels?*

I didn't think *Beneath* was, particularly; *Escape* I do, that was interesting. Then I saw the fourth one, *Conquest of the Planet of the Apes,* and I was *mezzo e mezzo* about it, so I never did see the fifth [*Battle for the Planet of the Apes*].

Would you have kept going with the series if you had been asked?

They asked me if I would do a guest shot on the TV series. And I said no, thank you. I was very glad I was killed off in the third!

Do you mind the fact that many fans remember you primarily for the Apes *series?*

No, I don't. The fan mail I get today, nine times out of ten relates to the *Apes* pictures.

You did a film called Dark August, *about a witch, that got little or no release.*

I think they tried to release it but couldn't—I heard that they released it in South America or someplace, and then I haven't the foggiest notion what ever happened to it. I don't think I ever saw it. It was about a guy who accidentally killed a child that ran out in front of his car. He was exonerated as far as the courts were concerned because of the nature of the accident, but the child's father never forgave him and put a curse on him. And the curse was working, so he had to find a "good" witch that would take the curse off of him. I was the witch and we had a séance to get rid of the curse. Well, we got rid of the curse all right, but I got killed in the process *[laughs]*!

Where was Dark August *made?*

We shot it all in Stowe, Vermont, and I do remember one thing about the shooting that was fascinating. Before they went up to Stowe, the director, Martin Goldman, had a pre-production meeting with a chap who was very knowledgeable about that sort of witchcraft business. Goldman said, "Let me tape-record this conversation that we're having, and the words that you use in describing the séance I can use in the script." Well, he had a whole tape from this man explaining the meanings of all the words and the whole rigmarole, Martin said goodbye to him, he went back to play the tape—and everything had been *erased!* So he brought him in again, and me at the same time, and had him go through it all a second time. This chap was very interesting—he said, "I do not know your schedule, but I suggest that you do not shoot this scene during the dark of the moon. Arrange your schedule so that you don't do that, because all the words that you'll be using are absolutely right—and you don't muck about with them!"

Well, the day that we went to shoot it, we were in an old barn that had been transformed into a house. It was a gorgeous day, absolutely beautiful when we started. We rehearsed and rehearsed because they were going to do the entire scene in a long shot before they came in for closeups. As the director called *action* for the take, there was *thunder* like you have never heard in your life, pouring-down *rain*—it went on throughout the entire scene! They did not say *cut*, fortunately, we went on and did the entire scene, and when the scene was over with, it all stopped! And there were some other little incidents that they mentioned—I wasn't involved in any of the others—when some very weird things happened. And then the film never got released. Well, maybe *it* had a curse on it, too *[laughs]*!

How about The Kindred, *with Rod Steiger?*

I know nothing about that, I've never seen it. I went out to L.A. for two days' shooting—I played a woman in a hospital bed—and left. Rod Steiger seemed to enjoy doing the picture, but it got such a bad review I wasn't eager to see it.

And your newest film is Two Evil Eyes, *a two-in-one Poe thriller.*

It's funny, but our director on that, Dario Argento, has a daughter who's living in this apartment building now—she just moved in a short while ago. The two directors, the Two Evil Eyes, are Argento and George Romero— Romero lives in Pittsburgh, but they brought Dario over from Italy and made the film in Pittsburgh. The segment I was in, along with Martin Balsam and Harvey Keitel, was *The Black Cat,* and I don't know how it turned out. All I know about Dario Argento is what I've been told, that the kinds of films that he makes are very bloody *[laughs]*! He brought his own cinematographer, and various others in the crew were his—some of them spoke English, some didn't. He speaks English a bit, but when he's working all the English words leave his head, so he has somebody around all the time to interpret. He would try to say what he wanted, but the way he worked you could tell that the camera angles and all of that were much more important to him than scenes.

So how did you get enticed into doing this one?

Oh, I just got asked if I would do it, and I said, "What the hell, yes." I think the reason Dario wanted me in particular was because he was a fan of Val Lewton, and he was very excited that I had been in *The Seventh Victim [laughs]*! That, I think, was the only reason he knew who the hell I was! All of it was done on location, and Martin Balsam and I play next-door neighbors who have a feeling something odd is going on in that house.

What do you think of newer horror films?

I don't go—I'm not sure I'm going to go see *Two Evil Eyes!* I don't like them that much, I don't really enjoy them. I get very nervous! I don't like gore particularly, and I don't like "scary."

Plans for the future?

Oh, I haven't the foggiest what they are. At this age, there aren't really that many roles, unless *Driving Miss Daisy* [1989] changes everything around *[laughs]* and they start writing for us again. But right now there aren't that many roles in films or television in general, although there still are bloody good roles in theater every now and then. When it comes to films, sometimes I do them simply because I want to work—I think that's true with *Two Evil Eyes,* 'cause I certainly had very little to do in it. I'm not retired, if that's what you're asking—not on purpose, anyway. I'm just unemployed *[laughs]*! I take it day by day.

KIM HUNTER FILMOGRAPHY

The Seventh Victim (RKO, 1943)
Tender Comrade (RKO, 1943)
When Strangers Marry (Betrayed) (Monogram, 1944)
You Came Along (Paramount, 1945)
Stairway to Heaven (A Matter of Life and Death) (Universal, 1946)
A Canterbury Tale (Eagle-Lion, 1949)
A Streetcar Named Desire (Warners, 1951)
Deadline U.S.A. (20th Century–Fox, 1952)
Anything Can Happen (Paramount, 1952)
Storm Center (Columbia, 1956)
The Young Stranger (Universal, 1957)
Bermuda Affair (DCA, 1957)
Money, Women and Guns (Universal, 1958)
Lilith (Columbia, 1964)
Planet of the Apes (20th Century–Fox, 1968)
The Swimmer (Columbia, 1968)
Beneath the Planet of the Apes (20th Century–Fox, 1970)
Escape from the Planet of the Apes (20th Century–Fox, 1971)
The Kindred (F/M Entertainment, 1987)
Two Evil Eyes (Taurus Entertainment, 1991)

Hunter's scenes were cut from *Jennifer on My Mind* (1971), although she can be spotted in some long shots. *Dark August* (1976) received no theatrical release in the U.S. Her 1979 TV movie *The Golden Gate Murders* received some theatrical play under the new title *Specter on the Bridge*.

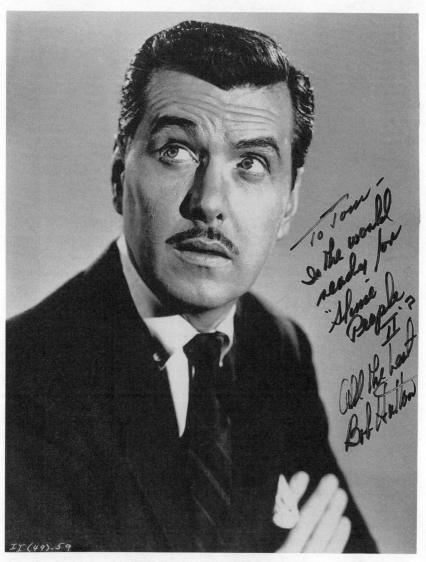

II (49) 59

When I went out to Hollywood
with a seven-year contract in my pocket
I never dreamed things would turn out the way they did.
The people I've met. The superstars I've worked with.
The friends I call true friends. My memories
of the Hollywood I knew are wonderful memories.

Robert Hutton

B FILMS SOMETIMES serve as a stepping stone for actors on their way up, but too often they're a refuge for players whose stars have slipped. A contract player at Warner Bros. in the declining days of the studio star system, Robert Hutton appeared in a string of Warners' 1940s productions and acted opposite many of the Burbank lot's top stars, but by the 1950s the B-movie mills had become his new stomping grounds. Bitterness, however, doesn't seem to be part of the Hutton vocabulary: Now a permanent resident at an upstate New York health facility, Hutton remains a man of enthusiastic perspectives and great personal charm, and he looks back with affection and candor on a film career that ran the gamut from A to Z, from *Destination Tokyo* and *Hollywood Canteen* to *Invisible Invaders* and *The Slime People.*

How did you become involved on The Man Without a Body?

I suppose, for money! W. Lee Wilder was Billy Wilder's older brother, and he was an interesting guy. I remember that we were in his office in Hollywood, and he told me about this picture *The Man Without a Body* that he was preparing to make in England. Willie offered me the lead by saying, "If you don't take the job, the hell with you, I'll get somebody else. It's as simple as that!" And he told me to make up my mind by six o'clock that night. He wasn't at all delicate about it; I was just another actor as far as he was concerned and I guess he felt we were a dime a dozen. A very cold-blooded type, but a nice guy; we had worked together previously on a picture called *The Big Bluff* [1955] with Martha Vickers, so *[laughs]* I guess he didn't hate me all that much! Well, I wanted to go to England, and there wasn't that much work going on in Hollywood, so I took the job. He gave me very little to live on in England, but he arranged for a beautiful London apartment for my wife, Bridget, and myself. And we saw England and had a lot of fun.

You had an illustrious co-star in George Coulouris.

He was a fine actor, and very nice to work with. I think he had been blacklisted in Hollywood, which is why he left and went to England. I knew him from Warner Bros., but of course his first really important picture was *Citizen Kane* [1941] with Orson Welles.

Did Coulouris seem pleased to be in a movie called The Man Without a Body?

Now, you see, over there in England it is completely different from Hollywood. Over here if you made a movie like that, they'd say, "The guy's washed up, he's finished." But over there the main thing is to *work.* They couldn't care less if the movie has a fifty-cent budget or a fifty-million-dollar budget, as long as you worked. That's why I enjoyed living there so much: You could play a lead one day and a cameo role the next, it made no difference whatsoever. There are dozens of English actors who worked that way.

Previous page: A contract player at Warner Bros. in the 1940s, Robert Hutton went on to star in no-frills SF flicks like *The Slime People, The Man Without a Body* and *Invisible Invaders* (pictured).

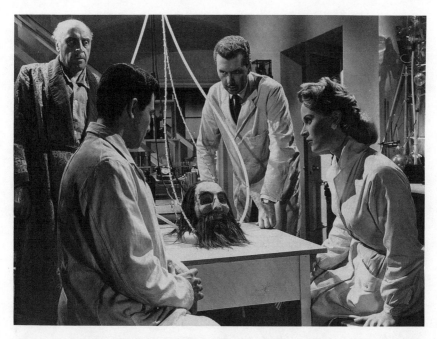

(Left–right): **George Coulouris, Sheldon Lawrence, Robert Hutton and Julia Arnall** manage to look quite serious in this scene from the risible *The Man Without a Body.* Poking up through a hole in the table is The Man (Michael Golden).

Why does The Man Without a Body *have a second director, Charles Saunders?*

In order to fulfill the quota requirements in England, there was a limit on the number of non–British resident personnel that could be employed on the picture. Charles was "in name only"; I remember him being on the set all the time, and not doing anything. To satisfy the union, they had to hire an English director because of the rules.

What did you think of the story of The Man Without a Body?

It was ridiculous — it was stupid, really stupid. And we felt stupid talking to that head — we would almost break up! The actor was underneath the table, with his head stuck up through a hole in the tabletop, and you felt like a damn fool talking to him.

What memories of The Colossus of New York?

To be quite honest with you, I had completely forgotten that I even made that movie until I saw it just recently on television. It was wonderful working with Otto Kruger — he was great, a fine actor. Except for that, it was not a very memorable experience *[laughs]*! I recall that Eugene Lourie was the director, but other than the simple fact that he was there, I don't have any recollections of him, either.

You're the third person I've interviewed that worked on The Colossus of New York, *and none of them remember the picture at all.*

On a movie like that, if you say the dialogue that they've written for you, or something rather close, they don't even care. The same thing, unfortunately, is also true of *Invisible Invaders;* that's another picture I really can't remember too much about. The thing I do remember about *Invaders* was a Jeep ride with John Agar—he damn near turned the thing over. We were doing a scene where we were driving up to the cave entrance in Bronson Canyon, and he made one turn where we went up on two wheels—he was a madman! But he was a very nice guy to work with, very quiet and very serious.

What do you think of horror and science fiction films in general?

I think there's a place for them, but not the ones they make today. They're well-made—my gosh, I can't believe the special effects—but they're too bloody, too gory, too much violence and killing. The kids, it must be so bad for them. As a kid, I went to see all the classics: *Frankenstein, Dracula, The Invisible Man,* all that stuff, and they were wonderful. They scared the daylights out of us *[laughs]* but they didn't give us nightmares or plant any crazy thoughts in our heads.

How did you become interested in being an actor?

Truthfully, I wanted to get away from my home town, Kingston, New York. It was a very quiet little town, and I was supposed to go into business with my father, who had a rather good business here. But one day I told him that I wanted to be an actor, and asked him if I could go to dramatic school.

Had you ever done anything in the way of acting?

No, nothing whatsoever. But I was a movie buff; I went to see every single movie that ever played in the area. And the life appealed to me. Beautiful girls, wine, women and song—I liked the whole idea! And my father said "Fine!" because he, too, was a big movie buff. I went to the Feagin School, in Rockefeller Center in New York. Some of their students were Angela Lansbury, Jeff Chandler, Susan Hayward—some pretty good names. I went there for two years, and after that I ended up at the Woodstock Playhouse, and did a season of stock. And during the summer I met two gals who kind of changed my life: They were Gloria Vanderbilt, Sr., and her twin sister, Thelma Furness. *Lady* Thelma Furness—she was married to Lord Furness, who owned the Furness Line, and she had been the mistress of the Prince of Wales [the future King Edward VIII]. They befriended me, and every free moment I had I would spend with them and listen to stories about another lifestyle, one that completely fascinated me. They suggested that I go to Hollywood, that I couldn't miss. My father agreed to sponsor me out there for one year, and so I drove to Hollywood to "knock 'em dead." I spent a year, and nothing happened. So I came back, and did another season of stock.

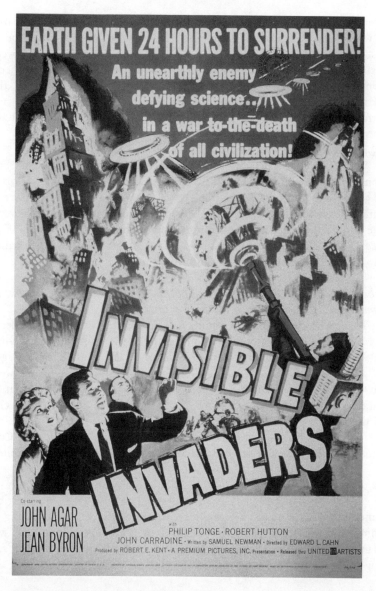

Hutton remembers little about *Invisible Invaders* except that John Agar nearly turned a Jeep over during a wild ride.

So how did you end up back in Hollywood?

My mother and father divorced, and I went from being a rich kid to a kid without a nickel to call his own. It was do-or-die, so I went to Manhattan and walked into the Louis Shurr Agency, which was the biggest at the time. They asked me, "What the hell do you want?" and I said, "I want to go to Hollywood, to get into the movies." And they said, "Give us two weeks." They got me a test with Paramount in New York, and I made what I'm sure had to be the worst test ever filmed. But Paramount wanted to sign me, for $200 a week, which to me was a magnificent sum. I wanted it, but the agent turned it down—which convinced me that he was crazy. Then, out on the Coast, they took the test over from Paramount to Warner Bros., and Warners gave me a contract for $250 a week. I went out with the contract, and that was that.

You were gone from Warner Bros. by the end of the '40s.

Warner Bros. actually got rid of all their contract people; people like Errol Flynn left, and so did Bette Davis. By the way, when Bette Davis left, nobody said goodbye to her, not a soul—that's a well-known story. I felt that the time for me to leave was then. Also, I had been offered a starring role with Franchot Tone and Charles Laughton and Burgess Meredith in *The Man on the Eiffel Tower* [1949]. I accepted it for less money than I should have got, but I wanted to go to Paris, which is where the film was made.

In the '50s, after you left Warners and got into a low-budget rut, you put the blame on an agent who stuck too high a price on you.

That's when television was coming in, and everybody was scared to death. All I wanted to do was work; I thought that was the most important thing. And, yes, after I got back from doing *The Man on the Eiffel Tower,* my agent was asking way too much money for me. Consequently I didn't work. Something else that hurt was the fact that I was very outspoken about my politics. I'm a Republican, and a very conservative one—always have been—and there was a period when I had a hell of a time getting a job because of that. The leftists had made real inroads into Hollywood, I was very anti–Communist, they knew about my feelings and I didn't work for quite a while.

Sort of a reverse blacklist.

Yes, it *was* a reverse blacklist. Those were bad days—they were terrible. I remember I was at a party one night at Ann Rutherford's, I was playing gin rummy, and directly in back of me, talking the way we're talking now, were two guys talking to Larry Parks, saying, "Larry, come on, join the party, it's the thing to do." And he joined the Communist party that night.

Did you like working with Jerry Lewis in the fantasy CinderFella?

CinderFella was a great experience from beginning to end. I got the part because I happened to go over to Paramount as a visitor to see Bobby Darin make a test. He was doing "Mack the Knife," and I was on the stage with some friends. Jerry came on with a pair of scissors, and he went around cutting everybody's necktie off *[laughs]*! He saw me—we had known one another since the Dean Martin days—and he didn't cut my tie; instead he took me by the arm and said, "You're just the guy I want to see." He took me back to his office,

Taking five at Bronson Canyon, Hutton, Philip Tonge and Jean Byron get ready for their next clash with the *Invisible Invaders*.

set me down and said that he was going to make the story of *CinderFella* — Cinderella in reverse. He had Dame Judith Anderson, Anna Maria Alberghetti, Ed Wynn, and he wanted me to play one of the stepbrothers. He said, "No agent involved, you just decide here and now, you don't read the script." Then, as far as money was concerned, he said, "You write down what you want — ten-week guarantee — and I'll write down what I'm going to give you. It could be more, maybe it could be less." I wrote down what I thought was a very fair amount, we exchanged these little pieces of paper, and his figure was double what I had written down! So we shook hands and that was it, right then and there. But that's what it was like to work with him, it was wonderful.

How did The Slime People *come about?*

A promoter by the name of Joe Robertson found some people who ran a string of launderettes, and got them to put up some money to make *The Slime People*. Joe and his wife had written the screenplay, but they wrote under made-up names ["Blair Robertson and Vance Skarstedt"] because they didn't want the credit — and I don't blame them! They needed a director and he knew that I was very anxious to direct — so anxious that I would do it for practically nothing.

The Slime People was a lot of fun to make — oh, we had a *ball*! We had a very, very low budget, but I'd always wanted to direct a movie and they gave me the opportunity. We only could afford to have two outfits made for the

**Bob Miles, Hutton's stunt double, gets tossed around by Slime Person Robert Herron.
The ultra-cheap *Slime People* was Hutton's first fling at directing.**

Slime People, and they were supposed to take over the world in the movie! We
had a drunk in the slime outfit, we had anything that could move! But it was
fun, and it made money, so that's all that really mattered.

Were you satisfied with the job you did as director?

I found out that directing was not that simple a job. There were a lot of
things I didn't know, and I don't think I'd ever want to do it again. But I did
it, and I had fun. And I did, I suppose, as much as anybody could do with
the amount of money we had—which was nothing!

How much is nothing?

I think our budget was $56,000, which *was* nothing, even back then! I
knew that I was in way over my head and I tried to fake it. In making the movie
I went to all my friends, because we couldn't afford to pay any kind of salaries.
We borrowed an office on Hollywood Boulevard to cast the female lead, and
the first girl who came in was Susan Hart. She had a sweater on and she looked

good, and I didn't ask her to read or anything; I said, "You've got the part!" And that was it! She was attractive, and I knew she was going to photograph well. Susan Hart did all right for us, and she went on to do some pretty good work; she later married one of the heads of AIP, Jim Nicholson. I got Les Tremayne because he was a friend — I said, "Please help me, this is my first chance as a director" — and we paid him scale. He helped me a lot.

Richard Arlen was originally going to play the professor. He was an old friend, and he had been having a real tough time — I think he had a drinking problem, and he hadn't worked regular for quite a while. He was doing this as sort of a favor to me, and I very badly wanted him to do it because he was a big star of yesteryear and that would have been good for the picture. At eleven o'clock the night before we started shooting, as I was going to bed, the phone rang, and it was a nurse from the hospital saying, "Mr. Hutton, we've got Mr. Arlen here and he's a very sick man. He wanted me to call and say he can't do your picture." So I got on the phone and called Robert Burton, asked him if he could take over the role and start work in the morning, and he said, yes, he could. He was a fine actor, too; he worked like a dog on the thing. He died shortly thereafter of a heart attack, and I felt very bad about that; he was a nice man. So we had good actors, even if it wasn't a very good movie.

Where did you dig up William Boyce, who played the young marine?

He didn't know anything about motion pictures. I think Joe Robertson found him walking down the street one day, asked him if he wanted to be in movies, the guy said yeah and that was it.

The film is listed as a Hutton — Robertson Production. Does that mean you had money in the movie?

Oh, no. Joe and I simply formed our own company to make it. We had great plans — we were going to go on, and make a lot of movies, but *[laughs]* it didn't pan out that way! And Robertson was completely crazy, like a little boy. He was producing a movie and he was as happy as I was directing. I remember driving down with him to pick up the monster costumes — the wolf's head masks and also the Slime People's outfits — which had been made in New York. He had them in his car and I was driving mine. And on the way back I stopped at a stoplight and looked over, and the damn fool had the head of the wolf on, and he was growling at me from his car *[laughs]*!

What's this about wolf's head masks?

That was something that they cut out of the movie. It was really the mask of a vole, which is some sort of burrowing rodent. I think the voles belonged to the Slime People, and they were brought along by them — for what reason, I don't know! We didn't do too much research on that movie; the only research involved was what manhole could these Slime Men come up out of without any traffic around?

Right around this time they had one of their yearly fires in Bel-Air, and some very beautiful mansions were destroyed—Burt Lancaster lost his home, Zsa Zsa Gabor, people like that. Joe called me and said, "Listen, I'll get a police pass and a 'wild' camera, we'll go up there, shoot the whole thing and use the scene in the movie." And we did. Thank God for that fire *[laughs]*!

Where else did you go on Slime People?

The airport scenes were shot at Van Nuys Airport. The TV station was KTTV—we got in because we knew somebody there. The butcher's shop was up in Lancaster, California, and *[laughs]* it belonged to my father-in-law! He said, sure, we could use the place, but he refused to shut off the refrigeration and we nearly froze to death in that scene in the meat locker. Man, that was cold! That was the scene where the voles came in—we hired a couple of midgets to put on these vole costumes, and had them jumping down from the ceiling onto people in the market. And my father-in-law didn't want to close the shop! We had paid him, but he didn't see the sense in closing up and losing business. So he didn't stop customers from coming in, and we frightened the daylights out of them for a while!

Were your Slime People costumes expensive?

Yes, they cost a lot of money; they ran us three or four thousand dollars, and that was a big chunk out of $56,000. I think we had two complete outfits, and then also those vole heads. Those costumes were pretty good—I mean, they were as good as any you'd find in that type of movie. I think they used too much fog in a lot of scenes, but on the other hand, that fog covered up a lot of sins, a lot of mistakes. We had fog machines going all the time and, like I said, a few times they laid it on a little too thick and you couldn't see anything—no scenery, no actors, nothing but fog.

Why does the second unit director, William Martin, get such a prominent credit?

After I had finished with the picture, Joe said they had to go back to do some added scenes and that William Martin was going to direct them, and would I share billing with him? I had a contract with Joe which stated that I was to get sole director's credit, and I insisted upon it. So that must be why he gets such a prominent credit.

I was told that you were never paid for directing and starring in The Slime People.

I didn't even get the first week's salary.

I talked to two of the stuntmen who played Slime Men [Robert Herron and Fred Stromsoe], and if it makes you feel any better, they weren't paid, either.

It does — makes me feel a *lot* better *[laughs]*! The man who played the monster the most often was a friend of Joe Robertson's, and he was drunk the whole time. And he was very good as a Slime Man, because he stumbled around and it looked real good! He also had a couple of bucks in the picture.

The Slime People *came out through a small outfit called Hansen Enterprises.*

Donald Hansen was the man who owned the launderettes. I think I brought that film in for $51,000 or $52,000, and what little money was left I would imagine they used for advertising. It took three weeks to shoot.

When did you move to England, and why?

My brother-in-law and I were together one night playing cards, and then all of a sudden, late at night, we started talking about making a movie and wouldn't-it-be-fun? And slowly it all came together and we co-produced this picture [*The Secret Door,* 1964]. We shot in Lisbon — I had already made one movie in Portugal, I liked the country and the people very much, and so I chose Portugal as our location. After shooting the picture we had to go up to London to do the scoring and editing and so forth, and while I was there I was offered quite a bit of work. And so I stayed on.

How did you get involved on The Vulture?

Jack Lamont was a producer I knew from Hollywood, and he asked me if I'd like to play the lead in *The Vulture* — it was that simple. English agents didn't make the rounds of the studios like American agents did. They waited for the phone to ring and for the producer to call them, rather than going out and seeking jobs for the actor, as I was used to. So most of the negotiating was done by me, with Jack Lamont — salary and all that. Also, I wanted to work with Akim Tamiroff, and Brod Crawford was an old friend of mine — we'd had the same agent in Hollywood and I'd known him for years and years.

In the movie Brod had a cane with a wolf's head on it, very highly polished. And I remember I had a long speech by a fireplace and he had to just sit there and listen to me go on and on. During rehearsal he played with that wolf's head and twisted it around and made it reflect the light. Stealing the scene. And I thought, "Now, that's not right, not while I'm talking — I've got a long speech here!" So just before we got to the actual take, I said, "Brod, are you going to play with that wolf's head, like you did in rehearsal?" And he said *[laughs]*, "No, I was just trying you out." He was a wonderful guy.

And how about Tamiroff?

He was just beautiful — such a fabulous actor! To be working with people like that was an honor. This may sound stupid, but sometimes I didn't think about money or anything like that; it was just fun to work and to know those people.

How did Akim Tamiroff feel dressing up in a vulture costume?
Stupid *[laughs]*! But he never argued, never complained. Again, you see—he was *working*. And he was really into the thing.

The Vulture really is the pits, probably the worst sci-fi thing you did.
The idea wasn't bad, but I think this was one film where they needed more horror. They talked about the Vulture all the time but you hardly ever saw the damn thing. It called for less talk and more horror. But, of course, that would cost money, and talk doesn't cost as much. I think *The Vulture* took five or six weeks; we even went out on location, down to Devon and Cornwall.

Were the people who made films like these open to suggestions, or were they only interested in getting the thing in the can?
I can tell you a story that I think will answer your question. In *The Vulture* there was a left-to-right move that I had to do that didn't make any sense to me. I asked the director, Lawrence Huntington, "Laurie, why do you want me to do this?" and he got all flustered! I said, "I don't want motivation or anything like that, just why do you want me to move there?" And he took me aside and said, "Bobby, please just do it. I don't care if it doesn't make sense, just do it." Laurie didn't care and Jack Lamont, who was also on the set, *he* didn't care, so I did it. And that's it. Why? Because it said in the script that the character moves from left to right at that point, and they just wanted to get the thing on film and forget it.

About this time you landed a small part in You Only Live Twice.
That was fun. [Producer] "Cubby" Broccoli and I kind of grew up together in Hollywood; there was a point where Cubby wasn't doing very much of anything, and he bought all of Ian Fleming's works. He got on the phone and called a whole bunch of people one day, just to say, "Hey, listen, you know what I did?"—and people in Hollywood laughed at him! Later, of course, the James Bond films caught on, which was wonderful for Cubby. And when I was over in England, I used to visit the sets a lot—they would take over the biggest stage at Pinewood and do miraculous things. One day I was there talking to some of the production people when I happened to say, "Boy, I'd love to be in a James Bond sometime," and they said, "You're in it right now!" They sent me to wardrobe, put me in a general's outfit and there I was! It was as simple as that.

Your next science fiction film was They Came from Beyond Space.
What I remember best about that picture was Freddie Francis, one of the nicest guys in the whole world, and a good director. He came to me, out to

Hutton *(second from left)* pals around with fellow cast members Jennifer Jayne and Michael Gough between takes of *They Came from Beyond Space.*

my home, said he was going to make the movie, gave me the script and asked me if I'd like to do it. We got along fine and became very good friends. We shot at Pinewood in Twickingham, that magnificent studio where some of the Bonds were done.

Sounds like you enjoyed the experience.

Yes, and also the film itself. A lot of the *Movies on TV*-style books call it a bomb, but I don't think it was bad. I know that it was selected by some group of scientists in America as one of the better science fiction movies, and they said this *could* happen. I also enjoyed working with Michael Gough, who was a good actor and a fine guy.

The picture reminded me quite a bit of Invisible Invaders.

That's right—aliens coming down from the moon, and dead bodies coming back to life. But *They Came from Beyond Space* was done a bit better; in fact, I thought it was done very well. One thing I could never understand was why my character drove that old car. I know I asked Freddie why, and he gave me an answer and it seemed reasonable at the time, but looking back now I still don't understand how I ended up with that miserable heap!

You worked with Freddie Francis again on Torture Garden.

Yes, that was Freddie again. Amicus made a specialty out of that sort of anthology horror film, but I think they're confusing, and I didn't care for them. You become involved in one story, and suddenly it's over and you're into another. And it takes a bit of time to build up interest again. Now, *Dead of Night* was a classic, just great, especially the episode with Michael Redgrave as the ventriloquist — that was scary. That apparently was the film Amicus was copying, but they didn't do as good a job. I later did another horror anthology film called *Tales from the Crypt,* but it was a very small part and I just don't remember it at all.

Most of your Torture Garden *scenes were with Beverly Adams.*

She was very nice, but she was a terrible actress. I know that when we did the scene where we disclose the fact that I'm made of steel, she had an awful time — she couldn't hit me or do any of the things she was supposed to do. But she was very, very beautiful, and a delightful person.

You got special "and" billing in Cry of the Banshee *but not a very good part.*

I had known Vincent Price for years and years but I had never worked with him*, so that's why I did it. It was shot at Grim's Dyke, which was the house that belonged to W.S. Gilbert of Gilbert and Sullivan fame. We were there in the dead of winter, and it was cold because they didn't have any heating! *Cry of the Banshee* was Vincent's 100th movie, and after shooting they gave a big party for him in the house. And they had a girl come out of a cake — a nude girl. This was another first for me, I had never seen that before. The poor thing was freezing to death, naked as a jaybird, and Vincent was very embarrassed because that isn't his cup of tea. A nude coming out of a cake, that isn't Vincent Price, not at all.

How about working with Joan Crawford on Trog?

I did that film because she asked me to; I lived right around the corner from Bray Studio, which is where *Trog* was shot. Joan and I were old, old friends from Warners, and to see her working on a picture like *Trog* was very, very sad. But, by golly, she worked hard and she gave it her all.

Joan couldn't stand the heat, and they didn't have air conditioning at Bray. So she had electric fans all over her dressing room, and she carried a little hand fan when she went on the set. I wasn't working one day, and I went over just to see her and talk about old times. I was in her dressing room waiting for

---

*Hutton and Price both appeared in *Casanova's Big Night* (1954), but not together.

her, because she was on the stage. She came in and she had a flowing dress on, a full skirt, and she sat down and complained about the heat. And she lifted up her skirt so that the fans could blow some fresh air, and a moth flew out. She roared with laughter, looked at me and said, "My God, it's been so long it's got moths in it!" *[Laughs.]*

Did you ever get to see Trog?

No. I don't think I'd want to see her in something like that; I'd rather remember her for *Mildred Pierce* [1945] and *What Ever Happened to Baby Jane?* and pictures like that.

A few years later you wrote a horror film called Persecution. *How did you come up with the idea for that?*

I don't like cats, and I came up with this idea about a cat that could destroy a family. The original title was *I Hate You, Cat,* which I thought was a much better title than *Persecution.* Everyone who read the script thought it was good. I sent it to Bette Davis, who complimented me on it, but she said that the lead character was *so* bad, *such* a horrible woman that she didn't dare play it, although she would like to. And she suggested other people.

I gave Freddie Francis a copy of the script. And from what I understand his son Kevin came over one night, picked it up, took it home and decided it was a good movie to break into the motion picture business with, as a producer. I must admit he did it—he went out and raised the money—but still I say he received the money on the basis of the script.

Did you like Kevin Francis?

I liked him, yes, but he was kind of a devious little fellow and I like him less now because of what he did, or what he allowed to be done. I wish you could see the original script. It was a great script, and they changed the whole thing. I figure if Lana Turner decided to do it, and Trevor Howard, who was a damn good actor, if the people who are in it decided to do it on the basis of my original script, it must have been pretty good. But then, you know what happens, "I want to change this" and "I want to change that," and all of a sudden they changed everything. I have both scripts, my original and the shooting script, and it's like day and night. What they did to it broke my heart.

The one thing the movie has going for it is the Lana Turner name.

Lana and I used to go together, but once we broke up we didn't see or speak to each other from about 1946 'til when they made *Persecution.* I didn't know that they hired her, I had nothing to do with that; by the time they got around to shooting *Persecution,* I was making a movie down in Madrid. I thought the thing to do was to phone Lana at the Dorchester in London, to wish her well on the movie, and so I made the call. I got through to her suite and I heard them say, "Miss Turner, Mr. Hutton's calling from Madrid." And she wouldn't speak to me. Maybe because of what was happening—I know that she didn't like Kevin Francis at all, and she didn't like the fact that he had never done anything before. I didn't hear from her until 1985, when she found out I was here and sent me a lovely letter—but never mentioned anything about *Persecution!*

In 1975 she publicly called it a bomb.
    I don't blame her!

Have you ever seen the movie?
    No. Some friends of mine saw it down in Sarasota, Florida, and they said it was all they could do not to walk out. Because they were friends, they stayed. It opened and closed the same night in that theater.

Reviewing Persecution, *Rex Reed wrote about director Don Chaffey, "Lock that name in a steel box, drop it overboard 200 miles out to sea and never mention it again."*
    I wish that Freddie Francis had directed *I Hate You, Cat*—he wanted to, he thought it was an excellent script, but his son got involved. Why Kevin didn't hire his father to direct it, I'll never know. Freddie would have made a doggone good movie out of it, I guarantee you—he would have shot what I wrote. And Lana Turner wouldn't be ashamed of it. And the whole world would be a different place today *[laughs]*!

What made you decide to come home to the United States?
    In 1972 I thought it was about time to come back to Hollywood, and on the way back I wanted to stop off in Kingston because I knew my mother and my aunt were not well. And I found out that they were much more *un*-well than I realized, or had been told. I figured that I just couldn't leave, and so I stayed on here. And then I broke my back. I was in the hospital here in Kingston for nine months, on my back, couldn't move—and had a *ball*!

Really!
    I did, I had a ball—it was a great experience! Everybody was so kind to me. And then they sent me to New York to have a real delicate operation which would allow me to sit up, and I was down there for five months. After that I needed complete rehabilitation and therapy, and they told me, "You can go to the Helen Hayes Institute, or a place up by Schenectady, or, there's a brand new place up in Kingston called the Health Related." I said, "The Health Related!"

What do you do to pass the time here?
    I wrote a book since I've been here, about Hollywood, about what it was like. I think every publishing house in New York has read it, and every one

turned it down with the same comment. That it was charming, delightful, wonderful reading. But nobody would buy it. And when I asked why, they said, "Because you *liked* everybody." Because I don't have anything rotten to say about anybody! I do know "provocative" stories about people that haven't been told—stories that involve big names that I was fortunate enough to call my friends—but I don't think it's right to divulge stories like that, and I'm not going to rewrite the book. Unh-uh. No way.

Y'know, it's strange. When I went out to Hollywood with a seven-year contract in my pocket I never dreamed things would turn out the way they did. The people I've met. The superstars I've worked with. The friends I call true friends. My memories of the Hollywood I knew are wonderful memories.

ROBERT HUTTON FILMOGRAPHY

Northern Pursuit (Warners, 1943)
Destination Tokyo (Warners, 1943)
Janie (Warners, 1944)
Hollywood Canteen (Warners, 1944)
Roughly Speaking (Warners, 1945)
Too Young to Know (Warners, 1945)
One More Tomorrow (Warners, 1946)
Janie Gets Married (Warners, 1946)
Time Out of Mind (Universal, 1947)
So You Want to Be in Pictures (Warners short, 1947)
Love and Learn (Warners, 1947)
Always Together (Warners, 1948)
Wallflower (Warners, 1948)
Smart Girls Don't Talk (Warners, 1948)
The Younger Brothers (Warners, 1949)
The Man on the Eiffel Tower (RKO, 1949)
And Baby Makes Three (Columbia, 1949)
Beauty on Parade (Columbia, 1950)
Slaughter Trail (RKO, 1951)
New Mexico (United Artists, 1951)
The Racket (RKO, 1951)
The Steel Helmet (Lippert, 1951)
Tropical Heat Wave (Republic, 1952)
Gobs and Gals (Republic, 1952)
Paris Model (Columbia, 1953)
Three Chairs for Betty (RKO short, 1953)
Half-Dressed for Dinner (RKO short, 1953)
Casanova's Big Night (Paramount, 1954)
The Big Bluff (United Artists, 1955)
Yaqui Drums (Allied Artists, 1956)
Scandal, Inc. (Republic, 1956)
Thunder Over Tangier (Man from Tangier) (Republic, 1957)
Showdown at Boot Hill (20th Century–Fox, 1958)
The Colossus of New York (Paramount, 1958)

Outcasts of the City (Republic, 1958)
The Man Without a Body (Budd Rogers, 1959)
It Started with a Kiss (MGM, 1959)
Invisible Invaders (United Artists, 1959)
Jailbreakers (AIP, 1960)
CinderFella (Paramount, 1960)
Wild Youth (Naked Youth) (Cinema Associates, 1961)
The Slime People (Hansen Enterprises, 1963) Also directed
The Secret Door (Now It Can Be Told) (Allied Artists, 1964) Also Associate Producer
The Sicilians (Butcher's Films, 1964)
Los Novios de Marisol (Marisol's Boy Friends) (Spanish, 1965)
Busqueme A Esa Chica (Find Me That Girl) (Spanish, 1965)
Finders Keepers (United Artists, 1967)
Carnaby, M.D. (Doctor in Clover) (Continental Distributing, Inc., 1967)
The Vulture (Paramount, 1967)
You Only Live Twice (United Artists, 1967)
They Came from Beyond Space (Embassy, 1967)
Torture Garden (Columbia, 1968)
Can Heironymus Merkin Ever Forget Mercy Humppe and Find True Happiness?
   (Regional Film Distributors, 1969)
Cry of the Banshee (AIP, 1970)
Trog (Warners, 1970)
Tales from the Crypt (CRC, 1972)
Persecution (Fanfare, 1974) Co-wrote story and screenplay
It Came from Hollywood (Paramount, 1982) Clips from *The Slime People*

. . . I don't think there's one film that I can point to
that really represents what I might have done. And consequently
there's not one film or role that I look at of which I'm proud,
nor one which I would recommend to anyone to see.
It's a very sad statement, isn't it?

Nancy Kovack

THE CALENDAR says it's been more than 20 years since she worked in pictures, but—impossibly—Nancy Mehta looks every bit as chic and lovely as she did when (as Nancy Kovack) she stepped off the set of her last film, *Marooned,* in 1969.

A native of Flint, Michigan, Kovack was a student at the University of Michigan at fifteen, a radio deejay at sixteen, a college graduate at nineteen and the holder of eight beauty titles by twenty. Her professional acting career began on TV in New York, first as one of Jackie Gleason's Glea Girls and then, more prominently, on *The Dave Garroway Show, The Today Show* and *Beat the Clock.* A stage role opened Hollywood doors for Kovack, who signed with Columbia Pictures and played in such studio films as *Strangers When We Meet* (1960), *Cry for Happy* (1961) and *The Great Sioux Massacre* (1965) as well as in Paramount's *Sylvia* (1965), UA's *Frankie and Johnny* (1966) and an imposing list of episodic TV credits (she was Emmy-nominated for a 1969 guest shot on *Mannix*). Her best-remembered role came early on in her career, however, as the alluring high priestess Medea in Columbia's landmark stop-motion adventure *Jason and the Argonauts* in 1962. Now she's the first lady of music, happily and busily married to world-renowned maestro Zubin Mehta of New York Philharmonic fame.

Do you recall how you became involved on Jason and the Argonauts?

Being a Columbia contractee, we just did what we were told. But I was very happy to go abroad at that time—I was very young. *Jason and the Argonauts* was shot at the exact place in Italy where the legend was set. For instance, when our *Argonaut* sailed around a certain cape, the real one had in fact sailed around that very same cape.

Did you enjoy working in Italy?

Oh, I loved it. We were there a long time, as I recall, longer than we expected to be, and I've had a very warm place in my heart for that part of Italy. It's like a second home. We were there for something like four months.

Do you remember meeting the producers, Charles Schneer and Ray Harryhausen?

Charles Schneer, yes, I knew him well and I thought he was wonderful. He was a civil man, congenial and humorous. I enjoyed his wife—she was there—and I think his children were there, too. It was a very family-like situation. And Ray Harryhausen was on the set constantly. A very dignified, noble, quiet, "still" man—I appreciated that, and had a great respect for him. A very gentle man as well. And the special effects which he added to the film were phenomenal—I don't even have to say that. For that period, they were unique, were they not?

How did you prepare for your dance scene in Jason?

Previous page: One of Nancy Kovack's better roles during her five-year stint at Columbia was as the high priestess in the fantasy adventure *Jason and the Argonauts.*

In *Jason and the Argonauts,* Kovack (as Medea) joined flash-in-the-pan actor Todd Armstrong in his quest for the Golden Fleece.

Charles Schneer sent me to Rome a week ahead of time to learn this so-called dance. But it wasn't structured very well; in other words, I wasn't given much instruction in it, and I thought it was a little weak. And I also thought, at the time and in retrospect, that it was meant to be suggestive and erotic, etc., and *[disapprovingly]* I find that's a great form of titillation in films. And that's all I have to say about that . . . !

Any other Jason *anecdotes?*

It used to be very cold in the morning, and we'd have to get up at four A.M. sometimes in order to be ready for a six A.M. sunrise. We were in the village of Palinuro, in the shin of Italy. It was freezing, and I had a purple sweater that was very warm. And I was told that I couldn't wear the sweater, because the color purple was offensive to the people of the village! Purple meant death, and I was asked not to wear it. I said, "But I love this sweater!" It was all I had, and we had no access to other clothing, etc. I also remember staying long times on that ship, because the shooting was very difficult. I can't say why particularly, but shooting took a long time. But in general I just remember a great deal of warmth from everyone involved and from the Palinuro people.

Any recollections of Todd Armstrong [Jason]?

He was a nice boy, the son of someone who was a friend of someone at Columbia—as I understand it, that's how he was given this part. He found it phenomenal that I learned a little Italian before I went there. He was always frustrated and seemed sometimes disturbed, I don't know why. He was reactionary. And subsequent to that I understand he left the business, and I don't know what he's doing now.

What do you think of the picture?

I think it's a fine record for the legend, and I think that is important. I also feel that it's important for young people to see these things as opposed to other things that we may be seeing today. I do feel that society is deteriorating because of many of the effects of films.

How did you get interested in becoming an actress?

I came to New York City for the wedding of a friend. I was to be here for two days, and a girlfriend asked me if I wanted to go on a cattle call. I didn't know what that was. She explained that Jackie Gleason was having a cattle call, and that I should go. So I went, and I became one of the Glea Girls. And that's how it began. Also I did Broadway—*The Disenchanted,* with Jason Robards, Jr. From the Broadway show I was signed by Columbia Pictures.

Early on, what kind of roles did you think you were going to play in films?

Harry Cohn, who was the head of Columbia when I was signed, felt that I was a replacement for Rita Hayworth—my hair at that time was darker and slightly red. But he died, even before I got to Columbia. So those areas never came about. I had really, desperately hoped to play some serious roles. They never came my way. That was before this feminism crept into the industry. There are many roles now for women that are serious and very realistic, instead of paper doll cutouts. I'm sorry to have missed this period.

You next appeared in a Vincent Price picture, Diary of a Madman, *for United Artists.*

I must have been loaned out for that, because I couldn't do anything other than what Columbia agreed to. I enjoyed working with Vincent Price on *Diary of a Madman;* he was very respectful and I found that unusual. I knew that I wasn't known, and yet he was very respectful of me and kindly—he didn't have to be. He was professional, and I appreciated that. I remember that just before the scene where he kills me with the knife, Vincent Price was tickling me and I was laughing, and I couldn't stop laughing after that!

Did you pose for the painting, sketches and bust of you that are seen in the film?

No, I think they took a photograph and used that to do the painting and

Sculptor Vincent Price wants just the right look from model Kovack in the dismal *Diary of a Madman*.

the bust. I still have the painting; I think the busts were broken in the picture.

You had a director from the old school in Reginald LeBorg.

I had great empathy for him and sympathy for him. He was a good director, a fine director, and I respected him highly. Subsequent to that he didn't do much in the way of films and he wanted to, and I felt very badly about that.

Diary of a Madman *really wasn't much of a picture.*

I think these are all kind of "light" pictures, and they didn't get heavier with time *[laughs]*! I was very happy to be working. I don't know if you know the debilitating feeling of being under contract and not working. You're not permitted to work anywhere else, and you're really their puppet. And if you're not working, it's so debilitating, mentally and emotionally. So I was just very grateful to work.

Do you spend much time looking at your own movies?

No, I never see them, never. I'm a little embarrassed—in fact, a *lot* embarrassed. And sometimes I can't bear to see them!

You worked alongside the Three Stooges and Adam (Batman) *West in Columbia's* The Outlaws Is Coming *(1965).*

I was stunned that I was working with the Three Stooges, because they were a household word. I really didn't know they were still working—and neither did they *[laughs]*! That's why they were grateful for this film, I suppose. I was pleased to watch them, because after many years of seeing them on film, then all of a sudden you're sitting around drinking coffee and talking with them . . . it was quite extraordinary for a young person. And I liked Adam West very much. I thought he was a very whole person, his feet on the ground, and very likable.

Why such a small role in The Silencers?

It was also Columbia Pictures. One's career could go right down the tube, being signed during that period when there was no studio head like a Harry Cohn. This was during the segue from "big studio-dom" into what we have today, where there's nothing. And it was kind of a deterioration. I'm not here to tell you that it was the studio's fault, but it is a fact, analytically, that at that time the studio was moving away from what it was known as. So I just did what I was told. But I had a lot of fun for the short time I worked on *The Silencers*. Dean Martin was a nice, funny guy.

You also did plenty of "fantastic" TV, including The Man from U.N.C.L.E., Batman, *many episodes of* Bewitched *and also* Star Trek.

I had a lot of fun on the *U.N.C.L.E.*s, I enjoyed doing them; it was quick work, and I love to be quick in my work. I was capable of doing that, so it worked nicely. What stands out in my mind regarding *Batman* is that the episodes I did came at the beginning of the series, and it was very difficult for many of the guest actors to understand in what ilk to play. We had not been used to playing farce, and we didn't quite know what farce was—but we didn't want to admit that we didn't know! And when asking what form this was taking, we were told to play it straight. So we played it straight, although with what I know now of farce I would surely have played it differently. I was in the *Bewitched* pilot, playing Samantha's [Elizabeth Montgomery] girlfriend, and this pilot was so popular that they kept bringing me back as the girlfriend. And on *Star Trek,* I remember that William Shatner was a very warm actor, and it was easy to act with him. I enjoyed doing it.

What do you recall about Tarzan and the Valley of Gold?

That I wanted desperately to work in the jungle, and I begged them to let me swing on a vine. Which they promised they'd let me do, lying about it, of course. I remember that I felt that there was great discrimination against the Mexican workers, and that was very disturbing to me. I also remember a helicopter nearly crashing, and that scared me because I had just gotten out of it *[laughs]*! Robert Day was the director—a little worried because he was behind schedule, a little nervous. A nice man. But I loved more than anything the animals—I loved so much that lion, and the snake that worked with us. I feel that I really became fast friends with them. When they couldn't find me or call me to the set, they'd say, "Oh, she must be with the lion." The lion used to put its head in my lap, and we would just sit quietly under a tree.

You shot part of that film in the ancient city of Teotihuacan, which caused a furor.

There were armed soldiers watching over us, making sure that we did only what we had announced we were going to do. Once we got our scenes shot, we had to slip out of the country with the film underneath jackets, just to get home! The Mexican government felt that we were desecrating in some way the image of their monuments.

Did you get along well with Tarzan *Mike Henry?*

Mike Henry was an extremely handsome man, and I felt one of the finest Tarzans physically, but I found him very cold and always disgruntled. He was always unhappy about something, and I didn't know why. He always seemed as though he were someplace else. Mike was angry with the chimp always, very angry, and hurt him—treated him very roughly. That very much disturbed me, and so I took the side of the animal! We didn't have any contention, Mike Henry and I, I don't wish to say that, but in all sets there's tremendous

Kovack in full wardrobe for Columbia's *The Silencers.*

Kovack poses with the Lord of the Apes (Mike Henry) and the King of Beasts during production of *Tarzan and the Valley of Gold.*

warmth and camaraderie, and there wasn't with him. It was my first experience like that.

On the next Tarzan *picture, the chimp ripped open Mike Henry's jaw.*
    I remember that—that happened in Brazil *[Tarzan and the Great River]*. That's because he worried the chimp, because he treated it so badly.

Around this time you also made several films in, of all places, Iran.
    I lived in Iran for nearly three years. I used Iran as a base for seeing all of the world east of there—Afghanistan, India, Cambodia, Japan, all those sorts of places. Then I'd come back, do another little film in three weeks, and went west to Kuwait, Israel, Turkey, etc. Another little Iranian film in two weeks, and then I went into Russia through Samarkand and Tashkent, and saw Russia from that view, which was very special.

What kind of country was *Iran in those days?*
    Just magnificent. I cannot tell people enough, how magnificent the people were, and still are, in my view, regardless of how we see what's going on

now. How beautiful I thought the country was, what expectations I had for the country. And I felt that the Shah and his politics, at that time, and given the development of the country, were correct for the moment.

Stateside you turned up in a small role in the borderline SF Marooned.

What I remember about *Marooned* is that I had severely damaged my leg and could hardly stand, and [producer] Mike Frankovich saying, "If you weren't an actress, you'd be in a hospital!" It was a very small part. *Marooned* was my last film. I met Zubin Mehta, and we were married.

Whose decision was it that you curtail your acting career?

My husband's. I do sometimes miss the camaraderie of show business, but I am so busy that there seems not to be any space. I love my marriage, I just try to be a good wife and do the best that I can in my marriage. That's all.

Throughout the ten years you were an actress, you kept busy and worked opposite a number of top stars. Are you happy with your career?

Oh, no—absolutely not! I feel it was very shallow, and that I never was able to play a real person. I was perceived as a girl with combed hair and lipstick, and no matter what I would do, they would not give me the role of a real woman. I wanted that, and I could have done that—easily, and well. But I don't think there's one film that I can point to that really represents what I might have done. And consequently there's not one film or role that I look at of which I'm proud, nor one which I would recommend to anyone to see. *[Smirks.]* It's a very sad statement, isn't it?

NANCY KOVACK FILMOGRAPHY

Strangers When We Meet (Columbia, 1960)
Cry for Happy (Columbia, 1961)
The Wild Westerners (Columbia, 1962)
Diary of a Madman (United Artists, 1963)
Jason and the Argonauts (Columbia, 1963)
The Great Sioux Massacre (Columbia, 1965)
The Outlaws Is Coming (Columbia, 1965)
Sylvia (Paramount, 1965)
Frankie and Johnny (United Artists, 1966)
The Silencers (Columbia, 1966)
Tarzan and the Valley of Gold (AIP, 1966)
Enter Laughing (Columbia, 1967)
Marooned (Columbia, 1969)

. . . At first I thought
I was going to be very intimidated
by [Boris Karloff], because I'd only
known him as the Frankenstein Monster. But he was
the kindest, sweetest, nicest, quietest man
I think I've ever worked with.

Anna Lee

ANNA LEE HAS far too much poise and class to be hung with the label of "scream queen," but the petite blond leading lady *has* appeared in horror, fantasy and science fiction films with some regularity since she first broke the ice in the genre in the mid-'30s. Her first fantastic film credit was the Christ allegory *The Passing of the Third Floor Back,* made on her native English soil in 1935, and in the half-century since she has not only established herself as one of Hollywood's great character actresses but also reinforced her genre status in many other fantasy and SF titles, including *The Man Who Lived Again, King Solomon's Mines, Flesh and Fantasy, The Ghost and Mrs. Muir, Jack the Giant Killer, Picture Mommy Dead, In Like Flint* and more. Horror film fans will remember her best as the spirited Nell Bowen, running afoul of sadist Boris Karloff in Val Lewton's classic historical thriller *Bedlam.*

The daughter of a clergyman, Anna Lee was born Joan Boniface Winnifrith and encouraged to pursue an acting career by her father. After training at London's Royal Albert Hall, she took to the boards and later began appearing in English films, first as an extra, then working her way up to featured parts and finally earning the unofficial title "Queen of the Quota Quickies." Lee and her husband, director Robert Stevenson, relocated to Hollywood in the late '30s, and Lee began starring in stateside productions as well as becoming a fixture of the John Ford stock company (she appeared in *How Green Was My Valley, Fort Apache* and a half-dozen others). In 1970 she became the seventh wife of novelist, poet and playwright Robert Nathan *(Portrait of Jennie, The Bishop's Wife),* and she remains active today, still radiantly charming and strikingly attractive, regularly playing wealthy Lila Quartermaine on TV's hottest soap opera, *General Hospital.*

I was born in England, in a very small village called Ightham. My father was rector of Ightham for about 25 years; I was born in the rectory and I grew up there until he died when I was ten. My real name is Joan Boniface Winnifrith but for obvious reasons I had to change it, because the moment I started doing a play they said, "We can't put that on a marquee, we can't even put it in the program!" And they told me to choose a name that was short and easy to remember. I was reading Tolstoy at the time and I thought Anna—from *Anna Karenina*—was very romantic, a lovely name. Then I was also reading American history and I thought Robert E. Lee was a rather good chap, so I decided to take the name Lee. The story that goes with that is, when they put in the paper that I had changed my name to Anna Lee, I had a telephone call from a writer friend of mine—he did all the Hitchcock pictures, his name was Charles Bennett. And he said, "Joan, if you had to change your name, why did you choose something that sounds like a Chinese laundry?" Of course it hadn't dawned on me *[laughs],* but Anna Lee *does* have a certain Chinese feeling. When I was making *Seven Women* [1966] for John Ford, we all had our dressing rooms on the stage and our names on the doors. One day I came back from lunch and I saw this little old Chinese lady gazing up at my name—we had a lot of Chinese extras in that picture. I came up to her and said, "Good

Previous page: **Anna Lee and horror great Boris Karloff in a moody two-shot from** *The Man Who Lived Again.*

After a series of glamorous leads in British and American films, Anna Lee matured into one of Hollywood's finest character actresses.

afternoon," and her face fell. She said, "*Yoooo* are Ah-na Lee?" I said I was, and she said, "Ooooh, I t'ought it was a *Chinese* actress!" *[Laughs.]*

So how did a rector's daughter end up in show biz?
    I believe it was really my father's fault. I think most clergymen, at least in England, are frustrated actors—Laurence Olivier's father was a clergyman, so was Matheson Lang's and, oh, about five or six others at the time. My father wanted one of his five children to be an actor, and I think because I was the one who showed off a lot, a very extroverted child, he decided, "Joan is going to be an actress." And so it never occurred to me that I was to do anything else!
    When I was about 15 I couldn't wait to start, and my mother, who was a widow by that time, was a little worried because she'd heard all these wild stories about what happened to actresses. So she took me to see my godmother, who was Sybil Thorndike, quite a famous actress in her own right. I was in boarding school then, and I went up to the Old Vic to see her in my gym tunic

and blue serge bloomers. I recited "There Are Fairies at the Bottom of Our Garden" and I don't know how she kept a straight face *[laughs]*! Anyway, she said, "I think you should go back to school, and once you've been properly educated I want you to go to the Central School of Speech Training and Dramatic Arts at the Royal Albert Hall in London." Laurence Olivier and John Gielgud and Ralph Richardson had all been students there, but before my time—about three years before I arrived. So I spent the rest of my school term just swatting away, trying to pass the exam, which I did. And so my mother had to let me go to the Albert Hall.

How long were you there?

About three and a half years, until I left in disgrace. I had heard that you could get a job as an extra at Elstree in a movie they were making, I went down there and I got a part—it was probably *Ebb Tide* [1932]. This got back to Elsie Fogarty, who was the head of the school. I was dragged in front of everybody and she said, "I regret to tell the class that one of our most promising pupils has prostituted her art by playing in the cinema!" In those days for a stage actor to work in the cinema was really considered rather demeaning. I was forced to leave the Albert Hall, but then I went to the London Repertory Company and stayed for quite a while. My leading man there was a man named Bernard Lee, whom years later I found in the 007 movies, playing James Bond's boss, M! He and I worked in two or three plays together. Then I went on tour in things like *The Barretts of Wimpole Street* and so on.

This was about the time that your film career was starting as well.

I did lots and lots of extra parts in what were called quota pictures. Quota pictures—"quota quickies"—were made to conform with some kind of law, and so they were all exceedingly low budget and very, very fast. Of course in those days we had no union in England, so we had to sit up all night many, many times in order to finish them. But they were good training. I must have done seven or eight of those.

I did a film called *Rolling in Money* [1934] for an American man, an agent at that time, Al Parker. Whilst I was doing that he wanted me to sign a contract and come to America as an actress. About a week before that, I had been sent for to go down to Gaumont-British to test for a part in a picture called *The Camels Are Coming* [1934], and they *also* wanted me to sign a contract. So, without thinking, I signed both contracts *[laughs]*! Well, fortunately, I was under 18 at the time so they were null and void, and I chose to stay in England. I was with Gaumont-British for five or six years.

Your early publicity is full of far-out stories about your running away to join a circus, and encounters with Chinese bandits.

Well, the circus story is more or less correct: I did fall in love with a lion tamer and I did run away to the circus. I thought I could get a job there, and the only job they could give me was as the girl who had knives thrown at her! So I was very briefly the girl who had knives thrown at her, until my father soon found out about it and I was dragged home in disgrace. That was my circus career. Chinese bandits? Again, they're on the right track. I had a rather wealthy godmother who decided that she didn't want me to go on the stage (it wasn't respectable) so she thought she'd take me out to China, where British mothers sent their daughters to find suitable beaux—there were a lot of soldiers and sailors stationed there at the time. We went to China, and whilst we were in Hong Kong we took a trip to Macao. And on the way there the boat that we were on was boarded by Chinese pirates. I was thrilled *[laughs]*—I wanted to go meet the pirates—but a British gunboat came by very fast and chased them away!

It was after you were in pictures a few years that you married director Robert Stevenson.

I was making *The Camels Are Coming* with Jack Hulbert—we made it out very near the Suez Canal, out around where the Sphinx is. We were supposed to drink Evian water, but the Egyptians who took care of us, all they did was go down to the Nile and fill up the empty bottles with Nile water *[laughs]*! So everybody came down with awful attacks of dysentery—except me, because I didn't drink the water. But at any rate they were all sick, and the production was almost at a total standstill. So Gaumont-British sent Bob Stevenson out as a troubleshooter. I remember I was riding across the desert on the little Arab pony which they had given me, and I saw this man who looked like something out of a Noel Coward movie. Everybody who was already there was looking so dirty by this time—they were unshaven, they were living in tents and everybody was half-sick. And this character came out wearing a white shirt and white shorts and white socks and white everything. We met and fell in love, and when we got back to England, I married him. We worked together quite a lot—actually, there were usually three of us on the team, Bob and myself and Ronald Neame, who was our cameraman. And now Ronnie is doing so well here as a director.

What memories do you have of the making of the fantasy The Passing of the Third Floor Back?

It was the first time I had worked with Conrad Veidt, and of course like all young girls I was madly in love with him. He was a big, very ... *[laughs]* strange man. He was a very egotistical man, I think—he was always admiring himself in a mirror, he had mirrors all the way around, rather like Marlene Dietrich. But he was very nice, and he had a great sense of humor. My mother was played by Cathleen Nesbitt, who of course at one time was the great love of Rupert Brooke, the poet. I had always wanted to meet her but I was a little shy at that time about asking her questions. But years later when I was out in Hollywood, about '72 or '73, I did a play here at the Westwood Playhouse and playing with me was Cathleen Nesbitt, who was then in her eighties. We had a wonderful time together, and remembered back to when she played my mother in *The Passing of the Third Floor Back*.

The film got some good writeups when it opened, but it really seems to have fallen through the cracks.

It's a strange picture, a little hard, almost impossible to describe. It was directed by Berthold Viertel, whom I also met again in America—he came out here when war broke out. He was married to Salka Viertel, who was Garbo's great love. Conrad Veidt played a Christ-like character who has an impact on the lives of the tenants of a London boarding house and *[laughs]* of course it always made people smile to think of Conrad Veidt, who always played such evil characters, playing Christ!

He once described it as his most difficult role.

I'm sure it was—quite sure. But he was good in it.

What do you remember about working with Boris Karloff on The Man Who Lived Again?

Of course at first I thought I was going to be very intimidated by him, because I'd only known him as the Frankenstein Monster. But he was the kindest, sweetest, nicest, quietest man I think I've ever worked with. He had a great love for poetry, and I did, too, and so we used to have a sort of jam session: He would start a poem, like, "Between the dark and the daylight, when the night is beginning to lower," and I'd go on, "Comes a pause in the day's occupation, which is called the Children's Hour." We went on for hours and hours doing this, seeing if we could stump each other! He was a very, very nice man.

Did Karloff enjoy his return to England?

Yes and no. He was very, very perturbed and frustrated to find out that there was no union. He said, "You've got to have a union! We have a union in California, and an actor should have a union." And I thought to myself, "Well—why?" I worked Saturdays and Sundays and everything else, and we'd never heard of anything like double time; we even did our own stunts. In a film called *Young Man's Fancy* [1939], I played Miss Ada, the Human Cannon-ball, and I was fired out of a cannon! Here in Hollywood they'd get an extra for that, but back then I was fired out of a cannon. Well, Karloff thought this was all wrong, and I remember that he lectured us all quite firmly on the fact that we must have a union.

Did he clash with the higher-ups on that picture?

I think they wanted us to work on a Saturday, and he said that, no, he would not work on a Saturday unless he was paid more for it. We all listened to him, because English actors had never heard of a union at that time.

What other recollections of the film?

We made that at Gainsborough, I remember that distinctly because the dressing rooms were rather small. And right next door to me, practically sharing my dressing room, were the monkeys—the chimpanzees that you see in the film. And they smelled awful! I remember holding my nose whenever I had to go into my dressing room!

How long did shooting take?

We took quite a long time, I think probably about eight to ten weeks—we very seldom got more than three sequences a day on that. I saw the picture again recently and I loved it, because it was so long since I'd seen it—I saw old faces like Frank Cellier, whom I played with several times after that, and Donald Calthrop and Cecil Parker. And I thought it was very well done, that it stood up remarkably well. I think it was one of Karloff's better pictures.

Certainly one of your best-respected films from this English period is King Solomon's Mines.

Everybody agrees that that was by far the best of all the versions they made. They made a second version [1950] with Deborah Kerr and Stewart Granger which was not as good as ours—and I wasn't the only person to say that, I heard that all around. And the third one [1985], with Richard Chamberlain, I think was a disaster. Ours was really very, very well done, in my opinion, and I love watching it again now.

Location photography was done in Africa.

But *we* never moved outside the studio! They had a second unit in Africa, but we had *our* desert in the studio. We had two of the largest stages at Gaumont-British, and we built that huge cavern you see in the film. All done in the studio! And I skinned my knees on those rocks—it was really a tough picture to do. I remember when we did that scene in the desert, where we're all dying of thirst, they wanted realism so they filled my mouth, and I think most of the other people's, too, with alum. And you could hardly open your mouth by the end of the day!

Non-Stop New York *was another highly entertaining film with fantasy elements.*

That film depicted the first trans–Atlantic passenger flight, which of course was still a few years in the future in real life. I remember that John Loder and I did a love scene which was supposedly set on a sort of veranda, built outside the plane. They had a wind machine blowing our hair, but the idea that this plane, which is supposedly going six hundred miles an hour, should have an open deck for passengers to stroll out onto...! But it was fun, that film, and there was a wonderful cast: We had Francis L. Sullivan and Athene Seyler, Desmond Tester and Frank Cellier.

Is it just coincidence that you made so many films [The Man Who Lived Again, King Solomon's Mines, Non-Stop New York *and others] with John Loder?*

No, I think Gaumont-British thought we made a good pair, Anna Lee and John Loder. He died only recently, at 90.

He was one of those actors that, when he died, everybody thought he had *been dead!*

I know, a lot of people did, it was such a shame. I did myself at one time! I last ran into him in London, about 20 years ago, and he was pretty old then. He had just gotten married again—he was always marrying rather expensive ladies *[laughs]*! My sister sent me a clipping out of an English paper, his obituary, which read, "Anna Lee, the actress, said, 'He was the most beautiful man I ever worked with.'" And he *was*, he was very beautiful at the time. He was the very youngest British Army officer in World War I.

Did you enjoy working so often with him?

I was madly in love with him before I met him, but he was rather heavily involved with a lady in London, and whenever I met him he was always married. He married four or five times at least! He was a very nice, sweet guy.

What made you decide to come to America?

I didn't decide to come to America. I had already turned down two Hollywood contracts, maybe three, because I was doing very well at Gaumont-British and I had a wonderful contract with them. I was very happy because my family was there, and I had no desire to go to Hollywood. But I was married to Bob Stevenson, and he had signed a contract with David Selznick to do the first American Ingrid Bergman picture.

Intermezzo *[1939]?*

I believe it was *Intermezzo*. Selznick took Bob to see (I think it was) the Swedish version of *Intermezzo* [1936], and Bob said, "Oh, she's got no sex appeal, she's just a fat Nordic broad." And I wanted to kill him *[laughs]* because I adored Ingrid Bergman, and I still do! But he wasn't really that interested in directing her. Anyway, before we left England he was trying to talk me into coming and he said, "Well, why don't you come with me just for the trip, and we'll bring the baby?"—our daughter Venetia was just 18 months old then. So I thought, "Well, maybe if I go over for three weeks..." So I took Venetia and my English nanny with me.

In those days you did things in such style (with Selznick). We went across on the *Normandie*, we were wined and dined in New York by Selznick's people and then put on the train to California. And they didn't let you disembark at Los Angeles; you had to get out of the train at Pasadena, because it was more beautiful. They didn't want you to see downtown Los Angeles *[laughs]*! All you saw when you disembarked were these beautiful orange groves and the snow-capped mountains in the distance. It was really a beautiful, beautiful place. Then they took you by limousine down to Los Angeles, to Hollywood. We arrived there and they put us up at the Garden of Allah, which was a sort of chic place in those days. It was lovely—it wasn't all that comfortable, but it was very exciting because Bob Benchley and Scott Fitzgerald and a lot of other interesting people lived there.

The night we arrived at the Garden of Allah, I remember I was very tired and we were unpacking when suddenly the telephone rang and it was Selznick. He told Bob, "I want you both to come to dinner tonight, I'm going to run a movie and I want you to see it." I said to Bob that I didn't want to go, I was so tired and I had all the unpacking to do, but he said it was a command because it's David Selznick and you mustn't say no to him. So very wearily I decided to go, and we went. The only other guests there were Clark Gable and Carole Lombard, and the film that we were to see was the rough cut of *Gone with the Wind* [1939]. So *[laughs]* it was worth staying up that late!

How long did you reside at the Garden of Allah?

The bungalow they gave us at the Garden of Allah was a little too small, so we moved over to a bungalow at the Beverly Hills Hotel. Next door was Marlene Dietrich and Erich Maria Remarque, and across the way was Edna Best and Herbert Marshall and their babies. It was a pleasant life; I was getting homesick, but I thought, well, I'll stay on a bit longer. This was August 1939. In September, war broke out in England, so I said, "Well, now I *am* going home." I went down to the British Consul and asked for a visa to get back, and he said, "I'm afraid we can't give you a visa because you're a married woman with an infant child." They had strict instructions that no married woman with infant children were to go across, because of the submarines and so on. I was very angry, and I went up to Canada to try to join the Red Cross, but they wouldn't take me, for the same reason! So I had to wait. Eventually I joined up with the U.S.O. and I thought, "This time I really *will* get back to England." Instead of that, they sent me with Jack Benny to the Persian Gulf *[laughs]*! Anyway, that was how I came to Hollywood—very reluctantly!

And after all this, your husband never did direct anything for Selznick, did he?

He was under contract to Selznick, but I think Selznick just sold him out. He never made a picture for Selznick, but Selznick loaned him to other studios. And Selznick got all the money!

You made your American starring debut in My Life with Caroline *[1941], then made your first of eight films for John Ford.*

How Green Was My Valley [1941]; there's a curious story about that, too. William Wyler was supposed to direct that picture, and I went to interview him at 20th. He was very nice, very polite, and he said, "I would love to have had

Anna Lee first worked with the John Ford stock company of character players in *How Green Was My Valley* (1941). The film and its director remain her favorites to this day.

you as Bronwyn, but I'm afraid I've just promised the part to Greer Garson." I thought, "Well, that's that." He did take me around, told me about this wonderful young English boy that he'd got, Roddy McDowall, and showed me some of the sets. But I went home and forgot all about it for six months. Then I got a call to say I was to go and interview John Ford for *How Green Was My Valley*. Somebody told me I wouldn't have a chance—Ford only liked Irish actresses and wouldn't work with anybody who was English—so thereupon I made up a purely fictitious Irish grandfather, and it was years before I told Ford the truth about it! I went in, and evidently he liked me. The only thing he'd seen me in was *My Life with Caroline,* and you can't imagine two roles more entirely different, Bronwyn and Caroline. But at any rate he hired me; I made a test with Roddy and the next thing I knew, I was playing Bronwyn.

Roddy McDowall, Maureen O'Hara, Patric Knowles and I are the only survivors of *How Green Was My Valley*—Patric called me the other day, to assure me that he *was* alive! I think everybody else is gone and, frankly, I'm starting to get a little bit worried *[laughs]*!

When people think of the John Ford stock players, they think of John Wayne and Ward Bond, Victor McLaglen, people like that. It's so funny to find you lumped in there!

They were all such dear friends, it was just like being in a repertory company again. I loved it. But then of course I learned the lesson that you must never, never refuse any part that you are offered by John Ford. He never lets you see a script; you might have three lines, or you might be playing the star part. *The Man Who Shot Liberty Valance* [1962], I was in there less than two minutes. I was attacked by Lee Marvin, right in the beginning of the picture, and you never saw me again! But you must never say no. Arthur Shields turned down a part, and he never worked for Ford again.

You seem more like the type that would turn up in, say, the occasional Hitchcock film.

I never worked for Hitch; I knew him quite well, and in fact he gave me away when I married my second husband in 1944, but I never particularly *wanted* to work with Hitch. I'd heard a lot of stories about him in England which had rather frightened me *[laughs]*; his humor was somewhat sadistic. Apparently he was much nicer when he came over here!

What about the horror stories that are told about Ford?

He was wonderful to me, I loved him from the moment I met him. But God forbid that you want to be a star with Ford, because he hated the very idea of a star—nobody is a star but John Ford. He said one day that the only three women he liked working with were Maureen O'Hara, Katharine Hepburn and Anna Lee. And to the people who say, "That was why you never became a star in Hollywood, because you joined the John Ford stock company," I say, "I would much rather have been a member of the John Ford stock company than the biggest star in Hollywood," and I really mean that. It was wonderful, really wonderful; I loved Ford, and he's godfather to all three of my sons.

Getting back to your fantasy films, you had a good supporting role in the best segment of Flesh and Fantasy.

That was at Universal, directed by Julien Duvivier. It was a little odd working with him, as all his directions were in French and had to be translated by somebody else. Edward G. Robinson played my suitor in that, and he was a

Their lives darkened by a fortune-teller's prediction of murder, Lee and Edward G. Robinson face a doubtful future in the anthology *Flesh and Fantasy*.

charming, delightful man. He may have been a bit miscast in that, because you always imagined him as a sort of typical gangster character, but he was exceedingly well read and he loved paintings, and we had a lot to talk about in the way of art and so on. And I remember wearing a lovely green and silver gown which I took with me overseas when I was entertaining the troops—and it was stolen by the Arabs *[laughs]*!

How did you get involved on Bedlam?
    After *How Green Was My Valley,* I think *Bedlam* is my favorite picture. I loved it. I knew Val Lewton quite well, because I had been close friends with Val and his wife Ruth—I used to go have dinner with them all the time. Val told me he was writing this story, this historical picture about St. Mary's of Bethlehem, but I forget exactly how I became involved; I suppose it would have to have been Val who wanted me to do it. I know Mark Robson, the director, had other ideas; he rather wanted Jane Greer for the part and Val wanted me. And finally I did it, on the condition that I change my hair from blond to dark, which is nothing unusual. Ford always said the same thing; anytime I went down there I had to be dipped into dye.

Lewton is rightly famous for these brilliance-on-a-budget horror thrillers.

Boris used to get quite annoyed when people referred to *Bedlam* as a horror picture. He said, "It's not a horror picture, it's a *historical* picture," and he was right, absolutely dead right. There was never any thought of making it into a so-called horror picture; it was exactly what happened at St. Mary's of Bethlehem, so much so that it was not allowed to be shown in England for a long, long time. In fact, only very recently have they permitted it to be shown over there. They felt it was a true but rather melancholy description of St. Mary's of Bethlehem.

But once a Karloff becomes involved in a picture like that, it automatically becomes "horror."

He used to get so annoyed about that — *[imitating Karloff]* "I'm not playing a horror part!" And he was so good in that, he was wonderful.

Bedlam was done on a very low budget, but I don't think it ever really showed because it was (*I* thought) so beautifully done. I remember I had very, very bad strep throat halfway through it, and we didn't dare stop because I had no insurance. There's one part, during the game of paroli, where you can hear my voice getting huskier and huskier *[laughs]*!

The film's publicists built it up as though it were a big-budgeter.

I always thought it was a low-budget film because of not having proper insurance and various other things. I know that my costumes were not made for me; the green velvet riding habit that I wore was Vivien Leigh's dress, the one she makes out of curtains in *Gone with the Wind*. I was always very happy about that *[laughs]*! And the lovely ball gown that I wore in the gardens was Hedy Lamarr's. So I wore all hand-me-downs from various actresses!

Can you tell me a little more about Lewton?

Val Lewton was a sweet, very kind, lovely man and I liked him very much. I don't think Val really thought of these pictures so much in terms of "horror," either. He started out with *Cat People,* of course, and that's still doing well today, and I think I did get the impression that he enjoyed doing these horror films. I know *Bedlam* was the favorite film that he did — he told me that again and again. It was based on the Hogarth paintings and it was all done so beautifully authentically, with the background of the Hogarth pictures and so on.

What can you recall about director Mark Robson?

I had never worked with him before. I had only known Val Lewton very well, but I was sure that if Val thought he was good, then he *was* good. Val had done such a fabulous piece of work on the script and the dialogue that it would have been tough for anyone to do a bad job, but I thought Mark did an excellent job of directing. As of the time that we made *Bedlam* Mark hadn't

Lee had one of her best and favorite roles in the Val Lewton thriller *Bedlam,* with Boris Karloff. The abused inmate on the floor is B-star-to-be Robert Clarke. (Photo courtesy Robert Skotak.)

yet done anything really in a big way, but I know that David Selznick saw the picture and immediately wanted to sign him. And I know that Robson's next picture was *Champion* [1949], which of course is very good. He went directly from so-called B pictures, right up to the top.

What do you remember about some of the other people in the cast?

Ian Wolfe, well, of course I loved him; I also remember dear Billy House, and Jason Robards, Sr. Richard Fraser, who played the young Quaker, I never heard of him again after *Bedlam!* We had a sweet little script girl on the picture who was dying to be an actress, and Mark Robson had sort of talked about it and we were all encouraging it. It was Ellen Corby—remember her? They gave her the part of "Betty, Queen of the Artichokes." She had this very bad stroke several years ago and she can't really talk very well, but I keep running into her and she always comes up and puts her arms around me. I also remember Robert Clarke, the actor who played "Dan the Dog," and also the man in the cage, "Tom the Tiger" [Victor Holbrook]. He wasn't an actor, I think he was a professional wrestler, but he was a very nice man. We had a great, wonderful cast.

You were at the Academy's "Centenary Tribute" to Karloff in 1988.

The Academy invited me. Mrs. Karloff was there—I had met her once before. Vincent Price was there, and Peter Bogdanovich and Mae Clarke, whom I hadn't seen since we made *Flying Tigers* [1942]—she lives out at the Motion Picture Country Home. The Academy was packed, and I think Mrs. Karloff was very pleased about it.

You certainly did have one of your best roles in Bedlam.

I really think it was one of the better parts that I had here, and I loved the film.

Did Bedlam *do well for RKO?*

No, unfortunately. RKO didn't put as much p.r. behind it as they should have done; they didn't promote the picture at all, maybe because they didn't like historical pictures. That was certainly true of RKO after Howard Hughes came in. Howard Hughes hated anything that was historical, he hated anything that was British.

You had a small but memorable role in The Ghost and Mrs. Muir.

I did have a very, very small part in that. The only condition under which my agent would let me do it was if they gave me twice my usual salary, because the part should probably have only run three days at the outside. I reported to work on the first morning and I was just getting my makeup on when a message came down that Gene Tierney had fallen down stairs and broken her toe, and therefore there could be no shooting that day. I was held on salary, which was quite a lot, for six weeks, so I made more on that picture than I'd made on a lot of pictures before that—

You sure you weren't behind *Gene Tierney on those stairs?*

[Laughs.] And all for this part which literally is just two or three minutes on the screen! But it's amazing how many people remember me in it, and recognize me in it. I played the wife of George Sanders—a *nasty* idea!—and he is running around with Gene Tierney. And apparently it is what is now called a "cameo"!

What did you dislike about George Sanders?

I disliked him because he was so supercilious and condescending in his attitude, particularly toward women. As a matter of fact, my friend Brian Aherne wrote a book about Sanders and he called it *A Dreadful Man [laughs]*, so evidently I wasn't entirely alone in my opinions! But my real dislike of him didn't come until after he died, because when I read that he had committed suicide because he was bored with life, I thought, my God, what an excuse! What a ridiculous, ridiculous thing to say!

Looks like you had another "cameo" in What Ever Happened to Baby Jane?

I've got mixed memories about that. I really enjoyed the experience because I've always adored Bette Davis; when I was offered the part, I told them that I would love to work with her. Who wouldn't? My dressing room was sort of "center stage" — Joan Crawford's was on the right and Bette's was on the left — so I got all the vibes that came across *[laughs]*! Of course Bette did everything in her power to antagonize Crawford, but in a very quiet way. She would put little notes on her dressing room door — "Of all my relations, I prefer sex the most" — and she thought that Joan would be shocked at that.

But it still sounds as though you preferred Davis.

It was a wonderful experience working with them both, because they were both big actresses, but I was particularly in awe of Davis. I remember my very first scene, where I come to the door with the flowers and it's opened by Bette, who is in her cups, very blowsy. Afterward the director, Robert Aldrich, came to me and he said, "Well, you passed muster. Bette came up to me and said, 'It's good to be working with a pro.'" I was very pleased with that.

Your daughter in that film was Bette Davis's real-life daughter, B.D.

That's right. And B.D. was very, very tall, much taller than I was, so we had to have all my scenes sitting down because if I had stood with her she would have towered over me!

That's the daughter that later wrote the tell-all book about Davis.

Yes, I know, and that's very sad because they seemed to be so close at that time.

What impressions of Joan Crawford?

She was very, very gracious, and she always had this big box of Pepsis outside of her dressing room door. And when my sons came to visit me on the set they made a horrible *faux pas:* They asked if they could have a *Coke.* And Joan, who was on the Pepsi board of directors, growled, "It's not Coke, it's *Pepsi!" [Laughs.]*

When I was sent the script of *What Ever Happened to Baby Jane?* I remember that when I got to the point where the rat is on the plate, I was shocked—oh, how horrible! But then there was nothing really offensive about my part, except I played a rather stupid woman. I was always out in the garden and poor Joan Crawford was throwing bits of paper down at me and I completely ignored it *[laughs]*! So I don't know that I liked my role, but it is a film that I am very glad that I was in.

Around that same time you also made a fantasy costumer, Jack the Giant Killer.

You know, I had never seen *Jack the Giant Killer* until just a few weeks ago? *Jack the Giant Killer* I remember for two reasons: First, I had a very nasty encounter with a raven. Do you remember the scene where I carry the raven to the window, and let it fly off? Well, this bird came into the studio one morning with its trainer, and the first thing I noticed was that the trainer had long rubber gauntlets on, and he had little marks all over his face. And I said, "Are you sure this bird is quite safe?" "Oh, yes," he said, "birds never hurt anyone. This is a perfectly trained bird." Well, I looked at him with a great suspicion *[laughs]*, because this was a nasty-looking creature. And I had to perch it on my wrist! I had no gloves on, but I did have this big emerald ring, and as it perched on my wrist of course before we even started the take, it had pounced on my ring and pulled the emerald out. Then later, right in the middle of dialogue, I was holding my hand up (with the bird perched on my wrist) and looking at the actor I was playing to, and suddenly this bird pounced down and bit my lip open! Blood was streaming down my face—and *[laughs]* I think the camera went on cranking! They rushed me off to the hospital and I had a tetanus shot and everything else. Normally I don't mind working with animals, but I think that was the only bird I ever did work with. Never again *[laughs]*!

The other thing that I recall was that, for the scenes where I turn into the witch, I had to be fitted with contact lenses. They weren't like the usual, they were opaque, great big things. When I went to the optometrist to be fitted with these things, he said, "Don't you wear reading glasses?" and I said, "No, I don't need them," and I showed him how well I could read. He said, "Well, at your age, in six months' time you will be back here asking for reading glasses." Well, maybe it was because the thought had been planted in my mind, but in six months' time I was back and I've worn reading glasses ever since *[laughs]*!

How did you like having to wear those contact lenses?

They were hideously uncomfortable, very painful. They were green and yellow, as far as I remember, and they didn't even allow little pinholes for me to see through. I was completely blind all the time I had those things in, and I was led from one part of the set to the other.

What do you think of the film now that you've seen it?

I was fascinated because I didn't realize in making it that it was going to be a special effects movie. The effects were not all that well done, but they were there!

How about Picture Mommy Dead?

[Groans.] Well, again, there's a story about that! I forget how I got involved; I think it was [casting director] Marvin Paige who got me to do that picture. He told me that Hedy Lamarr was starring and that my part would be a cameo and that Signe Hasso was doing a cameo and that it was going to be a great picture. The moment I heard the title, I thought, "Oh, no!" but I had to go along with it. I played my scene, and I can't even remember what I did except that I was at some kind of auction with a crowd of people behind me — eight or ten extras. The next thing I knew was, they called me up and told me that Hedy Lamarr was going to be unable to do the film, and they had an idea that they would like to replace her with me. I said, "Well, I've already shot two days on it," and they said, "Yes, that's the problem. We're going to have to count how many extras are involved, because it may be too expensive to reshoot that scene." And *[laughs]* they literally counted the heads that I'd worked with and decided that it would cost too much to reshoot that scene with somebody else!

Lamarr was replaced by Zsa Zsa Gabor.

And of course Zsa Zsa Gabor at that time weighed at least twenty pounds more than Hedy Lamarr, and they had to squeeze her into the wardrobe *[laughs]*!

You next turned up in a science fiction spy adventure, In Like Flint.

In Like Flint was a favorite and again, it has a weird story attached to it. I was cast in that and I'd been fitted for all my wardrobe, and four days before we were due to leave for Jamaica I was involved in quite a bad car accident. I had thirteen stitches in my thigh, I had ribs cracked, and I was taken off to a hospital in Canoga Park. I told them, "I can't stay in the hospital because I've got to go to Jamaica in four days' time." And the doctor said, "Oh, don't be ridiculous, you can't possibly go." I persisted, and he said, "Well, if you can walk down the corridor outside your room in three days, I will say you can go." So somehow or other I did, I walked down that corridor, and the next day I was on that plane. I had so much codeine in me — and then of course I drank on the plane, too *[laughs]* — that when I arrived in Montego Bay, we were met by the producer, Saul David, and I didn't know who he was!

Did you tell anyone that you had been in an accident?

No, I knew I couldn't tell anybody because the insurance people would have immediately sent me home. I had all these stitches in my leg but fortunately I knew that my wardrobe consisted of all pants and clothes that would

Lee in a 1950s pose.

keep me well-covered — I was black-and-blue from my head to my feet! The only person who knew was the wardrobe girl, who screamed when she saw me. I told her, "Don't you dare say anything to anybody!"

I managed to get along but later on I found that I couldn't turn the handle of a door or take a cap off a Coke bottle, things like that, so I knew there was something wrong. The doctor in Los Angeles had told me that, whatever happened, I must go and have the stitches out before 13 days went by, otherwise they'd turn . . . gangrenous or something *[laughs]*! I waited and bore the pain until they had enough footage in the can that I knew they wouldn't replace me, and then I very cautiously approached the assistant director and asked for the loan of a car, that I had to go and see a doctor in Montego Bay. So I went in, had the stitches out, and the doctor said, "I don't like the look of your arm, there's something wrong with it." Two days later I get a cable from the United States saying, SEE A DOCTOR IMMEDIATELY, YOUR WRIST IS BROKEN. And it was! So they gave me a sort of movable cast that could come off, and when I was working I took the cast off. If you watch the film again you'll notice the awkward way my hand goes up and down because I couldn't bend it! But at any rate I did the picture and I loved it.

In 1970 you married the well-known author and poet Robert Nathan.

That was when my life really started, because I always thought that the other two marriages were no good, but this was really a perfect marriage. The only sad thing was that we had so short a time; I was 55 when I married him and he was 75. I met him when I was rather down on my beam ends; I had three young boys to raise without benefit of any child support and I couldn't make enough money as an actress, so I was working as a sales clerk in a Beverly Hills silver shop as their expert on Georgian silver. I used to get terribly embarrassed when friends of mine came in. I remember Angela Lansbury came in one day and I practically burst into tears! Then another friend of mine, Joanne Dru, came in and she said, "Oh, Anna dear, we've got to find you a husband!" Joanne was giving a party for Barbara Ford's birthday—Barbara was John Ford's daughter—and she told me she wanted me to come because she had somebody in mind. So very reluctantly I went—I was so tired after doing a day's work, but I did take a change in clothes and I did go. And I never met the man that she had in mind for me, but I met Robert. He had been widowed fairly recently. We had dinner together and we discovered that we both had the same birthday, the second of January. The party was continuing, but we sat in a little room off the main room and talked and talked until around two o'clock in the morning, when the host and hostess came in to clean out the ashtrays or whatever *[laughs]*, and there we were! We were married three months later, and I always have said he was the one love of my life. I really feel we were soulmates in a way, because it was as though I had known him all my life and yet never had.

What can we look forward to in the near future?

First, I'm working on editing my husband's autobiography. I want to get that published, and also the last poems he wrote that were never published, a collection entitled *An Old Poet Speaks to His Wife*. Then next I'm off on my autobiography, which I want to write—I keep on getting pestered about it, but I want to do Robert's first and then, God willing, I'll get around to mine. And then of course *General Hospital*—they've re-signed me for the next two years and built up for me a very nice, funny storyline, so they must have faith in my longevity!

ANNA LEE FILMOGRAPHY

Ebb Tide (Paramount, 1932)
Say It with Music (British and Dominion Productions, 1932)
Chelsea Life (Paramount, 1933)
The King's Cup (British and Dominion Productions, 1933)
Mannequin (RKO, 1933)
Mayfair Girl (Warners, 1933)
Yes, Mr. Brown (British and Dominion Productions, 1933)
The Bermondsey Kid (Warners, 1933)
Faces (Paramount, 1934)
Rolling in Money (Fox, 1934)
The Camels Are Coming (Gaumont-British, 1934)
Lucky Loser (Paramount, 1934)
First a Girl (Gaumont-British, 1935)
Heat Wave (Gaumont-British, 1935)
The Passing of the Third Floor Back (Gaumont-British, 1936)
The Man Who Lived Again (The Man Who Changed His Mind) (Gaumont-British, 1936)
King Solomon's Mines (Gaumont-British, 1937)
Non-Stop New York (Lisbon Clipper Mystery) (Gaumont-British, 1937)
You're in the Army Now (O.H.M.S.) (Gaumont-British, 1937)
Young Man's Fancy (Associated British Films, 1939)
Return to Yesterday (Associated British Films, 1940)
The Secret Four (The Four Just Men) (Monogram, 1940)
Seven Sinners (Universal, 1940)
My Life with Caroline (RKO, 1941)
How Green Was My Valley (20th Century–Fox, 1941)
Commandos Strike at Dawn (Columbia, 1942)
Flying Tigers (Republic, 1942)
Flesh and Fantasy (Universal, 1943)
Forever and a Day (RKO, 1943)
Hangmen Also Die! (United Artists, 1943)
Summer Storm (United Artists, 1944)
Bedlam (RKO, 1946)
G.I. War Brides (Republic, 1946)
High Conquest (Monogram, 1947)
The Ghost and Mrs. Muir (20th Century–Fox, 1947)
Best Man Wins (Columbia, 1948)
Fort Apache (RKO, 1948)
Prison Warden (Columbia, 1949)
The Last Hurrah (Columbia, 1958)
Gideon of Scotland Yard (Gideon's Day) (Columbia, 1958)
The Crimson Kimono (Columbia, 1959)
The Horse Soldiers (United Artists, 1959)
This Earth Is Mine (Universal, 1959)
The Big Night (Paramount, 1960)
Jet Over the Atlantic (Inter-Continent Films, 1960)
Two Rode Together (Columbia, 1961)
Jack the Giant Killer (United Artists, 1962)
The Man Who Shot Liberty Valance (Paramount, 1962)
What Ever Happened to Baby Jane? (Warners, 1962)

The Prize (MGM, 1963)
The Unsinkable Molly Brown (MGM, 1964)
For Those Who Think Young (United Artists, 1964)
Bearheart of the Great Northwest (Pathe-Alpha/Medallion, 1964)
The Sound of Music (20th Century–Fox, 1965)
Picture Mommy Dead (Embassy, 1966)
Seven Women (MGM, 1966)
In Like Flint (20th Century–Fox, 1967)
Star! (Those Were the Happy Times) (20th Century–Fox, 1968)

*... Hitch was trying to determine which dummy of Mother
to use in* Psycho, *and so periodically when I would walk into
my trailer on the set, there would be this apparition there —
a dummy of Mother. There were various forms of Mother; I don't know
whether he was gauging the volume of my screams or what, but
I'm sure I had something to do with the decision
as to which Mother was used in the climax!*

Janet Leigh

A GENERATION AGO it wasn't entirely fashionable for a mainstream actress to lend her name and her talents to horror and fantasy film subjects, but through those years Janet Leigh brought her blend of charm and screen acting skill to a number of genre productions. She played the wife of the world's celebrated Master of Escape (portrayed by her then-husband Tony Curtis) in George Pal's production of *Houdini;* added a touch of romantic sophistication to John Frankenheimer's *The Manchurian Candidate;* played opposite her real-life daughter Jamie Lee Curtis in John Carpenter's *The Fog;* and took on the mantel of monster fighter in the hare-brained ecological thriller *Night of the Lepus.* Her best-remembered role, however, was and will always remain Marion Crane, the most grossly inconvenienced guest in motel history, in Alfred Hitchcock's landmark *Psycho.*

California-born, Jeanette Helen Morrison spent a movie-crazy youth in darkened theaters before being "discovered" by former MGM top-liner Norma Shearer. Signed to a Metro contract, the wholesome ingenue, now rechristened Janet Leigh, appeared in a succession of popular films (including *The Romance of Rosy Ridge, If Winter Comes* [1947], *Act of Violence* [1948], *Little Women* [1949] and *The Naked Spur* [1953]) which quickly propelled her into the front ranks of '50s stars. (The veteran actress recounted her experiences in these and other film classics in her 1984 autobiography *There Really Was a Hollywood.*) Leigh took a break from her current writing activities to reminisce about Pal and Hitchcock, escape artists, shower scenes and bloodthirsty bunnies in this interview.

How did the film Houdini *come about?*

As I understand it, the producer, George Pal, had wanted to make *Houdini* for a long time. He was the man who had done all those wonderful Puppetoons, as well as several features prior to *Houdini*—he was a brilliant man. George was very interested in having Tony [Curtis] play Houdini; Tony and I had just been married and so they wanted *me* to play Mrs. Houdini. My studio, Metro, was not very happy about the idea of loaning me to Paramount, but I was so excited at the thought of doing it. Eventually they made their deal, so that we could do it. George hired [mentalist] Joe Dunninger to do the illusions, and he also had [magician] George Boston to be on the set and to teach us some of the magic and escape tricks. It was fascinating to do. *Houdini* was the first picture either of us did for Paramount.

Did you enjoy working there?

Yes, it was a wonderful lot. It was like Universal—it was small, and very family-oriented. It was fun because you rode bicycles all over, everybody knew everybody and so on. I liked it a lot.

George Pal has a large following among fans of science fiction and fantasy films. What more can you recall about working with him?

He was just the sweetest, nicest, gentlest man—and, obviously, brilliant.

Previous page: A star in four dozen films, Janet Leigh is destined to be best remembered for her role as Marion Crane in the opening reels of Hitchcock's *Psycho.*

Very meticulous, very caring, always wanting everything to be *right*. He was just an extraordinary person, to be that brilliant and to be that gentle.

Was he a hands-on producer?

Yes, he was there on the set a lot. He was not an interfering type — he was there to make sure that everything went smoothly and that everything was right.

Wasn't Houdini *originally scheduled for black-and-white?*

That's right, it *was* scheduled for black-and-white. I remember that Edith Head, who did the wardrobe, and I were going through the first fitting together, and the costumes were just so beautiful and so colorful. Edith called George over to the fitting room and said, "You just look at these costumes. I mean, if these are not just wasted in black-and-white! It's ridiculous." And George, in his quiet way, said, "I know . . . I just came from the front office, and it's going to be in color." Of course it wasn't just the costumes that prompted that, he had also been thinking about the whole atmosphere of the picture — the magic and the sideshow settings and all the rest. If *Houdini* had been done in black-and-white, it *would* have been a waste.

What kind of shooting schedule was Houdini *made on?*

It was a fairly long one. *Houdini* didn't have a blockbuster-type budget, but it did take time to shoot some of the sequences. I don't remember the exact amount of time, but I imagine it was somewhere between six and eight weeks.

What was the necessity for you and Tony Curtis to learn actual illusionists' tricks when they could have been easily faked with camera trickery?

Oh, but that was the point, so that it *wouldn't* have to be done with camera trickery. When Tony "levitated" me, there were no cuts, and there were no cuts during some of the other tricks — they were done "legit." Now, when it came to the escape scenes, the roping and chaining and all, those scenes had to be fixed because Tony wasn't Houdini; he didn't have the ability to contort his body or to manipulate the locks like Houdini did. Houdini had tremendous spiritual energy; he could get his body into positions that were just *[laughs]* — not human, almost!

How closely did the film follow Houdini's life?

As much as it could; I mean, there was obviously some dramatic license. You have to be true as much as you can, but you still are making a picture that is supposed to be entertaining. Bess Houdini *was* a little "off" in reality, evidently — a little strange *[laughs]*! — and you don't want to depict that. But they did the best they could, trying to make an accurate yet still an enjoyable motion picture.

11495-23

Leigh and husband Tony Curtis in producer George Pal's *Houdini*.

In preparing for your roles, did you meet and discuss Harry and Bess Houdini with people who actually knew the couple?

Yes, with Dunninger, and with a couple of other people. We also read a lot of books about the life history of Houdini.

Orson Welles, who knew Houdini when he [Welles] was a kid, really used to put down Houdini, especially the fabricated ending. Did he ever say anything to you?

No, he never did mention that to us. I guess he felt it wasn't what it should have been—maybe he would have made *Citizen Kane* out of it *[laughs]*! Obviously he would have done it differently, which is fine—

everybody has a different approach. We couldn't depict what really happened to Harry Houdini [a college student suckerpunched Houdini, rupturing his appendix] because some of the heirs to the guy who did it were still alive, and they would have sued. That's why in the movie we had to have Houdini bump into a table! We *knew* that the guy had hit Houdini and ruptured his appendix—Houdini wasn't ready, he hadn't tightened his stomach muscles so that he could "take" the punch—but legally that was something we couldn't do.

Were there any dangers or risks connected with the film's stunt and escape scenes?

Not really. I do recall that there's a scene where Tony, in preparing to go into the Detroit River, sits in a bathtub filled with ice so that his body would get used to that temperature. Well, he got ice burn, and he broke out all over his body—that wasn't very pleasant. Also, there's an early scene where Tony and I are on a stage and everything starts going haywire, and a fishbowl falls and shatters. We actually slipped and fell on some glass—it was supposed to be a fiasco, and it was! But the scene itself really turned out well.

The first two-thirds of Houdini *is fun and colorful, but once the picture takes that turn toward spiritualism and heavy drama, it becomes a turnoff.*

There's where their strangeness came in; as I understand from what I read, Houdini spent the last part of his life trying to find out if he could reach his dead mother. Toward the end the film began to depict that part of their lives rather than his wonderful ability and the love between the two of them. It was very strong, and I agree with you; I feel that the last part of *Houdini* was much harder to pull off. Houdini was exposing the falsity of these charlatans [spiritualists], and I think it was more difficult for audiences to accept that phase of the picture, especially at that time—that was before Shirley MacLaine's book came out *[laughs]*! It was a little far-fetched for the audiences of that era. Of course, *now,* maybe not.

Supposedly Houdini left a secret message to his wife; the idea was that if a spiritualist could repeat that message after Houdini was dead, she would know that he was legit.

And she went to dozens and dozens of spiritualists, and apparently none of them knew that message. *They* hadn't read Shirley's book, either!

Exactly how did you become involved on Psycho?

Mr. Hitchcock sent me the book and said that he would like me to play Marion Crane. He said that the script was not quite finished, and there would be some changes—they would not change the fact that Marion got killed, but there would be changes in the character. The movie Marion would not be quite as mousy; in the book she was really quite plain, and Hitchcock didn't intend

Top: Vera Miles, John Gavin and Janet Leigh in a publicity photo for *Psycho. Bottom:* Leigh consults with the Master of Suspense during a break in the shooting of *Psycho*, as costumer Rita Riggs makes an adjustment to her wardrobe.

to do that. He wanted the love scenes between the characters of Marion and Sam to be very realistic. I read the book and I could see what was there, and just the idea of working with Hitchcock was enough for me.

How did *you enjoy working with Hitchcock?*
I loved him—just adored him. He was obviously the most prepared director. After I did get the script and I was signed, I went to meet him and he showed me how every shot in the picture was already worked out.

Psycho *was made quickly and inexpensively with TV technicians. How did you adjust to the more rapid pace?*
I loved it. The sophistication of the equipment had progressed by that time, so things didn't take so long. It's very difficult to "sustain" a character when you're waiting, forever it seems, between shots. So I absolutely adored it.

In your book you wrote that Hitchcock promised to let you alone and allow you to shape your own performance. Did he provide you with much in the way of direction or guidance?
If I needed it. But as long as what I did fit into his camera and fulfilled the piece of his picture I was supposed to fulfill, he let me pretty much alone. If I didn't come up to it—in other words, if there was more he needed—or if I went beyond it and should do less, he would tell me. But otherwise I was on my own.

Much has been recently written about the "dark side" of Hitchcock's personality, but you never seemed to be on the receiving end of any of this.
Nope. I assume that that is true, I can't say yes or no, I can only talk about what was with me. He couldn't have been better with me. One funny thing I recall is that Hitch was trying to determine which dummy of Mother to use in the film, and so periodically when I would come back from lunch and I'd walk into my trailer on the set, there would be this apparition there—a dummy of Mother. There were various forms of Mother; I don't know whether he was gauging the volume of my screams or what *[laughs]*, but I'm sure I had something to do with the decision as to which Mother was used in the climax!

Both Vera Miles and John Gavin got a dose of Hitchcock's displeasure.
I never worked with Vera Miles, I was done by the time that she started, and I only had that one opening scene with John Gavin. I remember John had a little trouble in the love scenes—it just wasn't as passionate as Hitchcock wanted—but I don't know first-hand whether or not John and Hitchcock had any subsequent run-ins.

The bathroom and shower scenes were well ahead of their time. Were you pleased with the history-making opportunity, or did you go in with misgivings?

I had no misgivings whatsoever. None. I knew how hard Hitchcock had worked and how he had manipulated the censor office to get certain things into the picture. He would put outrageous things in the script, knowing that the censors would tell him there was no way that he'd be allowed to do them; and then Hitchcock would say, "Okay, then I'll give *that* up, but I *have* to have *this*" — the things he had actually wanted all along.

Is it really true that Psycho *has turned you off on taking showers?*

[Ingenuously.] Uh huh — it is absolutely true. I'm a scairdy-cat *[laughs]*! I won't even take a bath in a hotel unless I can face out, even if I have to have my back to the faucets. It just scares me — I never thought about it before *Psycho,* but you are absolutely defenseless in that situation.

Did Hitchcock actually try to inveigle you into doing that shower scene in the nude?

That is b.s. There have been so many myths about that shower scene, and I've tried to put them to rest every time they've come up. What some people forget is that we had the Hays Office in those days. There was censorship. There was no *way* we could do it in the nude — no possible way! There *couldn't* have been a nude model, because it would not have been allowed in the picture. The only time that they used a stand-in for me was when Tony Perkins pulled the body out of the bathroom. Hitchcock said there was no sense in my doing that; no one could see who was wrapped up in that shower curtain, so there would be no purpose served by me getting dragged and bumped around in that scene. But getting back to what I was saying, those people don't realize what the censorship restrictions were like at that time, as compared to today. Today, of course, there'd be no fuss at all about a person doing a scene like that in the nude. But at that time we couldn't. The fact that I had a bra and a half-slip in that opening scene with John Gavin caused such consternation at the Hays Office, you wouldn't believe; Hitchcock had to fight like hell to get that into the picture. And you never see *anything* in the shower scene. That was the genius of Hitchcock. People swear they saw the knife go in, but they never showed that — it was not allowed. You saw a belly button, and even *that* was something that was very difficult, and was almost not allowed. But that's all you saw — you *thought* you saw more, but you didn't.

You received a death threat after Psycho *was released.*

Oh, yeah — several. Some of them were so bad that we had to turn them over to the F.B.I. There were several they wouldn't even let me look at. One really explicit one came from Chicago, just as we were leaving to go on a publicity tour to Chicago! And I was terrified. The F.B.I. traced it down and found the guy — he was sort of a "listed" nut — and they made sure that he was not loose while I was there!

The influence of Psycho *changed the face of horror films. What do you think of the new breed of gore-spattered horror films* Psycho *helped spawn?*

The brilliance of *Psycho* was that your imagination was allowed to flourish. Today, you don't have to use your imagination, they show you everything. I think the new horror films are not as good. Your imagination is much stronger than anything that they could graphically depict.

Do you see many new horror films?

No.

Did you see the Psycho *sequels?*

I saw *Psycho II* but I haven't see *III* yet — I should see *III*, because Tony Perkins directed it, but so far I just haven't. I didn't think very highly of *Psycho II;* it left nothing to the imagination. As I said earlier, what your mind conjures up is so vivid that nothing can match it.

In your opinion, what would Hitchcock have thought of these sequels?

[Looking heavenward.] Hitch, I hope I'm saying it right — here goes: I think he would have just been revolted. That type of film is just so contrary to what he believed in, which was suspense and mystery, imagination and titillation. And there's none of that in *Psycho II*.

Was there ever any talk of working with Hitchcock again after Psycho?

No. After the impact that *Psycho* had, you couldn't have Marion Crane in another Hitchcock picture — you just couldn't! Because no matter what role I played, it still would have been Marion Crane. So it just couldn't be.

If by some stretch of the imagination you had been offered a role in a new Psycho *film, would you have accepted it?*

No — and my daughter Jamie [Lee Curtis] didn't, either. She was offered a part in *Psycho II* [the Meg Tilly role].

What prompted her decision to turn it down?

[Laughs.] Wisdom!

In preparing for your role in The Manchurian Candidate, *did you read the original novel by Richard Condon?*

You want to hear something really weird? Before there was any talk at all about making *Manchurian Candidate* into a movie, I read the book on a chartered plane on the way to President Kennedy's inauguration ball. It bothered me so — I got so *mad* — that I threw the book across the plane! I had that same reaction reading *From Here to Eternity*—when Prew got killed in that book I was so upset that I threw the book. And as I said, that happened again with *Manchurian Candidate.* And Frank Sinatra was on the plane! I had no idea that Frank was going to do the picture or that I was going to be in it! All I knew was that I had a very strong reaction to that novel.

You did another especially good job of acting in that film.

I loved that part; it was a very difficult one. One of my most difficult roles, in fact—not in its length, but in its *brevity,* almost! The book had the luxury of being able to relate all of the characters' thoughts and what was happening within them, whereas in the movie everything is conveyed either through the visuals or through the dialogue. My character, Rosie, comes in around the middle of the film; all of a sudden there's this lady on the train! It was really difficult because I had to make an impact right away; the audience had to know, when I'm making these ridiculous non sequitur remarks, what I was trying to do. It was a very hard thing to do, and I was very pleased. For the kind of role that it was, I was very happy with it.

And it really is one of John Frankenheimer's best pictures.

He was such a strong, dynamic director—I really enjoyed working with him. We had lunch before we did the train scene, because that scene had to be so "on" and it had to have that impact. He was wonderful, and I liked him a lot.

In growing up, did you have a fondness for fantasy, horror and science fiction films?

I've always liked *all* movies, horror movies included. I remember there was one picture we saw, my girlfriend and I—we weren't supposed to go—and it was about a house, almost like the *Psycho* house in a way, and there was a crazy person on the third floor [probably Universal's *The Old Dark House*]. I'll never forget that one—we were scared out of our wits! And I remember *Dracula* and *Frankenstein,* and the other classics. I saw everything—I lived at the movie theaters.

What possessed MGM to make a film like Night of the Lepus?

[Shaking her head.] Don't ask me *[laughs]*! No, I take that back. I read the script, and I have to tell you that it read very well. *Night of the Lepus* was made at the time of science fiction pictures like *Willard* and *Ben* and *Frogs,* and I must repeat that the script read very well. No one twisted my arm and said I had to do it. What no one realized was that, no matter what you do, a bunny rabbit is a bunny rabbit! A rat, *that* can be menacing —so can a frog. Spiders or scorpions or alligators—they could all work in that situation, and they have. But—a *bunny rabbit?* How can you make a bunny rabbit menacing, what can you do? It just didn't work.

Leigh took on killer bunny rabbits in the infamous *Night of the Lepus*.

Wasn't a man in a bunny suit used in several scenes?

Yes, there was somebody they put a bunny suit on, to achieve some of the effects—I've forgotten as much as I could about that picture.

Did the rest of the cast and crew go in with good intentions and high hopes, or did everyone else know from Day One that it was a losing battle?

Oh, no—it didn't dawn on anyone until—

Day Two?

[*Laughs.*] It took about four or five days before we realized that perhaps we didn't have the ideal director. That was disheartening. And then it was not until the first scene with the big bunnies that we all realized that it was hopeless.

How did you land your part in The Fog?

I saw *Halloween,* Jamie's first picture and I thought that for $300,000 or whatever it cost, there was so much value on the screen that it was wonderful. I was anxious to meet [director] John Carpenter after seeing the picture; we met and talked, and became friends. He asked me if I would ever want to work in one of his pictures and I said I would love to do it. And that's when he wrote a part for me in *The Fog.* We shot *The Fog* outside of San Francisco, by Point Reyes, where the Sir Francis Drake Bay is.

How did you enjoy acting alongside your daughter?

Oh, it was fun—we didn't have enough scenes together, though.

Is Jamie Lee glad to have shed her "Queen of the Horror Films" image?

Jamie was very grateful for those pictures—*very* grateful!—but then after a period of time she felt that she didn't want to just do those. And she was fortunate enough to go another step, into another genre—the "body" pictures. Then, when it seemed like every picture had to have a nude scene in it, she realized that she didn't want to move from Horror Queen to Body Queen. That's when she started doing pictures like *Amazing Grace and Chuck, A Man in Love* [1987] and *Dominick and Eugene* [1988]. It's a legitimate kind of progression, and she's been fortunate enough to take these steps. She really wants to keep growing, because in this business that's what you hope you do, as a person and as an actress.

The Fog *is a very slick and good-looking film, but it really didn't come off very well.*

No, not as well as it should have. I, too, thought it was *done* well; I agree with you, but I don't know just what's wrong. The special effects came across and everything. Maybe it was just a little too farfetched. *Halloween* had a more understandable, basic kind of menace, whereas in *The Fog* they were really reaching. That probably was the reason that it didn't quite make it.

If you had to be remembered for just one film, would you want it to be Psycho?

[Laughs.] I don't know if I have a choice!

But isn't it unflattering for a star to be best remembered for a supporting part?

If you think about it, the rest of the picture, after Marion's been killed, is about trying to find Marion. So Marion is really there the whole time, even though you only saw her for X-number of minutes. Also, one picture does not

Movie-making is a family affair on the set of *The Fog*. From right to left are Janet Leigh, daughter Jamie Lee Curtis, writer/director John Carpenter and Carpenter's then–actress wife, Adrienne Barbeau.

a star make, and one picture does not a career make. For an actress to be remembered at all is very flattering.

JANET LEIGH FILMOGRAPHY

The Romance of Rosy Ridge (MGM, 1947)
If Winter Comes (MGM, 1947)
Hills of Home (MGM, 1948)
Words and Music (MGM, 1948)
Act of Violence (MGM, 1948)
Little Women (MGM, 1949)
That Forsyte Woman (MGM, 1949)
The Doctor and the Girl (MGM, 1949)
The Red Danube (MGM, 1949)
Holiday Affair (RKO, 1949)
Strictly Dishonorable (MGM, 1951)
Angels in the Outfield (MGM, 1951)

Two Tickets to Broadway (RKO, 1951)
It's a Big Country (MGM, 1951)
Just This Once (MGM, 1952)
Scaramouche (MGM, 1952)
Fearless Fagan (MGM, 1952)
The Naked Spur (MGM, 1953)
Confidentially Connie (MGM, 1953)
Houdini (Paramount, 1953)
Walking My Baby Back Home (Universal, 1953)
Prince Valiant (20th Century–Fox, 1954)
Living It Up (Paramount, 1954)
The Black Shield of Falworth (Universal, 1954)
Rogue Cop (MGM, 1954)
Pete Kelly's Blues (Warners, 1955)
My Sister Eileen (Columbia, 1955)
Safari (Columbia, 1956)
Jet Pilot (Universal, 1957)
Touch of Evil (Universal, 1958)
The Vikings (United Artists, 1958)
The Perfect Furlough (Universal, 1958)
Who Was That Lady? (Columbia, 1960)
Psycho (Paramount, 1960)
Pepe (Columbia, 1960)
The Manchurian Candidate (United Artists, 1962)
Bye Bye Birdie (Columbia, 1963)
Wives and Lovers (Paramount, 1963)
Three on a Couch (Columbia, 1966)
Harper (Warners, 1966)
Kid Rodelo (Paramount, 1966)
An American Dream (Warners, 1966)
Grand Slam (Paramount, 1968)
Hello Down There (Paramount, 1969)
Night of the Lepus (MGM, 1972)
One Is a Lonely Number (MGM, 1972)
Boardwalk (Atlantic Releasing, 1979)
The Fog (Avco Embassy, 1980)
Psycho II (Universal, 1983) clips from *Psycho*

I realize that . . . it's
almost impossible [to break away
from my image of being a "horror writer"].
I wrote that TV movie called The Morning After . . .
about an alcoholic, and it worked out well—it's a beautiful film
and they use it in hospitals. And one of the critics wrote
a review and said, "This situation is a real horror. And
who better to write the script than Richard Matheson."
And so I figured, "To hell with it!"
I'll never get away from it!

Richard Matheson

LONG RECOGNIZED as one of the deans of modern-day fantasy writers, Richard Matheson has been screenwriting many of his tales of terror for a third of a century—from the cobweb-festooned mansions of Edgar Allan Poe to the subconscious world of the Marquis De Sade, from the dark dens of ghosts and vampires to the submicroscopic haunts of the Shrinking Man. Still active within the genre, Matheson shows himself in this interview to be as personable as he is prolific and popular.

Born in New Jersey and raised in Brooklyn, Richard Burton Matheson first became a published author while still a child, when his stories and poems ran in the old *Brooklyn Eagle*. A lifelong reader of fantasy tales, he made his professional writing bow in 1950 when his short story "Born of Man and Woman" appeared in *The Magazine of Fantasy and Science Fiction*, and he continued to turn out a number of highly regarded horror, fantasy and mystery stories throughout that decade. Matheson broke into films in 1956, adapting his novel *The Shrinking Man* for the big-screen *The Incredible Shrinking Man*, and has gone on to write dozens of movies, TV movies and series episodes.

Where did you come up with the idea for your book The Shrinking Man?

I was in Redondo Beach, California, in a theater, and I was seeing a picture called *Let's Do It Again* [1953] with Jane Wyman and Ray Milland. There was a scene where Ray Milland is leaving this apartment in a huff, and by mistake he grabs Aldo Ray's hat, sticks it on his head and it comes right down over his ears. And I wondered, what if a man put on his *own* hat, and that happened? That was the genesis of it.

Did you peddle the story around to studios, or did Universal come to you?

I believed then, and still do pretty much, that the best way to break into the movies is to write something that the studios would want to buy and then say, "I want to adapt it." So, after the book was written, I had it submitted by my sometimes-agent out here, a man named Al Manuel, who had never sold anything of mine before. And Universal made an offer on it.

Was Universal the only studio to show interest?

I don't know. They were the first to make an offer, and it was all so stunning to me that I never even asked Al whether he had submitted it elsewhere! That was when I broke into screenwriting, when I told them that I wanted to do the script.

What were your impressions of producer Albert Zugsmith?

I ended up writing a couple of pictures for him [*Shrinking Man* and 1959's *The Beat Generation*]. He seemed typical of the ten-inch-cigar-smoking executive of the time. He came out of the newspaper field, and he always used

Previous page: Renowned for his continued presence at the leading edge of innovation in SF and fantasy literature, Richard Matheson has many times turned his hand to the writing of screenplays.

to say to me, "I'm gonna give ya a scriptwriting lesson, kiddie!" At that time I assumed that I would be using the structure of my book.

Why did Universal insist on dropping your book's flashback story structure?

That was not the way they handled things in those days. I mean, they couldn't do *Last Year at Marienbad* back then; the story had to be in chronological order, to begin at the beginning and progress from there. As a result of which, I think the first part of the film is the weaker part. I wrote it that way in my novel originally and it got tedious, so I decided I would structure it the way I had structured *I Am Legend:* start smack-dab in the middle and then, in flashbacks, bring the story up to date.

What changes did writer Richard Alan Simmons make when he came along?

Gosh, it's been so long that I can't really recall—I don't think I had the paint can sequence in my script, and there must have been other things as well. I remember that Universal asked me to share a writing co-credit with him, and I wrote some enraged précis of all the changes he had made, and insisted that he had done really nothing to it. I realized in later years that, since it was my first picture, and because he was a very nice man, he may well have just backed off and let me have the solo credit. I did meet him; as a matter of fact, he's the one that got me to join the Writers Guild. He came into my office at Universal, representing them, and since I was working then as a professional he said I should plan on joining the Writers Guild. He's a very talented writer.

Did you get to meet Jack Arnold at that same time?

Oh, yeah, sure. A little on the picture—not too much—but later on through the years we really met. As a matter of fact, I believe it was his wife that showed us the house where we're now living; she was doing some realty work at the time, and in fact they lived right around the corner from here. So we got to know them here and at conventions.

Did Zugsmith have anything to do with the picture? Arnold's always insisting that the man did nothing.

Well, if Jack says that, I believe it; I'm sure the film was Jack's "vision." Actually, it took me a long time to appreciate what the picture was. I have a tendency always to have in my mind an image of what a picture should be, and of course the picture almost never matches the image. So I'm always disappointed, and sometimes it takes me a long time before I look at it for what it is. *The Incredible Shrinking Man,* it took me forever! My son Richard finally got me to come around by pointing out to me how unusual it was for that time and how wonderfully visual it was. I had never compared it to the pictures that were being made at that time, especially by Universal. And that ending was not a typical Universal ending.

Another day, another dollar: Grant Williams punches in at Universal in a gag shot for *The Incredible Shrinking Man*. (Photo courtesy Mark McGee.)

Technically, was the film everything you hoped it would be?

Oh, yeah, you couldn't fault that, it was remarkable what they did. Visually it was a feast, and Jack Arnold did a very good job.

I went on from there and wrote a sequel because Universal wanted to use all those sets and giant props. It was called *The Fantastic Little Girl,* and it had his wife shrinking and joining him in the submicroscopic world. But Universal never made it.

You ended up writing a few scripts for Zugsmith that never reached the screen.

Zugsmith wanted to do *Gulliver's Travels,* and I did an entire screenplay in which a little boy played the part of Gulliver. Then after that, because this was about the time of *Around the World in 80 Days* [1956], Zugsmith wanted to get David Niven and Cantinflas to star in it, so I wrote another screenplay in which David Niven was Gulliver and Cantinflas was some little Lilliputian soldier. Needless to say, these were not made.

How did your Fantastic Little Girl *script end?*
    Oh, that one had a Universal ending. Something happened where the process was reversed and they ended up back in hearth and home, happy as a couple bugs in a rug *[laughs]*! I don't know why the sequel wasn't made; at that time they told me that only *To Hell and Back* [1955] and *Away All Boats* [1956] had made more money for that studio than *The Incredible Shrinking Man* did. It made a ton of money! The picture cost $800,000, which for that time I guess was quite a bit, but it made a lot of money and I have no idea why they didn't shoot the sequel. They had all those big sets, Grant Williams and Randy Stuart were available and Jack Arnold was available. They were crazy, they should have done it, because it would have made a bundle of money. They use some of those giant props on the Universal tour—or at least they did, a few years ago.

Did you visit those oversized sets?
    Oh, yeah. I was watching them the day they shot the flood scene, with the giant pencil and the water heater breaking and (Jack's famous anecdote) the prophylactics filled with water to get the effect of giant water droplets. Poor Grant Williams, that guy looked beat! He nearly killed himself; he was almost blinded by an arc light, he was nearly electrocuted, he was half-drowned...! Boy, did he work hard!
    In later years, when my agent told me they were going to do a remake of *The Incredible Shrinking Man,* in my naivete I said, "Well, I want to do the structure of the book now." And it turned out they were going to do *The Incredible Shrinking Woman* and make it into a comedy, so that was the end of that *[laughs]*!

What did you think of Shrinking Woman?
    I thought it was terrible. The fact that they were doing a parody, that was okay, that didn't bother me, but I just thought it was bad—not funny. I think *I* could have written a funnier comedy!

Who approached you to write the screenplay for House of Usher?
    American International—James Nicholson. Nicholson was my contact; we really got along very well and he liked what I did. I saw Sam Arkoff, of course, but Nicholson was my friend in court, my compadre. Nicholson had the desire to do better and better things. In the beginning I didn't know

An overworked Grant Williams catches his breath between shots on *The Incredible Shrinking Man*. (Photo courtesy Robert Skotak.)

American International; I didn't really know anything about these people. When I met Roger Corman, I assumed that *House of Usher* was his project. I didn't know that he was working for AIP, and he had this deal where he would be producer and director. I don't even remember exactly when I met Nicholson and Arkoff—probably during the shooting of the picture.

House of Usher *was AIP's first stab at a reasonably respectable picture.*
       I don't think they planned to make a "respectable picture"; it just turned out that way because I wrote a very good script. Maybe they wanted to go classy with Edgar Allan Poe, but if it had turned out like *Attack of the Crab Monsters* *[laughs]* I don't think they would have cared that much! As a matter of fact, from what I understood they were totally thrown off by the fact that *House of Usher* did so well. It was running all summer—it ran in a double-bill with *Psycho* in many places. The very fact that American International could make something that had some semblance of quality, and still make a lot of money, I don't think that had ever occurred to them.

At that point Corman had only a history of low-budget SF/action films. Were you aware of his rush-rush, fast-buck reputation?

I didn't really know his background, I was no fan of that kind of picture, so I had no idea where he came from. When I met him through *House of Usher,* I would say that to all effects it was the first time I had met him or even knew of him.

So you were never a follower of the kind of SF films that came out during the '50s?

No, I wasn't—I never cared for those "monster" movies, atomic radiation things or giant insects. There were a few good ones, like *Them!,* but it got very repetitive. I always preferred fantasy movies; when I was a teenager I was a big fan of Val Lewton's. Subtle types of horror pictures, not the smash-you-over-the-head-with-a-club type. To me the ideal fantasy film was *Rosemary's Baby,* which is just so realistic that it sneaks up on you.

So what's your verdict on today's horror films?

[Groans.] Oh, I don't even go see them! I don't write this stuff anymore; I have opportunities all the time, but I literally don't want to have anything to do with them. I mean, they're revolting—axes in heads and people's stomachs splitting open...!

What are some of the ins and outs of adapting a Poe story like House of Usher *to the screen?*

Except for maybe some of the short Poe stories I adapted for *Tales of Terror, House of Usher* probably came the closest to the original. I tried to stay close, but even at that I added a romance to it. Other people have made it exactly the way Poe wrote it, and it's a pretty moody piece. I really worked on it, I tried very hard to get the whole flavor. I did a long, complex outline, and American International was very pleased with it. Vincent Price was delighted, because he hadn't done anything good in quite a while. I think he really outdid himself in *House of Usher.* I had seen him so many times with a mustache that when I saw him for the first time on the set and he was clean-shaven, I was startled *[laughs]*!

Price really did have enthusiasm for House of Usher?

He had enthusiasm about a number of those films—or, at least, I spoke to him and he sounded enthusiastic. (Of course, he's a very genial man.) I think he was impressed by the scripts and he felt inspired, elevated to give an outstanding performance. When you're handed a potboiler script, your tendency is not to do an outstanding Shakespearean performance. I think he enjoyed *Master of the World,* and that he also enjoyed *House of Usher* because it gave him something to work with. Then later on I gave him comedy to do, which he was very good at. So I think he was very pleased with them; at least he has said so.

Sibling tensions flare as Myrna Fahey and Vincent Price lock horns in *House of Usher*.

The books say that House of Usher *cost $300,000, with $100,000 of that going to Price.*

As far as I know, they made it for $125,000 exclusive of salaries. I had the usual 5 percent of the net profit, and every time I got a statement from AIP the price of the picture had gone up. It was ludicrous. And I know they made millions and millions of dollars!

Corman used to threaten to take AIP to court all the time.

I should have done that, because I had the same thing happen on all their pictures. Finally I got tired of it and I let them buy my little 5 percents, on all my pictures, for a total of $10,000. I would have gotten back a lot more just out of TV residuals and video cassettes. Arkoff was a . . . shark. Someone told me that if while they were making a picture they went out to lunch, and on the way back Arkoff bought a pack of gum, the pack of gum became part of the budget *[laughs]*!

Did you ever see Arkoff on the sets of these movies?

No, he was strictly business. Although I do remember that on one of the cast parties (it may have been *House of Usher*), his wife cooked up all the food! AIP was still on that level. Arkoff's a strange man; he would go to New York, so I was told, rush from the airplane to Broadway, grab a hot dog and go to the theater. Which seems out of keeping with the image that he presents: all business, no taste. But it turns out that's not the case.

The story that goes around is that Arkoff was down on the idea of doing House of Usher *because there was no monster, no real selling point.*

I never heard that, but I wouldn't be surprised. I'm sure it was Nicholson's notion. I mean, anytime that anything of an artistic nature came up, and it was going to cost more than ten dollars, I'm sure Arkoff tried to veto it. They were a strange combination.

The punchline is that Arkoff had to be convinced that the house itself was the monster.

I remember writing lines like, "The house itself is evil" and stuff like that. That's probably what got Arkoff to get off the dime.

Did you have any say in casting?

No, I think Roger did that. Outside of Price, he had a little coterie of people that he kept using. As they got more into the oldtimers, the casts got better and better; in the early pictures the casting was not that good. But they tried—God knows they were sincere about it.

What were your impressions of Corman?

My impression of him was that he was a camera director. I never saw him talk to actors, he would just let the people determine their own performances. The only thing I ever heard him say repeatedly was, after he'd do a shot, he'd spin on his heel and say, "We're on the wrong set." Once he's done, he just wants his crew to get where the hell they're going *[laughs]*! That's how he saves so much money. I've known him for years and he's a funny guy. You'd think he just got off the ferryboat—he's got that sheepish smile, and he acts as though he just came out of the cornfield or something! But, Jesus, what a mind—a very smart man!

Charles B. Griffith, Corman's regular scriptwriter, was put out that he didn't get to write House of Usher. *Corman told him that no screenwriter who gets less than $50,000 a script is any good.*
   [Laughs.] Well, they sure didn't pay me $50,000—they paid me $5,000!

Did you visit the sets this time around?
   Hanging around sets can get extremely boring. You figure, the picture's going to be 80, 85 minutes long, and they had two-week shooting schedules. So 14 days, at eight to nine hours a day, to end up with 80 minutes means that there's a lot of time spent just setting up lights and moving sets and dressing people—and that's very boring. And then when they actually do a scene, it's very brief, half a page or something. But I was on the *House of Usher* set a little bit; I remember that they shot it at the old Chaplin studio. Mark Damon was playing, I guess, at being a method actor, and before he went on the set he would run in place and huff and puff *[laughs]*! Then he'd walk in on a scene where Price would be chatting with somebody, and Price would out-act the hell out of him!
   Then there was the only time that I ever saw Vincent Price angry. Mark Damon comes in and he's about to strike Price with an axe, he flings the axe down, and it bounces right off Price's shin! Price uttered the only profanity I ever heard him say, he left the stage, walked around the whole thing. And then when he came back, he was himself again. Really, he's an incredibly nice man—you never met a nicer man than Vincent.

What changes would you make in House of Usher *if you could?*
   I would like to have seen (let's say) Joseph Losey direct it *[laughs]*, and some of the performances were a little limited, I think.

It was a hit nevertheless.
   It made millions of dollars, and AIP was totally bowled over by it. It opened in June, I think, and it just kept running all through July and August and made millions. I don't think they had any plan to make a whole series of Poe pictures; if it had done the usual, they would have just moved on to something else.

Who came up with the idea to do Master of the World *at this point?*

They did. I didn't realize until just recently that in writing my screenplay for that I had combined two Jules Verne books, *Master of the World* and *Robur the Conqueror;* I didn't know I had done that.

And came up with a picture that most resembles the movie 20,000 Leagues Under the Sea.

The similarities were in the books: a man who has this enormous image of creating peace in the world. Incidentally, I thought *20,000 Leagues Under the Sea* was a marvelous picture. I was so impressed when I found out that the guy who wrote the screenplay for that picture [Earl Felton] had been with it, not only all through the writing but all through the shooting, under contract. Which, to me, is the obvious way to do a picture, but which they almost never do.

Isn't it frustrating to write a screenplay like Master of the World, *one that requires a champagne budget, for a Kool-Aid company like AIP?*

Oh, sure. AIP spent like a half a million dollars on it, which for them was just incredible, but it still had a limited look to it.

Charles Bronson was certainly miscast.

He was miscast, and he knew it; he was very unhappy. Testy is more the word. I remember a real strange day on the set: The first day I went in to watch them shoot, I walked up to him and said, "Hello, Mr. Bronson. I'm the writer of this picture—" And he said, "Oh, don't talk to me," and he walked away! Which, of course, really pissed me off. Later on he came back, I guess feeling a little guilty about it, and said, "Hey, I hear you're a very good writer." I said, "I am," then walked away from *him [laughs]*! Then after lunch, I went back to him and said, "Can we start all over again?" We chatted awhile; he said, "I hope you don't mind my playing it like a coal miner." And then the next morning he walked by me and never said a word. Vincent Price, who could make friends with a dead man—and very often *has*, in his movies *[laughs]*— said, "I can't get through to this guy. I cannot make friends with him." I guess Bronson's always been that way. Very strange.

Anytime I found actors to be unpleasant at all, they were always the younger actors. Either they were uptight, or they felt arrogant, or whatever. But the oldtimers, I never met one who wasn't really pleasant, congenial, very friendly.

Did you think that Price did a good job in Master of the World?

Yeah, I think he did a very good job. I only wish that they had had the budget of *20,000 Leagues Under the Sea.* What annoyed me most was all that damn stock footage that they rented from *The Four Feathers* [1939], for God's sake, and from *Henry V* [1945]—I mean *[laughs]*, history periods were jumping all over the place!

David Frankham, Mary Webster and Vincent Price don't care what composer Les Baxter is pointing at on the set of *Master of the World*. (Photo courtesy Robert Skotak.)

Do you remember encountering Henry Hull on Master of the World?

I think maybe very briefly. Now there was a real ham. Henry Hull was a very nice man, but I think he always had the tendency to overact; he came from the stage, and I guess he just never really was able to shed that.

How about William Witney, the director?

Yeah, sure—I had an argument with him in our first meeting! I have had so few arguments down through the years—I've been at it since '55—and we were at each other's throats in seconds! He had a demeaning attitude about the whole project—"Well, if you really want to do this stupid thing, I'll see if I can pull it together"—and I really got ticked off about it. Nicholson had to act as an arbiter. Witney had done gangster movies and serials, he was not suited to direct *Master of the World*. (I don't know who *was,* that AIP could have afforded, but he was not the one.) I'm sure that didn't do the picture any good.

Nicholson was the one who really got behind Master of the World *and pushed to make it, and Arkoff was very much against it.*

At that kind of cost, I'm sure he was.

Going by the box office receipts, which of them was right?

Oh, I think *Master of the World* made money — I don't think I ever wrote a picture for them that didn't turn a profit. Even *The Comedy of Terrors*, where it turned out that the title was self-defeating, it still made a profit. And most of the Poe pictures made a really good profit.

I always had the feeling that Nicholson had more of an affinity for this type of picture than Arkoff did.

As I said, Nicholson was my connection there, a very nice man, very genial, very appreciative. Again, on *Master of the World* and *Pit and the Pendulum*, they paid me $5,000 each on them. There was a writers' strike at the time, so actually I was doing pretty well — everybody else was starving. And Nicholson liked both those scripts so much that he gave me a bonus, which he didn't have to do. That was a nice gesture.

Many fans don't realize that you also wrote a lot of Western TV shows back in this era.

I love Westerns, and some of my nicest experiences, I think, were on a show called *The Lawman* — more than *The Twilight Zone!* There was a producer named Jules Schermer, and he would do my scripts word for word and he would get good actors — I mean, the guy who played the marshal, John Russell, was sort of like a monolith, but Peter Brown, who played his deputy, was good. Schermer got this good director who used to work with John Ford and he'd get good actors, and, really, there were some nice — *very* nice — pieces. I got a Writers Guild of America Award for the first one I ever wrote. Ray Danton played sort of a tired gunman who literally committed suicide, which you couldn't do on television! He just intimidated this marshal, insisted he was going to gun him down. And in the end the marshal shot him down, and Danton's gun was empty. He just wanted to die, but he didn't want to kill himself. The last one I did was with John Carradine, it was called "The Actor," and it was a charming piece. Carradine was this actor who finally ended up doing some noble thing and saving somebody's life, and he got shot. It's in a barroom, he's on a table, he does a death scene, he dies, the camera pulls back and a curtain comes down. That wasn't in my script, it was the director's idea, Richard Sarafian's — he was a very good director. I had never seen anything like that on television — what a wonderful little touch! And Schermer let it happen. So, yes, I've always loved Westerns; as a matter of fact, I'm submitting a Western novel right now to Spielberg, because he's said he wants to do films of every genre.

Pit and the Pendulum, unlike House of Usher, was a totally original screenplay.

Pit and the Pendulum was a lot more of a challenge — Poe's story was just one scene of a guy lashed to a table with a blade that's going to cut him in half.

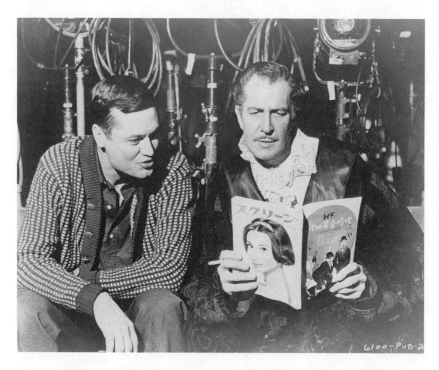

Roger Corman and Vincent Price are probably just looking at the pictures behind the scenes on *Pit and the Pendulum*.

And now most people ascribe what I wrote to Edgar Allan Poe! I mean, first there's Poe's short story; then I do the screenplay; then somebody writes a novel called *Pit and the Pendulum* which is based on my script. And so anybody who reads it thinks, "Hmmm, that Poe was a hell of a good writer...!"

Sounds like you were never a big fan of Poe's.
    Obviously I read his books, early on in life, but, no, I was not a big fan.

How about H.P. Lovecraft, whose stories formed the basis for some of the later "Poe" films?
    I never read Lovecraft until later on, after people told me about him, and then I didn't like him. His stories were just so thick and turgid; he would write about some abomination that was just too awful to describe, and then fifty pages later he'd take a crack at describing it anyway *[laughs]*! Stephen King says that he sort of grew up on Lovecraft and he assumed that that was the kind of stuff you had to write—full of crypts, that sort of stuff. And then when he read *I Am Legend,* he realized that you can set that type of story in a tract neighborhood, and then send it off in a different direction.

Did you meet Barbara Steele on Pit and the Pendulum?

No, I never met her. People in the business told me that her part had been dubbed in — they said her voice was not good enough for it. Whether this is true or not I don't know, but that's what I was told a number of times. And I was thoroughly astonished when I recently saw her name as producer on the mini-series *The Winds of War* and *War and Remembrance.*

Were you a visitor to this set as well?

I think I was there for the pendulum scene — that was a huge set, very impressive. That was a very well executed and well edited and very effective scene.

Was that all laid out, shot by shot, in your script?

It could very well have been. Years ago I learned that directors who have an ego problem don't pay any attention to shooting scripts, but right from the start I've always written them.

Now that he's attained some station in life, Corman insists that he liked his horror films Freudian — long scenes of people walking down corridors and that type of thing. But somehow I can't imagine him dictating to you, *or to anybody* else, *to put that stuff in there.*

Corman got his reputation in France because he had these constant shots of Jesus' mother holding the baby, and so they thought, "Ah, there's some religious significance here!" *[Laughs.]* I know for a fact that he had never used a boom shot until I wrote one into one of my pictures.

Did he have any input at all on your scripts?

Oh, yeah, sure, I would work with him on the scripts. I remember that American International always had me cutting; I went along with it, didn't argue. Then when they went to shoot it, it was too short! It used to happen all the time.

Even as early as Pendulum, *you were already reusing elements from* Usher. *Were these Gothic melodramas really your cup of tea?*

No, not at all, I was just trying to earn a living off of them. I was raising four children and the first film, *House of Usher,* did well, and so we went on from there. But as you can see, by the time I got to the third one, *Tales of Terror,* I couldn't take it seriously anymore and I started adding comedy to it.

So you prefer your more contemporary stories, then, like the ones you did for The Twilight Zone.

Oh, yeah. I have never written science fiction about the year 9000 or some distant galaxy, I just couldn't visualize that. I had to do it here and today, living in your tract house and there's a ghost next door, something like that.

Rise and shine! Vincent Price levitates from his deathbed in the Matheson-scripted Poe anthology *Tales of Terror*.

How much time would they give you to write one of these Poe scripts?

It probably wasn't long—they didn't take me that long! Maybe a month, month and a half. I mean, they shot 'em so fast they were practically standing outside my door waiting for new material so they could take it and run to the cameraman *[laughs]*! They always shot them word for word. And I stand by those scripts; what makes me wince is some of the performances!

Did you ever regret anything in a script written in haste?

In *Pit and the Pendulum* Vincent Price played Sebastian Medina, and I had all the characters calling him "Don Medina," which you don't do—it's "Don" and then the *first* name, so he should have been "Don Sebastian." And I made a terrible mistake on *The Incredible Shrinking Man*. In the film, and even in the book, I had him worrying about jumping from great heights, and then someone pointed out to me that at his size he would have just sort of floated down like an insect. I don't know why these little things stay with me, but I just hate to make mistakes like that!

When I asked Sam Arkoff what his favorite AIP movies were, the first one he named was Pit and the Pendulum.

Really? Well, I guess it *was* pretty clever, pretty intricately plotted. I guess he liked that.

Do you remember how you became involved on Burn, Witch, Burn?

Chuck Beaumont and I were friends, we went out one night to have a drink and we said, "Hey, let's write a movie together." We both loved the novel *Conjure Wife* by Fritz Leiber, and even though we knew that Universal owned the rights to it and had made a very poor picture [*Weird Woman*], we did it anyway. I took the first half, he took the second half, we got together and did a polish, and then we showed the script to Nicholson. He liked it, but because they had to get the rights from Universal to do it, we got very little money for it—I think we split $10,000. Then it went over to England, and it was made by a group of people who had made some very good pictures. And Chuck and I were delighted, we thought it was really well done.

Who came up with the British title, Night of the Eagle?

They did—I mean, either AIP or the people in England. Our title was *Conjure Wife*. And when the American release title ended up as *Burn, Witch, Burn,* we thought, "Hey, that's a little odd. What will Abraham E. Merritt's family think of this?"

In a TV interview, a writer named George Baxt talked about Burn, Witch, Burn *as though he was the sole writer.*

Obviously he's full of you-know-what. Stefanie Powers said the same sort of thing on *Die! Die! My Darling!,* that they had to rewrite the thing while they were doing it. And yet when I look at the movie, I see my script. I don't know why people do that.

And are you still happy with Burn, Witch, Burn?

I like it, I think it's excellent. Janet Blair, she's not bad. And the actor who played her husband, Peter Wyngarde, was the guy who played the ghost in *The Innocents;* his pants were a little too tight [*laughs*], but he was okay, too. The director, Sidney Hayers, did a great job.

Fritz Leiber had reservations about the film because you transposed the action to England.

That was necessary. But we followed his structure and his story very closely; I mean, that was the whole idea! You have a wonderful book, you try to follow it as closely as you can. That's what I did with *The Devil Rides Out [The Devil's Bride]*—so much so that Dennis Wheatley, the fellow who wrote the book, wrote me a letter thanking me for staying so close. There are so many wonderful books that have never been filmed the way they were written, it defies the senses.

Armed with stake and mallet, Vincent Price addresses the homeless problem in *The Last Man on Earth*.

Did you ever go over to England while any of the films you had written were being filmed?

No. I did go over to England, and I was there for about six weeks, adapting *I Am Legend* into a screenplay for Hammer Films, around 1957. I was working for Tony Hinds, who was going to be the producer. It turned out very well, then later he told me that the censor wouldn't pass it, and they finally ended up selling it to some guy in the United States, Robert Lippert.

I remember going to Lippert's house and having him tell me, "We're gonna get *Fritz Lang* to direct this thing [*The Last Man on Earth*]." And I thought to myself, "Oh, Jesus—how wonderful!" Then later I got a call, and they told me, "Now we're going with Sidney Salkow." And I thought [*in a sarcastic tone*], "Well, *there's* a bit of a drop!" The last I heard of him, Salkow was teaching at some college in the Valley, and he regards *The Last Man on Earth* as one of his masterpieces.

Why was that film shot in Italy?

It was cheaper, I guess. I'm sure it was a matter of price—financial, not Vincent. The film was released by AIP.

What's wrong with all the versions of I Am Legend, *that you're never happy with them?*

They never followed the book! *The Last Man on Earth* followed most closely, but it was inept—in fact, I put my pen name, Logan Swanson, on it. And that was one part that Price was not right for. I mean, they should do it today with, say, George Miller directing it and Harrison Ford playing the lead; it would make a wonderful movie. Of course George Romero has done it so many times now; the first time was *Night of the Living Dead.* I caught that on television, and I said to myself, "Wait a minute—did they make another version of *I Am Legend* that they didn't tell me about?" Later on they told me he did it as an homage to *I Am Legend,* which means, "He gets it for nothin'." *[Laughs.]* Dan Curtis is trying to get the rights, he's tried several times, since he'd like to do it.

What did you think of Night of the Living Dead?

It was . . . kind of cornball. At one point Roman Polanski had a contract at Warners, and my son Richard said, "Why don't you try and get him to do it?" Now, if Polanski did it, it would be wonderful; it should be done the way *Rosemary's Baby* was done, with a really outstanding actor as the star. But I don't think they'll do it. Why they keep making vampire movies, I don't know; if any monster has been "used up," it's the vampire.

Where did you get the idea for I Am Legend?

I think I got it before I came to California. I was watching *Dracula,* the old Universal film, and I thought, "If one vampire is frightening, what if the whole *world* was vampires?" That was the beginning of it.

How about the second "official" version of I Am Legend, *Warner Bros.'s* The Omega Man?

That one made me feel less bad because it was so far removed from the book that I believe it was almost unrecognizable. Too many cooks always spoil the broth.

Who now owns the rights to I Am Legend?

It's very complicated. What I was told was that Orion, being the ultimate offshoot of American International, owns the book rights whereas Warner Bros. owns the film rights. So whoever wanted to make it would have to offer both Orion and Warner Bros. something. It's not likely to happen.

Peter Lorre, who co-starred in your Tales of Terror *and* The Comedy of Terrors, *reportedly ad-libbed his way through these pictures.*

The rest of the actors in those pictures read my lines word for word; that dialogue was very well written, and they relished the way it fell trippingly off their tongues. Lorre just sort of gave the basic essence. Usually that kind of thing really bugs me, but he was such a nice man I couldn't really get fired up. He used to tell me that he drove Sydney Greenstreet out of his mind like that. Greenstreet came from the theater and would do every line down to the last semi-colon, and then Lorre would just sort of spew out some general reaction to it and Greenstreet would get all bent out of shape! And they were in a lot of pictures together.

People tell me that Lorre was on drugs throughout this period.
     He may have been, for physical pain. I think he had some serious physical problems. If he took drugs, it certainly wasn't just for the sake of taking drugs. Lorre was really a charming man.

The three-in-one Poe film Tales of Terror *gave you an opportunity to be more faithful than usual.*
     I must sound like I'm an egomaniac, but once again I thought that was a very good script. But on that first segment [*Morella*] the casting really bugged me—I always refer to that first segment as *Shirley Temple in the Haunted House.* In my script it was a really great character relationship between the two of them: Price was up to it, and I was visualizing someone like Nina Foch playing the dying daughter. But this girl that they got [Maggie Pierce] was terrible. And they also cut a lot out of it, so it just didn't work. The middle one [*The Black Cat*] had Lorre and Price and Joyce Jameson, who was marvelous. I enjoyed that middle one, I thought Price was wonderful and that the wine-tasting sequence was just delightful. And the last one *[The Facts in the Case of M. Valdemar]*—except for the lousy special effect at the end—I thought was very good, one of my favorites. They did a really nice job on that, very intelligent.

The omnibus approach was whose idea?
     American International's, I guess, I don't remember. I think I picked the stories that went into it.

In writing The Raven, *did you know which actors would be playing each role?*
     Sure, I wrote with them in mind, and I deliberately tailored the dialogue to fit their ways of speaking. In writing *The Raven* I didn't even have an original story to work with, they gave me a poem *[laughs]*, and I really had to start from scratch there! I couldn't take it seriously anymore and I did it as a comedy.

Lorre's ad-libbing threw Karloff for a loop.
     I'm sure that it threw everybody for a loop who was disciplined and followed the script. Short of firing him, though, there was nothing you could do about it—you couldn't talk him out of it. Of course I think his memory was failing anyway.

(Left–right) Sam Arkoff, Vincent Price, Jim Nicholson and Peter Lorre confab on the set of *The Raven*.

Karloff and Lorre appeared together on a New York talk show where Lorre said they had the time of their lives on The Raven. *But it was obvious from Karloff's reaction that* he *didn't think so!*

Karloff was always the essence of politeness, a very charming man. He was in great pain from some physical condition; I remember that he had to walk down these really precipitous steps in *The Raven* and he was in such pain. In most of his pictures after that, he just sat down most of the time. I really never did get much of a chance to know Karloff too well; I think he stayed to himself, he didn't just hang around the sets.

You gave Karloff opportunities to play comedy, which was something rare in his films.

You're right, comedy was something he almost never got to do in movies, and I thought he was very adept at it. He had a wonderful droll sense of humor that I thought came across very well in those pictures. It was delightful to watch him doing it.

Was the special effects duel at the end of The Raven *up to your expectations?*

No, no—I was very disappointed in that duel, it seemed very laborious to me. The effects were what I had written, it was just the way they were presented. Everything seemed too slow, it should have been a lot faster. People seem to enjoy it, but for a "duel of the titans" it seemed very, very heavy. With today's techniques, they could really do that right.

Was The Raven *a big moneymaker for AIP?*

I believe so. AIP was smart, they didn't reveal that it was a comedy, they let the word-of-mouth get around and so it made a lot of money.

Did you like the music Les Baxter wrote for these pictures?

Yes. It was very lush and very effective. He was great at big orchestral effects and melodies that were easily remembered.

Are your Poe pictures withstanding the test of time?

I think that there are a number of people who feel that they are. The fact that they are such period pictures helps; they don't age as noticeably as the contemporary pictures made back in the '50s and '60s, which became very archaic very quickly. If the Poe films have dated at all, it's just because of the way they do films today, more extravagantly and with more know-how.

Your screenplays; Floyd Crosby's camerawork; Dan Haller's art direction; Vincent Price's performances. Can you articulate exactly what Roger Corman's contribution was to these movies?

Traffic cop. I think he was good with the camera, he knew how to move with it, but as I said I don't think I ever saw him work with actors. He just cast them and assumed that they knew what they were doing. He was good at making pictures quickly and on a budget, and he gave an interesting look to his films. They were always crisp and fast-moving.

How did you get involved on The Comedy of Terrors?

I think I just told Jim Nicholson my idea about a couple of rascally undertakers who, when business is too slow, begin to murder people to get customers. That was enough to sell him.

Karloff was originally supposed to play the part Rathbone eventually got.

And Rathbone was going to play the father. They were approximately the same age, but Rathbone was really sprightly whereas Karloff by that time was really having pains. So Karloff requested that they switch parts, which was fine.

Did your continued leanings toward comedy sit well with AIP?

I think Nicholson liked it. Nicholson liked change, he liked variety. Arkoff probably would have done *Return to the House of Usher, Son of the House of Usher* and so on.

What extra responsibilities were entailed in your associate producer credit on
The Comedy of Terrors?

Probably very little, except that I was the one that got them to hire Jacques
Tourneur to direct. "Associate producer" is probably one of the most mean-
ingless titles in the motion picture business.

What turned you on to Tourneur?

I was a fan of his from way back—I wrote letters to Val Lewton when I
was 17, about *Cat People*. I'd always been a tremendous fan of Tourneur's; as
a matter of fact, even before *The Comedy of Terrors*, I had talked to Bert Granet
about hiring him to do one of my *Twilight Zones* ["Night Call"]. They said
the one reason they didn't want him was because he was a movie director, and
it would take him too long. Well, they hired him anyway, and Tourneur was
so organized that he shot the shortest *Twilight Zone* shooting schedule ever—I
think he had it done in like 28 hours. The man was a master, and he had great
taste, too.

The Comedy of Terrors *is also known as* Graveside Story. *Was that your
original title?*

[Laughs.] No, it was probably Nicholson. He had a penchant for very bad
titles. *West Side Story* [1961] had been a hit not long before that, so he might
have come up with it. I remember I was having a meeting once, I was going to
begin work on a screenplay based on my story "Being," and I said, "Well, you
know, you could call this picture *Galactic Octopoidal Ooze* — G.O.O. for short."
Next thing I know I'm looking through a trade paper and I see that G.O.O. is
the next picture they're going to be doing! I was just joking, but you must never
do that in this business because it'll backfire on you almost every time.

*People who knew Basil Rathbone toward the end say he was bitter over the fact
that he had become too closely associated with horror films.*

It's possible. I mean, look at the background of the man, the things he'd
done; he probably should have retired sooner if he didn't want to do 'em. I
always wonder at these stars who, just for the sake of continuing, will appear
in dreadful movies. They should retire, they should get out of the business.

Rathbone couldn't afford to retire.

Well, that's obviously the reason for his continuing on the way he did.
He didn't have to, he had made a lot of money, but he and his wife Ouida
lived awfully high on the hog and threw enormous parties and everything. But
he was very happy, I think, with both *Tales of Terror* and especially *The Comedy of Terrors*, because it was a great part. We had a luncheon before production began on *The Comedy of Terrors*, all the stars were there and they were
all really "high," Basil Rathbone especially, because they loved the script.

It's obvious that Peter Lorre has a stunt double throughout much of the film.

Oh, Lorre could do nothing. There were scenes calling for him to climb up on the roof and run around and drive the carriage, and he could do none of it. So they got this famous old stuntman, Harvey Parry, to stand in for him because he couldn't do any of this stuff. Rathbone did virtually all his own stunts.

You mentioned before that the title hurt the picture.

The public apparently did not like the juxtaposition of the words "comedy" and "terrors" (I think it's a great title), and that apparently hurt the box office. But it was the best of the lot, of course, because Tourneur directed.

In my last years with AIP I wrote some marvelous scripts — Nicholson had me really going for ambitious stuff — but none of them ever came to fruition. One that I kept turning down, and Nicholson kept wanting me to do, was about the pornography business in England. It was called *Public Parts and Private Places,* and it was just so black that I made this sort of *Dr. Strangelove* comedy out of it, really bizarre. And they never made it. Then there was another one, based on a novel called *Implosion.* It took place in England — I guess, because they were going to shoot it in England, I set it there, too — and it was about what happened when something got into the water and the majority of the women became sterile. Those who could have children were put into breeding camps, and one of the big ministers in the government has a wife who is one of the women that had to go to the breeding camp. It was such a good script that they gave me a three-picture deal after I wrote it — none of which I wrote. (Or maybe one, from my story "Being.")

Your script Sweethearts and Horrors, *which AIP never got around to filming, seems like it would have been a hoot.*

Yeah, that was very disappointing. It was going to follow up *The Comedy of Terrors,* and it had all of them — Karloff, Price, Lorre and Rathbone, plus Tallulah Bankhead. It was about a family called the Sweethearts. Boris Karloff was the host of a kiddie show, a very irascible host — always muttering curses under his breath; Basil Rathbone was an aging musical comedy star; Peter Lorre was a very inept magician whose specialty was a fire act, and every theater he worked in he burned down; Tallulah Bankhead was an aging Hollywood actress; and Vincent Price was a ventriloquist. They're all called back to their father's home, after he dies, for the reading of the will; the father manufactured gags, and the whole house is booby-trapped with gags. Then they start getting murdered off, one by one. It would have been a ball, because it was a very funny script; I was very happy with that script, and it would still make a very cute picture. As a matter of fact, I just recently sent a copy to my agent, because there are still a few of the oldtimers around — Price and Peter Cushing and Christopher Lee.

You worked for AIP one last time several years later, on De Sade.

I was very happy when I learned that *De Sade* would be directed by the man [Cy Endfield] who directed *Zulu* [1964], which to my mind is the best action movie ever made. But he was having a mental breakdown at the time — at least, that's what they told me. He was putting red crosses through script pages, which meant that they had been shot — but they hadn't been! So there was a lot of stuff that he literally hadn't shot. In my script, everything you saw was very inscrutable and had an interesting kind of texture, and it turned out ultimately to be what was going on in De Sade's brain as he was dying. And [Endfield] decided that, no, he wasn't going to do that, he wasn't going to make it a fantasy, he wanted a straight chronology. And yet he kept shooting scenes that I wrote, scenes that (except in a fantasy context) made no sense at all! Roger Corman ended up going over to Berlin and shooting some cheap orgy scenes.

The punchline to this story is that Jim Nicholson told me that he was talking to John Huston one day [Huston co-starred in *De Sade*], and Huston said, "Why didn't you ask me to direct it? I'd have been glad to direct it." That *[groans]* — that really made my day!

What do you recall about writing Die! Die! My Darling! *for Hammer?*

Tony Hinds sent me this book called *Fanatic,* and asked me if I wanted to adapt it. And I did. They were lucky enough to get the director who did *Georgy Girl* [1966], Silvio Narizzano, who did a very nice job. It got a little heavily melodramatic toward the end, but I thought it worked very well.

Early on there are scenes which at times are very funny.

Oh, sure. When something strange happens to people, if they have a sense of humor, they're going to try to respond to it; I thought Stefanie Powers did an excellent job of that. The situations were amusing to her character; only later did it gradually begin to dawn on her what the hell was going on.

Stefanie Powers's one complaint was that, in the scenes where Tallulah Bankhead beats her up, Bankhead didn't bother pulling her punches.

Oh, I can believe that; Tallulah Bankhead was a tough old broad. What that *Sweethearts and Horrors* would have been like on the set, with smiling Roger contending with her, would have been a picture in itself!

The business in Die! Die! My Darling! *about Bankhead having once been an oldtime actress is not well developed.*

That's not in the book at all, and I think they must have added that themselves. I didn't know Tallulah Bankhead was going to be starring in it, so I didn't make the lead character an actress; in the book she's like a little dumpy old lady who's just fanatical about her son. After they cast Tallulah Bankhead they might have just thrown in those other scenes.

Bankhead sued Columbia when they changed the title from Fanatic *to* Die! Die! My Darling! *for U.S. release.*

Well, I suppose they were looking to cash in on *Hush, Hush . . . Sweet Charlotte.* They're always so imitative, so slavishly imitative. *Fanatic* was the title of the book and the title I wrote my script under.

Hammer Films tend to be lionized by some fans but it's always struck me as being just a British AIP.

Yeah, I think they were pretty much alike, and that there are a lot of similarities between them. Maybe because their actors have an English accent, it just sounds nicer *[laughs]*. I was just talking recently to Michael Carreras, who is the son of the man who started the studio, and he is trying to get *I Am Legend* to make, the way I wrote it.

You worked for Hammer again on The Devil's Bride, *adapting Dennis Wheatley's book* The Devil Rides Out. *Was Wheatley offered an opportunity to adapt it himself?*

I have no idea. I thought I wrote a very good adaptation—I used the major sequences of the book, and it flowed together very well. Again, I thought the casting had some flaws in it, although I just saw it again recently and it wasn't as bad as I remembered it. Charles Gray was good, but I don't think I'd ever heard of a lot of the other people who were in it—maybe they chose them because they looked like they came out of the 1920s or something!

Did you write the screenplay knowing that Christopher Lee would be playing the hero?

No, I don't think so, but he did a fine job. It was the three leads who I found lacking—Tanith [Nike Arrighi] and Rex [Leon Greene] and Simon [Patrick Mower]. And that whole sequence where they're under attack was much more complete and much longer and much more interesting in my script than it turned out to be, because they didn't have the money to spend on special effects. They went for the big spider *[laughs]*—they always go for the goddamned big spider! That wasn't in my script. And the scene where they're in the attic and the great big black guy shows up, that wasn't that frightening—really good special effects would have added some more fright to it. But the picture had a nice period look to it, and the plot certainly zipped along. One of my favorite scenes in the film, probably *the* favorite, is where Charles Gray is reassuring the wife [Sarah Lawson] and gradually segues into getting control of her.

Variety *pointed out that two character names in* The Devil's Bride, *Mocata and Tanith, were "lifted" from* Rosemary's Baby.

Those names were in the original book, and it must have been *Rosemary's Baby* that lifted them. Wheatley wrote *The Devil Rides Out* in the '30s, long before *Rosemary's Baby.*

It's odd, after all those Gothic Poe pictures you wrote, that Hammer never approached you to write one of their Dracula or Frankenstein films.

No, they never did. But I wouldn't have done it anyway.

Who approached you to adapt your own book Hell House, *for* The Legend of Hell House?

Jim Nicholson again. He was starting his own company, and he wanted to do that as his first project.

Did you ever ask him why he had left AIP?

I think it was financial. He got divorced and he had to give half of his shares in AIP to his ex-wife, and I think he lost control. Previously he'd had enough control so he could fight off Arkoff, but when Arkoff had total control, I think he just knew he was going to be too unhappy. So he started his own company. He died shortly thereafter.

Were you happy with The Legend of Hell House?

It was made by some of the same people who were involved with *Burn, Witch, Burn.* When I first saw it, I didn't like it — as usual — because I had an image of it in my mind. Pamela Franklin seemed too young, and Roddy McDowall wasn't quite right, either; I thought the guy who played the doctor, Clive Revill, was good. The score I found a little inappropriate at first; it doesn't bother me now. When you see something over and over, you forget what you originally planned for it and how you saw it.

None of the "residents" of Hell House *are on display in the film the way they are in your book.*

I guess the filmmakers made up their minds that they weren't going to show anything — for instance, I had in the script what Pamela Franklin saw when the ghost makes love to her, and I had also described it very vividly in my novel. They chose not to show it in the movie, you just see the look on her face. But that was their choice, that was okay. It was intelligently done.

The Haunting *is probably the best haunted house film ever to use that "unseen" approach.*

I liked *The Haunting* a lot. What I didn't like was the way it copped out, the way it turned out to be in the mind of one of the characters who was there. I was so tired of that; that was part of the reason I wrote *Hell House.* But *The Haunting* was well-done and it was scary as hell — I mean, how about that scene where the wife's [Lois Maxwell] face appears through the trap door and the camera zooms in! That was one of the three moments in my moviegoing career where I actually recoiled in my seat. Another was when the shark appeared behind Roy Scheider while he's chumming in *Jaws,* and the third was in *Diabolique,* when the dead husband came up out of the bathtub.

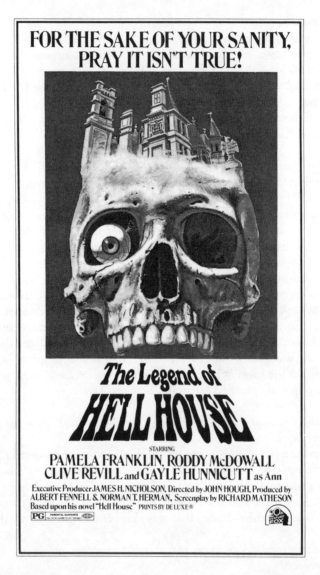

FOR THE SAKE OF YOUR SANITY, PRAY IT ISN'T TRUE!

The Legend of
HELL HOUSE

STARRING
**PAMELA FRANKLIN, RODDY McDOWALL
CLIVE REVILL and GAYLE HUNNICUTT** as Ann

Executive Producer JAMES H. NICHOLSON, Directed by JOHN HOUGH, Produced by
ALBERT FENNELL & NORMAN T. HERMAN, Screenplay by RICHARD MATHESON
Based upon his novel "Hell House" PRINTS BY DE LUXE®

PG PARENTAL GUIDANCE

Matheson got less than the dream cast he had envisioned when *The Legend of Hell House* went before the cameras.

Reportedly, Jim Nicholson had you dilute your Legend of Hell House *screenplay in order to get a PG rating.*

I cut out some of the sexual stuff; there was quite a bit left, but there had been a lot more. Originally I was going to do the picture with Stanley Chase, who produced that very good science fiction picture *Colossus: The Forbin Project*. He and I were going to do it and it was going to be really explicit — the book is extremely explicit. At one time I had in my mind a dream cast of Richard Burton and his wife Elizabeth Taylor to play the two mediums, Rod Steiger and his wife Claire Bloom to play the professor and his wife. Just after they made *The Legend of Hell House* people began making the really classy, A-picture-type horror films, starting with *The Exorcist,* so if I had held onto *Hell House* a few more years, it might have gotten that kind of treatment, too. It's a B-plus *[laughs]*, but it didn't make A!

Have you given any thought to trying your hand at directing?

Sometimes, when it's something that I've written or something that I know particularly well. But, as I've mentioned to other people in the past, I would probably get walked all over or I would turn into a Nazi. And I wouldn't want to do either one.

Did you have any misgivings when Christopher (Superman) *Reeve was cast in the lead of* Somewhere in Time?

No; as a matter of fact I thought at the time that he was probably the only actor around that could have pulled it off. Not because of his acting ability, although I liked what he had done in *Superman,* but because of his looks. In my mind it was essential to the story that the attraction between Richard [Reeve] and Elise [Jane Seymour] be a love-at-first-sight thing. I had breakfast once with Dustin Hoffman, who was interested in doing it, and I remember thinking, "Well, he would end up fascinating the girl but it would take like five *days*"—I mean, his personality would have to overcome his looks, so it would hardly be love at first sight! In that respect Chris Reeve was ideal, although my attitude toward his acting has sort of diminished through the years. But it was a nice experience; I spent more time on that shoot than on any other picture, over two weeks on Mackinaw Island, Michigan, where the Grand Hotel is. It was a lovely experience.

Did you adapt your own novel (Bid Time Return) *faithfully?*

In the novel, Richard's dying, because he has a brain tumor, and at the end his brother, who has analyzed the whole story, realizes that this type of hallucination was perfectly within the bounds of what Richard was going through—although the brother hopes that it had actually happened. Universal didn't want to do that. Also, to present Reeve, who had just played Superman, as somebody who was dying would have been kind of ludicrous.

Somewhere in Time *was the sort of gentle fantasy that's tough to "sell" to the public.*

And it *was.* They made a mistake in the way it opened; it should have opened in a few little theaters all over the country and got word-of-mouth working for it. Once word-of-mouth started working, it did very well. On the Z Channel out here, it was like the most popular picture; they would show it two times a day, it would be shown at Christmastime and so on. And the video cassette sales have been great. But the original box office was not that hot — maybe $15,000,000. But since it was made for five and a half, I guess it was still all right.

What can you tell us about Universal's Jaws 3-D?
Once again, I wrote an outline which was really very interesting — and I found out later, when the picture was done and I saw the credits, that they gave the credit for the story to some other writer! And I had never read anything by him!

I wrote a very interesting script. I would much prefer to write the second sequel to a popular film than the first sequel; when you're writing the first sequel, you're bound to directly follow what happened in the original film, but when you do a second sequel you can make a deviation. Universal made me put the two sons of Chief Brody [Roy Scheider] in the film, which I thought was dumb, but not only that, they wanted it to be the same shark that got electrocuted in *Jaws 2 [laughs]*!

Were you happy at all with the finished film?
No, not at all. I'm a good storyteller and I wrote a good outline and a good script. And if they had done it right and if it had been directed by somebody who knew how to direct, I think it would have been an excellent movie. *Jaws 3-D* was the only thing Joe Alves ever directed; the man is a very skilled production designer, but as a director, no. And the so-called 3-D just made the film murky-looking — it had no effect whatsoever. It was a waste of time.

You seem to be happier with your work in television than you are with most of the movies you've been associated with.
Oh, I've gotten much more satisfaction out of television. I did *Duel* for television, *The Night Stalker, The Night Strangler, Dracula, The Morning After* [1974] with Dick Van Dyke, *Dying Room Only* [1973] with Cloris Leachman — *Dying Room Only* is the one I always tell people was better than it deserved to be. It was just a simple, well-done suspense story, but the producer Allen Epstein put so much effort into it...!

Were you one of the instigators of Twilight Zone — The Movie?
No. I had lunch with Steven Spielberg and John Landis and Joe Dante, and they said they were going to make this movie. Landis was going to write his own segment and Joe was going to do "It's a Good Life" and Spielberg was going to do "Kick the Can." It seems to me that their initial plan was to use "Nightmare at 20,000 Feet" just as like a filler — I remember them talking about doing it in ten minutes, and I couldn't understand how they were going to do it. At one point they were going to get Gregory Peck for the "Nightmare" episode in the movie — they told me once that Gregory Peck was going to be

in *Duel!* So I wrote a whole script in which Peck was like the character he played in *Twelve O'Clock High* [1949] — he's familiar with the idea of "gremlins," he's heard pilots talking about 'em, and now he finally sees one for himself. Then, suddenly, it wasn't going to be Gregory Peck in the role. And then they hired George Miller to direct it — he's a wonderful director — but he decided to go back to scratch.

The movie version of "Nightmare" is slightly different from the TV version, and not nearly as good.

In my story, and in the original *Twilight Zone* episode, the guy had had a mental breakdown, but George Miller thought to make it just a guy who was afraid of flying. I can't say that I liked the characterization, but I must admit that John Lithgow was marvelous — I mean, to start out at 99 percent of hysteria and build from that is a little difficult, but he somehow managed to do it! Visually that episode was marvelous, although a lot of it I didn't care for. And I thought the monster in the movie was much better than in the television show.

How would you rate the other episodes on which you worked?

"Kick the Can," the one that Steven did, I thought was too treacly; "It's a Good Life," the one directed by Joe Dante, I liked the best. I was called to task by a lot of the fans on that one; they cannot stand happy endings, they love to have stories end on a bleak, dark, fatalistic note so that they can all shudder and go, "Ooo-oo-ooh, wasn't that *wonderful?*" I decided, "Oh, screw it" *[laughs]* — I wanted to see if I could put a positive ending on it. It didn't work too well, the way it was done, but I still stand by it; up 'til that point, I thought that Joe did a marvelous job.

Twilight Zone — The Movie *struck me as a yuppified, hotshot-director's movie that didn't suit the tone of the old TV series.*

They started the movie out with that little backroads bit with [Albert] Brooks and [Dan] Aykroyd that set a tone, which they never followed. And it was not a success.

*It's amazing what can be done with*out *millions of dollars or big special effects, but don't try telling that to most of today's filmmakers.*

When I was a teenager, as I have told you, I wrote a letter to Val Lewton and I told him I thought I had discovered their secrets of scaring people. One of them was a long period of absolute dead silence, suddenly broken by a noise. It could be anything — I remember a scene in *The Body Snatcher* where the hero is in a stable and suddenly this horse sticks its head into the shot and snorts, and everybody in the theater jumped out of their skin! Another way is to lead the viewer's eye across the screen and then all of a sudden something pounces in from the other side — they did that in *Wait Until Dark* [1967], which was another time that I jumped. It's so easy! I mean, you have to have the situation first and it has to be well done, but once you've got that, it's very simple. And yet they never do it.

Do you like to scare people?
    I used to; I don't now, because I have a different attitude. They say that horror films allow you to get things out of your system and help you deal with your own private terrors. I don't believe that anymore. I think that everything that's created on the screen, and that kids see, becomes rooted in their minds, it never leaves. And then it builds itself up. I think in the long run it does nothing but create a negative effect.

And that's why you sometimes appear to be trying to distance yourself from the image of being a "horror writer"?
    I realize that, out here anyway, it's almost impossible. I wrote that TV movie *The Morning After* for David Wolper, about an alcoholic, and it worked out well—it's a beautiful film and they use it in hospitals. It's probably the truest presentation of an alcoholic that they've ever done. And one of the critics wrote a review and said, "This situation is a real horror. And who better to write the script than..." *[Points to himself and laughs.]* And so I figured, "To hell with it!" I'll never get away from it!

*The producers hired a bunch of wrestlers to play the zombies,
and they caught me a couple of times within the film. They would
grab me and literally pick me up and throw me against a palm tree!
And I could hear my vertebrae just cracking, going down! . . .
That's what I remember about* Zombies of Mora Tau!

— *Gregg Palmer* —

EVERY WAR has its unsung heroes, and in the great 1950s onslaught of sci-fi beasties upon the world, many Hollywood actors risked life and limb (not to mention their professional reputations!) to preserve the human race. Another in the long line of classic monster fighters, Gregg Palmer took on the Creature from the Black Lagoon, the Zombies of Mora Tau and, perhaps most perilously, the Most Dangerous Man Alive, and has survived to tell the story of his heroic on-screen exploits.

Norwegian by heritage and a San Franciscan by birth (January 25, 1927), brown-haired, brown-eyed Gregg Palmer (born Palmer Lee) broke into show biz as a radio announcer. After an early '50s stint as a contract player at Universal, he turned to freelancing, closing out the decade by starring and co-starring in a number of detective, Western and science fiction adventures. In the '60s, Palmer drifted into supporting roles and much TV work, and reinforced his growing reputation with Western fans by becoming a regular member of John Wayne's latter-day stock company in *The Undefeated* (1969), *Chisum, Rio Lobo* (1970), *Big Jake* (1971) and *The Shootist* (1976). Big (6' 2"), beefy and robust in his sixties, this gentle giant kicked back to reminisce about his filmland skirmishes with Old West marauders and Atom Age monsters.

I was discharged out of the Air Force in 1946 and undecided about what to do, and I went back to college. One day my friend Frank called me up and he said that he had attended a radio announcer school, that he wanted to become a radio announcer, and would I tell him where [radio station] KGO was located in San Francisco? I told him, and he said, "Listen, why don't you join me, and afterwards we'll go to lunch?" So we went down to KGO, and they asked him to fill out some forms. And since I had asked a question or two, they handed me a form and asked me to fill it out, too. The following week when Frank came down he said, "I'm going for my interview. Why don't you join me, and we'll have lunch again?" So we went down there, he went in for his interview and he was in and out within four minutes or less. I asked him how he did, and he said, "I don't know, but they said they'd call me." Whereupon I heard *my* name called. Frank said, "Go 'head, see if they tell you the same thing they told me." I went in, and I was in there for an hour and a half *[laughs]* — reading all kinds of copy off the teletype and whatever. And as I was leaving, Noel Francis, who was a lady producer at KGO, said, "I would suggest you stay in the field of radio. I think that there's a future there for you." I thanked her for that and I went home, and one day when I came home from playing golf my mother told me that KGO had called, and they wanted to know if I would be interested in going to work as a radio announcer. I said, "Well, I don't have the experience for that" — I immediately thought of the millions of people out there listening to me fouling up and mispronouncing words and whatever. But I went in and told them, "I tell you what: I'll go to school, and after six months I'll interview again. And if you still feel that

Previous page: **Palmer's knife-in-the-throat attack doesn't even slow down the walking corpse — played by "Killer" Karl Davis — in Columbia's *Zombies of Mora Tau*.**

I have a future in the business, so be it." So I went to radio school and soon after got my first job in radio at Radio KEEN in San Jose—*[mellifluously]* "1370 on your dial, San Jose, California." I did shows emanating out of the studio and I would go out on remotes. I worked there for a period of about a year.

And shortly afterwards you tried your luck in the movies.
There was a columnist who worked in San Francisco by the name of Dwight Newton, and he and Noel Francis suggested that I try for the movies. I put that off for about eight months until finally one day they *drove* me on down to Los Angeles! I kept hanging around, hanging around—I drove a truck, bounced at the Palladium, did all the things that struggling actors in those days would do, and then went on my interviews. I can recall Paramount in the old days, they had what they call the fishbowl. You would go in there and bright lights would be on you. You wouldn't know who was sitting outside—a voice would say, "All right, go ahead," and you'd do your scene. And when you were finished, the voice would say, "Thank you, we'll be in contact." Now, that could be the janitor sitting out there *[laughs]*—you didn't know who it was—and off you would go! But these interviews were not too frequent; you might wait for four months, five months.

In 1949, before I got into the picture business, while I was still trying to find my way, I had an interview with two people at NBC Studios. One of them was Busby Berkeley, who was the choreographer for those big 1930s musical extravaganzas, and the other gentleman was Al Capp, who created the *Li'l Abner* comic strip. They told me that they were looking for someone to play Li'l Abner on TV, and they thought I had possibilities. I was introduced to a young lady, we rehearsed for a couple of days, then we went to a sound stage and we made the test, which I'll never forget. I was dressed as Li'l Abner, sitting on a log, she as Daisy Mae. She came up to me and she said, "Li'l Abner, I just inherited $24. Will you kiss me?" And I looked at her and I said, "I cain't. If 'n I kissed you for money, I couldn't face myself in the mornin'." She threw the $24 off-camera and she snuggled up, as Daisy Mae would, and she said, "Then kiss me without money." And I said, "I cain't. 'Cause without money, you ain't *worth* kissin'!" Now, as you laugh, do you know who the young lady was? She became Marilyn Monroe. And I've often wondered where that filmclip went to!

Finally one day I was about to chuck it and go back to San Francisco, and I was approached by an agent. He said, "Why don't we go over to Warner Bros.? I think there's a future here for you, Palmer." (I was still called Palmer Lee in those early days.) So we went to Warner Bros. and they said they had a war story coming up and I could play a navigator, and I said fine. And then they said, "Yeah, but it's about eight months away." I said, "Forget it!" Now, as we're going back over the hill, we pass by Universal Studios, and I went in there and there was some interest; they said, "Well, how 'bout coming back next week and reading for us?" I said, "No. If you promised to give me the *studios* next week, I wouldn't come back. I'm leaving Friday evening and I'm going back to San Francisco, go back to college and plan my future in another direction." So I was called in on Friday afternoon to read and Friday evening my agent called me up and he said, "Palmer, the studio would like to give you a seven-year contract." And I said [*disappointedly*], "Seven *years?* I don't know if I'd want that." Having just been out of the service a few years prior, I knew that would be like being tied up. But I sat with my cousin out on a curb in front of his house, we talked it over and finally I figured, well, all right.

It was a nice experience at Universal Studios. I met a lot of nice people and I enjoyed the time there. This was in 1951 that I signed there. Those were the days when they had a stable of people that they would train. We had training in voice, training in diction, training in tap dancing and ballet—if you can picture me doing ballet! Me with my size thirteen [*laughs*]! We were all submitted to these classes—Rock Hudson, Audie Murphy, Jeff Chandler, Clint Eastwood, Anita Ekberg, Piper Laurie, all of us. Many happy hours were spent there. We would maybe have a featured role in a picture, maybe we would star, maybe we would do a little cameo, but we were working. They were good and happy days.

You had your first role in a fantasy film when you appeared in Universal's Francis Goes to West Point.

There's a story that goes with that film, a story that begins about a year earlier when I had a bit part in an army comedy called *Up Front* [1951]. I was to play a binocular M.P. in a reconnaissance vehicle in *Up Front* and I really studied my one line, because I wanted to be good, to make a career in this business. The line was, "I think I see the truck up ahead, sir." I would sit at home in front of a mirror, as many of us actors do, pretending to be holding binoculars, reading the line different ways and so on. Finally the day came when I was going to do that line. I went over to the recon and I started to get in when the assistant director came over and he said, "No, wait a minute, Palmer, I want Alex to get in there." I said, "But I'm the binocular M.P., and—." "Don't worry about it," he said, "just get into this motorcycle sidecar here. Alex is going to do the line." Well, Alex was a friend of the assistant director. So I climbed into the sidecar and Alex did the line.

Three or four months later I signed the contract with Universal Studios, and I was assigned to *Francis Goes to West Point*. Arthur Lubin was directing it, Donald O'Connor and Lori Nelson were starring, and I was fourth-billed, as the football player. We went out to a local college stadium and we're standing out there in the early morning hours and Lubin was explaining to me the scenes that they were going to shoot that morning. All of a sudden he interrupted himself and said, "Gee, it's awfully chilly here, would you like a cup of coffee?" And he turned to the assistant director, the same one that took me out of the recon, and said, "Would you please go get Mr. Lee a cup of coffee?"

First a radio announcer, then a Universal contract player, Gregg Palmer turned freelancer in the mid-'50s and appeared in horror-action flicks like *Zombies of Mora Tau.*

So he walked *all-l-l* the way out of the stadium and came back with the cup of coffee for me. And now Lubin said, "Gee, it's gonna be a while before we start, you should sit down." And he turned to the assistant director again and said, "Would you please get Mr. Lee a chair?" So *[laughs]* out he walks again, *all-l-l* the way out, and he came back with this chair. When he put it down, I looked at him—I bore no animosity towards him—and I said, "Nice seeing you again. Remember me?" And he said, "Yeah . . . you never know, do you?" *[Laughs.]* And it's true, you never do.

Do you remember much about the scenes you shared with Francis the Talking Mule?

Yes, and that was interesting. I was quite taken by the way the mule would talk — that was done with wires. The wires, which were attached to the mouth of the mule, would be pulled and that would kind of irritate the mule, and he'd move his lips around. To which Chill Wills, who was the voice of Francis, would add the voice. We had personnel on the set at all times protecting the animals, making sure that they were not injured or mistreated. Even in Westerns, when we did horse falls, they want the ground dug up, softened up first, for the horse. *Not* for the rider *[laughs]*!

Why did you leave Universal?

I left 'em because they dropped my contract *[laughs]*! I was supposedly on my way, the next in line for the "big buildup" that they'd given to Rock Hudson and Jeff Chandler, Tony Curtis and Audie Murphy. I was told that, "Now the big push is on you, Palmer." But then, long about 1954 or '55, the policy changed. Instead of having the stable of talent there that would try to build, they brought in name stars — give them a piece of the picture or whatever. So I left, and within three months after I left they called me up and I went back to do another film for them at Universal: *The Creature Walks Among Us*.

Did you enjoy appearing in The Creature Walks Among Us?

I was fascinated by the Gillman, that costume that Bud Westmore had designed, and I often thought, "Gee, wouldn't it be nice to have a beach party some night and be sitting out there, and hire this guy to come out of the waves?" I had a young lady in for lunch one day and we were in the makeup room and I was showing her around, and in walked Don Megowan, who wore the costume in the film. He walked up behind my lady-friend and started breathing heavily, to give the effects of the gills working. She turned around, shook like an $18 television set, screamed and took off *[laughs]*!

Any memories of your Creature Walks *co-stars?*

Good memories. I saw Jeff Morrow not too long ago and we discussed *The Creature Walks Among Us* as one of the films we enjoyed making. Rex Reason, speaking of voices, is one person who really has a resonant voice — a wonderful guy. A few years down the road after the *Creature* movie, Rex left the business — took another avenue, and did well in real estate. He was a good actor, considerate and helpful. Both Rex and Jeff Morrow were professionals. They would stand off-camera and read the lines to you, and not let the assistant director or the dialogue director read them. I think that's a professional way to do it — I've always done it. You get more of a motivation out of looking at the person that you're doing the story with than you could with a person reading it out of a script.

Palmer first turned monster-fighter for Universal's third Gillman adventure, *The Creature Walks Among Us.*

How about the men who played the Creature, Megowan and Ricou Browning?

Ricou I don't remember too well, but Don Megowan was a very dear friend of mine. We would always kid one another about size and weight and all that sort of thing. I used to ask him, "Don, what do you weigh?" and he would say, "194 pounds." And I'd say, "No, no — with *both* feet on the scale!" *[Laughs.]* I remember that Don and I played brothers on an episode of *Gunsmoke,* there was a shootout at Dodge City and Don was hit. "Ma" told me, "Go git your brother," and I had to go out into the street, grab Don Megowan, pick him up, put him over my shoulder and carry him off. Well, when I draped him over my shoulder, his head was dragging and his feet were dragging, and it was a full day's work to make that ten steps off-camera with Don Megowan *[laughs]*! Don was a super guy. He died young.

One of the best scenes in Creature Walks *is when your party stalks the Gillman down that narrow channel in your motorboat.*

Yeah, that was kind of an ominous scene. At times you get "into" a scene — you know that this animal, this Creature, is out there, and all of a sudden the water breaks and this head pops out and reaches in for you — ! It was a frightening moment, an exciting scene, and I remember it well. That was all done on a sound stage at Universal Studios.

I liked *The Creature Walks Among Us,* I thought it was well-done, well-presented. And they still talk about it today. I travel around quite a bit and I have fans come up to me and talk about science fiction, and they always bring up *The Creature Walks Among Us* as opposed to some of the other sci-fi things that I did.

Were you a fan of science fiction films?
Oh, yes, I enjoyed them. I used to think of science fiction as being something that was different from being up in the hills — my claim to fame was a lot of Westerns and cavalry things. John Agar made a lot of these science fiction pictures, he would sit with me in the Universal commissary and we would talk about it and I'd think, "Gee, they're on a sound stage, they don't have to get up there in the wind and the blizzards or whatever!"
Zombies of Mora Tau I'll never forget, that's the one where I played a diver and we were diving for jewels that were protected by these zombies. The producers hired a bunch of wrestlers to play the zombies and they caught me a couple of times within the film. They would grab me and literally pick me up and throw me against a palm tree! And I could hear my vertebrae just cracking, going down! Then one of the wrestlers would say, "Come here, Gregg." I'd walk over to him, he'd turn me around and lift me up and pop my back for me, and put it back into place *[laughs]*! That's what I remember about *Zombies of Mora Tau!*

Do you remember how you got involved on Zombies of Mora Tau?
Sam Katzman was the producer on that, and the director was Edward L. Cahn. My agent set up an interview and I went over there to read. There were four or five other actors there, too, waiting to go in and try out. I went in and I read with Mr. Cahn — he was reading the other parts — and he said, "Now read this scene." And then, "Now, *this* scene." And pretty soon we're going through the whole script! Lenny Katzman, who was the nephew of Sam Katzman, came in and asked Cahn, "How long are you going to be? There's four or five more people out here." To which Mr. Cahn replied, "Send 'em home, I got the party right here. Palmer's gonna play it!"

Do you recall if Allison Hayes liked her role? She plays a zombie throughout much of the film.
I think she enjoyed it. We remained friends after the show for a period of time, then when I heard of her passing I was deeply moved by that. She was just wonderful, a really talented and beautiful person. And Morris Ankrum was in *Zombies of Mora Tau,* too — he was a great pro, was around a long time. That was shot out at the Baldwin Ranch, near Santa Ana Racetrack — Baldwin was an old pioneer and they used that ranch in many movies. We did the interiors at Columbia, on sound stages.
Another funny thing about *Zombies of Mora Tau,* which involves a fellow

called Joel Ashley, who played the fortune-hunter in the film. When you're working in a movie you get call sheets handed to you at the end of each day. Each actor would have a number—I would be #4, you would be #14, the leading lady would be #6—and you would match that number up against the scenes that they would be shooting the next day, to know when or if you'd be needed. So this one day on *Zombies of Mora Tau,* as we were leaving, Harry, who was the assistant director, handed out the call sheets; we accepted them and departed and came back the next day. Early that morning we're sitting in the dressing room when Harry came in and said, "All right, Scene #22 today, let's go." And Joel said, *"What?"* (That was his big scene.) "You didn't give me that, it wasn't on the call sheet!" And Harry said, "It sure was. Look at your call sheet." So Joel went over and took it out of his script and handed it to Harry, and said, "Do you see my number on there?" Harry looked at it and said, "No. But this is *Zombies of Mora Tau.* What's the title on *that* call sheet?" And Joel looked at it and cried out, *"The Man Who Turned to Stone*—!" Well *[laughs],* with that, sweat started to come out of Joel's forehead: Everybody was now waiting, the director was there, the scene was lit and so forth. Joel had to go in there and really work hard, and he's never to this day forgiven Harry for that!

Edward Cahn has a reputation as a lightning-fast director.
Edward Cahn was quick—in those days you had to be! But he knew what he wanted and he always had his shots all lined up. He was once a film cutter, and directors who have had film cutting experience know in their heads as they go in just how they're going to cut it and what they need. Those kind of directors are not around anymore. I remember doing *Death Valley Days* [on TV]—I made a bunch of those—and I would shoot one episode in two and a half days. We'd do 18 pages a day! When I started out we would make a movie in three weeks, five weeks, and they were good features. Today they go months.

How'd you end up with such a small part in From Hell It Came?
That was done at the request of my agent, Jack Pomeroy. We went over to the studio and the producers, the Milner Bros., told me about the part, and I said, "You want me to lay down and be staked out and have chickens around me? And then I turn into a tree?? Come *on*—!" But as I walked down the hallway Jack said to me, "Gregg, *do* this. A lot of people are going to see this—science fiction is coming around. I'll make it up to you." You always hear that in the business, *"Do* this, I'll make it up to you." So he kept chewin' on my ear, and the next thing I know, I was staked out on the ground and the chickens were all around me! I believe that was one day's work.

Did you get to see the tree monster prop while you were there?
Oh, yes, I saw the tree monster. I saw it in makeup and I saw it when it

Sacrificially slain and buried inside a hollow tree, Palmer returned to seek revenge in *From Hell It Came*.

came out to be viewed by the director. I didn't play the tree monster —
that was a "wrap" that day!

*Was it a whole new ballgame, now
that you were gone from Universal
and freelancing?*

It's different, yeah. The money
changes; you get more as a freelancer, considerably more. And some of
the offers you get are interesting. I
remember, after I left Universal
Studios, I was offered Tarzan. I was
on my way out to Culver City one
morning to meet with the producers
and sign a contract for Tarzan, and it
was a cold, chilly morning. And I got
to thinking, "I'm gonna have to
stand out in weather like this and go
a-woooo-a-woooo-a-woooo in a
loincloth? No, that's not for me!" So
I went up there and I told them, no,
I don't think I want to be Tarzan.
Then there was also an interest in me
for *The Lone Ranger.* Clayton Moore
had left and they needed another
Lone Ranger, my agent had me over
there and I made the test on it. And
after the test, he told them, "After
the shows are shot, we'd like to go
out and hit the rodeo circuit" — I
would ride around and say "Hiyo,
Silver!" and so forth. But they told us
we couldn't do that, so we passed on
The Lone Ranger and John Hart was
the one that got the part.

*You worked with a real "name"
director on* Most Dangerous Man
Alive, *Allan Dwan.*

Allan Dwan went back to the
days of silent pictures. I'll never
forget the day when I came up on the
set and I was introduced to Allan

Ad for *From Hell It Came.*

Dwan. We were in a lava canyon down in Mexico, he was sitting there, and I was introduced to him—"Mr. Dwan, this is Mr. Palmer. He's playing the police lieutenant." Dwan looked at me and then he turned to the wardrobe man, and he said [out of the corner of his mouth], "Where's his hat? Who ever heard of a detective without his hat?" I had never met Mr. Dwan, but I knew he had a reputation for being very firm. I said, "There's no problem, Mr. Dwan," and he said, "What d'ya mean, no problem? You gotta have a hat, Cowboy!" Where he got "cowboy" from, I don't know, but he hung that sobriquet on me [laughs]! I said, "Well, I'll use your hat." "My hat? No, no, no, no—you see all this stuff here?" and he took off his hat and revealed to me little sun spots on his forehead, from too much sun. So I called for property, they came over and I said, "Do you have an umbrella? A big beach umbrella?" They went off and they came back with a beach umbrella, and I remember struggling to jam this thing into the ground. Now there was shade covering Dwan, and I held my hand out and I said "Gimme the hat." So— reluctantly—he handed me the hat, he looked at me and he said, "Cowboy, this is my favorite hat. You damage this hat, and you got big troubles."

As I looked off in the distance I could see a car scurrying down the canyon, toward Mexico City, to find a hat—and they came back with maybe a dozen! Dwan picked one up and said, "This one here, Cowboy, this is your hat. Gimme my hat." And I looked at him and I said, "I'm afraid I can't do that, Mr. Dwan. This one's already established. You wear that hat." He again looked at me and he put it on and he said, "I'm telling you again, Cowboy. Injure that hat and you got big problems!" Well, the upshot of this story is that we became very good friends, and even after the show I was invited up to his house for dinner and so forth!

So you enjoyed working with Dwan.
Oh, yeah. He was a great man, a legend, just a super person. I enjoyed working with him and just being in his presence. We had a little gag going on *Most Dangerous Man Alive:* He would do closeups on me, which you would have to do in shooting a film. And after he'd get through with each closeup, I'd walk over and I'd give him a five-dollar peso. And he'd laugh, because that got people to thinking that I was paying Dwan to give me these closeups [laughs]! He was a great joker himself and he liked to kid around.

I'll never forget one scene in there where they used a bomb—it was sup- posed to be a tear gas bomb, in the scene where the police have the bad guys trapped in a power house. We were all concerned about our clothes and everything, but Ben Bogeaus, who was the producer of the show, said, "Don't worry about it, no problem." Well, cameras rolled, the bomb went off, and that liquid got on Tony Caruso's suit and my suit, and we had nothing but holes left in 'em! Another thing I remember is Morris Ankrum, who played my boss in the picture, he took ill, I guess from drinking the water. (We shot *Most Dangerous Man* down in Mexico City, at Churubusco Studios.) A lot of

Although he plays a machete-wielding sadist in *Big Jake,* Big Gregg looks jovial enough in this posed shot.

people fail to realize that in Mexico, even if you ask for bottled water, the ice they put in it is made from water that is not pure. And when you get the turistas, it brings you right on down to the ground — you couldn't be thrown faster, and you don't want to get up! It's an experience you'll never forget. And Morris Ankrum had that. Anyway, there was a scene that went for about a page and a half and it was decided that I would take all of Morrie's dialogue. They gave me the lines, and 15 minutes later I was before the camera. They were very appreciative about it, especially Mr. Dwan and Ben Bogeaus. But I'll never forget Morrie, so ill down there with that.

Fed up with L.A.'s smog and traffic, Palmer (seen here in a recent shot) is planning to head for the tall timber.

Just a few years ago you popped up in a Friday the 13th–*style film alternately called* The Outing *and* Scream.

What ever happened to that film, I'd like to know; I don't know where it went, but my guess is that it didn't go too far *[laughs]*! Some friends of mine approached me to do the picture and I said, "Well, why not?" Ethan Wayne was the star of it; Ethan was also in *Big Jake,* as the little tyke that Richard Boone and I kidnaped. A handsome young man—he's still in pictures today as an actor and doing very well. *The Outing* was about a bunch of campers turning up in a town where people are getting killed by various means. I played one of the campers, and I end up getting axed, I think *[laughs]*! We shot it at the Paramount Ranch here in the Valley. I read that it was released in New York and the first week, from what I read in the trades, it made a lot of money. But where it is now I don't know.

What would you say was the highlight of your career?

I would say that working with John Wayne was one of the highlights of my career. It was a pleasure working with this man—he was a legend. He was a person that gave you the bottom line, you knew where you stood with him. I can recall as a kid watching him in the movies, never realizing that someday I would be in his presence . . . acting with him . . . having him give me a nickname. "Grizzly" *[laughs]*—he hung that one on me! Six pictures I worked with him in. And I guess what I admired about that man most of all is his love for our country. He stood for the best in America and he always spoke very highly of it. He had that strength, and I'll never forget him for that.

Are you retired today?

Around the beginning of '89 I was taking the 405 freeway up over the hill, back into the San Fernando Valley where I live. I looked down at the bumper-to-bumper traffic and the smog and everything, and I just said to my wife, "Honey, that's a wrap." I called up the [Screen Actors] Guild and took my pension. Which doesn't mean that I can't go out and do other shows. My plans now are to go up into Oregon, or maybe Montana or Wyoming, and hunt and fish a little bit. But I still intend to do some more work; even though you draw your pension, you can still work seven days out of the month.

Overall, are you happy with your career?

I think that I had a very exciting career. I was able to meet a lot of nice people and I was fortunate enough to travel quite a bit. I made a few films in Durango, Mexico, a couple down in Mexico City and I've made films throughout the United States. I also went to Europe, and made a couple of spaghetti Westerns! I still have recognition, still have people that write to me. I've just recently gotten mail from Switzerland, Germany, England—even one from the outlands of Australia! When I look back now I think of some 50, 60-odd movies and close to a thousand television shows, and so, yes, I would say that I've been very lucky to have done as much as I have. I've had an exciting life.

GREGG PALMER FILMOGRAPHY

As Palmer Lee:

My Friend Irma Goes West (Paramount, 1950)
That's My Boy (Paramount, 1951)
Up Front (Universal, 1951)

The Cimarron Kid (Universal, 1951)
The Battle at Apache Pass (Universal, 1952)
Willie and Joe Back at the Front (Universal, 1952)
Son of Ali Baba (Universal, 1952)
Red Ball Express (Universal, 1952)
Francis Goes to West Point (Universal, 1952)
Meet Danny Wilson (Universal, 1952)
Sally and Saint Anne (Universal, 1952)
The Raiders (Universal, 1952)
The Redhead from Wyoming (Universal, 1952)
Abbott & Costello Go to Mars (voice only; Universal, 1953)
It Happens Every Thursday (Universal, 1953)
Column South (Universal, 1953)
The Veils of Bagdad (Universal, 1953)

As Gregg Palmer:

All American (Universal, 1953)
Francis Joins the Wacs (voice only; Universal, 1954)
Magnificent Obsession (Universal, 1954)
Playgirl (Universal, 1954)
Taza, Son of Cochise (Universal, 1954)
To Hell and Back (Universal, 1955)
The Creature Walks Among Us (Universal, 1956)
Hilda Crane (20th Century–Fox, 1956)
Footsteps in the Night (Allied Artists, 1957)
Revolt at Fort Laramie (United Artists, 1957)
From Hell It Came (Allied Artists, 1957)
Zombies of Mora Tau (Columbia, 1957)
The Female Animal (Universal, 1958)
Thundering Jets (20th Century–Fox, 1958)
The Sad Horse (20th Century–Fox, 1959)
The Rebel Set (Allied Artists, 1959)
Five Guns to Tombstone (United Artists, 1961)
Gun Fight (United Artists, 1961)
The Cat Burglar (United Artists, 1961)
Most Dangerous Man Alive (Columbia, 1961)
The Comancheros (20th Century–Fox, 1961)
The Absent-Minded Professor (Buena Vista, 1961)
Forty Pounds of Trouble (Universal, 1962)
The Prize (MGM, 1963)
Advance to the Rear (MGM, 1964)
The Quick Gun (Columbia, 1964)
Shenandoah (Universal, 1965)
The Rare Breed (Universal, 1966)
If He Hollers, Let Him Go! (Cinerama Releasing, 1968)
The Undefeated (20th Century–Fox, 1969)
The McKenzie Break (United Artists, 1970)
Chisum (Warners, 1970)
Rio Lobo (National General, 1970)
Big Jake (National General, 1971)
La Vita, A Volte E Molto Dura, Vero Provindenza? (Italian-French-West German, 1972)

Ci Risiamo Vero Providenza (Italian-Spanish, 197?)
The Shootist (Paramount, 1976)
Hot Lead and Cold Feet (Buena Vista, 1978)
The Man with Bogart's Face (Sam Marlow, Private Eye) (20th Century–Fox, 1980)
Scream (The Outing) (Cal-Com, 1985)

*I just loved good roles: I would love to have done
great big roles in great big A pictures, roles that had
meat in them. . . . It never quite happened for me in that way,
but I had some wonderfully satisfying experiences, I learned a
tremendous lot, I had a marvelous teacher, and who knows
what'll happen at this point? I don't necessarily
know that I've finished with acting.*

Mala Powers

TALENT AND BEAUTY go a long way toward helping a young actress up the ladder of stardom, but the elusive element of luck also plays a large part in the process. "Discovered" by Ida Lupino, Mala Powers co-starred in several prestigious films at the beginning of her career, including *Cyrano de Bergerac* (1950) with Oscar-winner Jose Ferrer, but after an illness interrupted her career momentum she fell into the clutches of the B science fiction and Western moviemakers. The mainstream's loss was fandom's gain, however, as brown-haired, gray-eyed Mala Powers has brought poise and charm to such genre productions as *The Unknown Terror, The Colossus of New York, Flight of the Lost Balloon, Doomsday Machine* and *Daddy's Gone A-Hunting*.

Do you remember how you became involved on The Unknown Terror?

I'm sure that it was simply a question of my agent calling me and telling me that they wanted me to do it. I do remember that I was pregnant then and that I didn't want anybody to know it at that point. I was eager to do as much work as I could, before I *couldn't [laughs]*! If memory serves, we shot *The Unknown Terror* at the old Producers Studio in Hollywood.

Did you consider a low-budget monster movie like The Unknown Terror *a comedown?*

You may read a script and say to yourself, "I wonder why this is being made at all." But if you need to work, if you need to stay in front of the public, if you need the money—whatever your reason is—and you say yes, at that point it is incumbent upon you to fall in love with the script and fall in love with your part. At that point you put on blinders that enable you to permit your love for your profession to shine a radiance over everything. This allows you to put all of yourself into it. I remember that our shooting title for *The Unknown Terror* was *Beyond Terror,* which I think might have been a better title.

Were you on hand for the scenes where the fungus is cascading down the cave walls?

Yeah, I was there. They used a lot of soap suds and some other stuff that was kind of like a plastic goo. It was a real conglomeration, and to find out exactly how it was done you'd have to go to Merlin the Magician *[laughs]*! The prop man was very inventive, and it was quite effective. It's quite different now that they have these special effects laboratories—it's much more sophisticated today. The effects in *The Unknown Terror* were just done by very good, inventive prop men.

Do you remember the fungus-men in the film?

Yes, they were made up by a makeup man. A lot of that makeup was just

Previous page: Mala Powers and Ed Wolff, *The Colossus of New York.*

Stalked by one of the fungus men in *The Unknown Terror,* **Powers wonders why the script was filmed at all.**

cotton, put on with liquid adhesive or spirit gum. Then they gave it a little glitter, to make it look more *[laughs]* . . . fungus-y! I don't know how it came out in the picture, but I do remember that at the time I wasn't really impressed with that aspect. When I "fell in love" with my part and so on, I guess I just ignored it!

Really, what I remember about *The Unknown Terror* is that I liked working with Paul Richards—he was a good actor—and I also liked John Howard [q.v.] very much. I thought the three of us worked well together. The director, Charles Marquis Warren, was pretty permissive, and he let us do whatever we wanted to do. It was just a very congenial set: John and Paul and I got along fine, and as far as I can remember, we all got along with Warren.

Was The Colossus of New York *the first film you made at Paramount?*

Yes, it was. But, you know, we shot a lot of that picture on location, in a house. It was a house not far from the studio—maybe 20 minutes away. We'd go to Paramount and get made-up there, get in the car and go to the location. Perhaps somebody thought it would seem more real if we did it in an actual house.

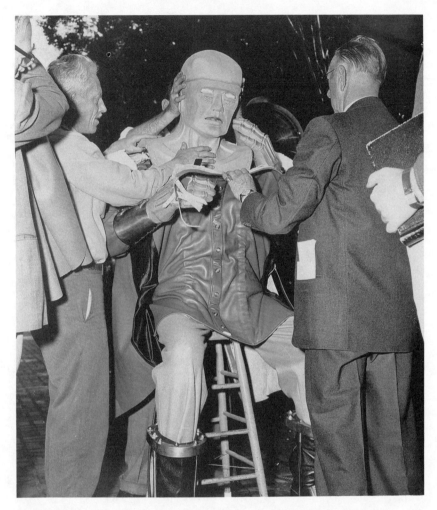

Eight-foot circus giant Ed Wolff is helped into (out of?) his robot suit backstage on *The Colossus of New York.*

Did you enjoy working with the director, Eugene Lourie?

I remember that I got along well with him, but really not too much more than that. I do remember that I always liked the producer, William Alland. He's a very pleasant man, and as I recall, whenever he came on the set, he did what I believe a producer should do: He made everybody feel that everything was fine. That's very important on a picture. If a producer comes on and he has a gloomy look on his face, everybody vibrates with gloom—it reverberates all the way around! My advice to any producer is always, if you come on the set unhappy about something, put on your best actor's face until you can handle it, because your face very materially affects the set.

Any special memories of your co-stars from that film?

I do have some very special memories of Ross Martin, because I later went out with Ross for a long time — it was on *The Colossus of New York* that we first met. I was very impressed with him on that film, and with the way he worked. After the first scene or two, he was only the voice of the Colossus, but he was really very impressive and a very, very good actor. And although he certainly had a great success, I always felt that he should have had even greater success, because he had the talent, ability and the training for it. I also loved working with Otto Kruger, he was so full of fun. Quite often he would play a menacing type of character, but he had this tremendous sense of humor — he was always coming up with some joke or something that caught you off-guard. I really liked him so much. *The Colossus of New York* was fun in those respects, but all in all it's not one of my favorite pictures.

At one point in your career you made the statement, "There are pictures I've made which I'd just as soon blank out of my mind." Were you mostly talking about these horror and science fiction films?

No, there were other pictures as well, for one reason or another. I can recall a picture I did called *Fear No More* [1961] where I really liked the script, and then all of a sudden in the last scene of the picture it falls apart so badly that the audience laughed at it. And the producers didn't have money enough to go back and change the ending. Up until the last scene it was a good picture, so that was a painful experience. There are various reasons why certain pictures weren't so pleasant to do, and others were great fun even if they weren't tremendous pictures!

How did you become interested in being an actress?

It started the summer my family and I moved down here to L.A. from San Francisco, where my father was an executive with United Press. This was in 1940, and it was the first summer that I had not been up at our summer home, on the Russian River near Guerneville. And for me it was pretty grim because I didn't know anybody. There was a drama school a few blocks away, the Max Reinhardt Junior Workshop, and my mother thought that it would be a good place for me to go for the summer, 'til school started, where I would meet other children. Also, she had always loved drama, and had done a lot of it when she was in college. So I went there for the summer, and while I was studying drama I did a play. And with the first play that I ever did in front of a live audience, that was it — I had the fever.

It still didn't occur to me that I was going to be an actress, I was just a kid, and I just went on being in amateur plays. At one point my parents were planning to send me to a private school, and my mother said to me, "We'll have to stop your dramatic lessons until next summer, because I can't afford to keep up with your lessons *and* send you to this school." And I said, "Then I don't want to go to that school!" And I got my way: We all talked about it and we found another school that was nearby, not so expensive, and that my parents felt was a good school, so I continued my drama lessons.

How did you break into pictures?

I guess close to a year later I was doing a play and an agent came back after the performance and asked my mother if he could submit me for a part in a movie. I'll never forget that night, because that was the first time it had ever occurred to me that I was going to be an actress — up until then, acting was just something that I loved doing. My mother said to me, "Well, what do you want to do?" and I said, "I want to *go!*" So I went out on the audition. It was a part in a Dead End Kids picture called *Tough as They Come* [1942] at Universal Studio. They wanted someone slightly older for the part that the agent had taken me out for, but they liked me and decided to write in the part of this giggly little girl at a party, and they gave me that part. And then they actually wrote it in for a second day, so I worked two days on it.

People talk about the smell of the greasepaint and the roar of the crowd; for me, it was the smell of the sound stage. It was just wonderful. And I knew that this was what I wanted to do.

Did you have any other roles as a child?

No, as a matter of fact, because very soon after that I started working with Max Reinhardt's wife, Helene Thimig, who was a great Austrian actress, and she more or less persuaded us to wait until I was at least in my teens, rather than to start out on the whole circuit of being a child actress. She felt that I should study and really prepare myself, and delay working professionally until a bit later.

When I was 16 I decided to try to break into radio, which I was fortunate enough to be able to do. I worked quite extensively for a couple of years, and was kind of making my mark in radio. I did everything that was out here in Hollywood: *Cisco Kid* and *Red Ryder, This Is Your F.B.I., Lux Radio Theater, Rocky Jordan*, that kind of show. During that process I did a *Screen Guild on the Air* where I met Ida Lupino, and she asked me to come in and read for her for a part in *Outrage* [1950], which she was directing and producing. When I read for her, she jumped up and said, "You're it, you're it! Read me another scene!"

Howard Hughes [then head of RKO] had to okay whoever it was that was signed to do the lead in the picture. So after Ida Lupino decided that she wanted me, she had me come in the next day and they took me into the portrait gallery, and I posed for portraits. They were shown to Hughes, and he asked to meet me. So my mother and my agent and I all went over to the Beverly Hills Hotel and had a meeting with Howard Hughes, in January 1950, in the outside court of the Polo Lounge. The chairs were all turned over and it was cold *[laughs]* — a very unlikely place to have a meeting, but that's where we had it! Hughes turned over the chairs and wiped them off with his handkerchief, and we all sat out there in the cold for about an hour and ten minutes, and he talked to me about the part. And I then did three pictures—*Outrage, Edge of Doom* and *Cyrano de Bergerac*—all within a span of four months in 1950.

Wasn't it soon after that when you became dangerously sick?

I was entertaining troops in Korea and I came down with a virus of some kind, and they gave me a drug called chloromycetin when I got back home. But I was allergic to chloromycetin, it destroyed a great part of the bone marrow, and I sort of stopped producing blood. I had a great many transfusions, and the doctors really didn't hold out a lot of hope for me as far as living was concerned. During that time I had a very wonderful spiritual experience in which I was told that I would recover, but what I had to do in order to recover. And that's really what I did. It took about nine months, but I did, obviously, get better.

But you were out of work all that time, of course.

Right. When I came back from Korea I was taking this medicine and I went to work on a film called *City Beneath the Sea* [1953] with Robert Ryan and Anthony Quinn and Suzan Ball. We were doing a lot of underwater scenes and earthquakes, and it was a fairly strenuous picture. I started to feel ill again and I called the doctor and asked for another prescription, which they sent to me. And while I was on the medicine I started to bleed under the skin and so on. The makeup man called the doctor, and I was taken off the picture and put into the hospital. I had finished all but one scene in *City Beneath the Sea,* and they wrote me out of that scene. Later the sound crew came to my house and recorded a telephone conversation which explained my absence from that scene. So from that point on, of course, I didn't work.

And do you blame your illness for your career losing its momentum?

Yes, unquestionably. I had two problems: One, there were a couple of good parts which came around a little bit later, and they wouldn't hire me because they were afraid I couldn't get insurance. That was ridiculous, because I could have gotten insurance—I mean, when I was well, I was well! But there were some problems like that. And then there was a whole kind of aura around me that persisted; instead of being known as "the actress," I was "the girl who was so sick." In fact, there came a point when I didn't want to talk about my illness and recovery any more for a number of years. But, you're right, I had a momentum going for me which somehow got slowed at that point.

You co-starred with Marshall Thompson in Flight of the Lost Balloon, *a film with some mild fantastic elements and a kind of Jules Verne flavor.*

I remember a lot about that picture. I loved the script, and so did Marshall Thompson. We knew it was Jules Verne and we knew it was tongue-in-cheek. But when we went to shoot it, we found out that we were the only people who

Powers and Marshall Thompson trooped down to the site of an old Puerto Rican leper colony for the Jules Verne-ish cheapie *Flight of the Lost Balloon.*

did know it! Marshall and I, and James Lanphier, who played the villain, were really the only people who knew that it was supposed to be done in that style, and it wasn't directed in that style. We also found out right away that the menacing elements in the picture weren't going to work out. They had men in gorilla suits, and also this poor giant who could hardly move because he was so big! To try to make him menacing was just ridiculous. The menacing elements should have been menacing, and of course they just weren't, so it became a neither-this-nor-that type of picture.

But you sound as though you still have a slightly soft spot for it.
     I have a soft spot for the script, not for the way the picture came out. But I loved my character—she was just so great, and I still like the moment at the end of the picture when she took this huge diamond from out of her mouth, where she had hidden it. And of course I had a wonderful time making the film because we went to Puerto Rico and we worked at some very interesting locations. We worked at the old Isla de Cabras—the Isle of the Goats—which used to be a leper colony! We shot a good deal of it there, and we shot in the castle in the bay in Puerto Rico, and then also in a jungle-type of location. I

remember the picture so well because the whole atmosphere of it was just fun and it was enjoyable to make. But I also found myself getting internally very angry because things weren't going right. Not angry *at* anyone, just angry because I felt like it had the potential to be a really fun, spoof kind of picture with some elements of menace and drama. But the menace just disappeared, and the sophisticated elements of the spoof were not capitalized upon.

Did you try to convey this to the director, Nathan Juran?

No, I didn't. What can you say when you get there in the morning and you see a man in a gorilla suit? Or what can you do when you sit down to watch the dailies and you see it's coming out just as you suspected it would? You can make your comments, but what are the producers going to do at that point? It was a low-budget picture — are they going to fly all the way back to the United States and prepare to start over? They're not.

A lot of stuff was getting shot, and as long as it was passable, they'd print it. That's not too unusual, but it was getting to me. And I remember saying at one point *[firmly]*, "No, I want to do it again." Nathan Juran said, "It doesn't make any difference," and I said, "It *does* make a difference. This is going to be on film a lot longer than I'm going to be alive, and I want to do it again." It was a scene on the edge of a cliff, with the ocean behind me, and it had really been a terrible take. And I just wasn't going to let it go that way.

What do you remember about the scene where you're chased by the angry tribe?

[Laughs.] That was great fun. They were all Spanish-speaking, and there were relatively few extras that spoke English. It was a very hot day — it was terrible! — and very, very humid. And there was also a fire in that scene, and that didn't help! I remember that the hairspray that they put on me would collect water, and my hair would get to be stringy and very difficult. And of course we were also perspiring, and it was impossible to keep the makeup on. Then there was bug spray *[laughs]* — the bugs would have eaten us alive in there without it! I remember the makeup people trying to keep me dry with powder going on over bug spray — it sounds like a horror film!

Did you ever actually go up in the hot-air balloon seen in the film?

We were in the basket of the balloon, of course, but it was just swung over a cliff by a big crane. So, no, we didn't actually go up. The background scenery in the flight scenes was simply rear-projection.

You worked again with Ida Lupino on TV's Thriller *and in an episode of* The Wild Wild West. *You've kept in touch with her through the years?*

Oh, yes, definitely, and we're still friends to this day. I loved working with her because I always knew that as a director she protected her people. In other words, you could dare to do things because you knew if it didn't come out right, she would not print it. I think that's one of the worst fears of actors today, and it was true then, too. Many shows are done so quickly that as long as you get the words out right, they print it! That means that you don't dare to be very original: Sometimes, when you create, it doesn't turn out right! If you've got a director that you trust, then you can be much more creative, but if you've got one that's going to print it no matter what, you tend to play it safe. And whenever you play it safe, it's not your best work.

Every time I worked with Ida Lupino, the crew loved her — she really made chums out of the crew. She used to call them "chum," and a lot of people called her "mum"! I just loved working with her because, first of all, I felt that she knew what was going on in me all the time, almost before I did. And I knew that she would protect me, and that she gave me confidence.

Any memories at all regarding those Thriller *and* Wild Wild West *guest shots?*

The *Thriller* episode was called "The Bride Who Died Twice," and I do remember that because any time that an actor lies in a coffin, they remember *[laughs]*! It was an interesting experience because I was interested in observing my own reaction to lying in the coffin. And working on *The Wild Wild West* ["The Night of the Big Blast"] was a ball because I did that with Ross Martin, and I was going with him at that point. We just had such a good time and so many laughs; it was so campy and so wonderful. And it was like old home week having Ida on the set as well; we didn't have a scene together in it but we were in the same episode, so of course we visited with each other on the set and so on. It was a very fun, very festive experience all the way around — it was fun-time, a playground. That to me was not work, it was sheer play, and I had a very good time.

How did Robert Conrad and Ross Martin get along together? Stories go around that they sometimes battled back and forth.

Well, you must remember that they worked together day in and day out, day in and day out. I know that basically Ross thought that Bob was a lot of fun, but I imagine that they had their tiffs occasionally. It wasn't an all-the-time fight: They had a whopper every once in a while, then they forgot about it and got along fine, and then something else would come up. But I never got the feeling that they were enemies.

What prompted you to accept a minor role in Daddy's Gone A-Hunting?

Mark Robson, who had directed me in *Edge of Doom* — I was still friendly with him. I was just about to get married when I went visiting at the Hal Roach Studio, and I saw an office door that said *Mark Robson*. I went in just to say hello, and he asked me if I was interested in being in this picture! It wasn't a real big part, he told me, but would I want to do it? And so I agreed that I would.

Not long after this I went on a trip to Europe. We were not scheduled to start shooting on *Daddy's Gone A-Hunting* for another ten days and I was just

For Tom —
Many thanks!
May a Rainbow of Happiness
be yours —
Always!
Mala Powers
29. 1988

Semi-retired from acting, Powers (seen here in a recent shot) has forged a new career as a writer of children's books.

arriving in London — my first trip there. And when I got there, there was a telephone message for me to call the studio immediately. I called, and they said I had to be in San Francisco in three days, that the schedule had all been changed! So I was in London exactly 24 hours, and got a plane direct from London to San Francisco and went to work. After that I didn't work on the picture again for another three or four weeks, and then I did a scene in Los Angeles. I went back to Europe in the meantime.

You enjoyed working with Robson?

I thought he was very creative, very warm, and that he had a very positive approach to things. He was firm, he knew what he was doing, but you could talk to him—he was not authoritarian. He came up with wonderful suggestions, and I really enjoyed working with Mark. I thought he was a first-rate director. *Daddy's Gone A-Hunting* was a good picture with a lot of suspense, and I enjoyed it.

In between your many film and TV appearances, you've done a lot of stage work. Do you prefer the stage to the screen?

I think they're two separate, very different things, and I love them both. I personally don't really like eight performances a week, month after month after month, so my preference would be limited runs as far as the stage is concerned. But I really do love working for a live audience; it's much more challenging in some ways. On the screen you can do short scenes and you can feel "that it was a little piece of art"—that's my teacher's, Michael Chekhov's, phrase. It has a beginning, a middle and an end, and you receive satisfaction from that, like a craftsman does. But the sustained experience of starting at the beginning of a play and moving all the way through it is also a very satisfying experience and quite different. And you get so much from a live audience which you have to work much harder to get on a sound stage. There are advantages to everything.

How do good actors get mixed up with the kind of filmmakers who'd make something like Doomsday Machine?

Doomsday Machine is a subject about which I could still scream. Once again, it had a certain premise that was okay. Then they ran out of money, twice. We had a director who was taken off the picture in the middle, and another director, Lee Sholem, was put on. The thing was not going well, and it was never finished because they ran out of money like two days before the end of the picture. One of the reasons I'm sure they were never able to raise the money to finish the picture was because of the really shoddy interior of that spaceship. The special effects hadn't been done yet, they couldn't sell it and they couldn't raise enough money to finish it.

Now is the point where I get really angry: A number of years later they had the audacity to sell that picture to someone who put doubles into spacesuits, and finished the picture with an ending that was never part of the script. I didn't even know about it until long after it had been shown on television, when somebody finally told me about it. They put somebody in a spacesuit—this was supposed to be me—and allowed them to speak without the Russian accent that I had used all the way through the picture! I just wanted to scream! I wanted to go to the Guild and start an action and see if anything could be legally done about it, but at that point I was simply too busy. I don't know that anything could be done, but that was my impulse. When I saw that on television, I was infuriated.

It's an unbearable movie to watch.

Absolutely. I don't think the whole thing was unbearable, but the special effects were . . . *so* . . . *bad*! They were added to the picture by the people who bought *Doomsday Machine* and decided to make money with it. But even the suits, the props and everything else that was in the picture while we were doing it were so junior-high-school, it was unbelievable. But we did have a good cast—Bobby Van was lots of fun; Denny Miller; Ruta Lee and I became real good friends; Grant Williams; Henry Wilcoxon I loved. We just had a good time.

Your last film to date is the Argentine-made fantasy Six Tickets to Hell *[1975], which has never been released.*

That was originally entitled *Temple of the Ravens,* and it was a co-production between Argentina and a group up here in the United States. It started out with a plane crash in the Andes; six people survive and trek across the mountains, and finally we find this abandoned monastery where one strange thing happens after another. I'm attacked by some kind of an invisible "thing"; you can't see anything but literally it's an attempted rape. Everybody has some sort of experience, 'cause we're kind of dealing with ghosts and so on. It becomes so frightening there that finally we leave, and we get to a city where no one can see us; we walk around and try to talk to people, but no one sees us! What finally happens is that we're captured by a strange group of people and end up in a kind of court where we are to be judged for our sins. The link between all of us is that all six of us had been responsible in various ways for the death of a human being; in my character's case, it was through my own selfishness and greed that someone committed suicide. John Russell plays a character that was actually supposed to be the Devil, and he wants to condemn us all, but because one of the other characters was found not guilty and because we had decided to be judged as a group, we were all exonerated. And the last shot in the film is of the plane wreckage, and now you see all six bodies there. So it really turns out to have been a purgatory story.

The whole film was shot in English, but nevertheless they still dubbed everything—none of the soundtrack was any good. So all of the scenes had to be dubbed, and we dubbed them in Argentina where there were no really professional facilities available to us. It was an impossible task.

What did you think of the film when you saw it?

I saw parts of it and it was so phony, so awful that I was glad that it was not released. It was a very interesting script, and photographically it was well done; the problem with it was that most of the actors were Spanish-speaking and they had to speak English phonetically. Which was very clever, except that the tempo of it was so different and so slow; when it was then dubbed into English, although their lips were making the proper shapes, it was so slow that it was ghastly! So it was one of those things where I enjoyed making it tremendously, and I thought it was an interesting story, but when I saw a rough cut of it I thought I would die. Everything was ruined by the dubbing, and again I admit that I was always glad that it was not released here.

Why didn't it get a U.S. release?
What happened with it was quite a story in itself, although I don't know all the details. At one point the group that had made the investments up here was indicted for having collected money for, like, 25 movies and only made 17, and pocketed the rest of the money. So all of the pictures were impounded, and as far as I know they have never been shown in this country; *Six Tickets to Hell* was shown in Argentina. The producer was a man by the name of Enrique Torres, who did a number of rather imaginative horror genre films, and the director was Fernando Ciro, who is a very well-known actor-director in Argentina.

How do you keep yourself active nowadays?
Right now I am in the midst of writing a play. I don't get very much time to work on it, so it's going to take me a while to finish it, but I'm enjoying myself. And I've been teaching the Michael Chekhov acting technique. I have a group that meets once a week, and I am really enjoying teaching, I'm really grabbed by it.

Which of your films are your favorites?
For various reasons—not necessarily because it was the best film—*Outrage.* I loved the part, and I think probably that has more to do with it than the quality of the film. Of course I think *Cyrano de Bergerac* is still an excellent movie, so from that standpoint it would definitely have to be called a favorite. The film I had the most fun on was *City Beneath the Sea* with Robert Ryan and Tony Quinn, and a crazy director—crazy-wonderful—by the name of Budd Boetticher. It was really fun making that movie, even though I became very ill during the filming.

Looking back over your film career, are there any major regrets or are you pleased with your Hollywood career?
That's a tough question. No, I'm not pleased with my career; yes, I am pleased with my *life.*
I just loved good roles; I would love to have done great big roles in great big A pictures, roles that had meat in them. Would any actress *not* like to play Scarlett O'Hara in *Gone With the Wind?* From a career standpoint, of course that's what I would like to have done. It never quite happened for me in that way, but I had some wonderfully satisfying experiences, I learned a tremendous lot, I had a marvelous teacher, and who knows what'll happen at this point? I don't necessarily know that I've finished with acting.

MALA POWERS FILMOGRAPHY

Tough as They Come (Universal, 1942)
Outrage (RKO, 1950)
Edge of Doom (RKO, 1950)
Cyrano de Bergerac (United Artists, 1950)
Rose of Cimarron (20th Century-Fox, 1952)
City Beneath the Sea (Universal, 1953)
City That Never Sleeps (Republic, 1953)
Geraldine (Republic, 1953)
The Yellow Mountain (Universal, 1954)
Rage at Dawn (RKO, 1955)
Bengazi (RKO, 1955)
Tammy and the Bachelor (Universal, 1957)
The Storm Rider (20th Century-Fox, 1957)
Death in Small Doses (Allied Artists, 1957)
The Unknown Terror (20th Century-Fox, 1957)
Man on the Prowl (United Artists, 1957)
Sierra Baron (20th Century-Fox, 1958)
The Colossus of New York (Paramount, 1958)
Fear No More (Sutton Pictures, 1961)
Flight of the Lost Balloon (Woolner Bros., 1961)
Doomsday Machine (Filmways / First Leisure, 1967)
Rogue's Gallery (Paramount, 1968)
Daddy's Gone A-Hunting (National General, 1969)
Six Tickets to Hell (Temple of the Ravens) (U.S. / Argentine, 1975)

Most of us thought that Superman *was just a job.
Even though it lasted season after season and I knew
it was popular, I never had any idea that its popularity
would last and that twenty-five years later we'd be
going to conventions where people would mob us!*

Robert Shayne

BORN IN turn-of-the-century Yonkers, New York, Robert Shayne (born Robert Shaen Dawe) worked at a variety of jobs before his interests ultimately turned toward acting. He appeared in a long succession of legitimate theater productions throughout the '30s and even got a false start in motion pictures, appearing in two 1934 features and a 1937 New York–made comedy short. In 1942 Shayne signed up with Warner Bros. and trekked to Hollywood, where he became a contract player at their Culver City studios. "I remember my arrival in California, walking through the Burbank Airport and out the front door," Shayne reminisces. "The sun was shining, it was warm, it was beautiful and I said to myself, 'Oh, my—this is for *me*!' And I've been out here ever since!"

Warners starred the newly arrived stage actor in a series of two-reel Westerns before graduating him to supporting roles in A features. Shayne appeared opposite many of the top WB stars of the day in pictures like *Shine on, Harvest Moon, Mr. Skeffington* (1944), *Christmas in Connecticut, Rhapsody in Blue* (1945) and many more. In 1946 he left the studio to freelance and several years later became involved in the infant medium of television, where he would win his best-remembered role as Inspector Bill Henderson in the syndicated TV series *Adventures of Superman.*

Do you recall how you landed the part of Inspector Henderson on Adventures of Superman?

My agent, Sam Armstrong, called me on the phone and said, "I've got a job for you at RKO-Pathe. Meet me on the lot at such-and-such a time." When we got there, we walked into the office of the producer, Robert Maxwell, and Sam said to Bob, "Here's the man I want you to have to play the Inspector." Bob took one look at me and asked, "How long have you been in the picture business?" and I told him I'd been in it about seven or eight years at the time. He asked if I minded graying my hair, to look older than George Reeves, and I said, "No, of course not, I'd be glad to." And Bob said, "Okay, you're it." That's how it happened.

What can you tell me about working with George Reeves [Superman]?

I found him a wonderful fellow to work with. George was an awfully nice guy. He was very sensitive and very friendly—he always gave me a birthday cake if my birthday came around when I was on the set. He was always thinking about other people.

What about some of the other regulars?

The one I got to know most was Phyllis Coates [Lois Lane, q.v.], although she was only with us for the first season. Later on, after *Superman,* we did a play down in Palm Springs, a comedy called *Never Too Late,* in which she played the wife and I played the husband. She comes down and visits every once in a while, and stays at my daughter's house—my daughter was in that same play. Phyllis is a good, professional actress.

Previous page: **George Reeves and Robert Shayne in a posed shot from the classic 1950s TV series** *Adventures of Superman.*

She lost interest in the show after that first season.

We were on layoff after the first 26 episodes, Phyllis had an offer to do another series, and she wouldn't give that up to come back to *Superman*. They had to get somebody to replace her, and they got Noel Neill, who was in the two original Kirk Alyn *Superman* serials at Columbia. Phyllis Coates was a much better Lois Lane than Noel Neill. Phyllis was believable whereas Noel Neill was never believable to me as a newspaperwoman. I didn't get to know either Noel or Jack Larson [Jimmy Olsen] very well, only professionally, from working with them on the lot. John Hamilton [Perry White] was a heavy drinker. He made the Brown Derby his club—he was at the bar always. But now let me quickly add that John never drank on the set, never drank before work or during work.

How did working in early TV compare to working in films?

Television was much more hectic. Sometimes in an A movie you would do one scene a day, shooting from various angles, close-ups and so forth, making sure the lighting was just right and so on. In TV, it's "To hell with the lighting, let's get in the can!" However, I don't think that this was quite the case with the *Superman* directors. It seems to me that every time I see a *Superman* episode, it's pretty well done.

What can you recall about some of the behind-the-scenes people on the series?

There's nothing much I can tell you about Bob Maxwell; he was my employer, I liked him and he liked me, but I didn't know anything about him personally. Whitney Ellsworth, who took over from Maxwell, I got to know fairly well because we were together much longer—Maxwell was only on the first 26 episodes. I remember that at one point Kellogg's wanted to drop me from the show, but Whitney stood up for me. This was during the blacklist period, and I was blacklisted. "He's done nothing wrong, I'm not going to fire him," Whitney told Kellogg's, and they backed down. I was out of the series for two or three episodes, then was back. That was a despicable era in Hollywood and in the United States, a despicable era.

It was so unfair. Being a Communist was not a crime, it was a legal political party in the United States then and it is now. All this hullabaloo about Communist influence in Hollywood was originally started by Bob Montgomery. He said he didn't want to be president of a union where, every time the union's name was mentioned, somebody would say, "Oh, that *Communist* union." Bob Montgomery was the one who really pushed the inquiry out here, and if you were subpoenaed, you were blacklisted, regardless of whether you were guilty of anything or not. This same thing would have happened again, in my opinion, if Reagan had had his way, 'cause he sees a Communist under every rug.

So what exactly had you done, to make them turn the heat on you?

Shayne (seen here in a publicity shot from *The Face of Marble*) was blacklisted in Hollywood after a run-in with the Joe McCarthy crowd, but he has still managed to rack up a long list of film and TV credits.

I hadn't done anything! The investigator told me and my wife, after everything had quieted down, "We had no reason to call you, I don't know why we ever did."

Did you maybe work for an organization that was linked with the Communist party?

Not to my knowledge. I was part of a group in Actors Equity [in New York] that fought for pay for rehearsals, minimum wages and better working conditions—and we got them. I was a rabid union man and I still believe in unions, although I'm not rabid anymore *[laughs]*! Maybe that was part of it. I was never active out here at all except when I was on the Board of Directors of the Screen Actors Guild for a while, and incurred the enmity of Bob Montgomery and Leon Ames and a few others because I was always trying to get something better for the actors.

Do you have a favorite among your many Superman *episodes?*

I have two favorites. One of them was about my son getting in trouble ["The Talking Clue," 1954], and in the other one I played a *Fr-r-rench* Inspec*teur* ["Peril in Paris," 1956].

Being that Adventures of Superman *was an action show, can you recall any injuries or near-misses?*

Not to my recollection—we were always too careful. The nearest I ever came to an accident was when I was making two-reel Westerns for Warner Bros. We were doing a scene in a barroom where I was lying on the floor, pulling a gun and shooting up at a heavy on a balcony. The director, "Breezy" Eason, came over and said, "Bob, you're not doing this quite right. I want you to do it *this* way." I had never used a gun on the stage, this was perhaps my first time. After he showed me, I pulled the gun out and inadvertently I squeezed the trigger, and the blank shot out and just went by Eason's face! I've never forgotten that.

Have you seen the four new Superman *movies with Christopher Reeve?*

No, I've never seen them. They didn't ask me to be in any, and I haven't gone to see them *[laughs]*! I understand that all those movies, especially the third and fourth, are predominantly special effects shows, with no storyline.

What are your fondest memories of working on Superman*?*

That's hard to say. I just enjoyed going to work, because everyone in the company was compatible. George and I worked so well together. We would come in every morning, he'd ask me, "Bob, do you know your lines?" I'd say, "No, not too well," and he'd say, "Well, neither do I! Come on, let's go into my dressing room and we'll run 'em." We'd sit in the dressing room and go over the lines two or three times, and then we'd be ready. That was the kind of relationship that I had with George—you don't have that with other actors or actresses as a rule. I never had it with any of the ladies I worked with. George was an easygoing, lovable guy.

Do you really believe that he committed suicide?

I don't believe he committed suicide, but I don't know who would have killed him, or anything else about it. There was some talk a few months ago that the case was going to be reopened, but not too long ago an interviewer told me that he had checked with the police department and that there was no intention of reopening the investigation.

What leads you to believe that he did not kill himself?

There was a man I met not so long ago who was a plasterer, and he told me that he went into George's house to plaster up the bullet holes. There was more than one bullet hole—they were all over the bedroom! Now, how could a man commit suicide and have bullet holes all over the room?

People say that Reeves was disgruntled over being over-identified with the Superman role.

No, no—George was making good money on that job and we had just signed up for another 26 episodes, practically all of them written. He was not wanting for work and he was not wanting for money. And if he was over-exposed as Superman, then I was over-exposed as a police inspector—but I got plenty of work after the show ended. So I don't think it holds up.

Fans of science fiction and horror films also remember you from many of those, beginning with The Face of Marble *in 1946.*

The Face of Marble was the first freelance picture I made after leaving Warner Bros. After we had finished it, I went to see a preview of it over in South Los Angeles somewhere, with my wife and another couple. We were near the back of the house, and as this picture went along I hung my head, I was so embarrassed by it! Finally, when the thing was over, I got out into the lobby before anybody else did, and I was standing against a wall with my wife and this other couple. Two young ladies came out and stood against an opposite wall, and they did a double-take when they saw who I was. And one of them came over to me and said *[wagging his finger]*, "Mr. Shayne, you ought to be ashamed to be in a picture like that!"

Did you enjoy working with star John Carradine?

That's a story in itself. We broke for lunch one day, and I came back early, onto the semi-darkened stage. John Carradine was on the dark stage spouting the dialogue of some character from Shakespeare, I forget which one, and I started to laugh, and poked fun at him. I said, "What the hell are you doing? Are you spouting Shakespeare?" He didn't like that, he didn't like my kidding him, and he got mad as hell *[laughs]*!

Your one starring sci-fi role was in 1953's The Neanderthal Man. *How did you land that part?*

The same way I got the job as Inspector Henderson on *Superman*. Sam Armstrong called me and said that the producers, Aubrey Wisberg and Jack Pollexfen, wanted to see me about a picture they were doing. I went in to see them with Sam, and I was hired. In those days, if you were a well-established actor, all the casting people and the producers knew of you and knew about your work, and you were hired on the basis of your name and reputation. You didn't have to go and audition, like they do today. The little secretaries sitting

MONOGRAM PICTURES *presents* "THE FACE of MARBLE"

starring JOHN CARRADINE *with* CLAUDIA DRAKE · ROBERT SHAYNE
MARIS WRIXON · WILLIE BEST

Directed by WILLIAM BEAUDINE   Screenplay by Michel Jacoby   Original story by William Thiele and Edmund Hartmann

Shayne's first freelance job after leaving prestigious Warner Bros. was a scientist role in Monogram's lowly *The Face of Marble* with John Carradine.

at the casting desks don't know a damn thing about pictures or the actors. When I'm called for an interview like that, I go in and the girl asks me, "What have you done lately?" and I say, "What have *you* done lately?" *[Laughs.]* But it's insulting, really—the people in the business should know who the actors are, and should know something about what they've done. It's professional.

Pictures aren't anything like what they were when I came out here, when the big studios were in existence and dominated the industry. Today the conglomerates own the business and they don't give a damn, so long as it makes money.

Did you play the monster in The Neanderthal Man, *or is that a double?*

No, they had a double for me. However, I did have to wear the makeup for the transition scenes. The transition scenes, me changing into the monster and vice versa, were all made on a Sunday. It was just me and the makeup man, Harry Thomas, and a camera crew. They were laborious shots: they'd put the monster makeup on me, shoot just a few frames, cut, and then the makeup man would step in and make me look worse. We were there all day long.

What was your opinion of the finished film?

Is it Shayne or a stuntman beneath the *Neanderthal Man* makeup? Only makeup man Harry Thomas knows for sure.

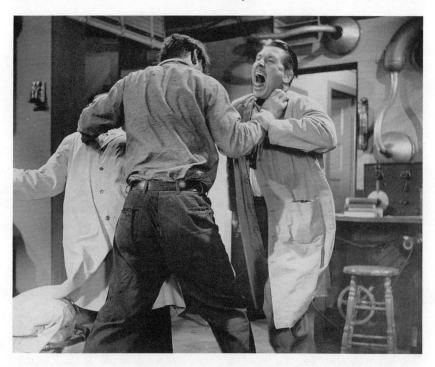

There's usually a price to be paid when medical science goes too far in a sci-fi film, as Joe Flynn and Shayne find out from *Indestructible Man* Lon Chaney.

If *The Neanderthal Man* had had good production, it would have been a good picture. But that was very cheaply done.

Many of the roles you played in science fiction films of the '50s were smallish or sometimes even bit parts — Invaders from Mars, Tobor the Great, Kronos, The Lost Missile *and others.*

Being a professional actor, it didn't matter much to me whether I was starred or if I played a much smaller part. I was interested in *work* — I had a wife and two young children to support at the time. I never had the ego that some of these so-called "name" stars have. But consequently I have a short memory on some of these science fiction things — after all, it's a long time ago.

One director you worked with on three occasions was Roger Corman.

Roger Corman was a driver. He made pictures on low budgets and made them fast, and I don't think he cared too much about the quality of the performances or the photography or anything else. He was more concerned with getting the film in the can, getting it out and getting the money! He may have changed — I have not worked with him since he's become a big-shot producer.

Shayne at home in 1987.

Certainly your most unusual role in a Corman film was as one of the Keepers of the Gifts in Teenage Caveman.

My son Bob, Jr., and daughter Stephanie wanted to be in that movie. I made a deal with Corman to put them in, and I would do a small part if I were disguised. Therefore, the heavy wig, beard, etc. No one knew it was me. It was a crappy little part.

You had a good-sized part in Sam Katzman's The Giant Claw.

I didn't see *The Giant Claw* when it was first released, I saw it somewhere later. And when I saw this giant bird, I said, "Oh, God!" to myself! They ruined that picture with cheap special effects. That was a classic piece of junk.

Did you ever get to meet Sam Katzman?

I got to know him fairly well. I remember that on one picture, I think it was *State Penitentiary* [1950], we were in Virginia City and the whole crew was gambling. I didn't gamble at all, so I came away with my salary, but most of 'em came away from that picture in debt to Sam because they borrowed not only their salaries, but money besides!

You've done stage, films, radio, TV—is there anything you haven't done?

I never shit on the captain's floor *[laughs]*!

Do you have a favorite part?

Among the A pictures that I was in, my favorite part was in *Christmas in Connecticut* with Barbara Stanwyck. So far as TV is concerned, I think my favorite part was on *Superman,* as Inspector Henderson—he was duck soup for me!

While working on the Superman *series, did you have any inkling that its popularity would be so long-lasting?*

Not the slightest. Most of us thought that *Superman* was just a job. Even though it lasted season after season and I knew it was popular, I never had any idea that its popularity would last and that 25 years later we'd be going to conventions where people would mob us!

ROBERT SHAYNE FILMOGRAPHY

Keep 'Em Rolling (RKO, 1934)
Wednesday's Child (RKO, 1934)
Off the Horses (Educational short, 1937)
Oklahoma Outlaws (Warners short, 1943)
Wagon Wheels West (Warners short, 1943)
Mission to Moscow (Warners, 1943)
Gun to Gun (Warners short, 1944)
Trial by Trigger (Warners short, 1944)
Roaring Guns (Warners short, 1944)
Hollywood Canteen (Warners, 1944)
Shine on, Harvest Moon (Warners, 1944)
Make Your Own Bed (Warners, 1944)
Mr. Skeffington (Warners, 1944)
Frontier Days (Warners short, 1945)
Law of the Badlands (Warners short, 1945)
Rhapsody in Blue (Warners, 1945)
Christmas in Connecticut (Warners, 1945)
San Antonio (Warners, 1945)
My Reputation (Warners, 1946)
Three Strangers (Warners, 1946)
Nobody Lives Forever (Warners, 1946)
The Face of Marble (Monogram, 1946)
Behind the Mask (Monogram, 1946)
Wife Wanted (Monogram, 1946)
I Ring Doorbells (PRC, 1946)
The Spirit of West Point (Film Classics, 1947)
The Swordsman (Columbia, 1947)
Backlash (20th Century–Fox, 1947)
I Cover Big Town (I Cover the Underworld) (Paramount, 1947)
Smash-Up, the Story of a Woman (Universal, 1947)
Welcome Stranger (Paramount, 1947)
Shaggy (Paramount, 1948)
The Strange Mrs. Crane (Eagle-Lion, 1948)
Let's Live a Little (Eagle-Lion, 1948)

Best Man Wins (Columbia, 1948)
The Inside Story (Republic, 1948)
Loaded Pistols (Columbia, 1948)
The Threat (RKO, 1949)
The Law of the Barbary Coast (Columbia, 1949)
Forgotten Women (Monogram, 1949)
Experiment Alcatraz (RKO, 1950)
Dynamite Pass (RKO, 1950)
Rider from Tucson (RKO, 1950)
Federal Man (Eagle-Lion, 1950)
Big Timber (Monogram, 1950)
When You're Smiling (Columbia, 1950)
State Penitentiary (Columbia, 1950)
Customs Agent (Columbia, 1950)
Missing Women (Republic, 1951)
The Dakota Kid (Republic, 1951)
Criminal Lawyer (Columbia, 1951)
Indian Uprising (Columbia, 1952)
Without Warning (United Artists, 1952)
Mr. Walkie Talkie (Lippert, 1952)
The Neanderthal Man (United Artists, 1953)
The Blue Gardenia (Warners, 1953)
Prince of Pirates (Columbia, 1953)
Flight Nurse (Republic, 1953)
The Lady Wants Mink (Republic, 1953)
Eyes of the Jungle (Lippert, 1953)
Marshal of Cedar Rock (Republic, 1953)
Invaders from Mars (20th Century–Fox, 1953)
Trader Tom of the China Seas (Republic serial, 1954)
The Desperado (Allied Artists, 1954)
Tobor the Great (Republic, 1954)
Double Jeopardy (Republic, 1955)
Murder Is My Beat (Allied Artists, 1955)
King of the Carnival (Republic serial, 1955)
The Eternal Sea (Republic, 1955)
Accused of Murder (Republic, 1956)
Indestructible Man (Allied Artists, 1956)
Dance with Me, Henry (United Artists, 1956)
Rumble on the Docks (Columbia, 1956)
Hot Shots (Allied Artists, 1956)
Spook Chasers (Allied Artists, 1957)
Kronos (20th Century–Fox, 1957)
Footsteps in the Night (Allied Artists, 1957)
The Giant Claw (Columbia, 1957)
Death in Small Doses (Allied Artists, 1957)
The Lost Missile (United Artists, 1958)
War of the Satellites (Allied Artists, 1958)
How to Make a Monster (AIP, 1958)
Teenage Caveman (AIP, 1958)
I, Mobster (20th Century–Fox, 1958)
Battle Flame (Allied Artists, 1959)
North by Northwest (MGM, 1959)

The Rebel Set (Allied Artists, 1959)
From the Terrace (20th Century–Fox, 1960)
Why Must I Die? (AIP, 1960)
Cage of Evil (United Artists, 1960)
Valley of the Redwoods (20th Century–Fox, 1960)
20,000 Eyes (20th Century–Fox, 1961)
Son of Flubber (Buena Vista, 1963)
A Tiger Walks (Buena Vista, 1964)
Runaway Girl (United Screen Arts, 1966)
The Arrangement (Warners-7 Arts, 1969)
Winning (Universal, 1969)
Tora! Tora! Tora! (20th Century–Fox, 1970)
The Million Dollar Duck (Buena Vista, 1971)
The Barefoot Executive (Buena Vista, 1971)
Cool Breeze (MGM, 1972)

*Of course, a lot of women believed I was really
like the roles I played. It was so funny—they would
practically rush with their husbands to the other side of the room
when they saw me! I thought to myself, "I didn't mean to be
that convincing!" I didn't know it was going to make
a social outcast out of me!*

Yvette Vickers

HAILING FROM Kansas City, Missouri, blue-eyed blond Yvette Vickers was the daugher of jazz musicians Charles and Iola Vedder. Vickers hit the road with her folks at an early age, but her career plans did not include show biz until she took an acting class at U.C.L.A. She subsequently began appearing in little theater productions and in revues as well as acting in TV and in commercials (as the dancing White Rain Girl).

Yvette was "introduced" into motion pictures via *Short Cut to Hell*, a 1957 crime drama directed by former movie gangster James Cagney, and some small film parts (*Reform School Girl, The Saga of Hemp Brown*, the Cormans' *I, Mobster*) quickly followed. Leading roles in *Attack of the 50 Foot Woman* and *Attack of the Giant Leeches* brought Vickers to the attention of science fiction fans, who later caught fleeting glimpses of their favorite pinup gal in pictures like *What's the Matter with Helen?* and TV's *The Dead Don't Die.*

How did you first become interested in being an actress?

I wanted to be a writer, and I was taking classes at U.C.L.A. to become a journalist. I needed an extra course, just to fill in, for three more units, and I took an acting class for that reason. I began taking the class, and I got very interested in the theater—there was something about it that seemed so natural. In Catholic school I had done a couple of plays and gotten a very good reaction, which is unusual because most of the time they don't suggest that you go into that field. The priest who gave the valedictory speech at my graduation actually encouraged me to go into the theater, and I thought that was really amazing. But I didn't do it at that time; I wanted to be a writer. Later, though, as a result of that one class at U.C.L.A., I got bit by the acting bug. I kept doing plays at school, and then outside of school—in the summer sessions I would do little theater at the Players Ring, and then professionally I would do revues. One thing led to another, I got on a roll and I just kept going with it. In fact, I didn't go back to school because I started really enjoying performing. I just kept working, and the next thing I knew I got a job as the White Rain Girl.

People ask me now how to get started, and I always say to them, "Go out and work in little theater, and perform in front of an audience." Now, I did have training in between all that—I was going to acting classes with Ben-Ari, I did a workshop with Anthony Quinn and so on. A lot of very, very good people were in my environment. I was very fortunate that way—I was always surrounded by top people. In fact, my first film, *Short Cut to Hell*, was directed by James Cagney—I mean, what more could a novice want? I didn't realize what a big thing it was at the time but, looking back, I'm amazed at my good fortune.

Was Cagney a good director?

Previous page: It isn't often that dramatic acting skill comes wrapped in a 34-20-34 package, but in the late 1950s actress Yvette Vickers embodied this piquant combination.

Yvette Vickers, '50s sex kitten *par excellence.*

He was just magnificent. But, as you know, the film just didn't turn out too well. I guess you've heard this fairly often, and it's really true: You can have the best ingredients, the greatest actors, the best director, a good story—and it can fall apart! And nobody ever knows why. While we were working on *Short Cut to Hell* we learned a lot from Cagney—he was so giving, he cared about actors so much. He was very serious about performing and about actors being respected and treated with dignity. Everything about him was wonderful. He encouraged me, and did a lot of press with me. Everyone who dropped by the set was curious to see *him*—he was really the star of the show—but he would always guide them over to the newcomers, especially myself and Robert Ivers, and say, "Now, *these* are the ones that are coming up." He was just generous that way. And, again, as far as the work itself was concerned, you couldn't have anybody that was more stimulating or more inspiring.

What about the press you got for being a beatnik during that era?

[Laughs.] There's a little bit of truth to that. I went to a lot of beatnik hangouts, and I used to go around with Mort Sahl—we'd go to bookshops and we'd go to coffee houses and listen to the music. I really liked that era, although I had a lot more fun in the late '60s and '70s as far as going out to clubs and so on. I was really working most of the time during that earlier era, and I didn't get to play very much. But I remember that beatnik era well, and I did enjoy those clubs—I went to Cosmo Alley, Chez Paulette, all of them.

You played your patented "bad girl" for the first time in AIP's Reform School Girl *[1957].*

One of the things I remember best about *Reform School Girl* was that I was scared of a snake that we used in one scene *[laughs]*, and that I told them I didn't think I could pick it up! But if something's required by a part, I can usually get up the courage to do it. I've played a deep sea diver, and I don't even *swim*—I've done a lot of things that I'm afraid to do!

I met Edd Byrnes on *Reform School Girl* and we became friends, and the same with Sally Kellerman—it was a good experience. There were a lot of people in *Reform School Girl* that were enduring in my life, and I thought that the show itself went very well. We were all very serious. I was reading *My Life in Art* by Stanislavsky at the time, and I remember one day on the set, while waiting for "action" to be called, whispering to Luana Anders, "Did you know that *My Life in Art* is out in paperback?" Acting, to me, was a serious business.

How did you become involved on Attack of the 50 Foot Woman?

I had started working a lot in television, and most of the time I did not have to go on interviews for work anymore. I'd been sort of established—I was a known quantity. They called my agency and asked for me, and we accepted. Of course I loved the idea of playing this vamp *[laughs]*—this *tramp,* this shameless hussy—and I still do! I think those are the fun parts. You get to do everything that you're afraid to do in life when you play those types, and I just had a ball doing it. I let out all the stops.

What do you remember about stars Allison Hayes and William Hudson?

Allison Hayes helped me a lot, because it was my first really large role. I'd been doing large roles on TV and on stage, but in film I'd never had a leading role. So I was a little insecure, and I used to go to her for advice. She gave me tips on how to behave on the set, that sort of thing. She was very, very helpful.

She came to a tragic end many years later.

Somehow Allison and I lost track of one another. We had been with the same agent, and of course that had a lot to do with my being cast in *50 Foot Woman*, too — they had already settled on her, and then since I was with that same office they made a sort of a package deal. I didn't know about her death until only a few years ago, and I was just shocked to hear about it.

And William Hudson?

He was fun. I think he's probably the only one that knew that *50 Foot Woman* was camp. Most of us were just playing it straight, but he had a little bit of a tongue-in-cheek attitude. I think he was a little wiser than the rest of us *[laughs]*, and seemed to know a little more what it was all about. He tried to guide me in that, too — I think he was tickled by how innocent I was. Here I was, playing this wild woman, and it was all pure acting.

Of course, a lot of women believed that I was really like the roles I played. It was so funny — they would practically rush with their husbands to the other side of the room when they saw me! Really, they'd just grab 'em and run! I thought to myself, "I didn't mean to be *that* convincing!" I didn't know it was going to make a social outcast out of me! And to this day I still have a little trouble with that — women see me as the husband-snatcher. Oddly enough, I've never knowingly dated a married man.

Knowingly.

[Laughs.] Twice I got fooled, but I claim the Fifth on that!

Do you remember working with the giant prop hand in 50 Foot Woman?

I was on the set just one day when they were using that. I don't know what it was made of — in the movie it looks like papier mache or something. And I don't know how they got it to move or anything. To be honest, I wasn't that interested in special effects at that time; my curiosity all tended to go into, "What is this scene about?", "What am *I* about?" and all that. I was pretty introspective about the parts that I played, and I was never that curious about the technical aspects.

Do you remember if you were around when Hudson was picked up by the hand?

No, I didn't see that. Of course I was there when *I* got killed, and that scene scared me to death. When the 50 foot woman started wrecking the cafe, I ran and hid under a table. All the people were screaming, lumber was falling into the room and so on. As soon as the scene was over, one of the prop men came up to me and said, *"Don't . . . move."* I looked around slowly, and there was a board with a nail through it, right at my ear! So from then on, when I had to do scenes like that, I'd go to the director and ask, "Are you *sure* everything's going to be all right?" *[Laughs.]*

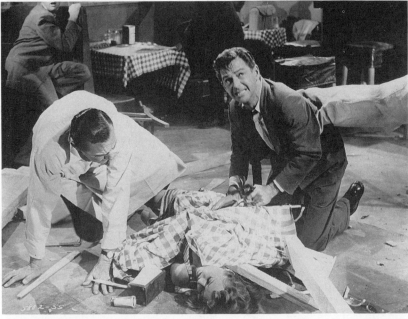

Scenes from *Attack of the 50 Foot Woman. Top:* William Hudson, Vickers and Frank Chase watch as the giant prop hand is swung through the door by offscreen stage hands. *Bottom:* Hudson is in the grip of the hand as Mike Ross checks over victim Vickers.

You can't believe what's happening in 50 Foot Woman *for a second, but the acting is really convincing while the story is not.*

People seem to get such a kick out of that, young people particularly. I've seen them watch the show at the Nuart Theater here in Los Angeles, and they respond to it. It's such a contradiction in a way: They watch this nutty movie and laugh at the special effects and so on, and yet they like the actors—Allison, Bill Hudson and myself. They come up to me afterwards and say, "I think you're a great actress," or, "I love your work." That's the response I'm getting, and I think they're really sincere when they say they like the actors. Maybe that's why *50 Foot Woman* has survived—maybe that's why the inadequacies of the special effects didn't really hang the picture up that much. Because the meat of the picture—the acting scenes—seemed to work.

Where was 50 Foot Woman *shot?*

We shot a lot of it over at a studio off of Cahuenga Boulevard. The bar scenes and my bedroom scenes were done there in that one building—it was almost like a TV setup. I'm sure right now it's probably a graphics studio. They did the location stuff at an old mansion in the Hollywood Hills. I was only up there for the driving-in and -out scene.

Was 50 Foot Woman *filmed quickly?*

Oh, yes—in eight days. A full, jam-packed eight days! But I kind of liked that—getting on with it, finishing and going on to the next thing. I think that's why the film had the momentum it did: We were just moving constantly and there weren't all those long waits you usually get. When I went to work on *Hud* [1963] at Paramount, I was just flabbergasted by all the waiting and waiting and *waiting* between setups. So that's why I liked *50 Foot Woman:* We shot fast and it was very intense, and that raised our energy level.

What do you recall about the director, Nathan Juran?

Very little, which I think means he's a terrific director. Everything was falling into place, and he let things happen. If there was help needed, he gave it, but he let work in progress be just that—he let it be. I think that was wisely done, and it turned out pretty well. Also, I thought his lighting was very good; it gave the picture some tone and style. I didn't know this at the time, but he had won an Academy Award for art direction for *How Green Was My Valley* [1941].

The producer, Jacques Marquette, told me that Juran was a producer's nightmare, that he was trying to make too much out of the picture.

As an actress I always want to make the most out of each part, so if he was doing that, too, I applaud him! I always want a picture to be the best that it can be; I don't ever think in terms of whether it's a low-budget film or a big-budget film. Whether it's TV or film, or whatever it is, I think if you're going

Vickers struts her stuff.

to work on that celluloid, you better do the best you can, because you never know who's going to see it or how long it'll last. I never dreamt that *Attack of the 50 Foot Woman* would come back the way it has.

Did you see 50 Foot Woman *when it was first released?*

No, I didn't, because I went to New York to do a Broadway play with Melvyn Douglas called *The Gang's All Here*. Oddly enough, I did see *Attack of the Giant Leeches* in New York — it was playing on 42nd Street. And, can you imagine, I actually got Melvyn Douglas and three or four other people from the cast to go over there with me, at midnight, to watch that movie! I told them, "I've got a movie playing over on 42nd Street," and they went, "Oh, my God!" But they came along: Melvyn Douglas, E.G. Marshall, Arthur Hill, Victor Kilian, maybe more. And they had a great time — they thought *Giant Leeches* was a lot of fun.

Some of those fellows used to be shocked that I would dare to do some of the things I did. I went up to the owner of that 42nd Street theater and told him, "You know, there *are* better pictures of me you could be displaying out there in front." But I was very young, and I would go up to anybody and say whatever I wanted. I'm trying to get back into that state of mind *[laughs]* — it's such a wonderful way to be!

Who hired you for Giant Leeches?

Again, I think that was a call to the agency — probably somebody who had seen my other work or heard about me. It might have been the director, Bernie Kowalski; I think he had seen me in something, and knew that he wanted me to play the part. I didn't have to go on an interview for it, I was just cast. That's my favorite way, because I'm not very good on interviews at all — in fact, I'm very bad! Bernie was just one of the best people I ever worked with; we really had a rapport, and got along very well. *Everybody* in that film did. It was one of the most cooperative groups of people I've ever seen.

What about the producer, Gene Corman?

Poor Gene almost died when we were doing the scenes over at the Pasadena Arboretum. We were there late one night, in the water, and he got violently ill — he caught pneumonia. Gene was such a nice person. I thought he was so helpful, so supportive, so *caring* about the actors. You *feel* that. I remember being on TV shows where "the New York people" would come on the set, and everybody would start shaking in their boots. It was time to shape up, shoulders back, chin up, like we were in the army. And I thought, "What are we, a bunch of trained animals or something?" We *are* human beings, and when a producer treats you like a human being they get a lot more out of you. I liked Gene Corman very much.

Interiors on Giant Leeches *were shot at the old Chaplin Studios.*

Right, over on Highland and Sunset. We did a lot of interiors there, including the scenes in the cave—which caved in! The tank that the water was in collapsed, the water went crashing across the sound stage and I remember seeing a camera whirling around really fast—luckily the cameraman jumped off in time. The water just carried everything to the back of the sound stage. Fortunately, one of the electricians pulled the main plug, which was smart because people could have very easily been electrocuted. I was up on a ledge in the cave set so I wasn't swept away, but it was really scary. The underwater shots of the dead bodies floating up toward the surface were filmed in somebody's swimming pool—it would have been pretty hard to get those shots out in the muddy waters of the Arboretum. Of course when my body surfaced and the guys pulled me up into the rowboat, we were shooting at the Arboretum. I remember that everybody was watching over me then, because I couldn't swim and I was afraid of the water.

Were your swamp scenes shot at night, or was that day-for-night?

A lot of it was shot at night, unintentionally. We started out shooting day-for-night but we went over, and we literally ended up shooting a couple of scenes by the light of flashlights and headlights from a car. Gene kept saying, "We gotta finish these scenes today, we gotta move!" So we kept going into the night, with whatever light we could find.

What were your first impressions of the leech costumes?

[Laughs.] Well, I guess the same as everybody else's: They looked like guys in plastic bags! Of course I'd seen the divers who played the leeches in their black scuba suits, so I knew who they were and I wasn't afraid of them—but I must admit that, in the cave scenes, when they crawled up to us and began to suck our blood, that I really was affected by that. A lot of people have told me that they saw *Giant Leeches* when they were ten or twelve years old, and that they were really scared by those cave scenes. And I can understand that—*The Blob,* that's my nightmare! But, again, when I first saw the leech actors on the set, I just thought they were not very well made. And those guys did have a little trouble in the water—they had to knock themselves out trying to make it look believable.

I understand that there was an effort made later to put together some better costumes, better special effects and so on, but for some reason the production end decided not to do it. They were actually offered the money to do better by those special effects scenes, because the show otherwise had turned out so well, but that never came to pass.

Were those swamp scenes any fun at all, or was it just hard, icky work?

It *was* hard work. That Arboretum does have a very swampy, jungle-like atmosphere—you felt like this was the real thing. So, yes, there were some uncomfortable moments, especially when Bruno Ve Sota forced us to wade

Spattered with swamp mud, Vickers strikes a glamorous pose behind the scenes on *Attack of the Giant Leeches*.

backwards into the swamp. I know I look scared in that scene, and I probably really was *[laughs]*! But I have to give Gene Corman credit again: He was waiting with the crew there on the sidelines, with army blankets and brandy, to keep us warm and to try and keep us healthy.

Bernard Kowalski told me he could tell you were unhappy about going into the swamp, but that you were a trouper.
    [Laughs.] Bless his heart, that's very sweet of him. As I mentioned before, I know that I can overcome almost anything. There are times when you want to be sure that everybody's protecting you, and I think it's good to be up-front

about things that you're a little frightened of. But in general I'll do whatever the part requires.

You were especially good in the scene where you explain why you're married to Bruno Ve Sota.

They *had* to explain that—I'm sure everybody was wondering why my character was married to this big fat guy. And then when you hear the reason it's very believable—things like that do happen, where somebody treats you with kindness and you cannot see them as being an ugly or unattractive person. I liked that scene a lot. I was recently on a local TV show where they showed a filmclip from *Giant Leeches,* and an artist friend of mine saw it and thought it was a Kazan movie *[laughs]—Baby Doll* or some real important film! And he said, "Gee, I didn't know you worked in those Tennessee Williams movies!" Some of the scenes that we did came across as being real thoroughbred scenes.

Did you like working with Ve Sota?

Oh, yes—we got along very well, and he was a fine actor. I loved working with him, and we respected each other a lot. I was just heartbroken when he passed away; [actor] Barry Brown told me he had died, and I attended his funeral. I was really sad, because I felt that he was one of the very good character actors of this town and should have had more credit. All of our scenes in *Giant Leeches* had a lot of heart and a lot of meat to them.

Your other co-star, Michael Emmet, really seems to have dropped from sight.

I don't know what's become of him, either. As you know, it takes a lot of determination to stick with the business. A lot of people get into it and do a few jobs, but if it doesn't take off they go into something else. I'm a diehard career person; I never really wanted to do anything else once I got started. But Michael was great—he was another Bill Hudson in that he was tickled by the whole thing. He thought it was amusing, and I think this comes through a little bit in his performance. I was playing it very seriously, but he had a little more sophistication and, like Bill Hudson, I think he knew a little better than some of the rest of us.

Early on you got typecast as schemy seductresses. What other kinds of parts did you want to play?

Of course I would have loved to do musicals and comedies—I think it would have been helpful to lighten up my image. I was up for quite a few things that I didn't get, TV series especially: I was up for *Gidget,* which Sally Field got, and I was up for a part in the movie *This Earth Is Mine* [1959] with Rock Hudson. That would have been pivotal; that would have represented a big step toward getting up to the next level. A girl named Cindy Robbins got the part—she was a friend of Rock Hudson's, and I think he felt more comfortable doing a love scene with her. Even though the producer and the director really wanted me, he just felt ill at ease since he had to do scenes that were romantic, and he wanted to be with somebody he knew. That was something I really was sorry to miss. Then Edward Dmytryk was very interested in me for a part in *The Carpetbaggers* [1964], and Martha Hyer ended up with *that* — there were quite a few. So, yes, I did want to play other kinds of parts and to go on into bigger pictures, but these things just eluded me — they slipped right through my fingers. Sometimes it was hard to accept, but I kept going.

In the early '60s you co-starred in an interesting-sounding play called Grand Guignol.

I was the leading lady opposite two real fine actors, Tom Troupe and Charles Macaulay. There were two one-act plays, and I played the lead in both of them. In the first one I was this Southern woman who was real trashy and down-dirty and all that, who henpecked her husband [Troupe], drove him crazy 'til he killed her with a drill in her neck. Then he cut her up — you see all this, through a scrim. Oh, it was grotesque, it was all the way *[laughs]*! Then in the end you see my head in this potbelly stove — actually it was the Shelley Winters head from *The Night of the Hunter* [1955]. It was a great head, and it looked enough like me that we could get away with it. The second one was a Hollywood story, very much a '20s or '30s period piece, where I played a Louella Parsons type. I found this old guy, this Phantom of the Opera type [Macaulay] — he's playing Bach on the organ when I come in to interview him — and it ended up with him trying to get a gorilla to kill me. They were fun, and I'm so sorry that we weren't able to keep it going. It did run several months, but we were thinking in terms of establishing a real institution, like it is in Paris: getting a Grand Guignol theater to survive in Hollywood. That was a good experience, it worked, but it didn't run.

You had a small part in the 1971 horror film What's the Matter with Helen?

The director, Curtis Harrington, knew me and knew my work, and wanted me to do that part. I did go on an interview for it, with Curtis and George Edwards, the producer, and the major part of that interview was, would I actually dye my hair henna red for the part? I told them I would, but I stipulated in my contract that they had to restore my hair afterwards to its blond color. They were so meticulous about getting everything right in that picture: They wanted to marcel and comb our hair into this certain '30s hairdo, they didn't want us to wear wigs, and in my case they definitely wanted the red hair. But I had fun being a redhead for a while — people were so amazed, I looked so different.

Everything went very well on *What's the Matter with Helen?* Debbie Reynolds was nice, it was a wonderful experience, and I enjoyed doing it.

Why aren't you mentioning Shelley Winters?

I never got to know her. Curtis had some problems with her — he had to

She was the July 1959 Playmate of the Month; today, Yvette Vickers is working to make a comeback as a singer.

go and bring her to the set a few times, she didn't want to come. She thought she was photographing too heavy, and—

No kidding!

[Laughs.] She was playing it as a character, with a character's attitude, but she didn't want to *look* like that! I found that hard to understand, because she is such a fine actress and she had done character parts before. At the wrap party I started to talk to her and she turned away from me, so I didn't pursue it. I never intrude on somebody if they don't look like they're open.

What about the TV movie The Dead Don't Die?

I did that as a favor to Curtis Harrington. I played a marathon dancer, and my scene was with Ray Milland, asking for work. He was very gracious—I love working with old troupers.

Recently you've been on the comeback trail again.

I've had about four comebacks *[laughs]*, and this one, I hope, will be the one that works. All those times in the '70s that I tried to get started again, I'd do a couple of jobs, but it just did not take off. I couldn't figure out what was happening, and I would get very depressed and unhappy about that. So right now I'm working on a cabaret act, since I do sing and dance. It'll be a kind of a reprise of the great Hollywood blondes—imitating and singing in the style of Mae West, Jean Harlow, Marilyn Monroe and so on. And of course I'm also looking to work more in movies and TV — that's a very good possibility as well. Lately there's been a lot of attention and a lot of interest in the appearances I have been making, so the time is right and it's up to me now to do my best and to find my place in the "new" Hollywood.

You just did a new horror film called Evil Spirits.

My part is quite nice for a "re-entry." I play Karen Black's snoopy neighbor and I stumble onto the fact that she is disposing of her tenants. The story is based on the Social Security check murders in Sacramento. I have a juicy scene with Karen during a party plus some fun scream stuff in her basement. We had a good time, lunched together and enjoyed working together.

Are you pleased with your cult actress status today?

Yes. I think it's very flattering, *remarkable* to be remembered for pictures that I did that long ago. I like people to know that I've been a little more active — a lot of people think that *50 Foot Woman* and *Giant Leeches* are all I ever did. I have done a lot of theater work, especially since then. But I'm just amazed and delighted and totally happy about the reaction I'm getting, and the fact that young people are so complimentary and so supportive and encouraging about my idea of working again now. It's very surprising and wonderful.

YVETTE VICKERS FILMOGRAPHY

As Yvette Vedder:

Sunset Boulevard (Paramount, 1950)

As Yvette Vickers:

Short Cut to Hell (Paramount, 1957)
Reform School Girl (AIP, 1957)
The Sad Sack (Paramount, 1957)
Juvenile Jungle (Republic, 1957)
Attack of the 50 Foot Woman (Allied Artists, 1958)
The Saga of Hemp Brown (Universal, 1958)
I, Mobster (20th Century-Fox, 1958)
Attack of the Giant Leeches (AIP, 1959)
Pressure Point (United Artists, 1962)
Hud (Paramount, 1963)
Beach Party (AIP, 1963)
What's the Matter with Helen? (United Artists, 1971)
Vigilante Force (United Artists, 1976)
It Came from Hollywood (Paramount, 1982) Clips from *Attack of the 50 Foot Woman*
Evil Spirits (Grand Am, 1990)

Many times I'd say to Jerry Warren,
"For God's sake, Jerry, let's do something
good for a change," and he'd say, "Why? People
aren't interested in anything good, they don't know
and they don't care. Just give them garbage!"
That was his philosophy.

——— *Katherine Victor* ———

WHAT BAD THINGS can be said about the films of Jerry Warren that haven't been said already? Everything that could be wrong with a motion picture afflicted the films of Hollywood's most notoriously underskilled auteur. His casts did the best they could under the circumstances, but they were defeated every time by the dirt-poor production values, lousy scripts and Warren's own "who-cares?" attitude. Warren (who died in 1988) more than lived up to his self-stated credo, "I have never seriously wanted to be a director, or to do great things"; yet even today, more than a quarter-century after Warren was in the heyday of his ill-contrived career, the films continue to turn up on TV, on pre-recorded tape and in the conversation of horror film buffs.

Among the cast members wading through the dullness of these films, Warren's most frequent star, Katherine (now Kathrin) Victor, gave color to stereotypic roles and turned in performances better than the production in flicks like *Teenage Zombies*, *The Wild World of Batwoman*, *Frankenstein Island* and the non-Warren *The Cape Canaveral Monsters*. Born Katena Ktenavea in the Hell's Kitchen district of Manhattan, the future TV and movie actress grew up in L.A. and began her acting career on the stage and on radio in the late '40s. She made her film debut in the dashed-off sci-fi adventure *Mesa of Lost Women* in 1952, and in 1957 she starred as the imperious Dr. Myra in Jerry Warren's *Teenage Zombies*, which led to a series of roles in Warren's impoverished productions. Always busy outside of acting (in modeling, real estate or, more recently, in various jobs in the animated cartoon business), she feels that the stigma of being a Warren regular has stymied her mainstream acting career, but is working to turn things around in her acting future.

Do you remember how you got your small part in Mesa of Lost Women?

In those days actors could stop by and visit producers and ask if there would be any work coming up. I just dropped in at Sam Goldwyn Studios, where Howco Productions had their office, and I met Ron Ormond, who was producing *Mesa of Lost Women*. He told me that it was coming up and I'd be right for it. Actually *Mesa of Lost Women* was a patch job: It had already been done, but it was unsalable because it was a mixed-up story. So Ron deleted a certain amount and put in new stuff to make it more cohesive — that opening part with me, that was new. My scene, which was set in the desert, had me driving up to a certain point in my car and then stepping out; we had to do it several times because I wasn't stopping right on the mark. A weed, that was my mark *[laughs]*! I had to stop on the mark and climb out of the car, and I didn't have time to put on the brakes or anything! I pulled the hand brake fast but it didn't hold, the car started to slip back and the door caught me. Ron said, "Obviously this is the first time that you've driven a car in a movie." (It was one of those great big old Cadillacs.) "You just have to pull the hand brake, fast, and jump out." The next time I did it I pulled it real hard and junped out, and it worked. Something always happens on a picture, so that was par for the course!

Previous page: **Notorious even among fans of *bad* movies, the awful *Wild World of Batwoman* continues to embarrass its star, Katherine Victor, to the present day.**

I also remember driving home from that location. We had done that scene in the Mojave Desert, at Red Rock Canyon, and it was hot, hot, hot. I was wearing velvet pants and a wool top, and it was very hot—I got sun-blindness from the reflectors and all of that sort of thing! There were other girls in the film—spider-women who wore skimpy undergarments *[laughs]*—and it was such a terribly hot day that on the ride home I wore one of the girls' costumes. Ron Ormond said, "If I had known you had such great legs, I would have put you on as one of the girls!"

How exactly did you come in contact with Jerry Warren for the first time?

I had just come back from New York, where I had been working in various phases of show biz—acting, modeling, singing in night clubs and dancing, keeping busy and making a living. Anyway, I came back and an old friend said, "I have some friends whose home is being used to shoot a picture, and the producer is looking for a leading lady." Now, when you hear that a fellow is ready to shoot a picture and doesn't have a leading lady, it strikes you as a little far-fetched *[laughs]*, but that's the way it was! So I went up to the house, which was on a five-acre estate in Mandeville Canyon, and that's where I met Jerry Warren. I told him my credits and showed him some pictures and he said, "You've got the part." That's how I ended up in *Teenage Zombies*. And then after that, over the years, he used me in a lot of different pictures.

The people I've talked to tell me that Warren disliked actors.

Jerry misused actors, he yelled at them . . . well, a lot of directors do. Jerry was one of those, and it was his style to yell at the actors. But he would not be very clear, and he'd yell repeatedly in order to make the actor nervous. I've worked with a lot of real professionals and big-name directors that do that, but I guess when they get to be big names and so forth it's their prerogative! George Cukor did that, and Paul Wendkos, that's just their style. But you'd think that since Jerry was using people on a low budget, that maybe he should be a little bit more compassionate!

When you say yell, do you mean yell instructions or belittle them?

He belittled them—belittled them to the point that it would make them very, very nervous. Now, he didn't do it to me, he told me that he respected me and that I was different from other actors because I earned a living in another field and I didn't "use" people. The average actor, in order to pursue his career, needs sponsorship and plugs away at it; I always kept a job going and didn't have to mooch off of people. Also, if an actor rubbed him the wrong way, Jerry wrote them out of the script or really reduced their part. In *The Wild World of Batwoman* the pretty brunette that was kidnaped at the beginning of the picture was supposed to be the lead girl, but for some reason Jerry thought she was getting too big for her britches and he gave all her lines to the

Victor, as the calculating Dr. Myra, in Jerry Warren's infamous rock-bottom *Teenage Zombies.*

girl in the leopard tights. Then on *Frankenstein Island,* Steve Brodie was drinking an awful lot and so Jerry had him killed off! Jerry used me because I was very reliable—he could give me hunks of dialogue and I could do my lines in one take. I wish now that things hadn't worked out that way, but they did!

Anyway, that's how I met him—it was a strange way to get a part, but I thought, "Gee, I've just come back from New York and isn't this great?" I was sure there were going to be better things coming because of the way this had worked out. And I wouldn't have to go through the casting couch bit and all that sort of thing!

Warren wasn't a casting couch producer?
He was strictly business and he never approached me in that way. He liked me and we were good friends, but he never made a pass.

How old was Warren at the time? He wanted me to believe he was in his early twenties then, but that's not possible.

We did *Teenage Zombies* in 1957 and he had to be in his early to mid-thirties, something like that. In talking to you he took off at least ten years.

Did the cast of Teenage Zombies *get together to rehearse?*
No, we met for the first time on the set. The first time we ever did the scenes it was right in front of the cameras, which were rolling! A lot of the actors that he used had been doing little theater and so forth, and they were good actors—Jerry always got competent actors. If he had had bad actors that couldn't remember their lines, he would have been in a world of trouble *[laughs]*! Most of the time it was one take, but occasionally he took a few. Jerry shot master shots, he would shoot a scene continuously for ten minutes and he didn't shoot closeups. In *Teenage Zombies* I think I had one closeup and the rest was master shots. That saved him money and saved time in editing.

Warren doesn't even allow you an entrance in the film. The first we really see of your femme fatale character is when you open that old screen door like a housewife.
Here I was, supposed to be the villainess, and he didn't introduce me at all; it was just terrible, me opening that screen door! In Jerry's last picture, *Frankenstein Island,* he tried to give me an entrance but he really wasn't very creative: First he showed the wine bottle I was holding, then he tilted up to the cleavage, and then up to my face. So he tried on that *[laughs]*! But, you're right, in *Teenage Zombies* he didn't dramatize it at all and I had a terrible entrance, really awful. Now, the funny part is that that house had a gorgeous front entrance—which they used for the sheriff's office—and they gave me the back screen door *[laughs]*!

Was making Teenage Zombies *a hectic experience?*
Yes, it was—very. There was a lot of dialogue and Jerry just wanted it done. There was no finesse, no chance to develop any characterization. As I said, I had one closeup in the whole thing and the rest was mostly master shots. Also, the sound was very, very bad; my voice came across very tinny because the recording equipment was bad. We didn't do scenes with an eye toward perfecting them, we just did 'em to get through 'em and to get it done fast. So, yes, it was frustrating; all of his shows were frustrating, because his manner was just yelling and intimidating everybody, from the crew to the actors.

What can you tell me about some of your co-stars?
Don Sullivan, who played the hero, was a very nice person, good to work with. He was a very handsome boy and I thought he had charisma and that he would do well. He made two or three movies afterwards but then I guess he just gave it up. I saw him on a talk show a couple of years ago and he was pushing his own Don Sullivan beauty products. His hair had a touch of silver

and he was a very handsome, distinguished-looking man. Don Morrison, who owned the house where we shot, played one of the enemy agents, the one with the glasses; he's passed away since. And Ivan the zombie was played by Chuck Niles; he's a disc jockey at KKGO here and he's been very prominent for years, a household name in L.A.

Warren's wife, Bri Murphy, was also in the cast.

She is now a very well-known cinematographer — in fact, the only woman cinematographer in Hollywood. Jerry was married to her and she was assisting him with this picture, and then they divorced right after *Teenage Zombies* and she went on to bigger and better things. She was a great gal. After Jerry, she married this fellow Ralph Brooke, who was also a filmmaker of sorts — he's since passed away. I remember I ran into them at one point and we got to talking, and Ralph asked if I would do one of his pictures. And Bri piped up, "No, Katherine doesn't do *that* type!" — it must have been a porno or something! Bri and (I think) Ralph did do a picture called *House of the Black Death* and it wasn't cohesive. So Jerry took it over and I think he made it *less* cohesive *[laughs]*! He put me into some added scenes.

How much were you paid on Teenage Zombies?

At that time I was paid a flat $300, which was a little bit over the Screen Actors Guild minimum at the time. S.A.G. at the time called for $285 a week. That's why I didn't hesitate to work for him, because it was in line with what S.A.G. called for. If he had offered to pay me like $200, I wouldn't have done it! (Jerry's were non-union pictures.) On February 1, 1958, the pay went up to $300 a week, and it was a two-year contract. And every two years it went up in $15 increments until 1970, and then it started going up $100 each time.

What sort of roles did you hope Teenage Zombies *would lead to?*

I was always the villainess; I had to be the Continental siren or "vamp." I looked very haughty and very aloof, that's the bearing I always had, and I was usually cast that way; my first TV show was a femme fatale role in *Lights, Camera, Action* way back in 1950. So I was hoping that *Teenage Zombies* would lead to some "other woman"–type roles.

Were you happy with your performance in Teenage Zombies?

No, I wasn't, I wasn't at all. As I said, it was just a matter of getting through the words, not giving it any nuance or characterization. I think the reason that *Teenage Zombies* has become a cult picture (if that's what you want to call it!) is because it did have an atmosphere that the kids liked. I saw *Teenage Zombies* for the first time at a grand opening in Long Beach; I went there, and I was invited to sign autographs. I didn't realize that I should look like I did in the picture; I dressed up in a white evening gown and put my hair up, wore a tiara and a lot of rhinestones — and nobody recognized me *[laughs]*!

Even though "Jacques Lecotier" gets screen credit for writing some of these Warren movies, weren't they written by Warren himself?

As far as I know, Jerry wrote the movies; he used two or three pseudonyms. He also did the music, and used pseudonyms there, too; on *Teenage Zombies* he used the name Erich Bromberg. Jerry was talented on the piano.

Bri Murphy divorced Jerry after *Teenage Zombies;* he found a girlfriend, Gloria, and she then became his wife. I liked her. She was a very naive girl but very sweet and nice; she thought Jerry was the greatest *[laughs]*, but that is the way it should be. Gloria was very, very good to Jerry, because he needed certain diets. Jerry had a problem with his health, I don't know exactly what it was, but during the time of the lawsuit on *The Wild World of Batwoman* he went to the Philippines, to one of those witch doctors who waves chickens over you *[laughs]*! Jerry was into spiritualism or metaphysics or something, and at one point, right after *Teenage Zombies,* he wrote a script, set in the Himalayas, in which he wanted me to play a high priestess. I read the script and I thought it was great. The whole cast got together and we had costumes made and were going to shoot up in Stockton. Then all of a sudden Jerry called it off, because he said he was really not ready to go into this sort of thing.

Do you remember how you got hired to do The Cape Canaveral Monsters?

Yes, I do. *Cape Canaveral Monsters* is in my opinion the best picture in my whole lot—but I looked the worst. Billy Greene, who was one of the actors on *Cape Canaveral Monsters,* told me that [director] Phil Tucker was going to be doing a picture and that he was looking for a leading woman. I went over to see him and he liked me. He told me that I looked beautiful, but of course when I got into making the picture I had to wear all that scar makeup and I was anything *but* beautiful!

On the first day of shooting *Teenage Zombies,* my dear Siamese cat died—I'd had that cat for years—and I was just crying and crying. That was the first day of *Teenage Zombies.* Then, the first day of shooting *Cape Canaveral Monsters,* I got word that my first cousin passed away, of cancer. And I began thinking, jeepers, every time I start something, a loved one dies, and I just maybe better not make any more pictures *[laughs]*!

Did you like working with Tucker?

It was a pleasure working with Phil and working on that picture. He had control of everything and he kept a firm hand, but he knew what he wanted. A group of dentists or doctors were putting up the money for *Cape Canaveral Monsters;* it was going to be in color and there was a nice budget. But then, just the day before shooting started, they cut the budget in half. The first thing that went, of course, was the color, and then other things had to go as well. But I think that in spite of everything Phil was very creative; it's just too bad that he didn't get the opportunity to do more, because he was good. He did the

Director of photography W. Merle Connell prepares to give Victor a closeup in *The Cape Canaveral Monsters.*

best he could under the circumstances. We shot the interiors at a small independent studio on Western Avenue in Hollywood. The cave scenes were shot in Bronson Canyon and the beach scenes at Malibu. I remember it was December and it was freezing!

The "look" they gave you in Cape Canaveral *certainly wasn't very flattering.*
    No, it wasn't. I wanted to wear something that might be flattering, maybe something tight-fitting, but, no, they told me I had to wear the costume that I did, which were like men's coveralls. If I had had my wits about me, I would have looked better—at least had eye makeup or something—but I just went along with what they wanted. They had a fellow, a monster makeup man, do the scar makeup on me a few times, and then when we ran out of money I did it myself.

Any other Cape Canaveral *recollections?*
    No, other than to mention again that Phil was very nice and so was

When the film's paltry budget could no longer support a makeup man, Katherine Victor applied her own scar makeup for *The Cape Canaveral Monsters.*

Richard Greer, who produced and did the editing. It was a very pleasant group, and it was sad that we ran out of money and had to cut back and make all those compromises. S.A.G. was up to $300 a week and Phil paid me $420 or $450, so I did a little bit better than I did with *Teenage Zombies.* Phil was broke about that time, and he came with me to the bank after he gave me the check and borrowed back half of it *[laughs]*! The poor guy, he was really flat broke.

You next turned up in added footage in Warren's Americanized versions of the south-of-the-border films Curse of the Stone Hand *and* Creature of the Walking Dead.

Those were just patch jobs. I remember *Curse of the Stone Hand* because we did that with John Carradine. We shot that in a beautiful home in the Los Feliz area; these people were friends of Jerry's. I remember talking to John Carradine and I asked him, "Why do you *do* pictures like this?" and he said, "The color of the money's the same!" For *Creature of the Walking Dead* we shot our scenes in a little studio on Fairfax Avenue. I really don't remember too much about that, again it was a hectic thing and just a matter of getting the words out. I worked with Bruno Ve Sota on that one, and Bruno was a great fellow, easy to work with. He was a very talented person and a natural actor.

What can you remember about The Wild World of Batwoman?

This was when the TV show *Batman* with Adam West was very, very popular. Jerry called me up and said that he wanted to do a Batwoman movie and asked me if I would play Batwoman. He said, "Look, we've got a great budget and we're gonna do it in color. You're gonna have your own Batmobile, you're gonna have your own Batboat, it's just gonna be great." And I thought, "Boy, this is terrific!" Then, as we got into it, little by little it all dropped away; I don't know whether his backers let him down, but I think he eventually put up all the money for it himself. Maybe when he was telling me about the color and the Bat-props and everything, that was just a story to get me to do it; I had told him I wouldn't be doing anything else for him unless we did a Class A movie.

Of course, if it was going to be first-rate, he would have hired a costume designer. But he asked me to bring what I thought would be good as a costume *[laughs]*! So I brought some things and also two or three different capes — he picked the one that he thought would be right, but on the rest of the costume he just went by my suggestions. I did everything. I wore a wig which I attached to the top of my head, and then I had red feathers that I just pinned into my hair. I wanted something that would look a little bit different, and *[laughs]* I guess I got it! I even designed the bat insignia on my chest; I made a cardboard form in the shape of a bat, I outlined it on my chest with a drawing pencil and then filled it in with black eyeliner.

Didn't Warren know he was heading for trouble, infringing on Batman's *copyrights like that?*

We kept telling him that DC Comics would bring a lawsuit because he was infringing, but Jerry kept saying everything would be okay and not to worry about it. I guess he thought he could finagle it — somehow or other, he thought, he could bluff it through. He was going to four-wall the picture in Philadelphia, to open in 30 theaters there, and I had a nice new velvet cape tailor-made for me because I was ready to go and make a weekend appearance in Philadelphia. But just a couple of days before this was all supposed to happen, Jerry called me and said everything was off — it was in litigation. I don't know who it was, whether it was 20th Century–Fox or [*Batman* executive producer] William Dozier or *who,* but they put a stop on the prints at the lab and that was it, period. But it had gotten that far—I had even seen coming attractions on TV, that it was going to open!

Jerry had to go back to New York, and he told me he went up in this skyscraper with all these huge offices and he said it was like getting the third degree. He said that was the worst experience he'd ever had in his life, because he went in this giant conference room and all of these V.I.P.s were hammering at him. At one point they even asked him if *I* was behind it—they asked, "This Katherine Victor, was *she* behind this? Did *she* do this for the publicity?" And Jerry said that, no, I had nothing to do with it. Which was very nice of him *[laughs]*, especially since I *didn't* have anything to do with it! They offered him a settlement of $330,000 to just stop the picture, because they didn't want any further publicity, and he thought, "Well, if they're offering me $330,000, maybe I can get a million!" So he turned it down and he asked for a million. It was a bad mistake. I don't know what he did settle for, but I know that he said that he should have taken the $330,000, because when the settlement finally came out, it was much less than that. I'm not sure what the final amount was, but it was something like $50,000, a small amount in comparison.

When did you see the film for the first time?

Jerry had a showing in some screening room in Hollywood, and

Victor designed her own costume for *The Wild World of Batwoman.*

there was a group of us that saw it. After the lights came up I remember there was this one fellow, I don't know if he was a backer or a distributor or what, but he was in a daze, absolutely dumbfounded—he was probably expecting something like the TV show. And Jerry said to him, "After all, this *is* a low-budget picture!" *[Laughs.]*

The film's a real stinker, just about the worst thing Warren ever did.
　　The production values were absolutely nil, really embarrassing. And I was horrified by the indoor sets. Of course Jerry is famous for that, for sets that are absolutely awful. And he doesn't know how to photograph them! You can photograph anything and make it look terrific if you know how, but when he moves the camera back and takes a master shot, it's terrible. He just didn't have the creativity to do anything like that.

I don't think it was a case of not being creative, it was a case of just not caring.
　　You're right, absolutely right. Many times I'd say to him, "For God's sake, Jerry, let's do something *good* for a change," and he'd say, "Why? People aren't interested in anything good, they don't know and they don't care. Just give them garbage!" That was his philosophy.

Bruno Ve Sota called him the only person in Hollywood that ever set out to make a bad picture.
　　That's it exactly. But unfortunately he would con the actors into thinking that he had changed and that each new film would be different. I kept coming back thinking that, but it never worked out that way. As a matter of fact, it was because of *The Wild World of Batwoman* that I took the two *es* out of my first name, and ever since that time I've been going around as K-a-t-h-r-i-n Victor. I wanted to have a new start, I didn't want to be associated with that film in any way! But now it's out on video cassette and it's back to haunt me, so it just goes to prove that you can't hide anything in your life. *The Wild World of Batwoman* has always been the skeleton in my closet.

You had other skeletons in your closet early in your life that also restricted your career, didn't you?
　　I was first-generation here and my mother was mentally ill and my father was a compulsive gambler. He left us and Mother was trying to raise us. I was the one in the family who had the talent—I was an artist, a musician and an actress, and acting was dearest to my heart. But my mother had paranoia and she had a possessiveness, and she wouldn't allow me to go out with people—she kept us tied down. My father started me on the violin when I was young and I got to be very good; I was asked to join a children's orchestra but my mother wouldn't allow me to do it. So I had to go out through a bathroom window and my sister had to cover for me! I had to do things like that because of my mother, and it was very difficult growing up. Also, there was no money,

Although she nearly torpedoed her own film career by becoming too closely associated with rock-bottom horror pictures, Katherine (now Kathrin) Victor is working on an acting comeback.

because my father had gambled everything away *[laughs]*! Finally we had to commit my mother, and not until we did that was I able to do something with my talent. But sometimes I wonder what would have happened if I'd had a decent family life and the support of my parents—I had to fight the family besides fighting the world. I always had continuous obstacles.

You seemed to drop out of films not long after Batwoman.

What happened was that I got married and my husband was very possessive—that worked out badly. I had never wanted to get married, but he chased me for about a year and a half, telling me that we'd be traveling all the time, and finally it began to sound pretty good. But then he said, "No more acting, because I don't want you running off with somebody else." The only thing I did do during the 13 years I was married, besides being a nursemaid to him (it turned out he was ill), a housewife and a mother to his three kids, was practice my piano. During that period I studied with Vladimir Horowitz's teacher, Sergei Tarnowsky, who was a tremendous inspiration. I put all my artistic effort into my piano.

Jerry Warren retired from pictures after that Batwoman *debacle.*
After the *Batwoman* experience he said that was it. That was a pretty harrowing experience and it really took a lot out of him. So he bought an avocado ranch down in San Diego. I'd go down about once a year and visit him, and then after I married, my husband and I would go down. We started to get after Jerry, to tell him that things had changed, and why didn't he try and do another picture? My husband was once a computer man, and he promised Jerry that he would handle all the computer stuff and special effects and it would really be authentic. Jerry began to get fired up and started to write a screenplay. Then when he actually called me to ask me to be in the picture *[Frankenstein Island]*, my husband said, "You're not going to *do* it, are you?" I said, "Yes!" and that's when things started going wrong with me and my husband. He was a great talker but when it came down to the nitty-gritty he backed out, and he was very unhappy about my being in it!

I was surprised to find that Frankenstein Island *was a semi-remake of* Teenage Zombies.
It was worse, because *Teenage Zombies* at least had a little bit of a story. *Frankenstein Island* is *Teenage Zombies* in color, but worse because Jerry tried to squeeze too much into it.

Where was Frankenstein Island *shot?*
Jerry had 20 acres down in Escondido, and he built the native village there. We shot some interiors in Jerry's house and the lab interiors at a studio on Seward Street in Hollywood. I shot about 10 days, and the four fellows who were the heroes, Robert Clarke and Robert Christopher and the two young actors [Tain Bodkin and Patrick O'Neil], shot about 20. Those fellows had it rough; they went to New Mexico and as I understand it they had a tough time there. They also did a scene where they were in a rubber raft, it was a one- or two-man raft and the four of them were crowded into it, and the thing nearly sank under them! Jerry ended up cutting all those scenes out and having the characters *talk* about what happened to them.
Actually, Jerry had a not-bad cast in that one: Cameron Mitchell, Andrew Duggan, Steve Brodie, John Carradine, Bob Clarke and Bob Christopher. Bob Christopher was the co-producer and he put up a lot of money, about

$85,000. Jerry also got a lot of young actors out of San Diego, little theater people, and they were all very competent. The dancing girls he got at a night club.

Bob Clarke never got paid for doing Frankenstein Island.

Bob *and* I did not get paid; we were the only two that didn't. Jerry kept telling us we were his best friends *[laughs]*, because both of us had worked with him several times before, but we're still waiting for our money!

He probably figured you were the two he could take advantage of.

Exactly. Which is kind of sad. Bob Christopher and Jerry's wife are still hoping to get some money out of the picture (the thing is in litigation right now) but I don't think anything'll come of that either. And Bob Clarke and I were shocked, because Jerry always did pay us in the past. I was supposed to get a thousand and Bob was supposed to get two thousand, but we didn't get anything. Bob I feel especially bad for, because as I said he went through a lot of hardships making those scenes that got cut out.

You also didn't get any sort of decent billing in the picture.

Everybody was very unhappy about that and said it wasn't fair. I confronted Jerry with that when we had the cast party at my home in Woodland Hills. I guess I had a little bit to drink and I said, "Jerry, you had me listed in the credits as a 'with'—I haven't been a 'with' for a long time." And he said, "I had too many stars." I pressed him and then he turned on me: "Who do you think you are anyway? Just because you got the star billing in *Batwoman*—." I said, "Jerry, what are you talking about? Who's ever going to see *Batwoman*?" It was crazy, but he threw *that* at me *[laughs]*! I just couldn't believe that Jerry would do that to me, but I guess some people do things like that to their friends, figuring they can get away with it. That's the only time we ever really argued.

Bob Clarke told me that when Warren found out he had lung cancer he didn't tell anyone except Robert Christopher.

And of course he told his wife, Gloria. Gloria told me that all the symptoms were there but that they didn't realize it; right in front of her eyes she saw him gradually disintegrate. Jerry used to have a terrific physique and a lot of muscle, and he would play tennis in his tennis shorts; she noticed that the muscles in his legs were disappearing and that he lost his backhand. She was with him when he died; in his last few days he couldn't even get out of bed. It was a Sunday afternoon. He could hardly talk but he told her to leave the room. She left and then she heard this awful sound, like a *whoosh,* and she went back and there he was, just slumped over in bed. It was very sad.

How happy are you with the way your career has gone?

I thought my career was off to a good start but it just went nowhere *[laughs]*! But then fans like Barry Brown, who interviewed me for the book *Scream Queens,* made me aware that people were interested and that I did have a lot of fans. That opened my eyes. I have started back in and I've done some stageplays and some dinner theater murder mysteries, but I still don't have an agent; they're looking for drop-dead-beautiful gals and gorgeous hunk guys 18-to-25. But I'm like an old firehorse and I'm still hoping that, the more exposure I have, maybe somebody will see me and there might be a part for me. I'm not going to break my heart over it *[laughs]*, I'm too old for that, but I do love acting and I would love to earn my living in acting and do something worthwhile and be remembered. Right now it's on account of the sci-fi pictures I did that I'm remembered, and I think that's nice. If I were to die tomorrow at least I've made my mark in the annals of horror and science fiction *[laughs]* — however dubious!

KATHERINE VICTOR FILMOGRAPHY

Mesa of Lost Women (Howco, 1953)
Sabrina (Paramount, 1954)
The Eddy Duchin Story (Columbia, 1956)
Teenage Zombies (Governor Films, 1960)
The Cape Canaveral Monsters (C.C.M. Productions, 1960)
Creature of the Walking Dead (Associated Distributors Pictures, 1965)
Curse of the Stone Hand (Associated Distributors Pictures, 1965)
House of the Black Death (Medallion, 1965)
The Wild World of Batwoman (She Was a Hippy Vampire) (Associated Distributors Pictures, 1966)
Justine (20th Century–Fox, 1969)
Frankenstein Island (Chriswar Productions, 1981)

Universal went into [The Land Unknown] *planning to
make it the biggest science fiction picture of its time.
But then the effects department and the makeup department
spent all their money! Universal spent so much on the monsters,
they didn't have any money left to make the picture.
They didn't know they couldn't make the biggest
show of all time without spending money!*

Virgil W. Vogel

NOW A RESPECTED and well-known TV director, Virgil W. Vogel cut his directorial teeth on science fiction films at Universal-International in the mid-1950s.
His initial assignment, *The Mole People,* pitted archaeologists against the
denizens of an underground civilization, while *The Land Unknown* found polar
explorers battling prehistoric animals in a lost world beneath the Antarctic ice.
These titles, together with the Swedish-made *Invasion of the Animal People,* have
made Virgil Vogel's a highly recognizable name among science fiction fans.

Vogel began his career at Universal in 1940, as an assistant editor. He worked
as an editor for many years, although by the mid-'50s he began to tire of the job
and pressed Universal executive Ed Muhl for a shot at directing. Because he was
known as a "special effects kind of fellow," Universal handed Vogel *The Mole People* with John Agar, and his capable handling of that film led to other assignments
at the studio. Still highly active on the Hollywood scene, Vogel fondly remembers
his early directing days of sci-fi/horror.

Were you pleased when Universal assigned you to The Mole People, *or would
you have preferred a more conventional film for openers?*

It really didn't matter to me, I just wanted to get out of the job I had and
get into directing. *The Mole People* seemed like a real challenge to me because
of all the special effects. Of course Universal never had a lot of money—it was
always a very inexpensive company, and I always prided myself on knowing all
the tricks and short cuts. For instance, for the mountain-climbing scenes I took
some footage of Sir Edmund Hillary climbing Everest, made a lot of plates and
such out of that, and *my* actors did all their climbing on the stage. And I was
real proud of the review I got out of *Variety,* which said that somebody deserved
a great kudo for the way the film was put together. We were able to put *The
Mole People* together on a 17-day schedule.

*Did you work with screenwriter Laszlo Gorog on the script, or make any script
changes?*

No, the script was given to me—Laszlo had written it under [producer]
Bill Alland's supervision. If I had known then what I know now, I would have
demanded some script changes, but at that time I thought the script was pretty
good. You've got to remember that I was a young man then, and I didn't know
too much what I was doing!

The scenes with the mole-monsters were the highlights of that film.

I can tell you a funny story about them. We went into a meeting, prior
to production, where they were cutting down the costs. They were trying to
cut the costs on the costumes for the monsters. Jack Kevan, the fellow who was
making them, detailed his expenses, and he mentioned that it was going to
cost X-number of dollars to make the rubber humps on their backs. Bill Alland

Previous page: **Virgil Vogel and the hydraulically controlled lake monster from Universal's** *The Land Unknown.* **(Photo courtesy Robert Skotak.)**

Vogel *(right)* **and director of photography Ellis Carter pose with the monster masks from** *The Mole People.* **(Photo courtesy Robert Skotak.)**

immediately said, "Well, take that money out." Kevan asked him, "You want to forget about the humps?" and Alland said, "No, no—we'll just put newspapers in there!" So instead of making rubber humps, they stuffed the backs of the monsters' shirts with newspapers.

Now here's the funny part I mentioned. There's a scene at the end of the picture where the mosnters revolt, and there's a giant fight between them and the palace guards. Even though I had never directed before, they had me directing this, the biggest scene in the picture, on my first or second day *[laughs]*—in Hollywood, that's normal procedure! Anyway, I'm up on a crane and the stuntmen start battling, and they put on a really good fight. When it was over I yelled, "Great! Cut! Print it!" That's when my asistant director Ronnie Rondell said to me, "But—look over on the stage!" There were newspapers all over the place *[laughs]*! The newspapers had fallen out of all their shirts during the fight, and we had to do the whole thing over!

What was your budget on The Mole People?
It must have been less than $200,000.

And was it a hectic 17 days of shooting?
Let's just say that I wasn't smart enough then to know how hectic it was!

What more can you tell me about producer William Alland?

Bill Alland was a brilliant young man, but to me he was an enigma. He had great ideas, and if he had had a little more push and just a touch more suavity about him, he probably could have been one of the top men in Hollywood. I liked Bill, but he thought a little bit too small. He did not know how to fight the studio hierarchy and he did not know how to take people on—he was always interested in making pictures within their budgets. Sometimes you just have to stop and say the hell with it, and fight for something better.

How did you get along with stars John Agar and Cynthia Patrick?

I liked working with John, he was a lovely man. But Cynthia Patrick, being quite inexperienced at the time, was a bit of a trial. You'll remember that in the picture the mole-monsters pull their victims down into the ground? What we did was, we had very stiff rubber across the top of an empty swimming pool—in fact, it was the same pool we later used as the lake in *The Land Unknown!* We slit the rubber and covered it with ground cork. That way, when the monsters pulled a body down through the slit, the rubber was so thick and stiff that it split just wide enough for the body—the cork couldn't all run through. There's a scene where Cynthia Patrick runs into the area where the monsters are working, and one of them grabs her and pulls her under the ground. As we were getting ready to shoot that, she came up to me and said, "I'm not going down through that hole." And I said *[sweetly]*, "Well, of course not, darling, a stuntwoman will do that. All I need you to do is run across there." She said she would do it. So I went to Al, the stuntman playing the monster, and I said, "Al, when she hits that god-damned hole you grab her legs and *pull!*" So he did it *[laughs]*—she screamed and yelled as she went down, but it was probably the best acting she did in the picture!

John Agar told me that he felt The Mole People *was just too far-out, and in fact he quit Universal right after it was made because he was fed up with sci-fi roles. Would you agree with his complaint?*

No, I wouldn't. I will admit, though, that when I saw the film at the preview I thought it was piss-poor. I was a little disappointed with my own dealing with people in those days—I thought actors could act, I didn't know that some of them take a lot of direction *[laughs]*! Now it's turned into kind of a cult picture and I'm proud of it, but 30 years ago I was ashamed of *The Mole People.* But it did do exceedingly well at the box office.

Let me tell you a story about the preview. The very first day of shooting, we had done the scene where the explorers climb down the vertical shaft, from the mountaintop to the land of the Mole People. One member of the expedition had fallen in there, and the other men climb down to see if they can help him. They find the body, roll it over and someone says, "He's dead." Universal gave me three 18-foot rocks, on rollers, and a lot of black velvet—that

Ad for *The Mole People.*

was my set. All I had to do this first day was shoot this one climb-down scene. But we worked so fast and so well that I actually finished everything I wanted by noon, so we spent the rest of the day shooting inserts — hands climbing, feet slipping, all that kind of stuff.

When the show was finished, we found that it ran five or six minutes short. So they told me, "That climb-down scene was so great, put some more of that in." And we did. Then, in the editing stage, we started cutting some stuff that was really bad — and every time we cut something out, we put some more climb-down in. Eventually we put in every bit of climb-down that I had shot — and *then* they said, "Well, now let's duplicate some of it, it's great!" So we put more and more in, and pulled some other crap out of the picture.

Now we're at the preview, and the climb-down scene is running. The suspense is terrific—you could just feel the tension in the audience, it really was good. The climbers went down deeper and deeper, into the very bowels of the Earth—it seemed like about five miles. They get down to the bottom, they turn the body over—and someone says, "He's dead." *Dead?* He should have been a *greasespot [laughs]*! There were about 1,500 people in this theater, and they all burst into incredible laughter! The assistant head of the studio, Jim Pratt, tapped my shoulder and said, "We've got a car waiting out back with the engine running, just for directors at times like this!"

How did you land your second science fiction assignment, The Land Unknown?

Jack Arnold was originally assigned to direct *The Land Unknown,* and I was helping him storyboard the picture. It was supposed to be in color, have an all-star cast—it was really going to be a big picture. In fact, one of the guys they talked about for the lead was Cary Grant, although I don't think they ever approached him on it. Universal sent me to New York, to the Astoria Studios, where I spent three or four weeks going through footage of the Byrd Expedition looking for stock footage we could use in *The Land Unknown.*

So what happened to the "epic" The Land Unknown?

Universal went into this planning to make it the biggest science fiction picture of its time. But then the effects department and the makeup department spent all their money! Universal spent so much on the monsters, they didn't have any money left to make the picture. They didn't know that they couldn't make the biggest show of all time without spending money! Jack Arnold found out that Universal was pulling all the money from *Land Unknown*—they took color away, they took the cast away—and Jack kind of lost interest in it. It was no longer going to be an epic, it was going to be a typical, cheap Universal picture. So Jack said, "I don't wanna do it, let Virgil do it!" I was preparing another show then which I wanted to do, a small musical, but being the lowest man on the 12-man directorial team at Universal at that time, they pointed a finger at me and said, "You have to do it because you're familiar with it." So that's the way I was assigned to *The Land Unknown.* They paid me a minimum salary, they cast it with their own stock company, who were paid minimum, too, and they went into it.

Was your lost world entirely an interior set?

All interior. Originally, when Jack Arnold was to do it, they were going to shoot it on the backlot. They had a big place called Fall's Lake, which was surrounded by big rock cliffs—they were going to use that in the picture. But when Universal decided they were going to pull the plug on the money it all went onto the process stage, which was the biggest stage they had. When we were on that big stage, we had a big cyclorama all the way around. That's a big

The Land Unknown. Top: Vogel (*in water, on right*) prepares for a low angle shot of the lake monster. (Photo courtesy Robert Skotak.) *Bottom:* The monster menaces Shawn Smith and Jock Mahoney.

piece of canvas, about 75 feet tall and about 300 feet long. It had the scenery painted on it and it hung all around the edge of the stage, like a backdrop in a theater. We also had that big pool in there, much bigger than an Olympic pool—it was 300 feet long and 100 feet wide. It's still there at Universal. To create the fog we had baby bottle warmers under each tree and put dry ice in them, and then we also had guys with fog guns running around in the background. And it was a tremendous task to get one shot—after we made a shot, we had to stop and clear all the fog out for an hour and a half, two hours, and then we'd get ready for the next shot. I'd get four shots a day.

And what was your schedule this time?
It was a 90-day shooting schedule—30 days first unit and 60 days second unit.

You had a number of impressive prehistoric monsters in The Land Unknown, *especially the Tyrannosaurus Rex.*
That was about 12 feet high. There was a man in the suit, but all he did was make it walk—it was a *heavy* piece of equipment. Everything was hydraulic—the eyelids, the mouth and so on. Small rubber hoses came from the end of the tail, six or eight of 'em wrapped together, and they were hooked up to a hydraulic console where a man would sit and operate the different things. They spent a lot of money on that elasmosaurus [the monster in the lake]—that was one that they spent a fortune on. That thing was on railroad tracks on the bottom of the pool, and it must have been 15 feet across, from wingtip to wingtip, and about six or eight feet high when it rose up out of the water. Again, that was all hydraulic—the mouth and the wings and everything were worked by a man on the shore. It was a magnificent monster. The miniature helicopter was about 15 feet long, a great-looking piece of machinery. All of these things were built for the "epic" *Land Unknown.* The pterodactyl was one of the cheapest things we had—it was a prop on a fish-pole!

What about the actual lizards seen in a few scenes?
Those were real monitor lizards, about eight or nine feet long. They were handled by a guy by the name of Jimmy Dannaldson, who was probably one of the best animal trainers alive at that time. He was a friend of mine. He brought these things in and, boy, he could handle them like crazy. Those lizards are worse than alligators, but he would walk out on that miniature set and pick 'em up by the tail—these things would be snapping at him—and just throw 'em on top of each other. It scared me to watch him.

Did the requirements of CinemaScope present any problems?
No. In fact, I was happy they gave it to me, because it added "bigness" to

the picture. I told them, "Look, you've taken the name cast and everything else away from me, I've got to have *something* to sell this show!"

Jock Mahoney's "hero" comes across as a pedantic and unromantic character.
You've got to remember that Jock Mahoney was probably one of the best stuntmen in Hollywood. Universal made him into a leading man. He was not a leading man, he was a stuntman. For a scene at the end of the picture where Henry Brandon is floating unconscious in the pool, they hired a stuntman [Saul Gorss] to take his place. But they had hired a stuntman who couldn't *swim!* We also had the two monitor lizards in the pool; that was kind of dangerous but I didn't care because I knew a good swimmer could get away from them. Also, we had a wire mesh 18 inches under the water, to keep the lizards from coming up on shore and taking legs off the crew. Anyway, this stuntman who can't swim starts screaming for help and so forth, and Jock, who was standing there alongside the camera, does a shallow dive into this foot-and-a-half of water, swam out there and pulled the guy to safety in nothin' flat. Jock could do any damn thing.

Were you happier with the results on Land Unknown *than you were with* Mole People?
Much happier. I thought that *The Land Unknown* had a lot of good special effects, which I was partially responsible for, and it was a great premise. I wish I could do it now, with what I know today.

How did you become involved on Terror in the Midnight Sun [Invasion of the Animal People]?
Gustav Unger, a Swedish newspaper columnist here in town who had been connected with the picture business for years, decided to make a science fiction picture in Sweden. He contacted a fellow in the Universal publicity department and asked him who was a good director. I had been very heavily connected with all the Universal sci-fi things, so this fellow recommended me. Universal had just gone broke, and just as they were closing up, this publicity fellow told me to call Unger, that he was looking for a director. So I did, and I went. We stayed in Riksgränsen in Northern Sweden, above the rail center in Abisko. It's a very interesting place up there—but colder than shit! We were up there in the wintertime, and it was 60 degrees below zero. I was very young then, but I don't think I've ever been so cold.
Gustav and his brother Bertil [the co-producer] are identical twins, and to this day they dress alike and they wear monocles. One wears the monocle in the right eye, one wears it in the left eye—they *are* characters.

What kind of money went into this film?
The American investment in that film was something like $20,000—that was supposed to have been half of it—and the Swedes put up the other

Top: The camera crew gets a worm's-eye view of the space monster in *Invasion of the Animal People* (a.k.a. *Terror in the Midnight Sun*). *Bottom:* Vogel and friend take five.

$20,000. But of course working above the Arctic Circle, work slowed down to a halt at times, and everything took longer than we'd anticipated. We went out one day and we did some aerial photography—really, we got some beautiful footage that day. When the picture ran out of money, they ran this footage for the lab, and the lab came up with some money for us because they thought it looked so good.

I could not ski, and there was no other method of transportation up there; if you didn't go on skis, you went by helicopter. One morning they put the cameraman and myself and two Arriflexes with tripods and batteries and film in the helicopter to fly us down to the location. As we were flying down we flew over the site of an accident: There had been an avalanche which had descended on an ore train, and it scattered the cars like matchboxes all over the white snow. The engines were all smoking, making lots of steam, and a few guys were running around. We flew over there and looked at it, and the cameraman pointed out to me how it happened and so on. Then we went down to Abisko and shot our scene. Later I realized how dumb I was—here I was, doing this story about a monster attacking the Northland, and all we'd have had to do was put the helicopter down and we could have made a whole sequence out of it. But we looked at it like a couple of tourists, and then went on about our business!

There's a lot wrong with Terror in the Midnight Sun, *but many fans like its strange, arty atmosphere.*

I had just worked with Orson Welles on *Touch of Evil* [1958, as film editor], and my heart was full of Orson *[laughs]*, so I did all I could. But then of course Jerry Warren, who released the picture in the United States, took as much of that out of the picture as he could! You should have seen it before he got ahold of it—it was a great piece of artistic work.

What do you remember about the man who played the monster?

He was a newspaperman, and he came in and did it as a lark. I think he also put some of the Swedish money in it. He just had the ball of his life.

Were you pleased with the other members of your Swedish cast?

The acting in *Terror in the Midnight Sun* was horrendous, but that's because we were dealing with Swedish actors, most of whom couldn't speak English and I couldn't speak Swedish. We had this great Swedish comedian, Bengt Blomgren, who did this one major role, and he had his English-language lines written phonetically in Swedish on *everything*—he had them hidden every place he was going to work. He would have a piece of paper with the phonetic lines wrapped around the barrel of his pipe! It was really tough on everyone. I hid the performances with production values—there was some really great, beautiful stuff I shot. We brought it home and I got my agent to look at the film, and he said, "The story's not worth a shit, the performances aren't any good, but visually it's a beautiful film. You've got a lot to be proud of here." It was released in Europe and did quite well, so Gustav and the guys in Sweden got their money out of it right away.

But there was a delay before it was released over here.
    There was a delay, yes. Why, I don't know, it was not my job to sell it. A lot of people who saw it thought it was a very, very artistic piece of work. As I mentioned before, some of the Swedish people who were speaking English were not the best performers because a lot of times they didn't comprehend what they were saying, but the effects were very good and the scenery was gorgeous. It had all the values; maybe part of the delay was the fact that it had no recognizable names in it except Robert Burton, and he was not what you'd call a major star by any manner or means. Finally Jerry Warren gave them $20,000 for the rights in the United States. He took the film and put John Carradine in it—Carradine sat around and just *talked* for half the show—and he cut out all this great stuff I had shot. Great skiing stuff and really fabulous scenery. He cut that all out and had people sit and talk. He also changed the title, to *Invasion of the Animal People.* The original show was a hell of a lot better.

Would you have any objections to tackling science fiction projects again in the future?
    I wouldn't mind it, if we had enough money. In 1986 I did a movie-of-the-week called *Condor*—it was made as a pilot, but it didn't really fly—but they ran out of money. It was a story about a futuristic cop whose partner was killed, and who gets a woman android as a partner.

Sounds a little like RoboCop.
    RoboCop was copied from it; they were both made by Orion. Ray Wise was the star—a fine actor—and he was also in *RoboCop,* by the way, in a minor role. I thought the first hour of *Condor* was really fabulous—I was really proud of it, I did some very innovative special effects in the first half of it. If you can get ahold of it I recommend it highly. Just turn it off in the last 15 minutes!

*Whenever you killed Vincent Price in a movie, he was
always so dramatic about it — he'd writhe around and scream
and holler and carry on. I remember I told Vincent, when he got
shot in* House on Haunted Hill, *"When someone gets hit with
a .45 caliber bullet, they fall backwards. You always
fall* forwards *when you get hit." And Vincent said,
"My boy, no actor falls* away *from the camera!"*

Robb White

OF THE SMALL GROUP of Hollywood filmmakers who made the ghost and horror film genre their specialty during the 1950s, the late producer/director William Castle was the most unusual. His name overwhelms the nostalgic film fan with vivid memories: a luminous skeleton sailing from the screen into the audience (*House on Haunted Hill*); the guarantee of a free burial, insured by Lloyds of London, should a patron expire from fright (*Macabre*); and, most remarkably, audiences being swept into a film's action by small vibrating motors affixed to the bottoms of theater seats (*The Tingler*). These were but a few of the unorthodox ploys engineered by Castle to lure thousands away from their TV sets and back into the faltering theaters of the era.

Too often overlooked by fans of the films of William Castle, writer Robb White was partnered with Castle during this most popular and productive period. Born in the Philippine Islands in 1909, White was a preacher's son who held a wide variety of odd jobs before landing in the Navy during World War II. White initially collaborated with Castle on the short-lived television series *Men of Annapolis,* then joined forces with the enterprising producer/director on the horror thrillers *Macabre, House on Haunted Hill, The Tingler, Homicidal* and the kiddie-oriented "chiller" *13 Ghosts.* A self-described "ol' country boy from the South" (he still has the Dixie accent to prove it), White has fond memories of this classic quintet as well as some *not*-so-fond remembrances of Hollywood's Abominable Showman.

How did you first come in contact with William Castle?

After seven years in the Navy I went back home to Thomasville, Georgia, back to my wife and children that I didn't know. One day a guy called up from Hollywood and asked me if I wanted to write for television. I told him no because I didn't think they'd pay me enough money; I was making a pretty good living then as a freelancer. My book *Our Virgin Island* was a best-seller for 18 weeks; I also got $186,000 for it from *Reader's Digest,* which was a lot of money in those days. So I told this guy, no, I didn't want to write for TV. Then he wrote and said he'd pay me $4,000 for a script for this series he was going to do. His problem was his series was called *Men of Annapolis,* and he didn't know anybody from Annapolis who knew anything about writing a TV script! So I went up to Annapolis to meet this fellow, William Castle. The first time I met him he was squeezing two tennis balls *[laughs],* and I thought, "What the hell is this?" Turns out he wanted to stop smoking, and that was the way he was gonna do it. He showed me a script, and it was idiotic! I went back to my hotel room, and by morning I had a script for him which was the first one that the Navy would approve.

I remember that after I had written about six or seven scripts for *Men of Annapolis,* I was talking to Bill one day when he happened to mention the Writers Guild and I said, "What's that?" You can't write for television without

Previous page: Robb White *(right)* confers with Vincent Price behind the scenes on *House on Haunted Hill.* Price's inscription on the photo reads, "Dear Robb, You wrote a great script. I hope we do it justice. Ever, Vincent."

White's partner, the self-proclaimed King of the Take One, was horror movie entrepreneur William Castle.

belonging to the Writers Guild, but how was *I* supposed to know that? He turned white as a sheet and went into a panic *[laughs]*!

One of the directors on Men of Annapolis *was Herbert Strock, and he told me that Castle didn't seem to know some of the most basic things about directing.*

Bill was a cut-and-print director. He'd say to the actors, "Do such-and-such a thing," and he'd never take another shot because it was too expensive! He liked to call himself the King of Take One. I wrote 28 episodes of *Men of Annapolis,* made a whole lot more money. And after that series was over I went out to Hollywood to talk to him because we agreed to go into business making horror movies. He said we'd go into it fifty-fifty — "finkty-finkty" was his term.

Bill was absolutely the coldest, most ruthless con man I've ever known. All he knew was promotion, he really could sell anything. The first movie we made was *Macabre,* based on a book called *The Marble Forest.* Bill got his old friend Howard W. Koch to agree to help us out on the picture, and I put up the money. Bill said he was gonna put up 50 percent and I was gonna put up 50 percent, but somehow he couldn't quite make it. So I put up the money, $86,000 cash, which is what the picture cost.

Who had picked The Marble Forest?

Bill had—he gave me the book and said, "Write a movie about this." *The Marble Forest* had been written by 12 mystery writers—each one of them had written a chapter—and so it was just a mishmash. I read the thing and I didn't like it, I didn't understand it and I couldn't see any point in trying to make a movie of it. So in writing my screenplay I just ignored it. I wrote a screenplay that had nothing to do with the book, and Bill never said anything about it! My screenplay did have the essence of the little girl supposedly being buried alive in the ground, but that was all I took out of it. And then these 12 mystery writers all got mad and said, why did I change this, that and the other thing? We paid them $2500, I think.

Were you on the set of Macabre?

Yeah. It only took six days, I think *[laughs]*—we did it in a hurry! As soon as production started I learned what Bill meant when he called himself the Earl of Deferral. We deferred everything, even the cost of the film! We didn't pay anybody, we deferred all the salaries, including the actors. Even [star] William Prince—I don't know why we got him. He came all the way from New York, I couldn't see that, but Castle wanted him.

I didn't know anything about making a movie, and I made myself unpopular right away. I remember one day I was talking to this old guy and I asked him, "Which one is the best boy, and what does he do?" And the guy said, "*I'm* the best boy!" He must have been at least 65 *[laughs]*! Then there was the script girl who claimed to be 35 and would never see 50 again. I asked Bill, "What the hell do we need with an art director?" 'cause I knew we weren't gonna be putting up any paintings! I didn't know a damn thing about the movies, but I learned.

Where was Macabre *shot?*

Most of the outside stuff was in Chino, California, the rest in the Ziv Studio on Santa Monica Boulevard. The fancy house where the blind girl [Christine White] lived was a wealthy playboy's mansion up in Beverly Hills. He had a swimming pool that went from inside to outside, he had five Ferraris in the garage—it really was an elegant place. Howard Koch got us that place for next to nothing—I think for $75. Later we got sued for messing up the carpet or something *[laughs]*, but they dropped it when they found out we didn't have any money!

There was lots of great atmosphere in the graveyard scenes.

Sudden shocks were the hallmarks of the William Castle thrillers. Here, Jacqueline Scott unexpectedly trains her flashlight on the propped-up corpse of Howard Hoffman in *Macabre*.

The graveyard was very simple. We went over to MGM and rented 12 tombstones that you could move around and make a huge graveyard out of 'em. The open grave was a box on the set, that you could shoot from above and below and stuff like that. Then we smoked up everything and shot the scenes, inside the studio at Ziv.

Where were you and Castle headquartered at this point?
In the Ziv building, upstairs, in a room where they had old files. We had a desk and two chairs.

Didn't Koch and his partners [Aubrey Schenck and Edwin Zabel] have money in the movie?
No. They had little pieces of it, they had a percentage, but they hadn't put any money in. Zabel was supposed to give us all the western theaters, because he was a big theater owner; Schenck just stood around and rubbed his

stomach. I guess they did something for us, but it wasn't visible to me. Koch came out to Chino as we were shooting the thing, and he got a lot of things done that Bill didn't know how to do, and I couldn't. He was a buddy of ours; he also found us a good editor for the picture, that sort of thing, and gave us good advice. Howard was the only guy I remember liking down in that town.

Part of the problem with Macabre *is the ho-hum cast.*

Yeah, and the fact that it was so sloppily, cheaply done. That cast was the best we could afford, because Bill didn't put up anything! The reason we were able to make *Macabre* so cheap was, I went around with a Volkswagen and khaki pants and a Southern accent, and people just didn't want to charge me the money that they'd charge a production crew from Columbia or Paramount or somewhere. As I said, we got that fancy house for $65, $75—they didn't know that we were going to tear it up, though!

One actor who did *do a good job in* Macabre *was Jim Backus.*

Yeah. He was a good, solid man, and he hated both of us! Bill promised him a big salary, which he didn't get, and that kind of thing. Originally Bill didn't want him because people might think he was Mr. Magoo. I liked Jim Backus, I insisted on him, so we had an argument about that.

Do you appear in any of these Castle films?

Yes, in *Macabre*. We had shot the scenes in the graveyard and we had forgotten to take a shot that we needed of somebody's feet walking on some gravel. So *I* walked on the gravel—my feet are in the movie *[laughs]*! But that was the only time I appeared in one of these films. I didn't want to have to join any more guilds!

One interesting touch in Macabre *is the way you cut back and forth between the action and the clock, to underline the passage of time.*

That was my idea. As a book writer, I know that you have to have a cliffhanger every now and then—you have to stop and start another whole thing, and let the last part sink in. That's what the movie needed, something to pace it. So we got the clock.

Did Castle have any trouble setting up the Lloyds of London insurance policy gimmick?

That I don't know; he was doing that while I was writing the screenplay down in Thomasville. He told me he had it all sewed up before I started, but you never could tell what was true with Bill. I do know that Bill was very pissed off that nobody died watching that picture *[laughs]*!

How did Castle treat his actors?

He was nice. The only time I saw him get mad at an actor was with the girl [Jo Morrow] in *13 Ghosts.* She was supposed to be playing a teenage girl, but she wouldn't wear a bra—she came flopping in there all the time. This pissed off Bill 'cause it made her look like the grown-up she really was—she was supposed to be playing a sweet little girl, not a working whore. And she was a method actress. I remember in one shot, she came in, stopped and said, "I don't know who I'm supposed to be." And Bill said, "All you're supposed to do is get your ass up here and put your feet on the mark!" *[Laughs.]*

Once you turned in a script, would Castle insist on changes?

No, very seldom. I do remember that I put one line in *Macabre* that didn't sit too well with him, though. One character's name was Polly, somebody asked her if she wanted something to eat and she said, "Yes, we haven't had a cracker all day." Well *[laughs]*, Bill didn't like that, and I don't blame him—it took away the "spellbinding" mood of the movie! But I thought it was funny.

When *Macabre* was finished, we invited Howard Koch and Schenck and Zabel to look at it, in a screening room on the Ziv lot. After we got through the end of the movie, Koch took me by the elbow and he said, "Come on out." We stood out on a balcony and looked at Los Angeles for a while and he said, "That is the worst movie I have ever seen in my whole life. I just advise you to forget the $86,000 it cost you, and take up another line of work." The problem with that suggestion was the choice of paying the deferrals or going to jail. So Bill and I trudged around Hollywood with our cans of film until at last Allied Artists agreed to handle it, putting up $5000 ad money and taking 30 percent off the top, leaving us 70 percent to pay the deferrals. The only thing the picture had going for it was Castle's Lloyds of London policy, but *Macabre* just took off and we made a lot of money. Bill told *The Saturday Evening Post* we made $6,000,000 on *Macabre.* The I.R.S. came roaring down to my house and said, "You didn't show that on your return!" Well *[laughs]*, they determined what the figure really was, and I didn't go to jail.

Once the money did start rolling in, did you and Castle split "finkty-finkty"?

No, it turned out that I didn't get my 50 percent, he got 75 to my 25 somehow or other. When it came to money, Bill could be very . . . careless.

If you disliked Castle, how were you able to get along with him as long as you did?

I didn't have to see him too often. One time I went to a party at his house; I never went there again. I really didn't want to see him socially.

About a year elapsed between Macabre *and* House on Haunted Hill. *Did you and he go your separate ways in the meantime?*

After *Macabre* was finished I went back to Thomasville; at first I didn't think *Macabre* was going to make any money. Then, when the money began to come in, Bill called up and asked me if I wanted to do another one.

By that time I was getting ready to get a divorce anyway—my marriage had gone to hell in a handbasket. So I went out to California again and rented an apartment in Malibu, where I did the script. This time we got some high-class people: We got Vincent Price, Carol Ohmart, Alan Marshal and Elisha Cook, Jr., and we made *House on Haunted Hill.*

Who came up with the basic idea for House on Haunted Hill?
    I came up with the whole story on that one. Bill and I discussed the an- cient plot of having somebody trapped in a house, couldn't get out—that was just so basic that I'd written short stories about that for several years *[laughs]*!

It also used the plot device of the errant wife, which seems to be a favorite of yours. A wife that's no good at all.
    Well, I've had two of 'em *[laughs]*!

Where did you shoot this time?
    House on Haunted Hill was shot mostly at Allied Artists. The exteriors were shot at Frank Lloyd Wright's Ennis House on Los Feliz, built during his Egyptian period. We were not allowed to shoot in there, but the guy who owned it let us look inside. And it was a weird house—the ceilings were 22 feet high! In one room there was a closet door that was 22 feet high and two feet wide with nothing in the closet to hold up clothes or anything else. The man who owned the house had furnished only one of the many rooms with a bed, a chair, a nightstand and, in the kitchen, a card table. He complained that the famous glass walls, which joined each other at the corner with only edges of the glass panes meeting, leaked when it rained and made a weird screaming noise when the wind blew. And there was nothing you could do about it! The swimming pool was about three feet deep; ten feet wide; a hundred feet long; and in the middle there was the statue of a horse! It was just god-damned ridiculous!

House on Haunted Hill *really is the* Citizen Kane *of low-budget haunted house movies. You did a great job on that picture.*
    I liked the whole thing, liked it right from the beginning. I liked Carol Ohmart, I was the one that insisted on having her. Vincent Price, we could have had him for $12,000, but Bill said, "No, we'll give him a piece of the movie." He got a tremendous amount of money out of it. I went to a party at his house after the movie was out, and he had just bought another painting for about $200,000. I said, "I'm glad we could afford it!" *[Laughs.]* Yeah, I loved Vincent Price, and I still do. Elisha Cook was also a great guy, just wonderful; he came down in a trailer, from up in Bishop or somewhere. I still

---

Opposite: White and producer-director William Castle collaborated on the *crème de la crème* of low-budget haunted house pictures, *House on Haunted Hill.*

write to him a lot. I remember that I objected to hiring the guy who played the hero, Richard Long, because he had a scar on his mouth which made him look like he was smiling all the time, even in the grimmest parts. But he turned out to be a good actor and I liked him very much.

How did Vincent Price get along with Castle?

Vincent was a professional get-along-wither. He knew his lines, he knew what to do, he didn't need much direction and he gave nobody any trouble.

The gimmick for House on Haunted Hill *was "Emergo"—the skeleton which seemed to appear right out of the movie screen.*

That thing operated from a fishing reel up in the projection booth—the projectionist's job was to pull the skeleton over from the stage, over the heads of the audience. We got the thing made and everything, rigged it all up, rented an empty theater and got in about 22 big producers—I mean, John Huston and people like that. We sat them down and ran the picture, and then this skeleton came out floating over them. Well, they thought that was great, until the line snapped and the skeleton fell straight down on top of them *[laughs]*! They all got up and walked out!

The government specified how much our skeleton could weigh and made us guarantee that they couldn't hurt anybody if they fell on them. We finally got it figured out so they worked all right, and then the kids shot them down—they'd come in with everything short of bazookas, and kill our skeletons! They cost us more than the movie!

How did you get interested in becoming a writer?

Damned if I know *[laughs]*! I just couldn't see anything that seemed more appealing—I liked it because it promised some freedom. I was a preacher's son and I didn't have the aptitude that people should have; I didn't see any use in going to work, that kind of thing. I started writing when I was 13. There was no money to go to college, so I went to the Naval Academy at Annapolis, Maryland, and I wrote all the time I was there. People thought I was crazy. When I graduated from the Naval Academy, I realized that writing and being a naval officer were not compatible; the Navy doesn't hire you nine to five, they own you all day long and all night, too. So I quit, and everybody got very mad at me for quitting—1931 was not the year to quit a cushy job as an officer in the Navy. But I did.

I went to Cleveland for some reason and found out that $700 doesn't last very long, so I had to get a job. I lived with a guy named Tex Wheeler, a sculptor, very nice guy. He drank a lot of corn whiskey and he had a funny habit: He got up in the morning, he'd put on his cowboy hat and his boots, he took a big shot of that whiskey and that's all he'd put on for the rest of the day! A lot of the rich Cleveland ladies liked to have him sculpt their horses, that was his specialty. One lady was sitting there one day watching him sculpt, she asked me what I did and I told her I was looking for a job. She said, "Well, go see so-and-so down at the Dupont plant." So I went down there and got a job as a draftsman, and I drafted a thing called a space ore roaster. I didn't know what the hell the thing was. Then the boss came in one day and said, "We're going to send you down to New Castle, Pennsylvania to put up this thing you been drafting!" *[Laughs.]* I struggled down there in New Castle for a long time, about a year and a half, and we got this thing built—turns out it made sulfuric acid.

Were you still writing and sending out manuscripts all this time?

Yes, I was. I worked for Dupont from eight to six, then from eight at night 'til two in the morning I did the writing, in a little boarding house. One day there was a letter addressed to me from a magazine: They had bought a story for a hundred dollars. That would be about 1933. So I went right up to Cleveland, to the head of Dupont, and I told him, "I quit!" Because I was a writer!

Anyway, the next job I got was on a schooner, up in Boston—a 72 foot schooner where we were gonna teach kids school. We were gonna take 12 kids as passengers, and this skipper and his wife and I were gonna run the boat. I was also gonna teach English. All the mothers came down with their kids, took one look at this boat, which was then 35 years old, and they said, "No way!" The only one that was left was this six-foot, 16-year-old kid that looked like something from outer space. So we

Vincent Price emceed a night of horror in the White-scripted *House on Haunted Hill.*

Skin and bones: Carolyn Craig and friend in a cheesecake shot from *House on Haunted Hill*.

took him, because we needed the money. The only trouble was, the skipper would not go out of sight of land *[laughs]*! I had a sextant and a chronometer and knew how to use 'em, but he wouldn't do it. So between Plymouth and Morehead City, North Carolina, we scraped bottom 108 times, because the thing had a ten-foot draft on it. It was a bastard to sail—a square-rigged schooner, 1,100 feet in the mainsail. This kid didn't do anything, and the wife just went around moaning all the time. We ran into a big storm that took all the masts out and things like that, and they decided that somebody had to swim ashore and get the Coast Guard. The wife couldn't go and the kid *wouldn't* go and the captain couldn't leave his ship, so I had to do it. I put a rope around me and wrapped the end around a cleat, and said, "If it's too cold, I'm coming back." So I swam a ways and it *was* too cold, so I pulled on the rope and all the rope came over 'cause he had untied the other end *[laughs]*! That was lovely. So I swam in, five miles, in the night.

After that I hitchhiked down to the West Indies, to Dominica, where I got a job with a British preacher who wasn't there but he had a plantation where he grew oranges and coconuts. I was the manager there but he never paid me anything, so I finally had to come back home. I got married in Thomasville, Georgia, and we went to the British Virgin Islands and rented a miserable place on Tortola—we paid $10 a month for this crappy little house. We started looking around for some better place to live down there, sailed around every day, went to different islands, and one day we ended up on this little island called Marina Cay. She went around one way and I went around the other, and we met on the other side—it was a little island, about six or seven acres. So we bought it, for $60. There was no water, no phone, no electricity—no nothing. We moved in and slept in a shed that we had put up and built a concrete house on the top of it, which is still there*. I kept on writing, I won a prize—one book called *Smuggler's Sloop* won for Best Juvenile Book—and I kept writing for magazines, any kind of magazines. I wrote for the Jewish Saturday magazines and the Catholic Sunday *[laughs]*; I wrote for *American Boy, Boys' Life;* I wrote as a woman in *True Stories*, and got raped in a hayloft about once a month! Things got to going pretty good, we lived there about four years, then the War started and I was back in the Navy.

The British government just took that island away from me; they said they didn't like something I wrote, but they never told me why. I just heard that the island sold again for $6,000,000, but *[laughs]* I didn't get any! They took everything I had.

Were you a fan of horror or science fiction films?

No, I hated 'em. And for years I didn't see some of these movies that I made with Bill Castle. I mean, they're so dumb—God! There's not a worm in your backbone when you get scared!

You're talking about The Tingler *now.*

Right. The only thing I didn't like about *House on Haunted Hill* was that it made enough noise around town to attract Columbia Pictures, who, when I didn't want to be bought, swallowed us like a shark.

Then why did you and Castle allow yourselves to be swallowed?

Columbia offered us fabulous things. Bill was very impressed with Columbia: We had a corner office, we had a bar, we had two secretaries, and it

*White's adventure on Marina Cay formed the basis for two of his books, *Our Virgin Island* and *Two on the Isle. Our Virgin Island* was made into the movie *Virgin Island* (1959).

cost us a fortune! But it upgraded Bill, it gave him character. Years before, he had been fired from Columbia for some sort of dereliction of morals or something—he never talked to me about it.

For some unexplained and mysterious reason Bill either couldn't, or wouldn't, or was not allowed to drive a car. This resulted in his late afternoon dance routine in every studio he worked. During the last half hour Bill would roam around trying to con somebody into driving him home to his house in the Holmby Hills. During this dance period everybody with a car ran around trying to either hide or disappear entirely. I had a Volkswagen—which Bill hated—but I was available to carry him around on his many errands. And he wanted me to put a phone in the Volkswagen! I wouldn't do that, so he bought—or ripped loose—a phone handset, which had just enough cord left on it to dangle down inside the VW. And as we'd drive along through Beverly Hills Bill would be talking into this handset *[laughs]*! He was a phony son of a bitch!

So moving over to Columbia didn't sit well with you.

No, but—I was sort of "unconscious" by that time. I was having a lot of fun down in Malibu, and I had more money than I knew what to do with. But the shenanigans that went on at Columbia were sometimes more than I could deal with. I remember we had a woman, a real high-class broad, assigned to us; Bill didn't know what she was supposed to do, and I certainly didn't. But at least she got us into trouble with the Executive Dining Room. You had to be in the Executive Dining Room on time, but at five minutes before the fixed time for lunch the woman would disappear into the ladies' room, asking us to wait for her, and then would not come out for 45 minutes. I sent my secretary in to find out what the hell she did in there, and she came out and said, "She strips to the waist, takes off her bra, washes her tits, then dries herself off and gets dressed again!" I never found out what that woman's job was, and I've never heard of her since.

How did you think up the idea for The Tingler?

The makeup guy that we had on *House on Haunted Hill*, Jack Dusick, had made a rubber worm. He showed me this worm one day, a horrible looking thing, about a foot long. In those days we didn't have the violent makeup and special effects they have today, but this worm, it haunted you—it scared you! I began thinking about that, and I told Bill, "Let's find out where fear comes from and we'll use this worm!" It was a lot of fun writing the script, but I didn't like the movie.

In one scene we wanted to have Vincent Price drop the worm, and we figured the best way was to have a cat leap up on the operating table, snarling and clawing, and startle him. The cat's fee was $1500, the trainer got $1000, the S.P.C.A. man cost $500, Columbia got a fee for having a cat on stage and the contract stipulated that if anybody stepped on that cat's tail the fine was $2000. Well, in one take that cat began screaming bloody murder, as though Vincent

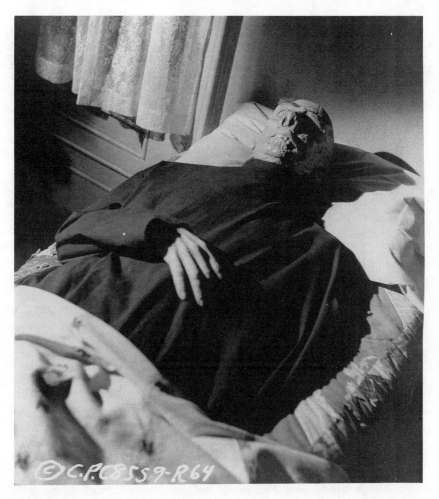

Philip Coolidge (or, more likely, a stand-in) in the ghoul-man get-up from White's *The Tingler*.

Price had stepped on its tail. The rushes made a liar out of the cat, but by that time our $2000 was long gone. The punchline to this story is, I'm in a bar one night someplace and I could hear this guy talking about his cat—it was the guy who owned the cat we used. And he said that this cat was trained to walk by somebody and scream and holler and writhe around. If I was a belligerent man, I would have gone over there and —!

The Tingler *is also the movie where Vincent Price goes on the LSD trip.*

I wanted something different from the typical shot or pill that you see in movie "trips." Aldous Huxley told me about a doctor at U.C.L.A. who was running an experiment on lysurgic acid [LSD]. So I went up there to see this man, Dr. Cohen, and he gave me some of it. He took me into a nice little room with a cot and a radio and he got something out of his refrigerator and gave me a shot. It was all legal then. I watched the grain in the wood writhing around and listened to the music. It was very pleasant, although I didn't ever want to do it again. I went back and told Vincent about it, what the real reaction would be—I just wondered if it wasn't something that Vincent could be dramatic about without falling around and all that stuff. He said, "Forget it." And when he took the shot in the movie, he jumped around and did the same god-damned thing he always did *[laughs]*!

Whenever you killed Vincent Price in a movie, he was always so dramatic about it—he'd writhe around and scream and holler and carry on. I remember I told Vincent, when he got shot in *House on Haunted Hill,* "When someone gets hit with a .45 caliber bullet, they fall backwards. You always fall *forwards* when you get hit." And Vincent said, "My boy, no actor falls *away* from the camera!" *[Laughs.]*

The gimmick this time was Percepto, with small motors on the bottoms of theater seats giving audience members a "tingle."

Bill's idea was to take the motors out of thousands of vibrators and screw them under the seats, then rig the wiring so that at crucial moments in the film the audience would suddenly begin vibrating in waves, six rows at a time. We didn't want to buy thousands of vibrators without knowing whether they would really work out, so we scouted around until we found a theater in the Valley that was running *The Nun's Story* [1959]—*The Nun's Story* was going to close on a Sunday night and *The Tingler* was going to open on Monday. We got in a huge crew of people to spend the day attaching the vibrators to the seats. But that night, just at the most tragic moment of *The Nun's Story,* somebody touched the master switch and the seats began vibrating in wave after wave. There was absolute pandemonium!

The other problem was the kids. They came and unscrewed the motors—broke them off and stole them. And they cost a lot of money. So that didn't work very long.

Did your films' budgets go up considerably now that you were at a major studio?

Yeah, Columbia charged us a lot, like $25,000 just to be there. Bill didn't tell me that at the beginning. And once we were at Columbia we never made the kind of money we did with *Macabre* and *House on Haunted Hill.* I also didn't hang around as much now that we were at Columbia.

13 Ghosts really was a departure, a very tame ghost movie which seemed like it was written for small kids.

[Laughs.] I didn't give a shit about that thing; I'd say it was my least favorite of the five films I made with Bill. *13 Ghosts* was his idea and I couldn't see any point in it at all. I don't think it made any sense and I've forgotten all

Neither the gimmicky "Ghost Viewer" nor a baker's dozen phantoms relieved the tedium of the disappointing *13 Ghosts*.

about it. Really, the only thing I remember about *13 Ghosts* was the lion that's in the picture. I had expected the King of Beasts, but what we got was an ancient, slightly mangy female. So we're shooting one of the lion scenes, when this old lion starts to pee! Lions don't pee in the same direction we do, they pee out the back, and it has a great deal more velocity and volume. As the stream kept coming, the lion made a slow, and I believe deliberate, turn through 360 degrees. She wet down everybody but the cameraman, who yanked a sheet of plywood out of the floor and used it as a shield. All hands took it very well except Jo Morrow, who declared she was gonna sue the entire state of California, starting with me!

The music in these films does wonders for them, really helps them to work. Did you get to meet any of these composures?

Yeah, I met Von Dexter *[House on Haunted Hill, The Tingler, 13 Ghosts]* and I thought he was a good guy. I saw him several times after that; he was a real estate agent last time I heard from him. He wasn't making it in the business and he didn't like it, either, and I'll bet he's making a lot more money now than he was then. Les Baxter, who wrote the music for *Macabre,* he was a pain in the ass. He wanted $10,000, he saw the movie and the only comment he made was, "Put a loud trumpet in there." I didn't like him and I didn't like his music, but this wasn't any of my business.

Homicidal *and* Psycho *have a lot in common but you claimed in a previous interview that you had no knowledge of* Psycho *going into* Homicidal.

Bill gave me the idea for *Homicidal,* and when I started to work on that screenplay he worked on it more than I did—more than he had on any other script that I did for him. It just felt very funny to me, that he was helping out so much, and that he wanted it exactly this way and that way and so on. One day after working at the studio I was on my way home when I saw that *Psycho* was playing somewhere in Santa Monica. I'd heard about the picture, I went in there and, Jesus Christ, I was afraid I was going to get arrested before I could get out! I was so embarrassed—he stole everything! And *Homicidal* was already in production by that time. But apparently nobody gave a shit that he had stolen it from Hitchcock.

You picked out some of the locations on Homicidal, *didn't you?*

Yeah, out in Solvang, California, a funny little place, totally Swedish. Somebody had told me there was a great old "haunted"-looking house there, so I went up to Solvang and located it. The script also called for a plant nursery, I found one up there and told them we were making a picture called *The Marble Forest.* We didn't want them to know it was really a horror movie. We tore up that nursery—God, we just ruined it! Solvang wanted to sue me and everybody else. I've never been back there, I'll tell you that *[laughs]*!

What do you think of the job "Jean Arless" [Joan Marshall] does in the film?

For years I tried to figure out, was that a girl or a guy? Now that I know it was an actress, I think she did a wonderful job.

Did you ever think about giving directing a shot?

No. I'm basically a book writer.

Homicidal *was your last film for Castle. Did you and he have some kind of tiff, or did you just drift apart?*

I just said I didn't want to work for him anymore. I didn't like working for Bill. Just as soon as I wasn't putting my own money into these pictures anymore, he got very bossy. Also, there had been the business about the

Homicidal script, the way he ripped off *Psycho* — when I found that out, I told Bill I would never work for him again. There was also a contract changed on me, on *Homicidal*. He said he'd give me 12 percent of it, he sent the contract down to me in Malibu and it said 12 percent and I signed it. But later, when it came back, there was a period between the one and the two — that was put in afterward! I wanted to talk it over with Bill, but he got "very sick" — he couldn't discuss it, he was "too sick." So I settled for my 1.2 percent, I didn't want to fight about it, but eventually I started getting awful tired of that bullshit. I figured, if I was going to work for a salary, I'd rather work with someone other than Bill. I never saw Bill again after *Homicidal*.

What did you do after leaving Castle?
    The first thing I did was to finish a book that I had promised Doubleday. Then I met the producer of *Perry Mason*, a fellow by the name of Art Seid. He lived down in Malibu, and I said, "Let me write one of those things." I wrote one script and they bought it, and then I kept on writing for them.

After you left Castle he floundered for a few years with lousy pictures like Zotz! *and* The Old Dark House, *then got back on track by hiring Robert Bloch.*
    Bloch talked to me about Bill one time, and he had the same opinion I did. That Castle was just impossible.

Did you follow Castle's career at all in later years?
    No. I did happen to see *Rosemary's Baby* and I asked Howard Koch what that was all about, and he said that nobody else wanted it.

In his autobiography Castle makes it sound as though every producer in Hollywood wanted it.
    Nobody wanted it, according to Koch. Bill didn't really do anything on that picture, he just filled a space. He didn't direct or put up any money or anything like that.

Looking back over the Castle years, was it an enjoyable time, or was there too much aggravation involved?
    No, I liked that experience. I had never done anything except some TV — *Men of Annapolis* and another series called *Silent Service* — and it was a relief to be able to whomp out all that stuff and then let the camera do the hard work. Writing a book is a hell of a lot different from writing a screenplay, a lot more work. Between movies I wrote three or four books while I was in Hollywood; I didn't socialize very much. I had a series of affairs that were nice — not serious. I didn't go to town if I didn't have to. I had a beautiful house in Malibu that kept sliding into the sea, and I spent a lot of time repairing that.

You ever think about writing another horror film?
    [Laughs.] Never!

Author's note: Robb White died at age 81 in November, 1990, as this book was in the final stages of production.

Index

Every movie title is followed by year of release. Television series, stageplays, etc., are identified as such in parentheses. The titles of novels, short stories, magazines, etc., appear in quotation marks. Page numbers in bold indicate photographs.

A